Essentials of Entrepreneurship

To the memory of my parents (Ruth and Bernard) who gave me
the gift of life,
And to Rebecca who ensured that I could retain it

Essentials of Entrepreneurship

Evidence and Practice

Robert A. Baron
Oklahoma State University, USA

Edward Elgar
Cheltenham, UK • Northampton, MA, USA

Published by
Edward Elgar Publishing Limited
The Lypiatts
15 Lansdown Road
Cheltenham
Glos GL50 2JA
UK

Edward Elgar Publishing, Inc.
William Pratt House
9 Dewey Court
Northampton
Massachusetts 01060
USA

A catalogue record for this book is available from the British Library

Library of Congress Control Number: 2013951853

ISBN   978 1 78347 177 5   (cased)
ISBN   978 1 78347 178 2   (paperback)
ISBN   978 1 78347 179 9   (eBook)

Typeset by Servis Filmsetting Ltd, Stockport, Cheshire
Printed and bound in Great Britain by T.J. International Ltd, Padstow

Contents in brief

Full contents

About the author

Robert A. Baron (PhD, University of Iowa) is Spears Professor of Entrepreneurship, Professor of Management, and Regents Professor, at Oklahoma State University. He has held faculty appointments at RPI, Purdue, the Universities of Minnesota, Texas, South Carolina, Washington, Princeton University, and the University of Oxford. He served as a Program Director at NSF (1979–81), and was appointed as a Visiting Senior Research Fellow by the French Ministry of Research (2001–02; Toulouse). He has served as a Department Chair and as Interim Dean and holds three US patents. He was the founder and CEO of IEP, Inc., a company that produced equipment for enhancing work environments. Baron's current interests focus on the role of cognitive and social factors in entrepreneurship. He has published 140 articles, 38 chapters, and 49 books. Professor Baron serves on the boards of AMJ, JBV, and JOM, and is an Associate Editor for SEJ.

Preface

The nature, foundations, and value of entrepreneurship: how ideas, sometimes, change the world

The title of this book starts with the word "essentials," and the choice of that term was far from accidental. On the contrary, it reflects several key goals I sought to attain in writing it. These are outlined—and clarified—below.

Goal 1: Prepare a text that "covers all the bases" (all major topics) but does so succinctly

The dictionary describes "essentials" as referring to a basic aspect of a particular subject or something that is absolutely necessary. Interestingly, this term is used in the titles of scores of books dealing with almost every imaginable subject—from human anatomy, Italian cooking, and strength training, through economics, psychology, and physics. All these books are entitled "Essentials of . . .," with the specific subject following. Why is this phrase so popular in so many different fields? Perhaps because in each there is an agreed upon "core"—a basic set of topics that anyone wishing to acquire a basic knowledge of that field—should be exposed to.

Does this principle apply to the field of entrepreneurship? Ten or perhaps even five years ago, the answer might have been "No." There was no agreed upon list of topics that should be included in any book designed to provide an overview of the field. This surprising fact, I believe, reflected the fact that entrepreneurship, as an academic field, had strong roots in several "parent" disciplines—economics, psychology, sociology, and strategic management. As a result, there was relatively little agreement about what topics and issues were central to the field and should be included in any text that sought to fully represent it.

Recently, however, this situation has changed considerably, to the point at which such agreement *does* now exist. Most individuals who teach courses or workshops in entrepreneurship (especially in universities), would, I believe, suggest highly similar lists of topics that should definitely be included in any comprehensive introduction to the field. That has been the guiding principle I followed in preparing this text, and choosing its content. All chapters deal with topics and issues that, I believe, would appear on the "must include" lists of most of my colleagues. And in fact, this list is not so long as to preclude a book that is relatively concise in length. As a result, the book does indeed focus on the *essentials*—the key topics and concepts that constitute the core of the field. The result is 12 highly integrated chapters that together do indeed reflect the dictionary definition of "essentials"—they present the topics and bodies of knowledge viewed as truly central to the field of entrepreneurship. While this was, perhaps, the central goal, several others too played a role in determining the context and form of this text; they are described below.

Goal 2: Fully represent the "nuts and bolts" aspect of entrepreneurship—the basic steps that are part of the process and must be accomplished for it to proceed

Entrepreneurship is, of course, a business activity, so any comprehensive text about it must fully represent this; in other words, it must include "how to" information, such as, for example, how to obtain financial support, how to form an effective founding team, how to write an excellent business plan, and how to obtain patents and other forms of protection for intellectual property. This basic information is included in several chapters, so it too is fully represented in the book.

Goal 3: Base the book, as much as possible, on actual evidence

As the field of entrepreneurship has grown (rapidly indeed!) it has begun to build a solid and expanding base of concrete knowledge about entrepreneurship—knowledge concerning such issues as "What motivates entrepreneurs—what are they really seeking?" "How do they recognize potential valuable opportunities?" "What skills and knowledge do they need to succeed?" "How do they deal with setbacks or failure?" and "How do they build the social networks essential for success?" Whenever possible, this book draws on such knowledge—on what *the findings of careful research tell us*. Certainly, the insights and information provided by experienced entrepreneurs can be very helpful and should *not* be ignored; in fact, doing so, would be somewhat absurd! But as explained in Chapter 1, there are important reasons why such input should be viewed with caution. So, whenever possible, the information presented derives from, and is supported by, knowledge provided by careful research.

Goal 4: Prepare a book that is useful both for students in schools of business or management and students from other schools who have no formal training in business

Interest in entrepreneurship has grown rapidly and is currently very strong in schools and departments outside the fields of business or management. For instance, many students in schools of engineering, science, social science, and education would dearly love to take a basic course in entrepreneurship. Unfortunately, they are reluctant to do so because (1) these courses are not available to students from outside management, and (2) the courses offered assume previous knowledge these students don't have. To address this issue, the present book is written in a manner that does *not* assume or require such knowledge. Thus, it is fully appropriate for business/management students because it reflects the basic fact that entrepreneurship's "home base" is certainly business or management. However, it is also accessible to students from other disciplines, and has been designed so that they too will find it informative.

Goal 5: Write a text that highlights the value of entrepreneurship—and how this value extends beyond purely economic factors

Most discussions of entrepreneurship—and many courses on it—seem to suggest that its main value lies in the fact that it generates economic gains, not only for the entrepreneurs who enact it, but also for many others (e.g., employees), and even for entire communities. Business plan competitions, for instance, emphasize that view; in general, it is the new ventures with high potential for generating profits that win the prizes and attract attention of venture capitalists and other sources of funding. Certainly this is appropriate. But do individuals choose to become entrepreneurs primarily for the economic gains it provides? A growing body of research suggests that, in fact, many choose entrepreneurship for very different reasons—to gain independence (e.g., to be their "own boss"), to escape from jobs they view as meaningless, to pursue personal interests and turn them into sources of income, and in some cases to do "social good", to help improve the quality of human life by providing products that make others' lives safer, more convenient, and more enjoyable. The key point is simply this: many persons choose to become entrepreneurs not primarily to become rich or famous (!), but because they want to improve the quality of their own lives, and perhaps those of others too. In short, they want to attain greater life satisfaction and increased personal happiness. These basic facts too are represented in the text and, once again, are based on the findings of systematic research, which, overall, suggests that entrepreneurial activity, like almost any kind of complex human behavior, stems from many rather than single motives.

Those are the major goals I have sought to attain, and I can honestly say that I worked hard to reach them. To assist in achieving these objectives, I have also included several special features in the book. These are summarized in Chapter 1, so there is no need to repeat that information here. Together, however, they are designed to illustrate key points in each chapter by providing intriguing examples of entrepreneurship in action (mini-cases, if you will; these are titled "The Entrepreneurial Quest") and by explaining how the principles discussed can be used to increase entrepreneurs' success (these are titled "The Effective Entrepreneur").

A few concluding remarks

By now this preface has violated the principle of conciseness that is so central to this book! But it is, perhaps, helpful to state these key goals clearly because in a sense they are the criteria against which its usefulness should be assessed. In any case, I fully appreciate the fact that only you—my colleagues, students, and other readers of this book—can tell me to what extent I have achieved them. So please feel free to share your thoughts, reactions, and recommendations with me at this address: Robert.baron@okstate.edu.

I look forward to hearing from you and will take your comments to heart in order to learn from my mistakes—as any entrepreneur should try to do!

Robert A. Baron
Stillwater, OK and Edmond, OK

Acknowledgements

Some words of thanks

Writing itself is a solitary task, best carried out in a quiet (and sometime lonely!) place. But despite this fact, many talented and dedicated people always contribute to the final product. Here, I'd like to thank some of these individuals.

First, my sincere thanks to my Editor, Alan Sturmer. His input helped shape the basic idea for this book and his support for it certainly made it possible to convert my ideas for it into reality.

Next, I want to thank Alison Hornbeck for preparing the manuscript for production and for her help with respect to the cover. Her assistance in these respects was both efficient and constructive.

Thanks are also due Dee Compson for a very careful job of copy-editing, which for me, personally is especially crucial. I know only too well that I make many errors, and calling these to my attention so that they could be corrected is an essential aspect of the process.

Thanks too, to Katy Wight for her help with the author information form—a short document, but one that includes important information.

And last, but *far* from least (!), my sincere appreciation to Jane Bayliss who oversaw production, and whose competence and expertise helped make this complex process both efficient and enjoyable.

To all these outstanding people, a warm "Thank you!"

Robert A. Baron
Stillwater, Oklahoma

Part I

Foundations of entrepreneurship

What is the basic nature of entrepreneurship and why is it so important? How do ideas for new products or services arise? What are the cognitive foundations of creativity and how can it be increased? What are business opportunities and how do future or current entrepreneurs take them? This part of the book focuses on these and related issues.

1

Entrepreneurship: Changing the world . . . one idea at a time

 CHAPTER OUTLINE

- Entrepreneurship: Why it's *not* synonymous with new venture formation – Entrepreneurs: the active element in change
- Why entrepreneurship is important: Economic growth, "giving back," and maximizing human motivation
- What do entrepreneurs seek? Wealth? Fame? Doing social good? Answer: All of the above
- Acquiring the knowledge we seek: Why the insights of entrepreneurs— even highly successful ones—are often not enough
- A roadmap to this book: Its special features

> *This defines entrepreneur and entrepreneurship—the entrepreneur always searches for change, responds to it, and exploits it as an opportunity.*
> (Peter F. Drucker, *Innovation and Entrepreneurship*, 1985)

> *The true entrepreneur is a doer, not a dreamer.*
> (Nolan Bushnell, entrepreneur and founder of Atari)

> *I never perfected an invention that I did not think about in terms of the service it might give others . . . I find out what the world needs, then I proceed to invent.*
> (Thomas Edison, US inventor and businessman, 1847–1931)

Years ago, I was on the faculty of a technologically oriented university that had what I considered to be a very inspiring motto: "Why not change the world?"[1] I truly admired that phrase and the idea it presented, but felt that, in a sense, it didn't seem to go quite far enough. It seemed to suggest, at least to me, that *education* (and specifically, scientific or technical education)

---

1 Rensselaer Polytechnic Institute.

was the key to world-altering change. Certainly, that's true to an important degree—change often *does* originate in knowledge and its applications. But I also felt then, and now too, that this is only part of the total picture. In addition, it's important to note that ultimately it is *people* who make change happen—individuals (or perhaps small groups working together) who, by combining knowledge (the fruits of education) with their own talents, creativity, and energy, generate major change. So in answer to the question "Why not change the world?" my reply might be: "Why not? But to do so we need *entrepreneurs*—individuals who not only formulate ideas for something new, useful, and better, but also who convert these ideas into reality, and by doing so, create value—economic or social, or both." That, in essence, is the definition of entrepreneurship adopted throughout this text, and it does, I believe, capture the essence of the true entrepreneurial spirit.

Actually, this suggestion is not very novel; in fact, it is quite close to what is perhaps, the most widely accepted definition of "entrepreneurship" at the present time. Slightly paraphrased, this definition (Shane and Venkataraman, 2000; Shane, 2012), suggests that entrepreneurship seeks to understand how opportunities to create something *new* (e.g., new products or services, new markets, new production processes or raw materials, new ways of organizing existing technologies) "arise" and are "discovered" or "created" by specific persons, who then use various means to "exploit" or "develop" them, thus producing a wide range of "effects" (including economic and social value).

In short, this definition suggests that entrepreneurship involves the emergence of ideas, their evaluation, and, ultimately, their conversion into something new and tangible by various means—essentially, actions carried out by one or a small number of persons. Often, this involves starting a new business to develop recognized opportunities in order to make them available to potential customers or users. But as Shane (2012, p. 12) suggests, creation of a new firm is just *one way* of developing recognized or created opportunities—just one means through which they can be used to create value, economic or social. It is the "recognition," "evaluation," and "development" of the opportunities themselves that together constitute entrepreneurship. This is an important point, so we'll pause here to consider it a bit more fully.

Entrepreneurship: Why it's *not* synonymous with new venture formation

At present, the term "entrepreneur" has a slightly romantic tinge, similar in some respects to that attached to the term "leader" (e.g., Meindl, 1995). It conjures up images of creative, active "doers" who, by converting their ideas into reality, do literally change the world in important ways. This implies that the term "entrepreneurship" refers basically to what entrepreneurs do—and in most people's minds, what they do is *start new businesses* (and then, perhaps, become incredibly rich!). As noted above, however, this view of entrepreneurship is slightly misleading. Yes, many entrepreneurs do start new ventures as a means of developing their ideas and the opportunities these suggest, but it seems clear that, as Shane suggests (2012, p. 12), entrepreneurship is broader than this: there are other ways of converting ideas into something real—and beneficial—aside from launching a new business. For instance, new ideas often emerge among employees of existing organizations who then seek to develop them internally—within that company (e.g., Parker, 2011)—although, in some cases, they take their ideas with them and depart, to develop them independently.

Alternatively, ideas for something new often arise among individuals working in various professions, who then seek to apply them to their work—again, without necessarily starting a new company. Here's one example. Consider a talented teacher who, on the basis of her or his experience has an idea for an improved way of teaching a specific subject (e.g., calculus, history, chemistry . . . the subject is unimportant). Having formulated this idea, the teacher may then evaluate it by trying it out, in a limited way, with her or his own students. If results are promising, she or he may then refine it further, and put it into a form that can be tried, and perhaps used, by other teachers. According to the definition above, this teacher is thinking and acting entrepreneurially, even if she or he does *not* start a new company to develop and promote the new teaching method—although, of course, she or he may decide to do that too. So to repeat: starting a new company is just *one* way—a very important one—of converting what starts as an idea into something tangible.

To recap, then, entrepreneurship, at its heart, involves identification, evaluation, and development of opportunities—new ways of creating economic or social value (Shane, 2012, p. 12), and it's important to note at the outset that this can occur in many different ways. Starting a new venture is probably the single most important and common route followed by entrepreneurs in their efforts to develop their ideas, but it is far from the only one. As Shane (ibid.; emphasis added) puts it: "firm formation is merely *one institutional arrangement for the identification, evaluation, and exploitation of opportunities.* The same acts of identification, evaluation, and exploitation of opportunities that occur through firm formation also can be undertaken by people in existing firms or through market mechanisms." In sum, although we will emphasize the importance of new ventures throughout this book, we'll also recognize that the entrepreneurial process itself is broader in scope than this, and can proceed in other ways too.

Entrepreneurs: The active element in change

Having made that important point, let's consider a somewhat different but related question: "How important are individual entrepreneurs in bringing about the kind of change mentioned earlier?" At a given point in time, won't many persons have the same basic ideas for something new, useful, and better? After all, people living at the same time and in the same culture are exposed to similar bodies of knowledge and often share many basic life experiences—experiences that may suggest to them needs that exist but are not being effectively met. To the extent that's true then it seems highly likely that *someone* will recognize these needs or problems, and formulate means of addressing them. Within this view, entrepreneurs are, in a sense, interchangeable "cogs in the machine," and who gets there "first" is not really crucial because ultimately, *someone* will.

Certainly, this is true in some instances; often, several individuals or companies are working, simultaneously on solving the same problems or meeting the same needs. This happened in Silicon Valley back in the 1960s, when many groups of engineers and scientists decided, concurrently to address the same sets of technological problems and issues; and it has happened in many other settings and at other times, too. Yet, despite this fact, history records many instances in which a potentially valuable opportunity existed for some time (years or even decades), but was *not* developed until a particular individual recognized it and took vigorous (often persistent) action to develop it. As Shane et al. (2003, p. 259) put it: "The entrepreneurial process occurs because people act to pursue opportunities"—not simply because "conditions are ripe" for some kind of advance or change. Here is, perhaps, one of the most dramatic illustrations of this point on record.

Have you used a copy machine recently? In all likelihood you have because making copies quickly and easily is something we now take for granted. But not very long ago (in fact, even very early in my own career), there was no such thing—or if such machines *did* exist, they were so expensive that they were kept under lock and key and were not available at that time (the late 1960s and early 1970s) to young faculty such as myself. By modern standards, the technology behind such devices is not tremendously complex and, in fact, it existed for decades before being put to practical use in modern copy machines. Why? Partly this delay derived from the fact that other means of making copies already existed (see Figure 1.1) and partly because few persons recognized the potential benefits of such machines. In fact, however, one entrepreneur—Chester Carlson—not only had the idea but also tried to develop it. Yet, despite his best efforts, several decades passed before he could persuade anyone to finance its development! Was he the only person to have the idea for a device that could make copies on plain paper? Probably not. But Carlson not only had the idea and recognized the opportunities it offered, he also worked long and hard to make it reality (Figure 1.1).

Sources: Left-hand photo: Fotolia #21237818; right-hand photo: Figure 3.1, p. 51, Baron, 2012.

Figure 1.1 Entrepreneurs: the individuals who make entrepreneurship—and change—happen

Good ideas—even ones with huge potential value—are *not* automatically developed. Rather, they often become reality only through the efforts of specific persons—individual entrepreneurs—who work long and hard to make them real. The concept of a machine that would make copies on plain paper, for instance, existed for decades but was not developed because few people recognized its value. They assumed, instead, that good methods for making copies already existed (left-hand photo). However, Chester Carlson pursued this opportunity for decades and finally did succeed in bringing it to market (right-hand photo). The result? This year, people all over the world will make more than *three trillion* copies using such machines.

How much change did Carlson's invention produce once it actually existed? Consider this statistic: this year, the world will produce more than three trillion xerographic copies and laser-printed pages—about 500 for every human being on earth. Would someone else have developed copiers if Carlson had suddenly disappeared or merely given up? Perhaps, but it is clear that in cases like this one, change does indeed happen because specific persons invest the effort to make it happen. And when such an "idea champion" is not available, the change may not occur. Here's another dramatic example of this fact. When the Spanish invaded South America and conquered the Inca people, they were surprised to find that this highly advanced civilization did *not* use the wheel for transport; instead, items being moved from one place to another (crops, manufactured goods, etc.) were loaded on the backs of animals, or pulled along behind them on sleds. Yet, the Inca *did* have the idea for the wheel: it was used on toy carts played with by Inca children. Why then didn't anyone have the idea of using the wheel for transporting items? We'll never know for sure, but history records that because no one seems to have made this connection and then acted to put it into practice, the Inca had to make do without the wheel for several centuries.

Having discussed these preliminary—but important—issues the remainder of this chapter will proceed as follows. First we'll examine the question of why entrepreneurship is so important—the various ways in which it contributes to human well-being. As we'll soon see, this goes far beyond its purely economic benefits. Second, we'll examine the reasons why individuals choose to become entrepreneurs, which are, in fact, much broader than is often assumed. Third, we'll turn the question of how we can obtain knowledge about entrepreneurship that goes beyond the informal suggestions and observations provided by entrepreneurs themselves. While these comments may be both insightful and informative, there are strong reasons for accepting them with a large degree of caution. We'll briefly explain what these are, and suggest alternative approaches for acquiring the accurate and reliable knowledge we week.

Why entrepreneurship is important: Economic growth, "giving back," and maximizing human motivation

In a sense, the early decades of the twenty-first century can be described as "the decades of the entrepreneur." Entrepreneurship is featured in countless magazine and newspaper articles, popular television shows (e.g., *Shark Tank*) and major films (*The Social Network*), universities have added courses, departments, and even schools of entrepreneurship to their offerings; and governments at all levels seem to be competing to develop programs and incentives to encourage entrepreneurship. A key reason behind this amazing popularity is the strong conviction that entrepreneurship is a powerful engine of economic growth. And in fact, considerable evidence indicates that it is. For instance, a major world-wide project, the Global Entrepreneurship Monitor (GEM), begun in 1999, reports that the level of entrepreneurial activity in various economies around the world is strongly and positively associated with subsequent levels of economic growth in those economies. When entrepreneurship thrives, so too does economic growth, and subsequent prosperity. Further, the same survey indicates that there are *no* countries with high levels of entrepreneurship that simultaneously show *low* levels of economic growth (Reynolds et al., 2002; OECD, 2010). Additional research demonstrates the same relationship with other data (e.g., Nickell, 2010). So, overall, existing evidence leaves little doubt that entrepreneurship is indeed positively linked with economic growth.

This, of course, is one reason why so many governments are currently making efforts to promote entrepreneurship: they recognize that it will, potentially, contribute to the wealth, standard of living, and well-being of their populations. This is not the only reason why entrepreneurship is important, however. Another—and one that is often overlooked—involves the strong propensity of entrepreneurs to "give back" to their communities and societies—to share the wealth they have accumulated by generous gifts, contributions, and similar actions. How important are such outcomes? Consider the following facts:

- In one recent year (2010), 13 of the 19 largest individual donations to various recipients in the United States (universities, medical facilities, cultural organizations) were made by entrepreneurs—founders or co-founders of highly successful companies. Among the familiar names on this list are T. Boone Pickens (business magnate and financier), Mark Zuckerberg (co-founder of Facebook), and Irwin F. Jacobs (founder of Qualcomm; see *Chronicle of Philanthropy*, 2010).
- *The Wall Street Journal* (2013), recently identified a number of famous entrepreneurs who have made public pledges to donate large portions of their fortunes to help address important social issues—ranging from efforts to rescue and revitalize "broken" pension systems (especially those for public employees), through dealing with the world-wide epidemic of obesity. Well-known entrepreneurs who have made such pledges (often to donate 50 percent or more of their personal wealth to special foundations they have created), include Warren Buffett (US magnate and investor), Paul Allen (co-founder of Microsoft), Sergey Brin (founder of Google), and his wife Anne Wojcicki, also a successful entrepreneur.
- A recently published compilation of the largest gifts ever bestowed on business schools by the Association to Advance Collegiate Schools of Business (AACSB) reveals that a large proportion of donors were entrepreneurs—individuals such as Philip Knight (co-founder of Nike), the Walton family (founders of Walmart), and Henry W. Block (co-founder of H&R Block).

Needless to add, not all large donations or charitable gifts are provided by entrepreneurs—far from it. But several sources of evidence combine to suggest that entrepreneurs' reputation for generosity is actually well deserved.

In addition, and this is crucial, entrepreneurs appear to be more generous in this respect than other persons of equivalent wealth. Long-term studies of what is often termed "giving by high net worth individuals" indicate that, in fact, entrepreneurs—as persons who have acquired their wealth through starting and running their own businesses—are more likely to make donations, and to make larger ones than persons who have acquired their wealth in other ways (e.g., inheritance, investments, real estate, etc.). In each of three recent years (2007, 2009, 2011), entrepreneurs made significantly larger donations, on average, than any other group—persons who acquired their wealth through real estate, investments, or inheritance. The magnitude of this difference was substantial in each year (although it varied considerably, reflecting shifting economic conditions). As shown in Figure 1.2, in 2007, for example, entrepreneurs donated almost $270 000 (on average), while the equivalent figures for persons whose wealth derived from inheritance ($84 000), real estate ($105 000) or earned income (i.e., salaries or other compensation; $65 500) were significantly lower. Other findings indicate

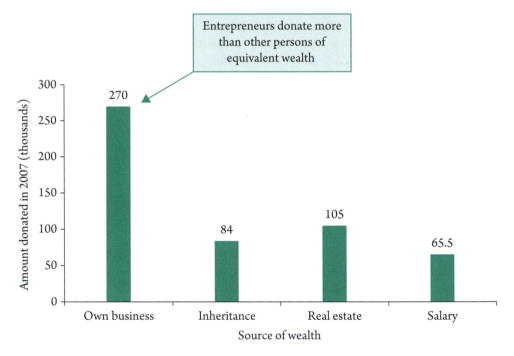

Source: Based on data from Bank of America study, 2012.

Figure 1.2 Entrepreneurs do indeed "give back" to their communities

As shown here, long-term studies of "giving" by people of high net worth indicate that entrepreneurs tend to make larger donations than persons whose wealth came from different sources (e.g., inheritance, real estate, salary, etc.). Data from one recent year are shown here.

that entrepreneurs were more likely than other groups to have a formal plan in place for continued giving (Bank of America, 2012). It is important to note again that these differences exist even when overall wealth is held constant, so it is not simply that entrepreneurs give more because they have more; rather, other factors (e.g., a desire to make amends for "cutting corners" on the way up; a desire to reduce feelings of being "over-rewarded"—receiving more than, perhaps, they feel they deserve, a desire to leave behind a lasting legacy) may be much more important (Baron and Hmieleski, 2013).

Whatever the specific reasons, however, entrepreneurs do appear to be unusually generous with their wealth, and since their prosocial actions (gifts, grants, etc.) produce major benefits for a large number of recipients (universities, medical facilities, etc.), this is another major contribution by entrepreneurs to society.

Finally, it is intriguing to consider, briefly, the relationship of entrepreneurship to human motivation, and, specifically, how it maximizes the motivation to work long, hard, and energetically. Decades of research on the questions of when and why people will exert effort at various tasks or jobs suggests that several factors are crucial: having specific goals to work towards (e.g., Latham, 2007), and cognitive factors involving the beliefs that (1) effort will result in improved performance and (2) excellent performance will be recognized and rewarded (Vroom, 1995). A large volume of research indicates that the stronger these beliefs, the stronger their work motivation. As Bandura puts it (1997, p. 129; emphasis added): "People regulate their level and distribution of effort in accordance with the effects they *expect* their actions to have."

In short, people work hardest and most consistently when they expect that doing so will result in the outcomes they desire—various rewards they wish to obtain. This is one reason why most organizations attempt to establish effective systems for evaluating and rewarding employee performance, and try to assure that these systems are viewed as fair and accurate by the persons being evaluated. Unfortunately, in many instances, these links between effort and performance and between performance and rewards are weak or even non-existent. And when they are, individuals conclude—rightly or wrongly—that there is little reason for working hard. And that, in turn, is often the "kiss of death" to motivation. After all, why should they work hard when doing so is unrelated to their outcomes?

Entrepreneurship, of course, is the antithesis of such conditions—or at least, most entrepreneurs believe that it is. In fact, as we'll see in the next section, one reason many individuals decide to become entrepreneurs is to strengthen links between their effort, performance, and outcomes. They believe that by running their own companies they *will* benefit from their own hard work and effort. A clear illustration of the importance of such beliefs is provided by the recent history of Russia, formerly the Soviet Union. Until the 1990s, agriculture in the Soviet Union was run by the state, either through state-owned farms or collective farms. In these organizations, individuals received wages, or a share of the farm's earnings. There was, however, almost no connection between individual effort and these rewards. As a result, despite huge investments by the government in providing modern equipment and raw materials, production was low—so low, that it rarely met projected goals. In sharp contrast, a very small proportion of land was set aside for "private" use: the persons who farmed it could keep the output and benefit directly from its use or sale. One result: although only 3 percent of all arable land was set aside for such use, it produced almost 25 percent of the total agricultural output! It was in short ten times more productive than the land farmed collectively. What was the difference? Primarily, observers agree, that the link between effort and reward was much stronger for the private plots than for the collective farms. After all, why should anyone work hard when doing so would not yield better outcomes? The answer was, apparently, "they wouldn't" (Figure 1.3). And as an anonymous government employee in Cuba put it recently (quoted in *National Geographic*, 2012): "They pretend to pay us and we pretend to work."

Source: Fotolia #1999616.

Figure 1.3
Entrepreneurship enhances human motivation

Entrepreneurs believe very strongly that the harder they work, the larger the rewards they will receive. In contrast, in situations where there is no strong link between effort and rewards, motivation is reduced, and performance suffers.

Of course, this is only indirect evidence—many other factors might well have played a role in productivity differences between "private" plots and collective farms (e.g., perhaps individuals working on private plots were younger, more energetic, and more ambitious than those working on collective farms). But overall, it seems clear that an additional benefit of entrepreneurship is that it maximizes strong links between effort, performance, and rewards—and in so doing, provides conditions for maximizing human motivation. Little wonder then that entrepreneurs often work long hours and devote themselves so passionately to building their companies—or, more broadly, that entrepreneurship itself is a such a powerful engine of economic growth.

What do entrepreneurs seek? Wealth? Fame? Doing social good? Answer: All of the above

Why do individuals choose to become entrepreneurs? Why do they take the steps needed to convert their ideas or dreams to reality, either by starting new ventures or through other means? The fact that acting entrepreneurially involves high levels of uncertainty and no guarantees of success suggests that this choice must involve strong underlying "motives"—internal processes we can't directly observe, but that strongly influence behavior and thought. But what, precisely, are these? It has often been assumed that the answer to this question is straightforward: entrepreneurs primarily seek wealth or fame, and view starting a new venture (or other entrepreneurial actions) as useful for attaining these goals. All too often this is the implicit message in courses on entrepreneurship. Examples and cases emphasize successful new ventures and the benefits they provide for their founders. Further, business plan competitions award substantial cash prizes to the winners, and—perhaps even more important—provide the entrepreneurs with introductions and access to venture capitalists, business angels, and other potential sources of funding. The overall result is that the term "entrepreneur" is now strongly associated, both in the public mind and in the field of entrepreneurship itself, with strong motivation for financial gain. Yes, the possibility that entrepreneurs seek other goals and proceed from different motives, is mentioned occasionally—for instance, the desire to leave something "behind" when their time on earth is through—something concrete that will survive their own demise. And it is increasingly recognized that some entrepreneurs—usually termed "social entrepreneurs"—want primarily to create beneficial outcomes for many other persons, rather than personal wealth. Overall, though, there is widespread belief that individuals become entrepreneurs to gain success, wealth, and fame.

Is this view accurate? Although it may apply to many entrepreneurs, it tends to ignore other motives that may be just as strong—or even stronger—than financial ones. For example, some individuals become entrepreneurs largely out of necessity rather than a desire for fame and wealth: they are downsized by their employers or lose their current jobs for other reasons, but are still too young to retire—or simply not ready to do so. If they are over age 50 they may be viewed as relatively undesirable in the job market, so such persons often turn to entrepreneurship as one possible option.

In addition, and even more important, many individuals choose to become entrepreneurs because they are seeking personal fulfillment—greater meaning in their lives. Tired of doing jobs they view as largely meaningless and that they don't enjoy (Figure 1.4), they choose instead to trade these positions (which may be stable and offer good salaries and fringe benefits) for the uncertainties of starting their own business. Taking account of these basic facts, Rindova et al. (2009) suggest that, in fact, many individuals become entrepreneurs because they are seeking what these authors describe

Source: Fotolia #9835092.

Figure 1.4
Why do many individuals become entrepreneurs? Not only because they seek wealth or fame

Many individuals choose to become entrepreneurs because they want to escape from dull, meaningless work and do something they enjoy and view as important.

as "emancipation"—release from social, economic, cultural, or institutional constraints that restrict their personal freedom or autonomy. As a prime example of such motivation, Rindova et al. (ibid.) point to Google, noting that its founders wanted to break free from constraints on the use of the internet that existed in the mid-1990s. Their goal was to shatter technological and cultural barriers, so that vast amounts of information would be available to virtually anyone. It is important to note that *at the same time* they also wanted to build a profitable company; as Rindova et al. (ibid., p. 483) note, "there is no opposition between emancipatory projects to create change and a hard-nosed business strategy." In fact, entrepreneurship—like all complex behavior—stems from multiple motives, often operating simultaneously. What's crucial, however, is to recognize that in many instances, wealth generation is not the only or even most important one.

Another way to express this view is to note that many entrepreneurs start new ventures or perform other entrepreneurial actions because they are seeking "self-realization." They want to grow and learn as a person, to exert leadership, motivate others, or fulfill personal visions and dreams. Evidence that such motives are important as a basis for becoming an entrepreneur is provided by research conducted by Cassar (2007). In this investigation data from a large national survey of entrepreneurs, the PSED (prospective, or nascent, entrepreneurs, more than 64 000 participants), was used, in part, as a basis for evaluating the relative strength of several motives that could, potentially, underlie entrepreneurship. Several different motives were also assessed, and as shown in Figure 1.5, results were clear: the desire for independence was stronger than the desire for financial success among both prospective and actual entrepreneurs. Still another motive, the desire for recognition, which is closely related to motivation for achievement, was also high in the ratings.

Similarly, it has been proposed by the present author (Baron, 2010) that individuals often become entrepreneurs because they are seeking the kind of working conditions identified by research on "job design" as ones that generate high levels of motivation, satisfaction, and performance (e.g., Baron, 2010; Grant et al., 2010). In other words, they become entrepreneurs because they are seeking *meaning* in their work, and this is provided by high levels of autonomy, task significance (tasks being performed seem important), task identity (entire tasks can be completed, not simply portions of them), and skill variety (many different skills can be exercised and put to good use). Clearly, the entrepreneurial role provides these conditions, and it may be that individuals who perceive that they can attain such outcomes by starting their own businesses or acting entrepreneurially in other ways, are especially attracted to this role. In essence, they become entrepreneurs in

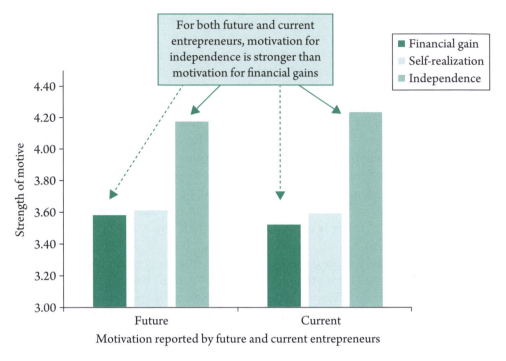

For both future and current entrepreneurs, motivation for independence is stronger than motivation for financial gains

- Financial gain
- Self-realization
- Independence

Motivation reported by future and current entrepreneurs

Source: Based on data from Cassar, 2007.

Figure 1.5 What motivates entrepreneurs? Evidence that financial gains are not at the top of the list

Growing evidence indicates that entrepreneurs have many different motives and that among these the desires for independence and self-fulfillment are often stronger than the desire for financial success.

a quest for "the perfect job or career"—one that will be closely aligned with their own strong desires for meaningfulness in what they do, and in this way will contribute to their personal happiness. For such persons, the decision to become an entrepreneur is certainly *not* the result, solely, or perhaps even primarily, of strong desires for wealth and fame.

In addition, some individuals choose to become entrepreneurs because they find the personal freedom this role provides (or at least, seems to provide!) highly appealing. In the past, I had the pleasure of team-teaching a course on entrepreneurship with a Nobel-prize winning physicist. He had started a company to develop his scientific ideas into useable products (e.g., one that could diagnose cancer on the basis of the electrical properties of cells). But, as he himself put it, he took virtually no steps to obtain adequate financing or build sales because being a scientist he had little or no training in business practices. Basically, he enjoyed working, whenever and however he wished in the university's Incubator Park, where as Nobel scientist he was always welcome and always treated with great respect (deservedly so). Clearly, he was *not* motivated by a desire for wealth or fame—he already had as much fame as most people could ever desire, and was well off financially, too. But he did greatly enjoy the role of "scientist-turned-entrepreneur" and it contributed yet another dimension to his sense of personal fulfillment and well-being.

Finally, some persons become entrepreneurs because they want to "do good"—to enhance human well-being, or at least the well-being of people in their own communities, regions, or countries. Such persons are often described as being social entrepreneurs, and although they realize that they must make a profit to stay in business, this is not their primary goal. Rather, they are primarily motivated by the desire to provide benefits for a large number of persons. For example, consider the work of two engineers— Pettie Petzer and Johan Jonker—who designed a product known as the Hippo Roller. What it does is simple: it provides a better means for individuals to move water from its source (e.g., a well or stream) to where it is used (in their homes). It is estimated that throughout the world more than one billion people must move water directly—they have no faucets they can simply turn on. The Hippo Roller (originally called the Aqua Roller) allows them to move water with much less effort than simply carrying it in pails or buckets (Figure 1.6). More than 50 000 Hippo Rollers have been distributed to approximately 21 countries, and here is the key point: *95 percent of these rollers have been donated (primarily by businesses)—they have not been sold for a profit!* To date, more than 400 000 people have benefitted in this way, and it is difficult to think of a better illustration of social entrepreneurship in action.

So, are all entrepreneurs seeking the wealth and fame we assume are the key motivators of their actions? Far from it! In fact, the more we learn about entrepreneurship and entrepreneurs, the clearer it becomes that they choose this role for many different reasons. Desires for self-fulfillment, personal growth, and helping others are often as important, or even more important, than motivation for financial gain. Further, it's important to recognize that various motives for entrepreneurship may exist simultaneously, and operate in combination. For instance, the desire for fame might combine with the desire to leave a lasting legacy, or the desire to acquire personal wealth might combine with the desire to do social good, since such wealth can provide the means for doing so. Whatever the precise patterns involved, however, it seems clear that the motives behind entrepreneurship are as varied and rich as those behind any other complex form of human behavior or challenging career choice.

Figure 1.6 Social entrepreneurship: enhancing human welfare

Far from seeking personal wealth and fame, some entrepreneurs turn their ideas into products or services that will contribute to human welfare—to enhance the quality of human life. A clear example of such motives is provided by the Hippo Roller—a product that provides a better way for individuals to move the water they need from its source to their homes. Large numbers of the Hippo Roller have been given free to the people who use them, so clearly, making a profit is *not* the key goal for the entrepreneurs who have developed it.

Some further thoughts about motivation

Although entrepreneurs clearly differ greatly in terms of interests, values, skills, personal characteristics, and many other factors, it seems clear that motivation is indeed central to the entrepreneurial process. Without it, ideas remain merely possibilities, and, as Locke and Baum (2007) suggest, nothing much happens! In their own words (p. 93; emphasis added): "A person may have sufficient technical skill and money to start a business, but without *motivation* nothing happens." In short, entrepreneurs are indeed the "active principle" in entrepreneurship, and it is their motivation to move forward with their ideas that makes the entire process.

Acquiring the knowledge we seek: Why the insights of entrepreneurs—even highly successful ones—are often not enough

There is an old saying suggesting that "if you want to know something, just ask an expert." Certainly, that advice makes a lot of sense in many situations. If you want to know about plumbing, ask a plumber; if you want to know about your health, ask a physician (especially the right specialist); and if you want to know about entrepreneurship, just ask an entrepreneur—preferably, a highly successful one. Certainly, that *sounds* like reasonable advice, and in fact it is the basis (although often implicit) behind many popular books on entrepreneurship—books that ostensibly tell readers how *they* can succeed in starting their own business by following the advice of the author—generally, an experienced entrepreneur who has "been there, done that."

Is this really a sound way to proceed? Can we really find out what we want to know about entrepreneurship by asking successful entrepreneurs? To some extent, perhaps we can; certainly, they do have a wealth of practical knowledge so paying attention to their advice *can* be helpful. But there are also important reasons for caution in terms of basing our understanding of the complex process of entrepreneurship on such informal and subjective foundations.

First, a large body of evidence indicates that, in general, we are far less effective than we believe in understanding our own behavior—in identifying the motives behind it, the factors that have affected our actions, why we made various choices or decisions in the past, or even why we like or don't like various objects, experiences, or even people. Basically, the bottom line of these all-too-human limitations is simply this: often, we don't know why we have acted as we did, why events turned out as they did, or what factors played a key role in their occurrence (Wilson, 2009). To the extent that's true—and a great deal of evidence indicates that it is (ibid.)—it is clear that we often *think* we know more about ourselves than we really do, and believe that we understand our own actions, motives, feelings, and the factors that influence them, much better than is actually the case (e.g., Nisbett and Wilson, 1977).

Further, and to add "icing to the cake" (although in this case, the "icing" is not necessarily a "plus") extensive literature on the nature and accuracy of memory suggests that this basic system for storing and retrieving information is far from perfect, is often highly selective in nature and is subject to a number of errors, and can easily be distorted. For instance, to mention just one pertinent illustration of these constraints, evidence concerning eyewitness testimony indicates that it is far less accurate than has been widely assumed (Loftus, 1996). Further, the accuracy of memory (and of self-knowledge generally) is often reduced by a wide range of cognitive biases—for instance, and again, to mention just a few of the more important ones—the "self-serving bias" (the tendency to attribute positive outcomes to internal factors and negative outcomes to external ones); the "optimistic bias" (the tendency to believe, to a greater extent than is rationally justified that positive events or outcomes will occur in many situations); and the "confirmation bias" (the tendency to notice and remember primarily information consistent with existing views or beliefs; Darley and Gross, 1983). The overall result is that most persons, much of the time, have only incomplete and somewhat inaccurate knowledge of the factors that actually affect (or have affected) their behavior, feelings, or thoughts (Kahneman, 2011). In view of this basic fact it seems appropriate to approach entrepreneurs' subjective impressions of why and how they succeeded with considerable caution. Certainly, the entrepreneurs may be doing their best to provide accurate information, but basic limitations in our cognitive systems suggest that their insights and conclusions can be misleading (Figure 1.7).

Perhaps, at this point, an example of the kind of research pointing to these conclusions about the need for caution in interpreting entrepreneurs' informal comments and advice would be helpful. In a classic experiment that vividly illustrates the limits of our understanding of the factors that shape our own behavior or thoughts, Nisbett and Wilson (1977) asked college students to memorize a list of word pairs. Some of these (e.g., ocean–moon) were designed to generate mental associations that would suggest specific words—ones closely related to these word pairs. For instance, participants were shown the words "ocean" and "moon," and were then asked to name a laundry detergent. A very large proportion came up with "Tide," which is clearly related to the ocean–moon word pair. But—and here's the key

Source: Courtesy of Robert A. Baron.

Figure 1.7 Memory is far from perfect: even eyewitnesses to crimes make errors in remembering what they saw

Because memory is subject to many errors and distortions, entrepreneurs' reports of what they did in the past, and how this influenced their success, should be viewed with a degree of caution. Eyewitnesses to crimes often make errors in identifying the criminals through line-ups such as this one.

point—when asked if the word pairs had influenced their answer, participants said "Absolutely not!" Instead, they insisted, they had come up with "Tide" because it is very popular, they use it at home, or other reasons. Was this true? Evidence indicates it was not, and that the word pairs had indeed affected their behavior, but the participants didn't, or couldn't recognize this fact. In a follow-up investigation, the same researchers asked participants to choose the best product from an array of products (e.g., the best radio, pens, etc.). Results indicated that participants had a strong "right-side preference"—they chose the items on the right-hand side of the display much more often than ones on the left. When asked if position had any influence on their behavior, however, they reacted with indignation: "Of course not!"

If we are not very good even at performing simple judgments such as these, can we be accurate in reporting the factors responsible for our success—especially since they may have existed years in the past? Please draw your own conclusion, but the weight of scientific evidence seems clear: "No, we are not very good at this task, and often make important errors." With this point in mind, can we view entrepreneurs' comments about *why* and *how* they succeeded as accurate—a firm basis for understanding entrepreneurship as a process? Perhaps, but again, a degree of caution seems essential. This does *not* mean that we should discount such information—far from it. It *is* often helpful and insightful. But these statements should always be evaluated against the backdrop of actual *evidence* concerning their accuracy—evidence gathered either through systematic research or imported from other fields where it already exists.

"But how," you may be wondering, can we conduct systematic research on entrepreneurship? It can't be studied in a laboratory, or by means of sophisticated scientific equipment. The answer is, in part, straightforward and rests on the methods developed by several branches of social science: instead of merely asking a few famous entrepreneurs to provide us with their personal insights, we can instead collect data from large numbers of entrepreneurs and new ventures using carefully designed measures, and then search diligently for patterns in these data. For instance, if a particular variable or factor is strongly related to various measures of new venture success (e.g., rate of growth, rise in profits, etc.), this provides evidence for the view that this factor plays a role in entrepreneurship. For instance, suppose we find that across many (e.g., hundreds) of new ventures, the ones headed by entrepreneurs who are "good with people" (i.e., high social or political skills) tend to be more successful than those headed by entrepreneurs who are lower on this dimension. That suggests that such skills may be one factor that plays a role in entrepreneurship. Or, alternatively, suppose we find that new ventures that adopt a strategy of seeking to be highly innovative and of being "first" to market with new products, tend to be more successful than ones that adopt a more cautious, "one-step-at-a time" approach. Again, we might conclude that this particular kind of strategy plays an important role in entrepreneurship and perhaps should be encouraged. And as a third example, suppose we find that new ventures headed by entrepreneurs with moderately high optimism tend to be more successful than ones headed by entrepreneurs who are either very low in optimism (they expect negative outcomes) or extremely high in this characteristic (they expect positive outcomes virtually all the time). This suggests that entrepreneurs' optimism may be related to the success of new ventures—but in a fairly complex manner. Can even highly experienced individual entrepreneurs tell us this on the basis of their own experience? The likelihood seems low. Given that entrepreneurship is indeed a complex process, affected by a wealth of factors relating both to entrepreneurs and to external (environmental) conditions, it seems clear that only systematic research, and the concrete evidence it yields, can help identify such relationships and provide the kind of accurate insights we seek.

For this reason, I will rely, whenever possible, on systematic evidence gathered by researchers in the field of entrepreneurship or, in some instances, imported by them from other related fields (e.g., the study of human decision-making, etc.) in discussing the many topics included in this book, and also as a basis for specific recommendations and guidance for current or prospective entrepreneurs. Doing so, I believe, will put our discussions on a firmer footing than relying, solely, on the subjective impressions and beliefs of individual entrepreneurs. Yes, these can be insightful and helpful, and they will certainly be included. But they are not, in and of themselves, enough for obtaining the accurate, reliable insights into the nature and outcomes of entrepreneurship as a complex process that we seek. Only data, gathered in systematic research, can provide *that*, and the upshot is that this book will be as "evidence based" as possible, but without—of course!—ignoring insights and information provided by experienced entrepreneurs.

A roadmap of this book: Its special features

This book has several special features designed to make it more useful. Several are fairly standard—chapter outlines, to help readers get the "big picture" of the content included, and summaries of key points. In addition, it also includes two unique features. First, each chapter also includes a feature entitled "The Effective Entrepreneur," which explains succinctly how the main points covered in that chapter can actually be applied by entrepreneurs to increase their own effectiveness—and success. Second, when appropriate, chapters include a feature entitled "The Entrepreneurial Quest." These case studies briefly describe the origins and activities of actual new ventures and are designed to illustrate, in concrete terms, how entrepreneurs use the principles discussed in the text in their efforts to convert ideas into reality. In a sense, they reflect the sub-title of this text: "Evidence and Practice," by helping to connect the findings of systematic research with efforts by entrepreneurs to create something new, useful, and better out of the "raw materials" of their own creativity, effort, experience, and skills.

SUMMARY OF KEY POINTS

1 In an important sense, entrepreneurs change the world—by converting their ideas into reality, they sometimes influence the lives of large numbers of people.

2 At its heart, entrepreneurship involves the emergence of ideas, their evaluation, and their development—conversion into something new and tangible by various means. Often, entrepreneurship involves the launch of new businesses that develop the opportunities and bring new products or services to market. However, it can occur in many other ways too.

3 Entrepreneurship is important for many reasons—it encourages

economic growth, entrepreneurs often "give back" to their communities in important ways (e.g., gifts, donations), and it is an arena in which the link between human effort and rewards is maximized.

4 It is often assumed that entrepreneurs' primary motive is gaining wealth or fame, but in fact they often seek other goals, such as greater autonomy or the opportunity to perform meaningful work.

5 It is often assumed that knowledge about entrepreneurship can be gained from the insights and comments of highly successful entrepreneurs. However, there are strong reasons for caution in terms of accepting such informal information as accurate. For instance, memory is far from accurate, and individuals often do not understand the motives behind their own actions very well. For this reason, such informal information should be supplemented with or replaced by evidence gathered through systematic research.

 REFERENCES

Bandura, A. (1997), *Self-efficacy: The Exercise of Control*, New York: W.H. Freeman.

Bank of America (2012), *Study of High Net Worth Philanthropy: Issues Driving Charitable Activities Among Wealthy Households*, Bank of America and The Center on Philanthropy at Indiana University.

Baron, R.A. (2010), "Job design and entrepreneurship: Why closer connections = mutual gains," *Journal of Organizational Behavior*, **30**(2–3), 1–10.

Baron, R.A. (2012), *Entrepreneurship: An Evidence Based Guide*, Cheltenham, UK and Northampton, MA, USA: Edward Elgar Publishing.

Baron, R.A. and K.M. Hmieleski (2013), "Cognitive and motivational foundations of entrepreneurs' prosocial behavior: Why they often choose to help," manuscript under review.

Cassar, G. (2007), "Money, money, money? A longitudinal investigation of entrepreneur career reasons, growth preferences, and achieved growth," *Entrepreneurship and Regional Development*, **19**(1), 89–107.

Chronicle of Philanthropy, The (2010), "Biggest gifts announced by individuals in 2010," 31 December, accessed 14 October 2013 at http://philanthropy.com/article/Biggest-Gifts-Announced-by/125775/.

Darley, J.M. and P.H. Gross (1983), "A hypothesis-confirming bias in labeling effects," *Journal of Personality and Social Psychology*, **44**(1), 20–33.

Drucker, P.F. (1985), *Innovation and Entrepreneurship*, Oxford: Elsevier Ltd.

Grant, A.M., Y. Fried, S.K. Parker and M. Frese (2010), "Putting job design in context: Introduction to the special issue," *Journal of Organizational Behavior*, **31**(2–3), 145–57.

Kahneman, D. (2011), *Thinking, Fast and Slow*, New York: Farrar, Strauss, Giroux.

Latham, G. (2007), *Work Motivation*, New York: Sage.

Locke, E.E. and R.J. Baum (2007), "Entrepreneurial motivation," in R.J. Baum, M. Frese, and R.A. Baron (eds), *The Psychology of Entrepreneurship*, Mahwah, NJ: Erlbaum, pp. 83–112.

Loftus, E.F. (1996), *Eyewitness Testimony*, Cambridge, MA: Harvard University Press.

Meindl, J.R. (1995), "The romance of leadership as a follower-centric theory: A social constructionist approach," *The Leadership Quarterly*, **6**(3), 329–41.

National Geographic (2012), "Cuba's new now," November, accessed 15 October 2013 at http://ngm.nationalgeographic.com/2012/11/new-cuba/gorney-text.

Nickell, S. (2010), "The unemployment challenge in Europe," *CESifo Forum*, **11**(1), 3–6.

Nisbett, R.E. and T.D. Wilson (1977), "Telling more than we can know: Verbal reports on mental processes," *Psychological Review*, **84**(3), 231–59.

OECD (2010), *Entrepreneurship and Migrants. Report by the OECD Working Party on SMEs and Entrepreneurship*, Paris: OECD.

Parker, S.C. (2011), "Intrapreneurship or entrepreneurship?", *Journal of Business Venturing*, **26**(1), 19–34.

Reynolds, P.D., W.D. Bygrave, E. Autio, L.W. Cox and M. Hay (2002), *Global Entrepreneurship Monitor, 2002, Executive Report*, Wellesley, MA: Babson College.

Rindova, V., D. Barry and D.J. Ketchen Jr. (2009), "Entrepreneuring as emancipation," *Academy of Management Review*, **34**(3), 477–91.

Shane, S. (2012), "Reflections on the 2010 AMR decade award: Delivering on the promise of entrepreneurship as a field of research," *Academy of Management Review*, **37**(1), 10–20.

Shane, S. and S. Venkataraman (2000), "The promise of entrepreneurship as a field of research," *Academy of Management Review*, **25**(1), 217–26.

Shane S., E. Locke and C. Collins (2003), "Entrepreneurial motivation," *Human Resource Management Review*, **13**(2), 257–79.

Vroom, V.H. (1995), *Work Motivation*, San Francisco: Jossey-Bass.

Wilson, T.D. (2009), "Know thyself," *Perspectives on Psychological Science*, **4**(4), 384–9.

2

Cognitive foundations of entrepreneurship

> *Creativity is just connecting things. When you ask creative people how they did something, they feel a little guilty because they didn't really do it, they just saw something. It seemed obvious to them after a while.*
> (Steve Jobs, Apple entrepreneur, in *The Wired Interview*, Wolf, 1996)

> *The chief enemy of creativity is common sense.*
> (Pablo Picasso, sculptor and painter, 1881–1973)

> *Innovation is the specific instrument of entrepreneurship . . . the act that endows resources with a new capacity to create wealth.*
> (Peter F. Drucker, *Innovation and Entrepreneurship*, 1985)

Where—and when—does entrepreneurship begin? In Chapter 1, entrepreneurship was defined as a process—one in which individuals (entrepreneurs) generate ideas for something new, useful, and better, and then take *action* to convert these ideas into reality—to give them tangible form and expression (Shane and Venkataraman, 2000; Shane, 2012). Given that definition, it seems reasonable to suggest that, in fact, entrepreneurship begins in the minds of individual entrepreneurs. One or more persons generate an idea that has the potential to create "value"—economic or social benefits (and sometimes, both). These ideas, which vary tremendously in scope, point the way to new products, services, means of production, raw materials, or ways of organizing current knowledge and technology. Whatever their content, however, they are definitely products of "human cognition"—human thought. Here's one example: what can people do with their old cell phones? Most just throw them away, thus wasting the useful materials the phones contain, and dumping items that will last thousands of years into landfills. After considering this problem, Mark Bowles came up with the idea of providing people with convenient places where they could trade their old cell phones for cash. He put this idea into operation by founding a new company (ecoATM) that placed kiosks that would accept not only cell phones, but also MP3 players and tablets, and pay the owners cash on the spot (Figure 2.1).

Source: Courtesy of ecoATM.

Figure 2.1 Ideas for something new, better, and useful: products of human thought

How do the ideas for new ventures such as ecoATM, which gives consumers a convenient way to trade their old electronic devices for cash (see above), arise? Clearly, they are the products of human thought and human creativity.

The result? The company now has 350 locations for its kiosks, with many more planned. It sells 75 percent of the phones to companies that refurbish them, and the rest to e-waste recyclers, who remove the valuable materials inside. Clearly then, the founder of ecoATM has come up with an idea for something new, better, and useful—and turned it into reality. To repeat what we said in Chapter 1: that is the essence of entrepreneurship.

But how did Mark Bowles come up with this valuable idea? To answer that question we must examine basic cognitive processes that underlie creativity, and its practical expression in innovations that people can actually use. Information on these processes will provide an important basis for our discussion of other important aspects of entrepreneurship, ranging from "opportunity recognition"—identification of new means of generating economic or social value that are not being currently developed by others (see Chapter 3 this volume and Baron, 2006) through "intellectual property"—legal steps entrepreneurs can take to protect their ideas (Chapter 9 this volume), so it is important to present it here.

In specific terms, our discussion will proceed as follows. First we'll examine the basic nature of human cognition, which, although tremendously impressive in many respects, also suffers from important flaws. Next, we'll examine the nature and origins of creativity—where and how ideas for something new and better originate, how creativity can be enhanced, the relationship between creativity and innovation. Finally, we'll look inside the minds of entrepreneurs, addressing the questions, "Do they think differently from other persons?" "And if so, how?" Now, to begin at the beginning, we'll turn to information about the basic nature of human cognition—how we think, remember, reason, make decisions, and—in essence—attempt to make sense of the world around us.

Human cognition: Its basic nature—and important limitations

Where were you when the terrorist-planted bombs exploded during the 2013 Boston Marathon, killing many people watching the race? Can you remember the first time you went to the dentist? The day you received your driver's license? When you experienced your first "crush" on another person? Can you dance? Speak more than one language? What are your plans for the future? Do you intend to start your own company some day? Are you happy in your current life? If not, how can you change it to *become* happy? This may seem like a totally unconnected list of items, but, in fact, they are related in a basic way: all involve, and depend upon, our basic cognitive processes—

our capacities to notice, store, remember, interpret, and use information—
processes that are a key aspect of being human. Without them, we would be
unable to remember the past or learn from it, to speak, read, perform any kind
of activity that requires skill, make plans, reach decisions, solve problems,
or even daydream. In short, our cognitive abilities underlie virtually everything we do, think, feel, or imagine. Knowing something about their basic
nature, therefore, is important for understanding the basic nature of entrepreneurship, which, as noted above, begins with processes that unfold in the
human mind. Research on human cognition has continued for decades, and
has uncovered an amazing array of facts about it—especially recently, with
the advent and use of techniques for measuring brain activity and function
(e.g., Amodio, 2010). Here, though, we'll focus on two topics that are highly
relevant to entrepreneurship: memory and a vast array of cognitive biases
that influence our thinking—and can lead us into serious error (e.g., Ariely,
2009).

Memory: How we store, recover, and use information acquired through experience

Some people—fortunately, very few—suffer from disorders in which they
cannot retain information for more than a few seconds. For such persons,
each day is like the start of a new life: they cannot recall anything that happened to them in the past. In most cases, they do retain the capacity to speak,
get dressed, and perform many routine tasks. But in other respects, their
minds are like blank canvases, waiting to be filled again each day.

In contrast, most of us possess functioning "memories"—cognitive systems
that allow us to store, retrieve, and use information we acquired previously.
As you can guess, these systems are crucial for many tasks, from solving
problems to making plans and thinking creatively, which often involves combining information in memory in new and unexpected ways (e.g., Sternberg
and Sternberg, 2011). Although in everyday speech we refer to memory as
if it were a unitary process, we actually possess three distinct kinds. One,
"working memory," holds a limited amount of information for brief periods
of time—perhaps up to a few seconds. If you look up a phone number and
then try to remember it just long enough to dial it, you are using working
memory. In a sense, working memory is where our current consciousness
exists: it is the system that holds the information we are processing or using
now.

Another and very different system is "long-term memory." This form of
memory allows us to retain truly vast amounts of information for long periods

of time. Research findings indicate that there are no clear limits to how much information long-term memory can hold or how long this information can be retained. Moreover, we retain the capacity to enter information into long-term memory throughout life—even as we age. So in that sense, learning from our experience is indeed a life-long process. Interestingly though, there are limitations on even this amazing kind of memory: recent research indicates that when we retrieve information from long-term memory, other information (that we don't recall) is lost—perhaps because it gets in the way! This sounds like a bad thing, but, in fact, discarding information we don't need or want to use can be one factor encouraging creativity because it helps us to "think outside the box" by forgetting what's already *in* the box but is not currently useful (Storm and Angello, 2010).

Long-term memory can hold many kinds of information—factual knowledge (e.g., what is the distance from New York to San Francisco? What is the formula for computing the area of a circle?). It also contains personal knowledge about events we have experienced in our own lives (what are known as autobiographical memories). Another kind of information retained in long-term memory, however, is much harder to express in words. For instance, a champion chess player can't easily explain how she or he anticipates opponents' moves, and a skilled bowler can't explain how they "know" the instant they release the ball whether it will produce a strike. Interestingly, experienced entrepreneurs often indicate that they can distinguish a potentially valuable opportunity from one that is probably unlikely to succeed very quickly—almost instantly—and, again, they can't describe clearly how they do this. As one described it to me: "I don't know how I know—I just do." This capacity is related to expertise (Baron and Henry, 2010), because one effect of becoming an expert in almost any field, from surgery to basketball, is that it provides the persons involved with amazingly rapid access to information stored in long-term memory. Since that system can hold vast amounts of information, finding it when it's needed is often a problem. Being able to do that very quickly—and accurately—may be one of the reasons why experts in a given field perform at such amazingly high levels.

This kind of memory—memory for information that can't be readily put into words—is known as "procedural memory" (Figure 2.2). Although it might seem that this kind of memory is only related to performing physical actions, research findings indicate that often our decisions, goals, and plans are strongly influenced by information stored in procedural memory, or in related aspects of memory that are outside conscious awareness. We can't describe such information and often are only dimly aware of its existence, but it still influences important aspects of our thinking. Such information under-

Figure 2.2
Procedural memory:
an important
component of
expertise

Procedural memory holds
information we can't
readily put into words,
but that plays a key role
in expert performance.
For instance, experienced
entrepreneurs often state
that they can distinguish
good opportunities from
ones unlikely to succeed very
rapidly, but can't describe
in detail *how* they do what
they do.

lies "intuition" and is also reflected in "tacit knowledge," knowledge that involves what is often described as "know-how"—knowing *how* to perform various actions without necessarily being able to describe this knowledge in words. Because tacit knowledge is represented in procedural memory, it is often difficult to share with others, who must learn from observing what we do, rather than from our descriptions of these actions and how we perform them.

Cognitive errors entrepreneurs should avoid—or at least reduce

Our cognitive abilities are definitely impressive, but it's important to recognize that they are far from perfect. In fact, they are prone to a wide range of errors—ones that can badly distort our judgment, decisions, and reasoning (Ariely, 2009). You already know from your own experience that memory is imperfect: on many occasions, we can't retrieve information we want, just when we need it most (for example, during an exam!). And when we do recall information it is frequently inaccurate. This is illustrated dramatically by research on eyewitness testimony: people who have witnessed a crime are often unable to recall important aspects of it, and report memories that, in fact, are far from accurate (e.g., Loftus, 1996). In addition, other evidence indicates that each time information is retrieved from memory and then returned to it, it tends to change—often so that it becomes more consistent or easier to interpret. For instance, I have been asked about my own experiences as an entrepreneur so many times that now when I try to recall these events, the information I retrieve from memory is almost certainly more flattering to me and my good judgment than is probably true. But errors in memory are only part of the problem, because many other factors that can undermine the accuracy or effectiveness of our thinking also exist. These can have devastating effects for everyone, but because entrepreneurs often operate under conditions where mistakes can be fatal (at least for their companies!), such errors are especially dangerous for them. So it's important for entrepreneurs to be aware of their existence and to take steps to avoid or reduce them. Below is a brief description of some of the most important of these potential errors.

The confirmation bias

Which kind of information is used more in making decisions or other kinds of thinking? Information that confirms the beliefs you already hold, or information that challenges these beliefs? In one sense, the latter: to make good decisions we need to take account of information contrary to our current beliefs. Despite this fact, we tend to show a strong tendency to pay most attention to, and remember, information that supports our current views or beliefs. As a result, we are in danger of becoming locked into the beliefs we already hold, while ignoring information that might lead us to change them so that they are more accurate. For instance, if entrepreneurs believe that customers are very pleased with a product supplied by their company, they may tend to ignore complaints or other information indicating that this is *not* the case. Clearly, that can be very harmful, so the confirmation bias is one "cognitive trap" entrepreneurs should try to avoid.

Heuristics: Quick-and-simple—but inaccurate—rules for making judgments and decisions

Often, we encounter more information than we can possibly process at a given time. This leads to a strong tendency to use "heuristics"—quick (and sometimes "dirty") rules for making complex judgments and decisions. Several exist, but two that are especially powerful should be briefly mentioned. The first, known as the "availability heuristic" or "rule," suggests that whatever we can bring to mind most easily tends to be viewed as most important or accurate. So, if we can remember information easily, it has a powerful impact on our current thinking. Unfortunately, such information is sometimes easy to recall because it is vivid or unusual, not because it is particularly useful or revealing.

Another heuristic—and one that is especially important to entrepreneurs—is the "anchoring-and-adjustment heuristic." This refers to our powerful tendency to accept an opening price or position as an anchor (a reasonable starting point) from which adjustments can be made. In fact, such initial offers or positions may strongly favor the persons who propose them, yet they still influence subsequent discussions or negotiations. This is why realtors try to set the price of a property at an ideal point: high enough to influence buyers to pay more, but not so high that they find the initial price unreasonable and walk away. If you have ever watched the popular television show *Pawn Stars*, you have seen the anchor-and-adjustment heuristic in operation. In this show, the owners of a large pawn shop attempt to negotiate the price of various items people bring to sell. Usually, the owners ask the would-be sellers to name a starting price—mainly so they can indicate, immediately, that this is completely unreasonable. (The phrase one of them uses says it all very succinctly: "Ain't gonna happen"—meaning that there is no way he will pay the asking price.) After this, the owners of the store name a price of their own, and the sellers—who are usually far less experienced as negotiators—usually adopt this as an anchor and then try to make small adjustments to it (in their favor of course). The outcome is almost always the same: the pawn shop owners (the experts) buy the items for a very favorable price. The moral: beware of the anchor-and-adjustment heuristic, because it can prove very costly in negotiations—a process of major importance for entrepreneurs.

The self-serving bias

Another strong tendency in our thinking is to attribute favorable outcomes to our own effort or talent, while negative outcomes are attributed to external factors beyond our control. The result is that individuals do not learn from their errors—because they don't see them as errors; instead, they perceive negative outcomes as "not their fault," and so discount them instead of examining them very carefully. This bias can also lead to considerable friction between partners (e.g., founders of a new company), since each assumes that *they* are primarily responsible for positive outcomes, while their partners are responsible for negative ones, and it may lead successful entrepreneurs to conclude that *they* are responsible, single-handedly, for the growth of their companies—in other words, to suffer from an exaggerated view of their own special talents and contributions (Hayward et al., 2013).

Optimistic bias and planning fallacy

People are, by and large, very optimistic: they tend to believe that things will turn out well, even if there is no rational basis for such beliefs. Closely related is the tendency to underestimate the amount of time needed to complete a given task, or to assume that more can be completed in a given period of time than is feasible. Together, these cognitive biases can lead to serious errors in planning, development of effective business strategies, and many other activities. Moreover, growing evidence indicates that they are a basic aspect of human thought—tendencies "built in" to the functioning of our minds and brains (e.g., Sharot, 2011). Recent research indicates that the optimistic bias is directly relevant to entrepreneurship and in ways that seem to contradict widespread beliefs: the more optimistic entrepreneurs are, the *poorer* the performance of their companies, especially in rapidly changing industries (Hmieleski and Baron, 2009). Why? Apparently, because high levels of optimism interfere with setting appropriate goals and with effective processing of relevant information, thus interfering with effective decision-making (Figure 2.3).

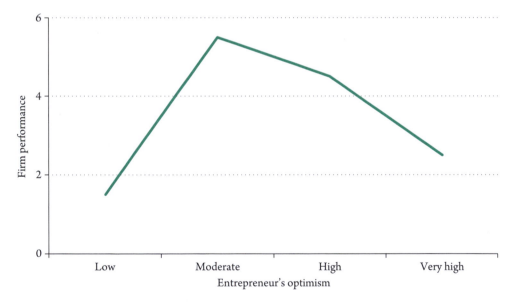

Source: Based on suggestions by Hmieleski and Baron, 2009.

Figure 2.3 The optimistic bias—can it interfere with entrepreneurs' effectiveness?

In general people tend to be optimistic—to expect positive outcomes even when this is not justified. Recent evidence indicates that when this tendency is very strong (i.e., when entrepreneurs are extremely optimistic) this can interfere with their effectiveness—and with the performance of their companies.

Affect infusion: How feelings shape thought

If we were totally rational beings, our feelings and emotions would not influence our decision or judgments. Do they? Of course! A large body of research evidence indicates that feelings, and even mild and subtle shifts in moods, often exert powerful effects on our thinking. For instance, when we are in a good mood, we tend to recall mostly positive information; when we are in a bad one, we tend to remember mostly negative information. Clearly, what we recall can strongly influence our decisions, so affect infusion—the tendency for our current feelings to influence key aspects of our cognition—is another potentially important source of cognitive errors. And since entrepreneurs have been found, in recent research (e.g., Baron et al., 2012), to show very high levels of affect or emotion, they may be especially prone to such effects.

Sunk costs: Getting trapped in bad decisions

Have you ever repaired a used car, only to have it break down again very soon? What do you do then? Rationally, at some point, you should "walk away" and write off the money you have already spent on the car as wasted. But in fact, most people find it very difficult to do this. Instead, they feel psychologically committed to their previous decisions, and *can't* walk away. They get trapped in what are called "sunk costs"—the resources they have already invested in a failing course of action. This is a very powerful tendency, and can badly distort the thinking and actions of individuals who become its victim. Among entrepreneurs, it can be very costly if it leads them to stick with plans, products, or courses of action that are not succeeding and have little chance of generating better outcomes in the future.

Fast thinking effect: Why risk-taking increases when the clock is ticking

It has often been assumed that entrepreneurs are risk-takers: they are more willing to accept high levels of risk than other persons. Although evidence on this suggestion is mixed (in fact, some indicates that entrepreneurs are less accepting of risk than others, e.g., Miner and Raju, 2004), recent findings indicate that a basic aspect of our cognitive systems may tend to encourage risk-taking among entrepreneurs. Specifically, it has been found that when people think quickly—as, for example, when they face deadlines, or in situations that require quick responses—their tendency to accept high levels of risk increase (Chandler and Pronin, 2012). Why? Perhaps because fast thinking signals a need for immediate action, and this encourages daring behavior. Fast thinking may also tend to elevate mood, and more positive moods may increase confidence, and so reduce the perceived levels of risk present in a situation (e.g., Baron et al., 2012). Whatever the basis, this is certainly a cognitive bias with potentially dangerous effects for entrepreneurs.

Many other cognitive errors and biases exist as well but by now the main point should be clear. Partly because of the limitations of our own cognitive systems, we are far from being totally rational as information processors. On the contrary, we are susceptible to many errors and biases that together often interfere with our capacity to make accurate and effective decisions, judgments, and choices. As shown in Table 2.1, and as noted throughout this

Table 2.1 Cognitive errors: potential dangers for entrepreneurs

All these cognitive errors are common, and are ones of which entrepreneurs should be aware.

Cognitive Error	Description	Relevance for Entrepreneurship
Confirmation bias	Tendency to notice, process, and store only information consistent with current beliefs	Reduces capacity to be flexible in the face of changing conditions, and capacity to respond to negative information
Heuristics	Rules of thumb for making decisions and judgments quickly	Efficient in terms of reducing cognitive effort, but can lead to serious errors when more systematic and detailed analysis is required
Self-serving bias	Tendency to attribute positive outcomes to one's own talent, effort, etc., but negative ones to external factors beyond one's control	Reduces capacity to learn, since negative outcomes are perceived as generated by external agencies or factors
Optimistic bias	Tendency to expect more positive outcomes than is rationally justified	Leads to unrealistically high goals and aspirations, and to underestimating the amount of time or effort needed to complete various tasks
Fast thinking effect	Faster speeds of thinking enhance risk tasking	Entrepreneurs must often make decisions rapidly and this may increase their tendency to assume high risks
Affect infusion	Influences emotions and feelings on key aspects of cognition (e.g., decision-making, evaluation of various alternatives)	Can seriously distort judgments and decisions by entrepreneurs in a wide range of contexts
Sunk costs	Tendency to get trapped in bad decisions or failing course of action	Can prevent entrepreneurs from "cutting their losses" by walking away from poor decisions or strategies

discussion, it is important for entrepreneurs to be familiar with them, and to guard against their impact. Doing so can add significantly to their entrepreneurial excellence in several different ways.

How can entrepreneurs reduce the impact of cognitive biases?

If these potential errors in our cognitive systems are general in scope—they are, in a sense, "built in" to our cognition—how can they be reduced? Fortunately, several techniques for doing so exist. Often, simply knowing about the existence of these errors can be very helpful. For instance, Ariely (2009, p. 244) suggests that once we understand our susceptibility to such mistakes, and their basic nature, we can reduce or avoid them by being vigilant and actively trying to think in ways that minimize their impact. For instance, we can try actively to avoid the confirmation bias by seeking out information that is contrary to our current views. Technology too can help; for instance, it can remind us—vividly!—of the strengths of competitors, and the odds of failure for new products in highly competitive markets. This can help to reduce our strong optimistic bias. As another researcher puts it, once we are made aware of our optimistic illusions, we can act to protect ourselves. In essence, enhanced self-knowledge may be one basis for mitigating the impact of our built-in tendencies to fall prey to cognitive errors. Only future research will reveal whether, and to what extent, that is the case, but it is consistent with other evidence suggesting that "to be forewarned is, often, to be forearmed" (e.g., Baron and Branscombe, 2012). In short, the fact that you are now familiar with some of the most important forms of cognitive errors may help you to resist them. So please: do carefully consider the information in this discussion, and the summary in Table 2.1. This may well help you to avoid telling yourself "I should have known better . . ." when, looking back, you consider your own mistakes and bad decisions!

Creativity: Where entrepreneurship begins

Creativity is one of those terms that is hard to define but easy to recognize, like "love" or "justice." We know it when we see it, but can't easily explain *why* we view an idea, invention, poem, painting, or anything else as creative. As a result, we often fall back on a social definition of creativity: something is creative if most people (or at least most experts in a given field) agree that it is creative. In short, we conclude that Einstein, Picasso, Mozart, Shakespeare, and Thomas Edison were highly creative because most people (and again, experts in their fields) agree that this is so. Unfortunately, this is a kind of circular reasoning: creative people produce creative ideas or products, and we know these are creative because we view them (both the people themselves and the products of they generate) as creative! As we'll soon see, there are ways of escaping from this kind of circularity, but as one author put it (Freyd, 1994, p. 125): "This circularity [with respect to creativity] does not prevent us from appreciating—and being stunned by—its novelty and value." With these thoughts in mind, we can note that most efforts to understand creativity emphasize two things: creative ideas or products involve "novelty" (they are now in some way new) and "value" (they are useful in the sense that they can generate economic or social value, i.e., profits or enrichment of human lives). As we'll note in Chapter 9 these are similar to the criteria used by the US Patent and Trademark Office to evaluate applications for new patents.

Now that we've commented on the complexities involved in defining creativity we'll turn to (1) its origins in basic cognitive processes, (2) factors that affect it, and (3) ways of enhancing it.

Origins of creativity: Generating the "new"

As noted earlier, long-term memory can hold a vast amount of information. That's a major advantage, but it comes with an equally important cost: there is so much information in this cognitive system that, as we noted earlier, it runs the risk of getting lost—like a file we create on a computer but then can't locate, perhaps because we can't recall the name. To reduce this problem, information in memory is "organized" in various ways—it is grouped together in internal frameworks that enhance the ease with which it can be recalled. Several types of mental frameworks exist and are useful, but the ones most relevant to creativity are known as "concepts."

Concepts and creativity

Concepts are a kind of mental "container" for objects, events, or ideas that are somehow similar to each other. For instance, the words automobile, airplane, and boat are all included in the concept "vehicle" because they all share certain key features: they move people around, have controls to start and stop them, to change direction, speed up or slow down and so on. Similarly, consider the words shirt, jeans, hoodies, and shoes. All fit within the concept "clothing" because they share several features: they are worn by people, can be put on or removed, cover various parts of the body, and so on. A key feature of concepts—and one closely related to their role in creativity—is that they all get "fuzzy" around the edges. Consider the concept of vehicle once again. Does elevator fit? Probably it does—it carries people and can start and stop, but it can't ordinarily change direction. But what about escalator? Roller skates? Similarly, think about the concept "clothing." Shirts, jeans, and shoes are at the core of this concept, but what about a wig? And what about tattoos—they cover parts of the body, but do not fit well within the concept "clothing."

The fact that concepts get "fuzzy" at the edges is closely related to their role in creativity. Briefly, concepts can encourage creativity when they are "expanded" or "combined" in various ways. The fact that they get "fuzzy" at the edges can greatly facilitate these processes.

First, let's see how concepts can be combined to generate something very new. Do you use a "smart phone"? If so, you know that such phones combine many concepts into a single product: they are phones, GPS devices, cameras, music systems, and with appropriate apps, can be used for an almost infinite number of purposes, from learning the prices of various products in nearby stores and reading bar codes, through translating words from one language to another. Clearly, smart phones represent a combination of several (many) concepts (communication device, camera, and so on) and this combination is so useful to many people that they can no longer imagine life without these phones. In instances like this, creativity is greatly enhanced through the *combination* of several initially separate concepts.

Another route to the same goal is "concept expansion." This happens when existing concepts are mentally stretched so that they generate ideas for new applications. For instance, consider a piece of equipment that is now used by virtually every chef on TV, and millions of amateur chefs at home—the microplane (Figure 2.4). It is used for grating almost anything—from lemon peel to hard cheeses, and is based on the combination of two seemingly unrelated concepts: "rasp"—a kind of file used to produce a smooth finish on wood, and "grater." Rasps are ancient—they were used in Egypt 5000 years ago, and can take many different shapes depending on the task they are used for, but the idea of combining this concept with one from cooking did not emerge until the 1990s (Figure 2.4). Once it did it was adopted by cooks all over the world very quickly, so that today it is used by famous chefs on every cooking show shown in TV.

Clearly then, the existence of mental "bins" or containers in our minds—concepts—can be a major "plus" in terms of enhanced creativity, but they have an important "downside" too. If they are very strong, concepts can lock us into traditional ways of thinking—what I personally describe as "mental ruts." Unfortunately, these "mental ruts" can be very deep so that people find it very difficult to escape from them. Here's one intriguing example. In the 1960s, engineers at Sony Inc. were given the task of developing a new

The microplane

A rasp for smoothing wood

Source: Left photo, Robert A. Baron; right photo, Fotolia: #15669504.

Figure 2.4 Expansion of concepts—an example

The microplane, a very popular new product, was derived from the basic concept for a rasp—a tool used to smooth wood since ancient times. By expanding this concept, a new and highly useful product was produced.

means for storing music. Working with the technology available at the time they came up with an early form of the CD. It worked, but was rejected as a potential product for one simple reason: it was far too large to be portable. Why did the engineers make this mistake? Because they were trapped, by their own experience with large long-playing records into assuming that this new storage device also had to be 12 inches in diameter! In sum, concepts can either encourage or obstruct human creativity; the key task is to use them as a basis for creative ideas, while avoiding the mental ruts into which they sometimes direct our thinking.

Fortunately, our cognitive systems (especially memory) seem to have a built-in way of reducing these restraining effects, which can get in the way of creativity. As noted earlier, research findings indicate that when we retrieve information from memory, other information that is related to what we want to recall is forgotten, perhaps because of competition between this information and the target information we want to remember and use (e.g., Storm and Angello, 2010). Although this might seem to be a negative outcome, it can actually increase creativity. Why? Because the information that's forgotten may be precisely that which locks us into thinking in familiar and routine ways. In a sense, and as Storm and Angello (ibid., p. 1264) put it, to "think outside the box"—to break free of the restraining influence of strong, existing concepts, we must "forget part of what's in the box"—information in memory relating to these concepts. Overall, then, creative people may be ones who readily forget irrelevant information—information that they do not need and are not currently using! For a startling example of how expansion of concepts can foster creativity, please see "The Entrepreneurial Quest" case study below.

CASE STUDY

The Entrepreneurial Quest

Finding lost masterpieces: Concept expansion in action

Each year, a number of paintings that *might* be ones done by famous artists are discovered. This raises a key question: "Are they real?" In the past, art experts have relied largely on intuition and their own experience to answer this question. As art expert Bernard Berenson explains: "It is very largely a question of accumulated experience. When I see a picture, in most cases, I recognize it at once as being or not being by the master it is ascribed to" (PBS, 2012). Is there a better way to solve this problem—one that is more reliable than experts' intuition? One intriguing answer has emerged in recent years, and seems to involve a totally

CASE STUDY *(continued)*

unrelated topic—fingerprinting. Fingerprints have long been used in law enforcement to identify criminals; they fall within a concept of "personal identification," which includes other methods such as handwriting, voice analysis, DNA matching, and retinal scans, to name a few. Can this concept be expanded so that it can be used for identifying the individuals who produced art, such as paintings? One individual—Peter Paul Biro—came up with the idea for doing just that.

Careful scans of famous paintings often reveal fingerprints, ones left—it is assumed— by the artists who painted them (such fingerprints often exist because artists can't help touching the canvas as they paint it or move it). This led Biro to reason: why not look for fingerprints in newly discovered paintings, to see if they match the ones found on well-documented masterpieces? This constitutes concept expansion because fingerprints would now be used not identify people but in a sense to identify physical objects (paintings) and answer the question "Who painted them?" To find out, Biro applied this technique to several paintings that resembled ones done by famous artists, but for which conclusive evidence for their origins (provenance) was lacking. He found—amazingly—that at least in some cases, he could match the fingerprints on these painting to those on ones known to be done by famous artists.

The most famous—and controversial—example of this new use of fingerprinting occurred with respect to a recently discovered painting, which was, after careful examination by several experts, attributed to Leonardo Da Vinci—one of the most famous painters of all time. If this initial assessment was accepted by the art world, the painting (known as "La Bella Principessa"—"The Beautiful Princess") would be worth many millions of dollars, and would be the first new painting by Leonardo discovered in more than a hundred years. To fully implement this method of identification, Biro developed a new kind of camera that scanned paintings with many different forms of light (infrared, ultraviolet, etc.). This enabled him to obtain clearer images of fingerprints on it—prints that were often blurred and hard to see with normal light. The result was startling: he *did* find fingerprints that matched those on famous paintings known to be produced by Leonardo. Biro then went on to found a company using this technique, and it offered this new service to the art world (Figure 2.5).

Sadly, the story does not have a totally happy ending. Questions about the technique soon arose—for example, even if the fingerprints on new paintings match those on famous paintings. this is no guarantee that they were left by the same artists; other persons such as apprentices might be responsible. In addition the fingerprints were often very hard to see, even with the new technology, so whether they really matched ones on well-known paintings was difficult to determine.

Whatever the final outcome though, it is clear that (1) the idea for using fingerprints in this way is highly creative, and (2) it derived, at least in part, from expanding an existing concept. It's difficult to imagine a more dramatic example of the role of basic cognitive processes in human creativity—and therefore, in entrepreneurship.

CASE STUDY *(continued)*

Source: Fotolia#54677889.

Figure 2.5 Concept expansion as a source of creativity: another— and ingenious— example

Are newly discovered paintings masterpieces created by famous artists, or simply clever forgeries? One way of finding out involves the use of fingerprints: if prints left on the new painting match those on paintings known to be produced by famous artists, this provides evidence that they are genuine—both were created by the same artists. Was the painting shown here produced by a famous Renaissance painter (e.g., Raphael?). This technique can help answer this question.

Analogies and creativity: Transferring information from one domain to another

Most of us use Velcro every day: it is a very convenient and effective way of holding things together. For instance, I use it on a porch to hold sunshades in place when it is windy. How did the idea for this useful and creative product arise? The answer is that George de Mestral, a Swiss inventor, noticed that his dog's fur was covered with burrs (which contained plant seeds). He wondered how they clung so strongly to the fur so he put them under the microscope and discovered that they had tiny hooks that attached readily to the dog's fur, clothing, or almost anything else! He reasoned that this could be used as a new, effective kind of fastener—and Velcro was born! This is an example of analogical reasoning: de Mestral reasoned that what worked for plants might also work in other domains too—and it did. Such reasoning is another important source of creativity. We should note that analogies are often very useful in science. For instance, you have probably seen Bohr's model of the atom, which looks like a miniature solar system. (It is, of course wrong, but helped scientists to conduct valuable research on the basic nature of matter.) Similarly, viewing the system of arteries and veins in our bodies as a kind of "plumbing" was very helpful to anatomists and physicians in their efforts to understand how our bodies worked. In sum, this basic kind of thought provides another route to enhanced creativity.

Factors that promote creativity: Evidence on what really works

Now that we've considered the origins of creativity in basic cognitive processes, we'll examine some of the factors that seem to encourage its occurrence. Get ready for some surprises, because several of these—uncovered in recent research—are indeed, unexpected.

Affect and creativity: Does being in a good mood help?

There is a large body of research (Ashby et al., 1999; Lyubomirsky et al., 2005; Kaplan et al., 2009) indicating that experiencing positive affect (i.e., positive moods) has many beneficial effects including: increased energy, enhanced cognitive flexibility, greater confidence and self-efficacy, improved performance on a wide range of tasks (Kaplan et al., 2009), and can even contribute to increased career success, enhanced personal health, and formation of personal relationships (Lyubomirsky et al., 2005). Several of these effects—especially enhanced cognitive flexibility—are related to creativity, and in fact there is considerable evidence that the tendency to experience positive moods often and in many situations *is* related to creativity (e.g., Baron and Tang, 2011). Why is this the case? Because positive moods speed cognition and allow us to make a broader range of associations—connections—between various kinds of information (e.g., De Dreu et al., 2008).

Does this mean that cheerful, up-beat people are more creative than other persons? Perhaps. But recent evidence (Bledow et al., 2013) indicates that the situation is a bit more complex than that. While positive affect offers important benefits, it can also lead individuals to ignore negative information and to jump to conclusions because they are thinking so rapidly. In contrast, negative affect (i.e., negative moods) can slow thought so that attention is more focused, and available information is examined in detail. Combining these points, Bledow et al. (ibid.) proposed that creativity is actually facilitated by a *change* in mood from negative to positive. This occurs because negative affect draws attention to problems and indicates that effort is needed to solve them, while positive affect, when it occurs later, enhances activation (i.e., energy) and cognitive flexibility—thus generating creativity. Research evidence (ibid.) supports this view, so basically we can conclude that there *is* a link between affect and creativity, but that that being "up" is not always beneficial; creativity is increased when we shift from a positive to a negative to a positive mood. So to put it simply, negative moods help us think deeply about the present situation, while positive moods then provide the energy to act on our conclusions.

Inspired distraction: Why creativity is enhanced by taking a break

Down through the ages, many highly creative persons—Einstein, Newton, and many others—have reported that their major new ideas occurred not when they were focused on specific problems, but rather when they were "taking a break" and doing other things. Until recently, however, there was no concrete evidence that this is actually the case, merely these anecdotal, personal reports. Recently, however, research findings have offered direct support for the benefits, from the point of view of enhancing creativity, of shifting attention away from the problem at hand to other, unrelated tasks or activities. To find out if taking a break really works in terms of enhancing creativity, Baird et al. (2012) asked participants to work on a standard measure of creativity—finding unusual uses for common objects (the "Unusual Uses" Test). Then they either performed a highly demanding task (one that required careful attention), an undemanding task (which provided a break from working on difficult cognitive tasks), no task at all, or kept working on the measure of creativity (no break). Finally, all participants completed the measure of creativity once again. Results were clear: those who performed the undemanding task (i.e., took a break) showed the biggest improvement in creativity from the first measure to the second, while those who performed the demanding task, or took no break at all showed no improvement, or actually demonstrated *lower* creativity.

Why does "taking a break"—and especially working on an undemanding task during this period—increase creativity? The term "creative inspiration" seems appropriate because apparently what happens when people work on an undemanding task is that this allows cognitive processes below the level of conscious awareness to proceed without interference, and this in turn, contributes to creativity. This is similar to the experience many people have of trying to think of a name or word and failing only to have it pop up in their minds at a later time, when they are doing other things. The bottom line is this: it *is* often useful to take a break while working on a problem or task that requires creativity. Doing so can encourage cognitive processes that enhance the inspiration we seek.

Distrust as a spur to creativity?

People differ greatly in terms of their trust for others: some begin with the idea that most other people can be trusted—unless they do something that calls such confidence into question. Others are mistrustful from the start, and assume that others are *not* to be trusted until they demonstrate that they deserve it. Do these contrasting mind-sets have anything to do with creativity? Surprisingly they do. When people adopt a mistrustful mind-set, this generates negative affect (moods), and as noted earlier, this, in turn, can increase their recognition that there is a serious problem to be solved, effort to do so, and more focused thinking generally. The result can be increased creativity. In fact, precisely these kinds of effects were observed in research by Mayer and Mussweiler (2011). They found that persons encouraged to adopt a mistrustful approach to others did indeed demonstrate higher levels of creativity than those who were not induced to be mistrustful. The reasons for these findings were also clear: when experiencing mistrust, individuals show greater cognitive flexibility, and broader, more inclusive categories (concepts). These factors, together, contribute to higher levels of creativity. Does this mean that to be creative it's necessary to be mistrustful of others? Not at all. But it does suggest that certain kinds of mind-sets—ones that cause us to focus on the problem at hand in a persistent and directed way—can sometimes help us to generate the new ideas we seek.

Other factors that boost creativity

Many other factors, too, play a role in creativity. One is the capacity to integrate different bodies of knowledge (Cheng et al., 2008). This makes very good sense: since creativity often involves combining concepts or other kinds of information stored in memory, we would expect that being able to do so would facilitate creative thought. Another factor is searching for, and identifying, the "obscure"—aspects of a situation or problem that have generally been overlooked before (McCaffrey, 2012). For instance, consider a classic problem often used to study creativity. Individuals are given matches, two candles, and two metal rings, and told to come with a means of connecting the rings together. The rings are too heavy to be joined by melted candle wax—a solution most people generate very quickly. So how *can* they be fastened together? The correct solution requires that individuals notice that the candles have wicks, which are string, so if the candles are broken apart the wicks can be extracted, and used to tie the rings together. As you can see, coming up with this solution involves overcoming the tendency to view the candles in, forgive me, a new light. In short, people seeking to solve this problem in a new, creative way, truly do not see the candles as unitary objects, but as ones consisting of two parts. Again, research findings support the suggestions that doing so can boost creativity (ibid.).

In sum, many different factors contribute to creativity, and to the extent they are present and active the greater the likelihood that creativity—novel and useful ideas and products—will emerge. These factors are summarized in Figure 2.6.

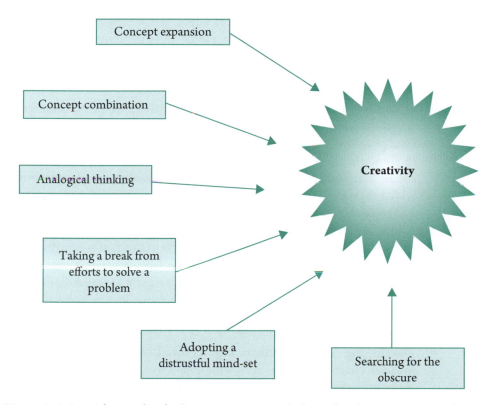

Figure 2.6 Some factors that facilitate creativity—including a few that are unexpected!

As shown here, several different factors—some of them unexpected—have been found in careful research to facilitate creativity.

Further thoughts on encouraging creativity: The confluence approach

Creativity—and how to encourage it—is a very popular topic at present. In fact, it is emphasized at virtually every level of education, from kindergarten through university. The university where I work has a special Creativity Institute, dedicated to encouraging creativity among students and faculty alike. And if you visit a bookstore or website that offers e-books, you will find scores of books that promise to increase your creativity. Unfortunately, many of these are based largely on the informal observations of their authors; a much smaller number rest on the firmer foundations of actual research such as that described above. The findings of that research then can certainly be applied to increasing creativity—for instance, taking "breaks" when seeking creative solutions or ideas, adjusting our affective states to maximize their beneficial impact on creativity, seeking ways to combine or expand existing concepts. In addition, other research has adopted a more general perspective, and attempted to identify both personal and environmental factors that contribute to creativity (Sternberg and Sternberg, 2011). Overall, this work suggests that creativity stems from a convergence (confluence) of several personal and environmental factors. To expand on the discussion above, we offer a brief summary of this work. It suggests that to enhance creativity, the following steps and conditions are helpful:

- **Obtaining a broad knowledge base**. Creativity does not emerge in an information vacuum; rather, to come up with something truly new (and potentially useful) a broad array of relevant knowledge is generally required. In the absence of such information, individuals run the real risk of "reinventing the wheel"—proposing ideas that already exist but of which they are unaware. So knowledge is a key ingredient in creativity, and acquiring it is a key step on the road to this process.
- **Adopting an appropriate thinking style**. Creativity is often encouraged by what is known as an "inventing" style of thought—one that seeks new and better ways of doing things. This is in contrast to an "implementing" style, which involves execution of existing ideas and methods. To the extent that individuals show a preference for inventive thinking and an ability to "see the big picture" they can escape from mental ruts, which are the antithesis of creativity.
- **Developing creativity-enhancing personal attributes**. Creativity also involves characteristics such as willingness to take risks and to tolerate ambiguity; these tendencies help individuals to consider ideas and solutions others may overlook. It's important to note that such attributes are *not* inherited, or "set in stone"—they can be changed, so that ones conducive to creativity are encouraged.

- **High motivation**. Even if people possess high levels of successful intelligence creativity-enhancing styles of thought and characteristics, nothing is likely to happen unless they also have high levels of "intrinsic, task-focused motivation." They must *want* to generate something new and better, so motivation too is a key ingredient.
- **Seeking environments that encourage rather than discourage creative ideas**. Creativity is enhanced by environments that encourage it. What are these like? Basically, they are ones that do not impose uniformity of thought but rather help individuals overcome their basic reluctance to seek or implement change. One way of accomplishing this is to emphasize the fact that maintaining the status quo involves definite losses—things are not being done as efficiently or effectively as possible. A focus on losses, in turn, tends to enhance people's willingness to accept risk by taking a chance on something new; in contrast, a focus on real or potential gains tends to make people risk-averse—and so to be less likely to think outside the box and seek change.

To the extent these conditions exist, creativity can flourish. In any case, existing evidence suggests that creativity is *not* a characteristic that people have or do not have. On the contrary it can be nurtured and encouraged by a combination of favorable factors.

Creativity and innovation: From ideas to reality

Many inventions are definitely "new"—nothing like them existed before. But only a small proportion of these inventions also have "value"—they can be developed into products or services that people will want to buy and use. A few examples of such inventions are shown in Figure 2.7; certainly some are creative in the sense of being novel and perhaps generating a smile or two. But as one expert on creativity has stated (Amabile, 1996, p. 143; emphasis added), "the products of creativity—new ideas, principles, or concepts— serve as the *raw materials* for innovation." In short, innovation involves the application of creativity to something useful—something that is actually feasible, both in the sense that it can really be made into something real, and in the sense that it is something that can generate sales and perhaps profits.

Basically then, a high level of creativity on the part of entrepreneurs does *not* assure that the companies they found will demonstrate an equally high level of innovation—developing products or services that are not only new but practical too. It's important to note that innovativeness is often a basic strategy adopted by new ventures because the founding entrepreneurs recognize that a steady stream of new products is necessary for survival—and

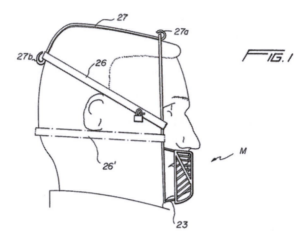

Dieting mask—to help people diet

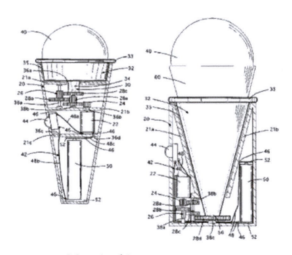

Motorized icecream cone

Source: US Patent and Trademark Office.

Figure 2.7 Not all ideas or inventions generated innovations

All of the inventions shown here received US patents, thus they were judged by a patent examiner to be novel and potentially useful. What do you think? (None ever resulted in an actual product.)

growth—in today's highly competitive markets (e.g., Lumpkin and Dess, 1996; Covin and Lumpkin, 2011). Thus, it has long been assumed that there is a link between creativity at the individual level and innovativeness and, in fact, research indicates that it does exist (Baron and Tang, 2011). In fact, as shown in Figure 2.8, and consistent with a large body of research

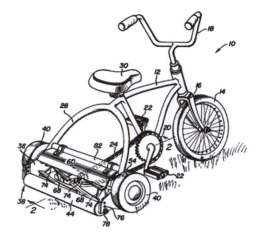

Combination tricycle and lawn mower

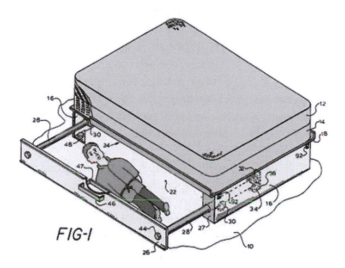

Hurricane protective bed

Figure 2.7 (continued)

findings, positive affect on the part of founding entrepreneurs contributes to their individual creativity, and creativity in turn facilitates firm-level innovation. This is just one illustration of the fact that individual entrepreneurs do indeed matter—their personal characteristics often strongly influence the success of the new ventures, and their creativity appears to be one factor that plays such a role.

Source: Based on findings reported by Baron and Tang, 2011.

Figure 2.8 Does individual creativity lead to innovation by new ventures?

As shown here, research findings indicate that positive affect on the part of entrepreneurs encourages creativity, and that individual creativity, in turn, contributes to innovations by new ventures. However, as discussed earlier, the link between positive affect and creativity may be stronger if entrepreneurs first experience negative affect and then shift to positive affect—as, for example, if they first experience setbacks followed by positive results such as growth in sales.

Entrepreneurial cognition: Inside the mind of the entrepreneur

Do entrepreneurs think differently than other persons? Researchers in several different fields who investigate various aspects of human cognition generally make the assumption that the basic processes that allow us to notice, store, retrieve, and process information are much the same for all human beings everywhere. For instance, consider memory: it is widely assumed that it operates in basically the same manner for all persons in all cultures and has done so since the appearance of human beings as a unique species. In other words, everywhere, regardless of geographic location, memory—which emerges from complex interplay between many parts of the brain—provides the foundations for noticing, storing, and later retrieving information among all human beings. Serious illness, injury, poor nutrition, or other biological factors can interfere with its operation, and people do differ greatly with respect to key aspects of memory. Overall though, memory itself is a process about which we can seek to obtain general, enduring knowledge, just as, for instance, physicists seek to obtain general knowledge about the nature of the universe and the laws that govern it.

If that's true—if memory and other cognitive systems operate in basically the same ways among all human beings—the following question arises: is entrepreneurial cognition—how entrepreneurs think—really unique in various ways? The most reasonable answer, we believe, is that although the basic *processes* are much the same (i.e., memory functions in the same basic ways in entrepreneurs and other persons), the *environments* in which entrepreneurs operate are so distinct and so unique, that they virtually require certain shifts in modes of thought and other aspects of cognition. In addition, entrepreneurs—or at least the ones who continue in this field—are something of a "special" group: they are selected by the same forces that select persons in other occupations or activities. For example, consider emergency room physicians. Only some people—

and in fact, only a small proportion of medical students—are attracted to this field, and only a small proportion of these find it to their liking and finally end up in this role. The same is true for entrepreneurs: only some people are attracted to this activity—others want the greater security of "regular" jobs. And only some people who give entrepreneurship a try find that they are suited to it and enjoy it. So, for these reasons—the unusual conditions entrepreneurs face and the fact that they are indeed a "special group"—their cognitive processes in fact differ from those of other persons.

What conditions and personal factors might contribute to such differences? Turning first to the unusual conditions entrepreneurs face, these include: (1) highly complex situations in which they must process large amounts of unfamiliar information overload; (2) very high time pressures (something "new" often remains new only for a relatively short period of time); and (3) high levels of "uncertainty"—that is, information needed for effective decisions or formulating useful plans simply does not exist, and therefore cannot be obtained. For instance, with respect to a brand new product, it is impossible to know with any confidence how it will be received by potential customers. Similarly, it may be impossible to obtain information on how competitors will respond to the new product that threatens to reduce their own business or market share. Predictions can be made but, basically, crucial kinds of information are simply not available. Together, these unusual conditions have important effects on entrepreneurs' cognition, shifting it into patterns and approaches not commonly observed among other groups of individuals. Below is a brief overview of some of these outcomes.

With respect to personal characteristics, entrepreneurs as a group have been found in recent research (e.g., Zhao and Seibert, 2006; Hmieleski and Baron, 2009; Baron et al., 2012) to be very high in the tendency to experience positive affect, optimism, self-efficacy (the belief that they can accomplish whatever they set out to accomplish), achievement motivation, conscientiousness (being organized and orderly), openness to new experience, and extraversion (being expressive and outgoing).

What differences in cognition do these unusual conditions and personal characteristics generate? Here are a few. First, entrepreneurs may be more likely to depend on "heuristic" thinking than other persons—thinking that relies heavily on quick "rules-of-thumb" for making decisions and planning future actions (e.g., the availability heuristic). Why? Because such thinking is almost a necessity under conditions of high information overload and high uncertainty. Second, entrepreneurs—especially ones who start several ventures—often develop "expertise" in the fields in which they work. As noted by McMullen and Shepherd (2006), entrepreneurs usually move ahead with efforts to develop ideas *only* in areas (industries, fields, etc.) they know well. In a sense then they are often experts in these fields even before they launch new ventures. Once they decide to proceed, of course, they devote many hours to running their businesses and to increasing their knowledge and skills with respect to various tasks they must perform, with the result that they become expert in at least certain aspects of starting and running new companies. As we noted earlier, the development of expertise in many fields is related to profound shifts in cognitive systems such as more rapid access to information in long-term memory (Ericsson, 2006).

Third, growing evidence indicates that entrepreneurs often think about the task of converting their ideas into something real in highly distinctive ways. According to several authors (Sarasvathy, 2008; Venkataraman et al., 2012) entrepreneurs often do *not* adopt standard cause-and-effect logic; they do *not* focus on trying to predict the future and on attaining specific goals. Rather, they use a very different approach in which they recognize that if they can shape or control future events they do not need to predict them; rather, they can focus on the resources they currently have available or can readily secure as a starting point, and move ahead from there. In a sense then they do not discover opportunities for new ventures—they create them. Current evidence, although still far from conclusive in nature, suggests that, in fact, entrepreneurs (especially highly successful ones) do tend to adopt this alternative means-driven kind of logic, at least to a degree (e.g., Wiltbank et al., 2009a, 2009b), although, again, existing evidence on this point is somewhat mixed (e.g., Baron, 2009). In any case, effectuation does suggest other important ways in which entrepreneurs think, reason, and plan differently from other persons.

Finally, entrepreneurs seem to focus to a greater extent than individuals in other careers on searching for connections between various events or trends in the external world—on attempting to recognize "patterns" that link seemingly unrelated events. While everyone engages in this kind of activity from time to time, research indicates that entrepreneurs tend to engage in it more frequently (Baron and Ensley, 2006), and in fact, build it into their normal activities, so that they are constantly searching for patterns others have not discovered (e.g., Tang et al., 2012). Such patterns when they emerge may constitute an important source of ideas that can be used to create value—a core task of entrepreneurship. (We'll return to this process, "opportunity recognition" in more detail in Chapter 3.)

In sum, although basic cognitive processes operate in much the same manner in all human beings, there are indeed grounds for suggesting that entrepreneurs think, reason, make decisions, plan, and set goals in relatively unique ways. In a sense, they develop a "mind-set" (way of thinking) that assists them in applying their creativity to making constructive changes in their work, their communities, or their entire society (e.g., Ireland et al., 2003), which is often defined as the ability to rapidly sense, act, and mobilize, even under conditions of uncertainty. In other words, entrepreneurs are especially sensitive to potential opportunities, are disposed to taking overt action to pursue them, and do so even under conditions that might tend to discourage other persons (e.g., high uncertainty). Understanding this basic fact offers important insights into the mind of the entrepreneur—and that is an important step on the road to understanding the complex process through which they create something new and useful from ingredients that have sometimes been described as "nothing," but are, in fact, very close to the essence of the human spirit: creativity, ingenuity, energy, and passionate commitment.

THE EFFECTIVE ENTREPRENEUR

The information presented in this chapter suggests several concrete steps you can take to become a highly effective entrepreneur:

- Always remember (!) that memory is imperfect and that the information it supplies can be inaccurate and biased in various ways (e.g., just the act of recalling it on different occasions may change it in various ways).
- Be aware of, and try to minimize, important cognitive biases or errors that can lead to bad decisions, inaccurate conclusions, and other problems: the confirmation bias, the optimistic bias, the self-serving attributions, sunk costs, and many others.
- Many steps can enhance your creativity: focus on concept expansion and combination, analogical reasoning—these can be important sources of new ideas. In addition, be sure to take a break every now and then when seeking creative solutions to problems, try to identify— and focus on—aspects of a problem that are *not* obvious (that is, are obscure). Also, be sure to broaden your knowledge base because it is an important foundation for creativity.

- Always remember that creative ideas do *not* necessarily lead to practical innovations—ones that can be converted into new and useful products or services.
- Recognize that as an entrepreneur you will be exposed to very challenging environments that may shift your cognition in several ways—some of which are helpful (e.g., toward searching for patterns in changing conditions), and some of which are not (e.g., over-dependence on heuristic thinking).
- Together, these principles may help you to "beat the odds," which are heavily stacked against new ventures, and become one of the effective entrepreneurs who succeed.

SUMMARY OF KEY POINTS

1 Entrepreneurship begins in the minds of specific persons, who generate ideas for something new, better, and useful.

2 Memory provides us with a cognitive system for storing, retrieving, and using information. It involves three distinct components: working memory, long-term memory, and procedural memory. Long-term memory can hold vast amounts of information—so much, in fact, that it is sometimes difficult to find the information we seek.

3 We are far from totally rational. In fact, our thinking is subject to many important forms of error, including the confirmation bias, the optimistic bias, the self-serving bias, and reliance on heuristics. It is important for entrepreneurs to be aware of, and avoid, such errors.

4 Creativity is hard to define, but is generally viewed as involving two key dimensions: novelty and value. Creativity often originates in concepts: mental "bins" for holding related information. Expanding concepts or combining them can yield creative outcomes. Analogical thinking is also important in this respect.

5 Additional factors that affect creativity include affect, taking a break while working on a problem, and attempting to focus on non-obvious (i.e., obscure) features of a problem. In addition, several personal and environmental factors combine to influence creativity.

6 Innovation refers to practical applications of the ideas generated by creativity. Basic cognitive processes generally operate in the same way for all human beings. However, because entrepreneurs possess a relatively unique combination of personal characteristics, and face relatively unique environmental conditions, their cognition too may be relatively unique in certain respects.

 ## REFERENCES

Amabile, T.M. (1996), *Creativity in Context*, Boulder, CO: Westview Press.

Amodio, D.M. (2010), "Coordinated roles of motivation and perception in the regulation of intergroup responses: Frontal cortical asymmetry effects on the P2 event-related potential and behavior," *Journal of Cognitive Neuroscience*, **22**(11), 2609–17.

Ariely, D. (2009), *Predictably Irrational: The Hidden Forces that Shape our Decisions*, New York: Harper Collins.

Ashby, F.G., A.M. Isen and A.U. Turken (1999), "A neuropsychological theory of positive affect and its influence on cognition," *Psychological Review*, **106**(3), 529–50.

Baird, B., J. Smallwood, M.D. Mazek, J.W.Y. Kam, M.S. Franklin and J.W. Schooler (2012), "Inspired by distraction: Mind wandering facilitates creative incubation," *Psychological Science*, **23**(10), 1117–22.

Baron, R.A. (2006), "Opportunity recognition as pattern recognition: How entrepreneurs 'connect the dots' to identify new business opportunities," *Academy of Management Perspectives*, **20**(1), 104–19.

Baron, R.A. (2009), "Effectual versus predictive logics in entrepreneurial decision making: Differences between experts and novices: Does experience in starting new ventures change the way entrepreneurs think? Perhaps, but for now, 'caution' is essential," *Journal of Business Venturing*, **24**(4), 310–15.

Baron, R.A. and N. Branscombe (2012), *Social Psychology*, 13th edition, Boston: Pearson/Allyn & Bacon.

Baron, R.A. and M.D. Ensley (2006), "Opportunity recognition as the detection of meaningful patterns: Evidence from comparisons of novice and experienced entrepreneurs," *Management Science*, **52**(9), 1331–44.

Baron, R.A. and R.A. Henry (2010), "How entrepreneurs acquire the capacity to excel: Insights from basic research on expert performance," *Strategic Entrepreneurship Journal*, **4**(1), 49–65.

Baron, R.A., K.M. Hmieleski and R.A. Henry (2012), "Entrepreneurs' dispositional positive affect: The potential benefits—and potential costs—of being 'up'," *Journal of Business Venturing*, **27**(3), 310–24.

Baron, R.A., K.M. Hmieleski and J. Tang (2011), "Entrepreneurs' dispositional positive affect and firm performance: When there can be 'too much of a good thing'," *Strategic Entrepreneurship Journal*, **5**(2), 111–19.

Bledow, R., K. Rosing and M. Frese (2013), "A dynamic perspective on affect and creativity," *Academy of Management Journal*, **56**(4), 432–50.

Chandler, J.J. and E. Pronin (2012), "Fast thought speed induces risk taking," *Psychological Science*, **23**(4), 370–74.

Cheng, C.Y., J. Sanchez-Burks and F. Lee (2008), "Connecting the dots within: Creative performance and identity integration," *Psychological Science*, **19**(11), 1178–84.

Covin, J.G. and G.T. Lumpkin (2011), "Entrepreneurial orientation theory and research: Reflections on a needed construct," *Entrepreneurship Theory and Practice*, **35**(5), 855–74.

De Dreu, C.K., M. Baas and B.A. Nijstad (2008), "Hedonic tone and activation level in the mood–creativity link: Toward a dual pathway to creativity model," *Journal of Personality and Social Psychology*, **94**(5), 739–56.

Drucker, P.F. (1985), *Innovation and Entrepreneurship*, Oxford: Elsevier Ltd.

Ericsson, K.A. (2006), "The influence of experience and deliberate practice on the development of superior expert performance," in K.A. Ericsson, N. Charness, R. Hoffman and J. Feltovich (eds), *The Cambridge Handbook of Expertise and Expert Performance*, New York: Cambridge University Press, pp. 683–703.

Freyd, J. (1994), "Circling creativity," *Psychological Science*, **5**(3), 122–5.

Hayward, M., R.A. Baron and R. Cropanzano (2013), "The shift from authentic to hubristic pride: Why CEO performance often declines over time," manuscript submitted for review.

Hmieleski, K.M. and R.A. Baron (2009), "Entrepreneurs' optimism and new venture performance: A social cognitive perspective," *Academy of Management Journal*, **52**(3), 473–88.

Ireland, R.D., M.A. Hitt and D.G. Sirmon (2003), "A model of strategic entrepreneurship: The construct and its dimensions," *Journal of Management*, **29**(6), 963–89.

Kaplan, S., J.C. Bradley, J.N. Luchman and D. Haynes (2009), "On the role of positive and negative affectivity in job performance: A meta-analytic investigation," *Journal of Applied Psychology*, **94**(1), 162–76.

Loftus, E.F. (1996), *Eyewitness Testimony*, Cambridge, MA: Harvard University Press.

Lumpkin, G.T. and G.G. Dess (1996), "Clarifying the entrepreneurial orientation construct and linking it to performance," *Academy of Management Journal*, **21**(1), 135–72.

Lyubomirsky, S., L. King and E. Diener (2005), "Benefits of frequent positive affect," *Psychological Bulletin*, **131**(6), 803–55.

Mayer, J. and T. Mussweiler (2011), "Suspicious spirits, flexible minds: When distrust enhances creativity," *Journal of Personality and Social Psychology*, **101**(6), 1262–77.

McCaffrey, T. (2012), "Innovation relies on the obscure: A key to overcoming the classic problem of functional fixedness," *Psychological Science*, **23**(3), 213–18.

McMullen, J.S. and D.A. Shepherd (2006), "Entrepreneurial action and the role of uncertainty in the theory of the entrepreneur," *Academy of Management Review*, **31**(1), 132–52.

Miner, J.B. and N.S. Raju (2004), "When science divests itself of its conservative stance: The case of risk propensity differences between entrepreneurs and managers," *Journal of Applied Psychology*, **89**(1), 3–13.

PBS (2012), "Economic inequality and fakery in art," accessed 15 October 2013 at http://www.pbs.org/newshour/businessdesk/2012/08/economic-inequality-and-fakery.html.

Sarasvathy, S.D. (2008), *Effectuation: Elements of Entrepreneurial Expertise*, Cheltenham, UK and Northampton, MA, USA: Edward Elgar, New Horizons in Entrepreneurship Series.

Shane, S. (2012), "Reflections on the 2010 AMR decade award: Delivering on the promise of entrepreneurship as a field of research," *Academy of Management Review*, **37**(1), 10–20.

Shane, S. and S. Venkataraman (2000), "The promise of entrepreneurship as a field of research," *Academy of Management Review*, **25**(1), 217–26.

Sharot, T. (2011), *The Optimism Bias: A Tour of the Irrationally Positive Brain*, New York: Random House.

Sternberg, R.J. and K. Sternberg (2011), *Cognitive Psychology*, Cincinnati, OH: Cengage.

Storm, B.C. and G. Angello (2010), "Overcoming fixation: Creative problem solving and retrieval induced forgetting," *Psychological Science*, **21**(9), 1263–65.

Tang, J., K.M. Kacmar and L. Busenitz (2012), "Entrepreneurial alertness in the pursuit of new opportunities," *Journal of Business Venturing*, **27**(1), 77–94.

Venkataraman, S., S.D. Sarasvathy, N. Dew and W.R. Forster (2012), "Reflections on the 2010 AMR decade award: Whither the promise? Moving forward with entrepreneurship as a science of the artificial," *Academy of Management Review*, **37**(1), 21–33.

Wiltbank, R., N. Dew and S. Sarasvathy (2009a), "Marketing under uncertainty: A knock on the door," *Journal of Marketing*, **73**(3), 1–18.

Wiltbank, R.N., S. Read and S. Sarasvathy (2009b), "Logical frames in entrepreneurial decision making: Differences between experts and novices," *Journal of Business Venturing*, **24**(4), 287–309.

Wolf, G. (1996), "Steve Jobs: The next insanely great thing," *The Wired Interview*, accessed 15 October 2013 at http://www.wired.com/wired/archive/4.02/jobs_pr.html.

Zhao, H., S.E. Seibert (2006), "The big five personality dimensions and entrepreneurial status: A meta-analytical review," *Journal of Applied Psychology*, **91**, 259–71.

3

Opportunities: Their nature, discovery, and creation

 CHAPTER OUTLINE

- **Opportunities:** Their basic nature
- **Opportunities:** Discovered, created, or both?
- **Opportunity recognition:** The role of information, experience, and social networks
  - The role of information in opportunity recognition
  - The role of experience and social networks in opportunity recognition
- **Individual differences in opportunity recognition:** The nature and impact of alertness
- **Cognitive foundations of opportunity recognition:** Pattern recognition, structural alignment, and regulatory focus theory
  - Pattern recognition: Finding opportunities by "connecting the dots"
  - Structural alignment: Coordinating markets and technologies in the quest for opportunities
  - Regulatory focus: Seeking success—or avoiding failure?
- How entrepreneurs can become skilled at recognizing opportunities

A pessimist is one who makes difficulties of his opportunities and an optimist is one who makes opportunities of his difficulties.
(Harry S. Truman, 1884–1972, 33rd President of the United States)

To hell with circumstances; I create opportunities.
(Bruce Lee, 1940–73, martial artist and actor)

One secret of success in life is for a man to be ready for his opportunity when it comes.
(Benjamin Disraeli, 1804–1881, twice Prime Minister of Great Britain)

What "bugs" you in your daily life? What little things annoy or irritate you even though they are fairly trivial in nature? Here's a few that sometimes drive me to distraction:

- items that are sealed in clear-plastic containers so strong that they can only be removed with tremendous effort—and risk of cuts, bruises, and so on (Figure 3.1);
- little pieces of soap that are too small to be useful, but still too large to throw away;
- people who get on the "speed" lines in grocery stores but have many more than the maximum number of items in their carts;
- drivers who never ever signal that they are about to turn;
- directions for assembling or using some product that are totally incomprehensible.

These are only a few of the things that "bug" me on a regular basis; certainly you have your own list. But what does all this have to do with the major topic of this chapter—opportunities? The answer is simple: often such situations are the stimulus for the ideas that ultimately lead to new ventures. Some individuals are not content to put up with these and many other small irritations so they think about ways to remove or reduce them—and that is often the start of the process. Of course, entrepreneurship often arises from other sources too: people have "big ideas" generated by their own creativity that have little or nothing to do with the petty annoyances of life. But many new products or services *do* start out in this way. Do you remember a product called the microplane, described in Chapter 2—a new, and very useful, kitchen utensil? The idea for it arose when the inventor's wife was baking and needed to grate a large number of lemons; she remarked to her husband that she was tired of hurting the tips of her fingers in the grating process, and he, being a skilled wood-worker with a mail-order business supplying various items to other craftspeople, connected this to tools he had long used. Further, he realized that if he could solve this problem in a simple way, there would be a large market for this product.

And that is the essence of business opportunities: as we noted in Chapter 1, they involve the recognition, evaluation, and development of ideas for something new, better, and useful that can create economic or social value (Shane and Venkataraman, 2000; Shane, 2012). But take note: this definition seems to imply that all opportunities exist "out there" in the external world, and are just waiting for someone to discover them. In fact, as we'll soon note, opportunities are sometimes *created* by the actions of entrepreneurs; in other words, the opportunities don't really exist until someone (an entrepreneur) takes the actions that produce them. We'll examine this question of "discovery" or "creation" and the basic nature of opportunities in the first section of this chapter. As we'll soon note, it seems clear that both processes play a role in providing the opportunities entrepreneurs develop. After that, and reflecting

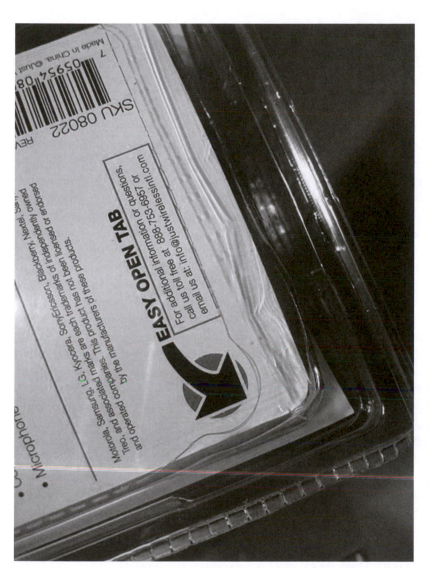

Figure 3.1 One item on my personal "bug" list

Items sealed in plastic so strong that it can only be removed with a knife, box cutter, or sharp scissors is a petty annoyance, but it annoys many people and might suggest an opportunity—some way of protecting such items without making them almost impossible to unwrap. In fact, recently some "user-friendly" packages such as the one shown here have begun to appear.

the emphasis in most research to date, we'll examine several factors that play a key role in opportunity recognition, including ones related to basic cognitive processes. Finally, we'll examine the ways in which the findings of that research can help entrepreneurs to recognize potentially valuable opportunities.

Opportunities: Their basic nature

"Opportunity" is defined in the dictionary as "a chance, especially one that offers some kind of advantage," and synonyms for it are "opening" or "break" (as in "lucky break"). More formally, business opportunities have been defined (Baron, 2006, p. 107) as a perceived means of generating economic value (i.e., profit) that has not been and is not being exploited, and is socially acceptable in the society where they exist. This last criterion is an important one because many ways of creating economic value are either illegal or viewed as illegitimate—something that might obey the letter of the law, but violate its spirit, and are not viewed as appropriate by members of the society in which they are developed. For instance, suppose that a scientist came up with a drug that made people crave a particular kind of food—for example (to choose a relatively inexpensive item), peanut butter. She or he could sell this chemical to the companies that make peanut butter, who might add it to their products, and so increase sales. This would not, perhaps, be illegal—especially if the new drug was declared safe by the appropriate testing agencies—but it is *not* something that most people would approve of, so for that reason it is *not* a bona fide opportunity. Conversely, sometimes a drug useful in treating some disease is legal in one country but illegal in another. In this case, people might approve of the sale of the drug, but entrepreneurs who supply it would be engaging in illegal activities. As noted by Webb et al. (2009) many such situations involve and are sometimes developed by individuals, but since they fall outside the "formal" legitimate economy (involving activities that are both legal and viewed as legitimate), they should not, perhaps, be viewed as opportunities. So to repeat (and this bears repeating!): business opportunities—the foundation of entrepreneurship and the new ventures they often generate—are defined as perceived means of generating economic or social value that have not previously been exploited, and are socially acceptable in the society where they exist.

Opportunities: Discovered, created or both?

Now that we have defined the basic nature of opportunities, it's important to consider another question: are opportunities discovered or created? Do they exist in the external world and remain only a potential until someone (an entrepreneur) recognizes and develops them? Or are they actually *created* by entrepreneurs' actions? This issue has been debated at length in recent years (e.g., Dimov, 2010; Venkataraman et al., 2012; Alvarez and Barney, 2013) and convincing arguments can be made for both ideas. That some opportunities exist "out there" and, in a sense, have an existence apart from the persons who recognize them, seems true in many situations. For instance, consider the giant of the online shopping domain, Amazon.com. Before it existed, people seeking specific items—especially unusual ones—had to search long and hard to find them. This often required many phone calls, personal visits to stores, and other inconvenient, energy-wasting activities. Sometimes, prospective customers were so discouraged by this situation that they simply gave up and did without the item in question. The founders of Amazon.com reasoned that if such need could be met effectively, doing so would offer a huge opportunity. Jeff Bezos, Amazon's founder, tackled this problem and realized that the tools for solving it either existed or could be readily developed: growing numbers of people had access to the internet, and many retailers were seeking new markets for their products or services. By combining these ingredients with new software and new physical facilities (e.g., huge warehouses for assembling and shipping products), Amazon boomed—and it did so because its founder recognized an existing opportunity and had the talent, knowledge, and dedication to develop it. I use Amazon all the time for hard-to-find items and a few of the things I've purchased there recently are shown in Figure 3.2.

On the other hand, consider the booming sales in tablet computers. If you went back in time to, for example, the year 2005, you would not find people expressing a strong need for such a product. They already had desktop computers, advanced laptops, and smart phones. So what was the need for something else? In 2010, however, Apple introduced the iPad and, in a sense, *created* a market for such devices, which quickly grew beyond even the high expectations with which it was launched (Figure 3.3). In fact, tablet computers were so successful that they were soon developed by Apple's major competitors (e.g., Samsung).

What does this suggest? That, as Venkataraman et al. (2012, p. 26), put it: "In other words, both processes of making and finding [opportunities] are intertwined in the practical reality of how opportunities come to be." In essence, opportunities can indeed exist before they are recognized and developed, but they can also be created by actions entrepreneurs perform and in fact, often, the two processes unfold together.

The fact that opportunities are both discovered and created raises another interesting question: are there circumstances where one is more likely to

Figure 3.2 Hard to find items that are readily available on Amazon.com

Jeff Bezos, founder of Amazon.com, recognized a need among large numbers of consumers: how could they obtain products that were not available in local stores? By meeting this need very effectively Amazon.com has attained tremendous success. Shown here are such items—an Italian espresso maker, coffee for it, and small cups in which it is served—all were available on Amazon.com, not offered in local stores.

Source: Fotolia # 53693799_M.

Figure 3.3 Tablet computers: an example of an opportunity that was *created* by the actions of entrepreneurs—and large companies

Sales of tablet computers have boomed tremendously since they were introduced in 2010 and even young children now use the devices. In fact, they now outsell regular computers. But only a few years ago, few people expressed a need for such a device. In a sense, therefore, tablet computers created an opportunity once they were introduced.

occur than the other (Alvarez and Barney, 2007, 2010). Recently, it has been proposed that opportunity discovery is more likely in situations involving *risk*—ones in which information concerning the probability that a recognized opportunity can be successfully developed exists and can be obtained. In such situations, it makes sense to generate detailed plans for developing the opportunity (business plans—see Chapter 5). This process doesn't proceed until an opportunity is discovered or recognized. In contrast, opportunity creation is more likely to play an important role in situations involving *uncertainty*—ones in which information useful in making decisions or planning future actions is *not* available and cannot be obtained because, in fact, it doesn't exist. In such situations, it makes little sense to formulate detailed plans; rather, it is more reasonable to adopt a broad and flexible view of the business that entrepreneurs wish to create and then "test the waters" by taking preliminary actions to see what might be possible (Wiltbank et al., 2006). In concrete terms, recent research (Hmieleski et al., 2013) suggests that opportunity discovery is more likely to occur in stable industries where change is not rapid and detailed planning based on actual, available information makes sense. Opportunity creation is more likely in dynamic industries where rapid change occurs and formulating detailed plans makes little sense, since conditions—and customer needs—may change in an instant, and information useful in predicting these shifts is not available (i.e., uncertainty is high).

So, are opportunities discovered or created? The most reasonable answer is: *both*, but entrepreneurs are more likely to follow one or the other of these routes in different situations, industries, or contexts. Despite this fact, however, most research to date has focused on recognition of opportunities that already exist rather than on the creation of new ones by entrepreneurs. Reflecting this fact, the discussion that follows will focus primarily on the processes involved in opportunity recognition rather than those involved in opportunity creation.

Opportunity recognition: The role of information, experience, and social networks

A key question that has emerged and re-emerged in efforts to understand opportunity recognition is this: "Why are some people better than others at this task—why are they and not others able to recognize specific opportunities?" If we can understand why certain people recognize opportunities that others don't identify, this may potentially provide key insights into how this process occurs—and how, perhaps, it can be enhanced. A focus on "information," both access to it and its effective use, provides important insights into this question so this basic perspective will now be briefly reviewed.

The role of information in opportunity recognition

It has often been suggested (and confirmed in research findings) that specific persons gain an advantage with respect to opportunity recognition by having enhanced access to relevant information. They can acquire such access in several ways. For example, they may have jobs that provide them with information on the "cutting edge"—information that is not widely available to others. Jobs in research and development or marketing appear to be especially valuable in this respect. Similarly, entrepreneurs often gain enhanced access to information through a large social network (Ozgen and Baron, 2007). Other people frequently serve as a valuable source of information and the information they provide cannot be acquired easily in any other way (Alvarez et al., 2012).

Greater access to information is only the beginning of the process, however. Entrepreneurs who recognize opportunities do not merely have greater access to information than other persons, they are also better at *using* such information. In other words, cognitive skills or abilities also enter the picture. As a result of having greater access to information, some persons have especially rich and well-integrated stores of knowledge—for instance, more information (retained in memory) about markets and how to serve them. This, in turn, enhances their ability to interpret and use new information because not only do they have more information at their disposal, it is also better organized, too.

Other aspects of cognition relating to the effective utilization of information also play a role. For instance, persons who found new ventures tend to be higher in intelligence than persons who do not, but such intelligence is broader in scope than the analytic intelligence measured by standard IQ tests—it involves what is often termed "street smarts"—practical and creative intelligence as well (e.g., Baum and Bird, 2010). Additional evidence suggests that entrepreneurs are especially likely to be higher than other persons in successful intelligence—a combination of analytic, practical, and creative intelligence (ibid.). Finally, entrepreneurs tend to be higher in creativity than other persons (Baron and Shane, 2008). In other words, they are more adept at combining the information at their disposal into something new through concept expansion or combination, as described in Chapter 2. In sum, it seems clear that a key component in opportunity recognition is information—greater access to it and possession of better cognitive tools for putting it to use.

The role of experience and social networks in opportunity recognition

Another factor that plays an important role in opportunity recognition is prior experience in a specific industry or from having been an entrepreneur previously. Industry experience may be especially valuable in contexts where opportunities are discovered, because it can help entrepreneurs both to identify specific opportunities relating to their experience and to formulate plans to develop them. It may be somewhat less valuable in situations involving opportunity creation, because in such situations the entrepreneurs are, in a sense, moving into "unknown territory" and can't really use information gained in the past. On the other hand, entrepreneurial experience, although valuable in a wide range of situations, may be especially helpful in contexts where opportunities are created by the entrepreneurs' actions. Why? Because experienced entrepreneurs have learned how to proceed without large amounts of information—which, in such situations, may not be readily available (Hmieleski et al., 2013).

In addition, other, more general kinds of experience such as that gained through having had many different jobs and worked in many different organizations also may be valuable because, in a sense, it provides the "raw materials" for recognizing some opportunities. For instance, an engineer who has worked for several different companies may have gained a wider array of information than another engineer who has worked in only one.

Finally, as noted earlier, the breadth of entrepreneurs' social networks is also important. Other persons are often a valuable source of information, and this can come both from people the entrepreneurs know only slightly (persons they have *weak* ties with), and from persons with whom they have much deeper and relationships (e.g., close friends, family; *strong* ties; see Jack, 2005). In short, where opportunity recognition or creation is concerned, *who* you know may be just as important (or perhaps even more important) than *what* you know.

In sum, considerable evidence confirms the importance of information—access to it, its effective use, its presence in prior experience, and its acquisition through social networks and other sources—in effective opportunity recognition. In short, what entrepreneurs know and who they know are ingredients in their capacity to identify potentially valuable, socially acceptable opportunities.

Individual differences in opportunity recognition: The nature and impact of alertness

Are some people better at recognizing opportunities than others? Interestingly, although economists are not typically concerned with differences between individuals, it was a well-known economist—Israel Kirzner—who first emphasized this possibility. In fact, Kirzner (1979) suggested that some individuals—and some entrepreneurs—are simply very good at this task: they are able to recognize opportunities that most other persons overlook. Kirzner described such persons as high on a dimension of "alertness," and added that since noticing opportunities is a crucial first step to deciding to pursue them, alertness is a key variable in entrepreneurship. People do indeed differ in a seemingly countless number of ways, so on the face of it this was a very reasonable suggestion. But being an economist, Kirzner simply called attention to this variable and went no further in trying to understand its origins and nature. Why, in other words, are some persons more alert to opportunities than others? Is it something about their past experience that equips them with this enhanced capacity, something about the ways in which they search for opportunities in the external world, a particular skill they have acquired, or something else?

Recently, research has been conducted to investigate the basic nature of alertness, and to integrate it with broader efforts to understand the role that basic cognitive processes play in opportunity recognition (e.g., McMullen and Shepherd, 2006; Alvarez and Barney, 2010). The results of this research now provide a much more complete and useful picture of the nature of alertness and how it operates.

Perhaps the most informative work on these issues to date is that reported by Tang et al. (2012). These researchers conducted several carefully designed studies to clarify the nature of alertness and its role in opportunity recognition. On the basis of existing evidence, the studies proposed that alertness actually involves three basic dimensions: (1) alert scanning and search—searching the environment for opportunities (new ways of creating value that are not currently being exploited); (2) alert association and connection—efforts to connect or integrate various sources of information, to perceive links between them and use these as a basis for creating something new and useful; and (3) evaluation and judgment—efforts to distinguish between opportunities offering low and high potential for creating value, and choosing the most promising among them (Figure 3.4).

To measure individual differences in these three aspects of alertness, Tang et al. (2012) developed a questionnaire and tested it extensively to determine if it does indeed measure the core features of alertness. Results indicated, in fact, that these three dimensions were observed among a large group of CEOs. That is, the higher the CEOs were on these dimensions, the more opportunities they recognized. Thus, alertness does indeed seem to involve these three basic aspects.

Additional research using this questionnaire was then conducted with large samples of entrepreneurs to see if the three components of alertness were

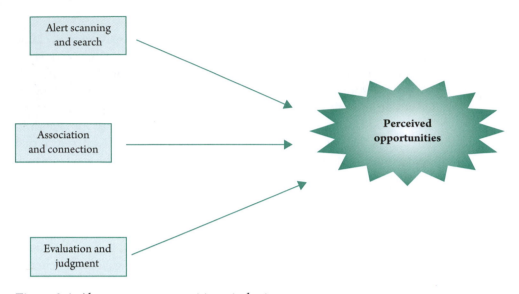

Figure 3.4 Alertness to opportunities—its basic components

Research findings (Tang et al., 2012) indicate that alertness to opportunities reflects the three basic aspects shown here.

related to other aspects of entrepreneurship. For instance, it was predicted that alertness (all of three basic dimensions) would be related to innovation in new ventures and to research and development expenditures in these companies. These predictions were confirmed. Further, it was predicted that the more "upbeat" entrepreneurs were (i.e., the higher they were in dispositional positive affect), the higher they would score in terms of alertness, since positive affect is related to broadened perceptions of the external world (e.g., Fredrickson and Branigan, 2005). Overall, findings were consistent with these and other predictions, so it appears that the framework offered by Tang et al. (2012) does clarify the basic nature of alertness and confirms its important role in opportunity recognition. As Kirzner (1979) suggested, people do indeed differ in their capacity to recognize opportunities, and this reflects differences in their tendencies to engage in careful, continuous scanning of the environment (an active search for opportunities), their capacity to perceive connections between seemingly unrelated information and events they encounter, and their ability to evaluate the potential of the various opportunities they identify. All of these components can be strengthened with practice and effort, so the upshot of this research is highly encouraging. Alertness, it appears, represents a cluster of skills that can be acquired or enhanced, so strengthening it may be one important step actual or would-be entrepreneurs can take to tip the odds of attaining success in their favor.

Cognitive foundations of opportunity recognition: Pattern recognition, structural alignment, and regulatory focus theory

The suggestion that information deriving from past experience plays an important role in opportunity recognition is very helpful, but it largely ignores a central question: how does opportunity recognition actually *occur*—what cognitive processes underlie the emergence, in the minds of specific entrepreneurs, of ideas for new products or services that they believe they can then successfully develop? This question, in turn, reflects the basic assumption that recognition of specific opportunities is an event that occurs primarily in the minds of individual entrepreneurs. If that is so, then the following and potentially valuable approach to enriching our understanding of opportunity recognition is suggested: why not adapt existing and often well-validated theories of cognition to the task of understanding opportunity recognition? This has been a basic theme in recent efforts to understand the essential nature of opportunity recognition and its key role in entrepreneurship. To represent this recent research and its important implications, we'll focus on the role of three basic cognitive processes in opportunity recognition: "pattern recognition" (e.g., Baron, 2006), "structural alignment" (Grégoire et al., 2010; Grégoire and Shepherd, 2012), and "regulatory focus"—an aspect of the cognitive processes individuals use to regulate their own behavior (e.g., Hmieleski and Baron, 2008; Tumasjan and Braun, 2012).

In discussing alertness, Tang et al. (2012) note that association and connection play key roles. Entrepreneurs search for connections in information they acquire, seeking to use these perceived connections as a basis on which to formulate ideas for something new and useful that is not now available—the core of opportunities. How does this search actually proceed? Basic research in the field of cognitive science offers important insights. To describe the implications of this research for understanding opportunity recognition, we'll now focus on the two basic topics mentioned briefly above—pattern recognition and structural alignment, and will also consider the role of one aspect of self-regulation (ways in which individuals regulate their own actions)— regulatory focus. All three involve a search for similarities and patterns in available information, but they take somewhat different forms.

Pattern recognition: Finding opportunities by "connecting the dots"

The term "perception" as used in cognitive science, refers to the complex process through which we interpret information brought to us by our senses and integrate it with information already stored in memory (e.g., Baddeley et al., 2009). If some opportunities exist in the external world as complex patterns of observable events or stimuli, then perception must, logically, play a role in opportunity recognition. Basically, there is a pattern of observable events or stimuli in the external world that entrepreneurs can perceive and whether this pattern is or is not recognized is, in a sense, a central question in opportunity recognition.

Basic research on perception refers to this task as "pattern recognition" (e.g., Matlin, 2004), and involves a process through which specific persons perceive complex and seemingly unrelated events or stimuli as forming "identifiable patterns." As applied to opportunity recognition then, pattern recognition involves instances in which specific individuals notice or mentally construct these links and so observe specific patterns (Alvarez and Barney, 2007). The patterns they perceive then become the basis for identifying new business opportunities. For instance, consider an entrepreneur who noticed the following facts: (1) in large cities, many people use taxis to get them to their destinations, (2) finding a taxi is often difficult, and can take lots of time, (3) at the same time taxis spend lots of time cruising the streets in search of fares (Figure 3.5)

Together, these facts suggest an important need: how can people wanting a ride and available taxis find each other? One ingenious solution was developed by three taxi drivers and three entrepreneurs, who together founded a new venture known as Hailo. They produced a mobile app that connects taxi drivers and potential customers. The app provides information on where each taxi is located and is first given free to taxi drivers in a given location. When enough taxi drivers have signed on to use the app, it is provided to potential customers—also free. Users can then hail a cab using the app, and when they pay for the ride with their credit cards, they are charged a small fee (ranging from $0.99 to $3.00) for using the service. In cities where cab fares are higher, Hailo receives a 10 percent commission instead. The result? Both taxi drivers—who waste less time cruising for fares—and customers— are happy! And the solution involved linking several factors together into a pattern that suggested a valuable business opportunity.

The same process—noticing that several events, needs, or trends can be linked together to form the basis for an opportunity—happens over and over again. Here's another example: medical costs have risen rapidly in the United States—to the point where even with new legislation, many people cannot afford to have all the medical help they need. This is especially true for what are known as "elective" conditions—ones that don't require treatment for health, but which people strongly want—for instance, plastic surgery. At the

Source: Fotolia # 12331234_M.

Figure 3.5 Finding a taxi when you need one is not always easy—but one new venture offers a solution to this problem

Together, taxi drivers and entrepreneurs came up with the idea for a new venture—Hailo—that provides drivers and customers with a free app they can use to connect. This saves the drivers from wasting time and fuel cruising for fares, and saves customers from having to search long and hard to find an available taxi. Everyone gains, which is often the sign of a valuable opportunity.

same time, an increasing number of Americans have traveled abroad, and are comfortable with doing so. Finally, there are many skilled physicians in other countries—especially ones where the cost of living is still relatively low—who can provide medical services for a fraction of the cost in the USA. Putting these trends and facts together suggests a valuable opportunity: medical tourism. People wanting medical services travel to countries where they are available at relatively low cost, and all the details of their travel are arranged for them by the company providing this service. Again, combining several different facts or trends points to a valuable business opportunity.

Does pattern recognition actually play a role in opportunity recognition? Several lines of evidence indicate that it does. First, many opportunities exist for years before they are noticed and developed. For instance, consider wheeled luggage of the type that is now used by a large majority of all air travelers. Such luggage was used for decades by air flight crews before it was introduced into the market for general sale. Why? Perhaps because no one "connected the dots" between several seemingly unrelated, but pertinent trends: a large increase in the number of passengers, growing problems with checked luggage, expansion in the size of airports, and so on. Once these trends were combined into a unified pattern in the minds of several different entrepreneurs, a product that would help meet the needs of a large and growing market was suggested. As soon as such luggage appeared it came to dominate the market and drove earlier models to extinction (Figure 3.6)

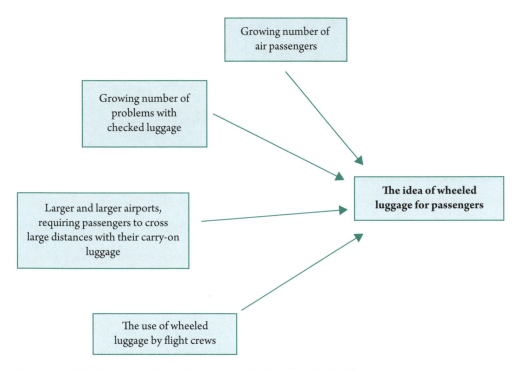

Figure 3.6 A clear example of "connecting the dots"—wheeled luggage

Once entrepreneurs connected the trends shown here into a recognizable pattern, the idea of wheeled luggage for passengers was suggested. Such luggage, once introduced, soon took over the luggage market.

Second, there is a large body of evidence in cognitive science suggesting that pattern recognition is a basic aspect of our efforts to understand the world around us. That is, we do indeed expend considerable effort searching for patterns among various events or trends in the external world. To the extent that opportunity recognition also involves perceiving links or connections between seemingly independent events or trends, it may be closely related to this basic perceptual process. Third, there is empirical evidence indicating that predictions derived from models of pattern recognition are accurate and that, therefore, such models offer important insights into the nature of this process (e.g., Baron and Ensley, 2006; Santos et al., 2013).

Overall then, it seems clear that many opportunities are discovered when entrepreneurs "connect the dots"—when they perceive patterns in events, trends, or ideas that have not previously been linked. For yet another—and perhaps more dramatic—example of how pattern recognition can lead to recognition of opportunities (in this case, a huge one!) please see "The Entrepreneurial Quest" case study below.

CASE STUDY

The Entrepreneurial Quest

Can mushrooms save the world—or at least free it from dependence on plastics that last forever?

Several years ago, Eben Bayer, a graduate student at a technological university, was working on his family's farm. The farm produced maple syrup, and one of his chores was moving wood chips used to fuel the fire for boiling the sap collected from maple trees. He noticed that one large pile of chips had become wet, and as result, it had sprouted a kind of mushroom. He also noticed that the mushrooms had produced filaments that bound the chips together very tightly. Bayer had a class project that involved making insulation from a mineral (perlite) that comes in small pieces about the size of cooked popcorn. Thinking of the mushrooms on his farm, he ordered a grow-it-yourself mushroom kit and placed spores from the kit, perlite, and water in a glass jar. He put the jar in his basement, and when he came back a few days later he found a solid white disk of perlite. The mushroom had bound the small pieces of perlite together, and the result was a totally biodegradable product—one that, unlike plastics, would *not* last forever (or at least, for hundreds of years). Where did the idea for this break-through product come from? From Bayer's connecting several seemingly unrelated strands: wood chips stuck together by mushrooms, the need for biodegradable products, and the ready availability of waste organic products that could allow the mushrooms to grow—and do "their thing."

Excited by this discovery, he teamed up with a close friend, Gavin McIntyre, to see if this process would work with many different kinds of organic waste, such as corn husks, wood chips, and even lint from a dryer. In each case, the mushrooms (or rather, the mycelium, the part of fungi that digests organic matter; funguses do not make their own food like green plants) produced solids in the shape of the mold into which they were placed. In short, Bayer and McIntyre had come up with a means of producing solid materials that could take the place of many plastics—especially Styrofoam (the white polymer widely used in everything from coffee cups to packing materials); and, in contrast to Styrofoam, this new kind of product would disappear (in about a month) in landfills. Styrofoam and related plastics are a tremendous and growing problem: they collect in landfills, in the oceans (they are found thousands of miles from land), and even in the stomachs of animals, which interferes with their digestion of food (Figure 3.7).

CASE STUDY (continued)

Source: Fotolia # 12331234_M.

Figure 3.7 Styrofoam and other plastics—a major ecological problem facing humanity—and one that creative entrepreneurs may have just solved

Two entrepreneurs—Eben Bayer and Gavin McIntyre—"connected the dots" between seemingly unrelated factors, and came up with a new way to produce materials that can replace Styrofoam and similar plastics. Unlike these plastics, which may last for hundreds or even thousands of years, their product is totally biodegradable, and disappears in landfills in about one month.

Recognizing the huge potential value of their invention, Bayer and McIntyre founded a company, Ecovative. They did not seek funding from venture capitalists or other sources, but instead set out to obtain the capital they needed by winning prizes in competitions for new inventions designed to reduce CO_2 emissions and so slow global warming. In one of these competitions, they won 500 000 euros (about $800 000), and this allowed them to proceed with development of their company. Once word of their new process spread, they were deluged with offers from venture capitalists who wanted to fund the company, and with orders from many large companies who recognized the benefits of a totally biodegradable substitute for Styrofoam.

So, where did the basic idea for this new product—one that promises to solve a major problem facing humanity—originate? From the fact that Eben Bayer recognized a pattern that many other persons—even experts in mushrooms and other fungi—had overlooked. Yes, people knew that fungi could bind organic materials together, but no one had perceived the potential uses of this natural process. In short, Eben Bayer "connected the dots," and the result was a product that seems certain to create both economic and social value.

Structural alignment: Coordinating markets and technologies in the quest for opportunities

Pattern recognition is a very basic cognitive process and appears to play a role in many important activities, including opportunity recognition (e.g., Baron, 2006). However, it is not the only cognitive process that underlies the identification of potentially valuable business opportunities. Another is what is known as "structural alignment" (Grégoire et al., 2010). Basically, this refers to the cognitive processes through which individuals attempt to identify similarities between new information and information currently present in memory. This can occur at several different levels: at a superficial level in which specific attributes or features are considered. For instance, with respect to a new technology, this could involve a focus on the basic elements of the new technology, who developed it, or its major parts. With respect to markets, it might involve the products or services currently available, the individuals who make up the market, and similar features. More important than these comparisons of superficial features or attributes, however, are higher-level comparisons that focus on aligning features of the new technology and features of the potential markets. For instance, the benefits and advantages of the new technology could be considered in relationship to the problems they will solve in specific markets.

Recent research (Grégoire et al., 2010; Gregoire and Shepherd, 2012), indicates that the search for higher-level structural alignment may underlie the identification of many opportunities. For instance, Grégoire and Shepherd (2012) conducted research in which senior executives who had previously founded new ventures were asked to "think aloud" as they tried to imagine opportunities that could be based on two new technologies and the markets these technologies would serve. Careful analysis of their comments were then used to identify the executives' thoughts about structural alignment between the technologies and potential market uses. Results indicated that in many cases the participants in the research did generate opportunities as a result of their efforts to align these two important factors. In other words, when they encountered new technologies, the executives (former or current entrepreneurs) searched actively for ways in which these technological advances could meet important market needs, and used this as the basis for identifying opportunities that could be developed with these technologies.

These findings, in contrast to those of earlier research (e.g., Baron and Ensley, 2006), were based on what and how entrepreneurs (or senior executives) actually thought as they attempted to identify opportunities, rather than on their memories of such cognitive activity in the past. Thus, these findings provide additional information on how the process of opportunity identification actually occurs, rather than reports of how it occurred in the past. In short, in trying to identify opportunities, individuals do consider similarities between new information and information already present in memory and how it can be aligned, as well as how this new information will prove useful in various situations. As Grégoire et al. (2010, p. 425) put it:

> [W]e found that in their efforts to recognize opportunities, participants considered the alignment between how a technology operates and the cause-and-effect principles explaining the benefits and advantages of a technology, with what individuals in a market do, why they do it, and . . . the unsatisfied needs and problems in that market.

The search for opportunities, in short, is anything but simple and often involves deep and complex thought on the part of the persons engaged in this quest. Given the stakes involved in identifying truly valuable opportunities, however, this appears to be effort well worthwhile (see Figure 3.8 for an overview of these suggestions).

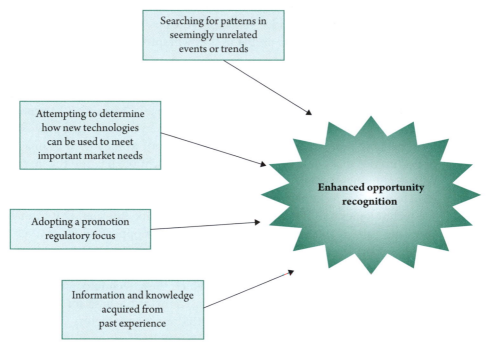

Figure 3.8 How opportunity recognition actually occurs

Research findings indicate that entrepreneurs identify opportunities in several ways: by searching for patterns in seemingly unrelated events or trends, and by searching for ways in which technological advances meet important market needs. In addition, a promotion regulatory focus on generating many hypotheses and obtaining positive results is positively related to identifying many new opportunities. As shown here, additional factors also play a role, including experience and knowledge in a given field.

Regulatory focus: Seeking success—or avoiding failure?

As we'll see in more detail in Chapter 8, individuals often regulate their own behavior in order attain important goals. This involves a number of specific skills, including self-control—doing what's necessary to reach these goals while refraining from other activities (including ones that are more enjoyable!), delaying gratification so as to maximize it when it occurs, and a high level of persistence—exerting effort until goals are reached (e.g., Baumeister and Tierney, 2011; Baron, 2013). One aspect of self-regulation involves what is called "regulatory focus" (Higgins, 1997; Eitam et al., 2013). This refers to two different ways in which individuals regulate their behavior. One, known as a "promotion focus," occurs when individuals focus on their ideals—what they would like to attain or the kind of person they would like to be. As a result, when individuals adopt this focus, they concentrate on obtaining positive outcomes. In contrast, a "prevention focus" occurs when individuals view their goals as duties or responsibilities that they should fulfill. This leads them to concentrate primarily on avoiding negative outcomes or losses.

Regulatory focus has important implications for understanding opportunity recognition. When individuals adopt a promotion self-focus they seek to generate many hypotheses and to explore all possible means of reaching the goals they desire. In short, they want to consider every feasible way of attaining positive outcomes. When individuals adopt a prevention focus, in contrast, their ultimate goal is safety—avoiding negative outcomes. As a result of this focus, they tend to generate fewer hypotheses and concentrate on avoiding mistakes. This suggests that persons who adopt a promotion focus are more likely to search actively for opportunities, as they attempt to test their various hypotheses about the best ways to attain success. In other words, they tend to be high in an important aspect of alertness—engaging in active search. In contrast, when individuals adopt a prevention focus, they generate fewer hypotheses and focus instead on what is safe or predictable, so that errors can be avoided. Overall, then a promotion focus may be positively related to opportunity recognition, while a prevention focus may be negatively related to finding new opportunities.

Evidence that this is indeed the case has been obtained in several studies (e.g., Hmieleski and Baron, 2008; Tumasjan and Braun, 2012). In the study by Tumasjan and Braun (2012), a large sample of entrepreneurs in the United Kingdom were presented with a set of problems relating to actual products (specifically, footwear), and asked to generate solutions for the problems. These solutions were then rated by a panel of judges in terms of the number of opportunities identified by the entrepreneurs and the innovativeness of these opportunities. The entrepreneurs also completed a questionnaire that measured their regulatory focus—the extent to which they typically adopted a promotion or a prevention approach to reaching key goals.

Results indicated that as expected, the higher entrepreneurs' tendency to adopt a promotion focus, the greater the number of opportunities they discovered. On the other hand, there was no relationship between participants' tendency to adopt a prevention focus and the number of opportunities they discovered.

In sum, regulatory focus—or at least, one aspect of it (promotion focus) — provides another clue as to how the process of opportunity recognition actually unfolds. Apparently, individuals who are focused on attaining positive outcomes are either more willing, or better, at finding new ways to attain these goals than persons who are focused, instead, on avoiding negative outcomes or losses. In sum, it is individuals who focus on attaining success and achieving important goals (a promotion focus) that are more likely to find new ways of actually doing so than ones who, instead, focus on avoiding losses (a prevention focus). But is it always best to adopt a promotion regulatory focus? Perhaps not. Such a focus can lead individuals to ignore important obstacles or potential pitfalls as they focus on attaining positive outcomes. So, the best results may be produced by a combination of both a promotion and prevention focus. The promotion focus encourages individuals to search for opportunities, while the prevention focus helps them avoid unnecessary risks and "fatal" errors. The moral? In entrepreneurship, as in many other areas of life, the best results may be obtained by a balanced approach in the quest for opportunities.

How entrepreneurs can become skilled at recognizing opportunities

It has long been observed that some entrepreneurs are much better than others at identifying potentially profitable opportunities. One source of such differences may lie in the fact that some have "better" (i.e., broader, more fully developed, more interconnected) cognitive frameworks than others, and so are more successful at "connecting the dots" into patterns that suggest new products or services (Baron, 2006). Similarly, research on "alertness" (Tang et al., 2012) suggests that important individual differences also exist with respect to active search, the capacity to notice connections, and to evaluate various opportunities, and may play a key role in opportunity recognition. This raises an intriguing question: can these findings help entrepreneurs to develop their capacity to identify and then develop excellent opportunities? A large literature on the nature of "expertise" and "expert performance" suggests that they can. This research indicates that in many different fields (e.g., sports, music, science, medicine, financial forecasting, creative writing) some individuals are able to rise above ordinary or "average" levels of performance and achieve true excellence. Further, a large body of evidence indicates that they do so *not* because of genetically determined talents, but largely as a result of engaging in a special kind of practice—practice that is highly focused, very effortful, and specifically designed to improve their performance. As a result of such practice (generally known as "deliberate practice") they obtain consistently superior levels of performance in whatever tasks they are performing (e.g., Ericsson, 2006). Again, it's important to note that, contrary to what common sense suggests, attaining such performance does *not* derive primarily from high levels of talent or even from the amount of time spent in a given activity. In fact, in most fields, most people do *not* continue to show improved performance as their time in that field increases. Rather, most reach a plateau within the "ordinary" range, and only a few individuals move beyond this level and demonstrate truly exceptional performance. Only those who engage in deliberate practice manage to exceed what is "average." As Michael Jordan, the star basketball player once put it: "I'm not out here sweating for four hours every day because I like to sweat . . . " Clearly, he understood very well that his participation in vigorous deliberate practice played a crucial role in his exceptional performance.

How does deliberate practice generate exceptional levels of performance—the kind shown by famous athletes, world-class musicians, or amazingly skilled surgeons? Apparently, by enhancing basic cognitive systems in several ways. First, persons who engage in deliberate practice gain increased amounts of "domain-specific information" and enhanced cognitive frameworks for storing and processing such information. The value of such information has been well documented in past research on entrepreneurship, where, as noted earlier in this chapter, the greater entrepreneurs' knowledge of a given field or industry the greater the likelihood that the new ventures they launch will be successful (e.g., Fiet and Patel, 2006).

Second, deliberate practice provides individuals who engage in it with enhanced "self-regulatory and meta-cognitive skills." Self-regulatory mechanisms—skills we'll examine in more detail in Chapter 8—are aspects of cognition that assist individuals in monitoring, regulating, and enhancing their own performance. These skills are useful in a wide range of contexts, including becoming truly excellent at performing various tasks. Recent findings (Duckworth et al., 2010) indicate that individuals high in such skills are better able to engage in deliberate practice, and so to attain superior performance.

Third, and perhaps most dramatic, deliberate practice provides individuals with actual enhancements to basic cognitive processes. For example, persons who engage in focused, effortful cognitive activity in a given domain may develop improved "perceptual skills" in that domain: they notice more than novices and are better at recognizing complex patterns (e.g., Ericsson, 2006). This is consistent with the role of pattern recognition in opportunity discovery. Further, persons who engage in extensive deliberate practice may also experience changes in "working memory," the memory system where, as we noted in Chapter 2, information currently being considered is held and processed (e.g., Ericsson, 2006). Although working memory has severely limited capacity, engaging in deliberate practice can effectively increase this capacity by strengthening links between working memory and long-term memory. As a result, experts in almost any field acquire enhanced capacity to locate and retrieve information stored in long-term memory. This enhanced access, in turn, can greatly improve performance by permitting experts in a given domain to use this information to guide their current performance and to better anticipate future events. The end result is that individuals who have developed expertise in a particular field through deliberate practice can make more rapid and accurate judgments than other persons because they essentially have greater access to vast stores of useful information held in long-term memory. These skills, in turn, can contribute to the evaluation and judgment aspects of alertness to opportunities.

As an example of how the benefits resulting from deliberate practice can contribute to opportunity recognition, the words of a famous and highly successful entrepreneur known to the author are revealing. When he was asked how he managed to identify one highly profitable business opportunity after another, he replied: "I just know. When I consider an opportunity, I can 'see' hundreds or thousands of others in my mind's eye . . . And when I see how this idea compares with *those*, I know instantly whether it will work." So, this expert entrepreneur—who had, in a sense, practiced evaluating opportunities for many years appeared to have gained the enhanced access to information stored in long-term memory that such practice provides.

Together, the benefits provided by deliberate practice may enhance entrepreneurs' ability to recognize opportunities, to accomplish this task quickly and efficiently, and to choose from among many opportunities those that offer the greatest potential economic potential. Of course, entrepreneurs cannot ordinarily engage in deliberate practice in the same way that it occurs in many other domains (Baron and Henry, 2010)—they cannot practice the same piece of music or a special kind of tennis serve over and over again. They *can*, however, focus attention and effort on engaging in active scanning and search for opportunities, identifying connections between trends, events, and changes in the external world, and on accurately evaluating potential opportunities. Finally, it's important to note that entrepreneurs can gain some of the advantages provided by deliberate practice in a vicarious, rather than direct manner—that is, by carefully studying the experiences of other entrepreneurs and opportunities they identified.

Together, all this information points to an encouraging conclusion: current or future entrepreneurs *can* enhance their own capacities to identify valuable opportunities by engaging in vigorous efforts to develop the basic skills on which successful opportunity recognition rests.

THE EFFECTIVE ENTREPRENEUR

Opportunities, whether recognized or created by entrepreneurs are a key initial step in the entrepreneurial process. In fact, starting with a good, potentially valuable opportunity is often a firm foundation for attaining success. How can entrepreneurs perform this important task effectively? Here are some key points that can help:

- It's almost impossible to recognize or create a valuable opportunity in a field or industry where you have little or no experience. So, concentrate on the ones you know best.
- In order to find or create valuable opportunities, it is usually essential to search actively for them. This means, among other things, being alert to things that "bug" you or other people. Hidden inside these annoying experiences may be potentially important opportunities.
- In situations where information about the potential value of opportunities (e.g., the size of possible markets) is available, it is useful to engage in detailed planning about how they can be developed. In situations where such information is available and can't be obtained because it does not exist (!), it is better to begin with a general idea about the opportunity you want to develop, and then fill in the details as you proceed.
- Opportunities often emerge out of changes in the external world—in technology, demographics, markets, government policies and regulations, shifting public tastes. Seeking ways to connect these can often suggest excellent business opportunities, so practice such pattern regulation because the results may be the emergence in your mind of an opportunity no one else has noticed.
- Adopt a promotion regulatory focus and concentrate on obtaining positive outcomes; *but* temper this with a healthy dose of prevention focus to help you avoid costly, and perhaps—for your new venture—fatal mistakes.

➡

- Develop broad and high-quality social networks, because other people are often an invaluable source of information on which opportunities are based.
- Most generally, seek to broaden your knowledge and experience in every way you can. The more you know about a field, industry, or domain the more likely you are to be able to identify opportunities in it. And this includes learning vicariously, from carefully observing the actions and results of other entrepreneurs—and thus, developing your expertise in several respects.

SUMMARY OF KEY POINTS

1 Opportunities are defined as a perceived means of generating value—economic or social—that have not been and are not now being, exploited and, in addition, are socially acceptable in the society where they exist.
2 Opportunities can be recognized or created by entrepreneurs, depending on the situation or context in which they operate (discovery is more likely in stable environments, while creation is more relevant in dynamic rapidly changing ones).
3 Opportunity recognition is influenced by information (e.g., about an industry) and past experience. It can also be encouraged by broad social networks, because other people are often an important source of information.
4 Individuals differ with respect to their likelihood of discovering opportunities; those who are high in alertness—persons who engage in active search for opportunities, are good at recognizing links between various changes in the external world, and are good at evaluation of opportunities, are better at this task than persons lower in these skills.
5 Several basic cognitive processes play a role in opportunity recognition: pattern recognition, structural alignment, and an important aspect of self-regulation, regulatory focus. Entrepreneurs can learn to be more effective at opportunity recognition by developing expertise with respect to this task in several ways—for instance, by carefully examining a large number of opportunities other entrepreneurs have recognized.

REFERENCES

Alvarez, S.A. and J.B. Barney (2007), "Discovery and creation: Alternative theories of entrepreneurial action," *Strategic Entrepreneurship Journal*, **1**(1–2), 11–26.
Alvarez, S.A. and J.B. Barney (2010), "Entrepreneurship and epistemology: The philosophical underpinnings of the study of entrepreneurial opportunities," *Academy of Management Annals*, **4**(1), 557–83.
Alvarez, S.A. and J.B. Barney (2013), "Epistemology, opportunities, and entrepreneurship:

Comments on Venkataraman et al. (2012) and Shane (2012)," *Academy of Management Review*, **36**(1), 154–6.

Alvarez, S.A., J.B. Barney and P. Anderson (2012), "Forming and exploiting opportunities: The implications of discovery and creation processes for entrepreneurial and organizational research," *Organization Science*, **24**(1), 301–17.

Baddeley, A., M.W. Eysenck and M.C. Anderson (2009), *Memory*, Hove: Psychology Press.

Baron, R.A. (2006), "Opportunity recognition as pattern recognition: How entrepreneurs 'connect the dots' to identify new business opportunities," *Academy of Management Perspectives*, **20**(1), 104–19.

Baron, R.A. (2013), *Enhancing Entrepreneurial Excellence: Tools for Making the Possible Real*, Cheltenham, UK and Northampton, MA, USA: Edward Elgar.

Baron, R.A. and M.D. Ensley (2006), "Opportunity recognition as the detection of meaningful patterns: Evidence from comparisons of novice and experienced entrepreneurs," *Management Science*, **52**(9), 1331–44.

Baron, R.A. and R.A. Henry (2010), "How entrepreneurs acquire the capacity to excel: Insights from basic research on expert performance," *Strategic Entrepreneurship Journal*, **4**(1), 49–65.

Baron, R.A. and S. Shane (2008), *Entrepreneurship: A Process Perspective*, Cincinnati, OH: South-Western/Thomson.

Baum, J.R. and B.J. Bird (2010), "The successful intelligence of high-growth entrepreneurs: Links to new venture growth," *Organization Science*, **21**(2), 397–412.

Baumeister, R. and J. Tierney (2011), *Willpower: Rediscovering the Greatest Human Strength*, New York: The Penguin Press.

Dimov, D. (2010), "Nascent entrepreneurs and venture emergence: Opportunity confidence, human capital, and early planning," *Journal of Management Studies*, **47**(6), 1123–53.

Duckworth, A.L., T. Kirby, E. Tsukayama, H. Berstein and K. Ericsson (2010), "Deliberate practice spells success: Why grittier competitors triumph at the National Spelling Bee," *Social Psychological and Personality Science*, **2**(2), 174–81.

Eitam, B., P.M. Kennedy and E.T. Higgins (2013), "Motivation from control," *Experimental Brain Research*, **229**, 475–84.

Ericsson, K.A. (2006), "The influence of experience and deliberate practice on the development of superior expert performance," in K.A. Ericsson, N. Charness, P.J. Feltovich and R.R. Hoffman (eds), *The Cambridge Handbook of Expertise and Expert Performance*, New York: Cambridge University Press, pp. 683–703.

Fiet, J.O. and P.C. Patel (2006), "Evaluating the wealth creating potential of business plans," *Journal of Private Equity*, **10**(1), 18–32.

Fredrickson, B.L. and C.A. Branigan (2005), "Positive emotions broaden the scope of attention and thought-action repertoires," *Cognition and Emotion*, **19**(3), 313–32.

Grégoire, D.A. and D.A. Shepherd (2012), "Technology–market combinations and the identification of entrepreneurial opportunities: An investigation of the opportunity–individual nexus," *Academy of Management Journal*, **55**(4), 753–85.

Grégoire, D.A., P.S. Barr and D.A. Shepherd (2010), "Cognitive processes of opportunity recognition: The role of structural alignment," *Organizational Science*, **21**(2), 413–31.

Higgins, E.T. (1997), "Beyond pleasure and pain," *American Psychologist*, **52**(12), 1280–300.

Hmieleski, K. and R.A. Baron (2008), "Regulatory focus and the exploitation of dynamic entrepreneurial opportunities: A moderated mediation study," *Strategic Entrepreneurship Journal*, **2**, 285–300.

Hmieleski, K.M., J. Carr and R.A. Baron (2013), "Integrating discovery and creation perspectives: The role of founding CEO intangible resources in contexts of risk versus uncertainty," manuscript under review.

Jack, S.L. (2005), "The role, use and activation of strong and weak network ties: A qualitative analysis," *Journal of Management Studies*, **42**(6), 1233–59.

Kirzner, I.M. (1979), *Perception, Opportunity, and Profit*, Chicago: University of Chicago Press.

Matlin, M.W. (2004), *Cognition*, New York: John Wiley and Sons.

McMullen, J.S. and D.A. Shepherd (2006), "Entrepreneurial action and the role of uncertainty in the theory of the entrepreneur," *Academy of Management Review*, **31**(1), 132–52.

Ozgen, E. and R.A. Baron (2007), "Social sources of information in opportunity recognition: Effects of mentors, industry networks, and professional forums," *Journal of Business Venturing*, **22**(2), 174–92.

Santos, S.C., A. Caetano, R.A. Baron and L. Curral (2013), "Testing a bi-dimensional model of business opportunity recognition and decision to launch venture," manuscript under review.

Shane, S. (2012), "Reflections on the 2010 AMR decade award: Delivering on the promise of entrepreneurship as a field of research," *Academy of Management Review*, **37**(1), 10–20.

Shane, S. and S. Venkataraman (2000), "The promise of entrepreneurship as a field of research," *Academy of Management Review*, **25**(1), 217–26.

Tang, J., K.M. Kacmar and L. Busenitz (2012), "Entrepreneurial alertness in the pursuit of new opportunities," *Journal of Business Venturing*, **27**(1), 77–94.

Tumasjan, A. and R. Braun (2012), "In the eye of the beholder: How regulatory focus and self-efficacy interact in influencing opportunity recognition," *Journal of Business Venturing*, **27**(6), 622–36.

Venkataraman, S., S.D. Sarasvathy, N. Dew and W.R. Forster (2012), "Reflections on the 2010 AMR decade award: Whither the promise? Moving forward with entrepreneurship as a science of the artificial," *Academy of Management Review*, **37**(1), 21–33.

Webb, J.W., L. Tihanyi, R.D. Ireland and D.G. Sirmon (2009), "You say illegal, I say legitimate: Entrepreneurship in the informal economy," *Academy of Management Review*, **34**(3), 492–510.

Wiltbank, R., N. Dew, S. Read and S.D. Sarasvathy (2006), "What to do next? The case for non-predictive strategy," *Strategic Management Journal*, **27**(10), 981–98.

Part II

Gathering essential resources

Even the best ideas cannot be transformed into actual products or services without the financial, human, and social resources needed to develop them. How do entrepreneurs obtain these resources? And how, before starting this process, do they determine whether a specific opportunity is "real" and worth developing, or, instead a kind of "financial black hole" into which they will pour their time, energy, effort, and reputations with little, if any, chance of success? What is the role of careful planning in entrepreneurship—for instance, writing a detailed business plan? And how important, in attaining success, are improvisation and related processes? This part of the book describes current evidence concerning these important topics.

4

Feasibility analysis . . . and other essential information: What entrepreneurs need to know before they begin

 CHAPTER OUTLINE

- Is the opportunity worth pursuing? Basic dimensions of feasibility analysis
  - Product or service feasibility: will it work, can it be produced—and at what price?
  - Market feasibility: Who will be the customers, can you reach them— and support what you sell?
  - Competitor analysis: Who's already out there—or soon will be?
  - Organizational feasibility: Are the founding team's management skills sufficient?
  - Financial feasibility: Are essential financial resources available?
  - Is a feasibility analysis always necessary?
- Industry analysis: Why some industries are more favorable for new ventures than others
  - Industry structure: The costs of entry and the number and size of competitors
  - Industry life cycles: New ventures do better in young industries than mature ones
  - Why certain kinds of markets favor new ventures
- Other essential information: Being familiar with key government policies and regulations
  - Regulations concerning employment practices: Preventing discrimination
  - Regulations concerning the health and safety of employees
  - The Affordable Health Care for America Act: What it means for new ventures

The only way of discovering the limits of the possible is to venture a little way past them into the impossible.
(Arthur C. Clarke, Clarke's Second Law, *Profiles of the Future*, 1973)

It's the possibility that keeps me going, not the guarantee.
(Nicholas Sparks, *The Notebook*, 1996)

Have you ever heard of an electronic device known as the Fuze? Perhaps, but perhaps not. It was introduced by Microsoft in 2006 to compete with Apple's iPod. Despite a huge marketing effort, sales were disappointing, and although it's still available it has never reached the goals set for it by Microsoft. Why not? That's hard to say, but it was somewhat "clunky" in appearance, could not use Apple's iTunes, and lacked the iPod's ease of use.

What about an Edsel? It was an auto introduced by Ford in 1957. It was under development for several years, and was supposed to be a tribute to Edsel Ford, Henry Ford's only son. Unfortunately, when people saw and drove it, they viewed it as totally ordinary, except in appearance, which few people liked. It was not priced in a way to attract a specific market and, in fact, many potential customers viewed it as a Mercury (another Ford brand) with a slightly different look. The car was a dismal failure, and after a few years was discontinued by Ford.

Why do I start with these failed products? To illustrate the importance of gathering crucial information before moving forward with a new product— one that is, supposedly, significantly different and better than what currently exists. Clearly, neither of these products—and many others, too—met these criteria. They were *not* viewed by potential customers as better than what already existed, and therefore attracted few buyers. If this can happen to huge companies like Microsoft or Ford, which have almost unlimited information at their disposal, think about how much more likely—and dangerous!— such outcomes can be for entrepreneurs. The basic point then is simple but important: do *not* proceed to develop an identified opportunity until several kinds of information concerned with its *feasibility*—whether there is a reasonable likelihood that it will succeed—have been gathered. To obtain such information, entrepreneurs should perform what is known as a "feasibility analysis." This is a very important activity, so we'll consider it in detail. But the information obtained from a feasibility analysis is not the only kind that entrepreneurs need. In addition, they should carefully consider the industry they plan to enter—whether it is large or small, whether it is growing, and whether it currently has many or just a few competitors. Finally, because governments are an important fact of life for all companies—and especially small ones—entrepreneurs also need information on policies and regulations that may influence their ability to successfully develop an opportunity. Overall, the main point is that it is usually wise to follow the old saying, "Look before you leap" and that is the key theme of the discussion that follows.

Is the opportunity worth pursuing? Basic dimensions of feasibility analysis

A common problem in many fields is this: does something that *appears* to exist really exist? Perhaps an example will help clarify this statement. Suppose that an engineer has the task of inspecting a bridge and finds some indication that it may have a serious structural weakness (Figure 4.1). The evidence is far from conclusive, so the engineer faces a dilemma: should she or he close the bridge, thus inconveniencing many drivers, or keep it open, running the risk that it may collapse? As another example, consider a radiologist who obtains scans (e.g., MRIs, CAT scans, etc.) that seem to indicate that a patient has a dangerous medical condition that can only be corrected by major surgery. Again, though, the evidence is not conclusive. As a result, the

Source: # Fotolia, 54863908_M.

Figure 4.1 Does something that seems to exist *really* exist?

An engineer checking the safety of this bridge is not certain whether a structural flaw exists. What should the engineer do? Close the bridge or keep it open? Entrepreneurs face the same kind of question with respect to opportunities: do they really exist, or only appear to exist?

radiologist too faces a dilemma: should he or she recommend the operation or not? The operation itself has real risks for the patient, but if the medical condition is really present, it too poses a serious threat. In both of these cases, the people trying to decide whether or not something exists—a flaw in a bridge or a serious medical condition—must weigh the "pros" and "cons" of each decision very carefully, using all the information at their disposal.

In a sense, entrepreneurs face the same predicament: they *think* they have identified a potentially valuable opportunity, but can't be sure. Should they proceed to develop it? Or should they, instead, stop immediately and try to find another? While there is no perfect answer to this question, the entrepreneurs should at least try to tip the odds in their favor by obtaining as much relevant information as possible. And the way to do this is through a careful feasibility analysis. Such an analysis involves several distinct kinds of information, and all are important.

Product or service Feasibility: Will it work, can it be produced—and at what price?

Some ideas look very good on paper—they appear to offer an excellent opportunity for developing a new product or service that will generate significant value. Yet, when efforts are made to do so, the result is failure. As we'll note below there are many reasons for such outcomes, but among these are failing to carefully consider such a question as (1) will it really work—will it deliver what it promises? (2) Can it actually be produced or supplied? And if so, (3) will the cost of production be such that it can be sold (or provided) at a price that seems reasonable in its potential market and that people will be willing to pay? If the answer to any of these questions is "No," or even "Maybe," it is time to think again. But how can information useful in answering these questions be obtained? Fortunately, ways of doing so exist that are *not* complex or costly.

First, will the product actually work? This can be addressed through careful testing as it is developed. If development costs are high this may be difficult to accomplish, but the more information on the product's performance the better. Second, whether the product will be perceived as useful or attractive by potential customers can be obtained through a "concept test." This involves presenting the idea for the new product to industry experts and potential customers to determine if they think the basic idea makes sense, what they like and dislike about it, and whether it fills an existing need. It is also useful to obtain information on costs of production and use this as input for estimating an actual selling price. In short, the basic idea is find out as much as possible whether the product is indeed feasible—one that can be produced, sold at a reasonable price, and will have an actual market.

Do all entrepreneurs obtain such information before proceeding? Definitely not. For instance, consider a start-up designed to teach Gaelic (the Irish language) over the web. The basic idea was that people would receive a lesson each day for 30 days. The lessons would consist of e-mail text messages, each containing a small "bite-size" sample of the language. Its founders forged ahead—and only after launching the company discovered that most people trying to learn a language want to *hear* it, not just read it. Here, paraphrased, is what one of the founders says about the way they proceeded: "I hadn't thought about who would be using the service and how they would interact with it. I focused on the marketing site, and liked creating graphics that could call attention to the "small bites" (of information) at a time. I didn't begin paying attention to feedback from customers for a couple of months—and that was deadly."

The result was predictable: failure, and the key lesson is: make sure your product or service works before moving ahead.

Market feasibility: Who will be the customers, can you reach them—and support what you sell?

Information on product feasibility is an important part of a feasibility analysis, but only part of the total picture. It's also important to consider the potential market too. The basic question is this: "Does a market for the product or service really exist?" To find out, it is usually helpful to present the basic concept of the product or service both to experts in the industry in which it will be introduced, and also to persons in the target market—those whom, the entrepreneur believes, are most likely to find the product useful and attractive—and to ask them to indicate their intentions about purchasing it, once it is available. (An example of such a survey is provided in Figure 4.2.) Social networking makes gathering such information far easier than in the past and can provide entrepreneurs with feedback from a large number of persons *before* they proceed further. Many techniques for obtaining information about potential markets exist, and some are relatively expensive, for example, conducting "focus groups" in which groups of persons, usually paid for their time, are exposed to the product and asked about their reactions to it, their attitudes, beliefs, and opinions. The focus group members engage in discussion and to the extent they reach a consensus, their input can be very helpful in assessing the size of the potential market, or in changing the product or service in ways that will enhance its appeal.

SAMPLE CONCEPT TEST

1. What do you like or find attractive about the product described above?

2. What do you *dislike* about it?

3. What would make it better?

4. Do you think this idea is feasible—that it can be produced and sold at a profit?

5. Do you have suggestions for increasing its chance of success?

Figure 4.2 An example of a concept test

A concept test provides valuable information on whether a market for a proposed new product or service actually exists. It usually includes questions such as the ones shown here, and can be presented (with slight modifications) both to experts in the industry and to potential customers.

A related issue entrepreneurs should consider as part of examining market feasibility is this: "What happens after the sale?" Customers expect service of various kinds so entrepreneurs should consider this issue carefully. Will they be able to service what they sell or provide? If not, the result will be angry, disgruntled customers. And again, given the popularity of social networks, this can be deadly to a new venture.

Competitor analysis: Who's already out there—or soon will be?

Another key aspect of a feasibility analysis involves identifying actual, or potential, competitors (a "competitor analysis"). This involves identifying existing companies that now, or perhaps soon, will seek to fill the same customer needs as the proposed new venture. A thorough competitor analysis gathers information on dimensions such as financial resources, human resources (i.e., the pool of talent they possess), technical resources, reputations, and so on. Rating each competitor on the basis of such information can help entrepreneurs understand the challenges they will have to face once they enter their chosen market. A basic rule of thumb is that existing competitors will *not* readily surrender market share to a new "upstart." Rather, they will use their resources—which can be considerable—to block new ventures quickly. If a competitor analysis indicates that the new venture will be going up against existing companies that have a very positive reputation and large financial and technical resources, it might be better to choose another opportunity rather than enter a contest the new venture is unlikely to win. Only if the new venture has a truly superior product—and, perhaps, one protected from imitation by a patent or other legal protection (see Chapter 9)—does it stand much chance of success under these conditions. Instead of trying to compete directly with giant competitors, a new venture can adopt a different strategy: it can seek to attract a small segment of an existing market by developing a specialized "niche"—a market large enough for the new venture to succeed, but too small for the large existing competitors to be concerned about retaining. This is true, for instance, in the biotech industry with respect to what are known as "orphan diseases." These are medical conditions that are relatively rare, so that large drug companies do not find it profitable to provide medicines for them. For a small start-up company, however, such markets can be large enough to offer a valuable opportunity.

Organizational feasibility: Are the founding team's management skills sufficient?

Identifying a good opportunity—that really exists!—can be a strong beginning. But to develop it, entrepreneurs must start, and run, an operating company. This means that in order to succeed, entrepreneurs need more than creativity and a high level of motivation—they also need "management knowledge and skills" (see Chapter 10). For instance, suppose that a group of engineers come up with a good idea for a new product; the idea is a unique one and the product does in fact work, and is useful, so it has a large potential market. But once they launch a company to develop it, they must be able to run it. This means that they need skills useful in hiring employees, keeping adequate financial records, developing marketing and sales campaigns, negotiating agreements or contracts with suppliers and customers (e.g., other companies), and many other functions. Given that all the founders are engineers, it is possible that they have no training or experience in these matters, and unless they attain outside help, will soon experience serious difficulties.

For instance, I once knew a Nobel-prize-winning physicist who started a company to develop and sell products based on his research. After launching the company, he and his partner received a letter from the state government informing them that since they had not filed the proper financial forms, they were being fined $50 000! The founders did not even know that this requirement existed because they were trained scientists with no management background or training. The situation was resolved when they hired an accountant, but it was a near thing in terms of the new venture's limited resources. This is why, in building a strong founding team (see Chapter 7), it is helpful to attract members who have complementary skills and knowledge, rather than where all members have the same background and training. Unfortunately, that's harder to do than describe, because many founding teams consist of friends who have almost identical stores of knowledge and experience. Do you recall Ecovative—the company described in Chapter 3 that is developing a substitute for Styrofoam? The founders were both engineers and in fact, close friends. As a result, they had little knowledge of how to run a company. By adding persons with such knowledge to the company, however, they succeeded in dealing with this problem. But in many new ventures, the result of a lack of management skills is a serious problem. The bottom line? Entrepreneurs should carefully assess their management skills as part of a careful feasibility analysis.

Financial feasibility: Are essential financial resources available?

Yet another issue entrepreneurs should consider very carefully is financial feasibility. This involves several different issues. First, how much cash will be needed at the start (start-up funds). These costs can be considerable, and unless funds are available to cover them, the new venture may have a very short life! What do such costs involve? Everything from rent and utility costs, through materials and supplies, legal costs, and the costs of purchasing essential equipment (e.g., computers, printers, copiers), and—of course!—the large "miscellaneous" category. It is the last category that is hardest to estimate and often results in rapid draining of the company's initial resources. A general rule is that whatever the estimated costs of getting the company started and running, *triple* these and perhaps you will be in the "ballpark."

Where are start-up funds obtained? Many entrepreneurs use their own savings, credit cards, or obtain loans from friends or family. And recently, many have used "crowdfunding," which involves raising funds over the internet in several ways—for instance, small loans from large numbers of people or selling small amounts of equity to investors, again over the internet (Mollick, 2013). We'll consider the possible sources of financial resources in more detail in Chapter 6, but for now the main point is that start-up funds can be obtained in many ways.

Another issue to consider as part of a financial feasibility analysis is the financial returns earned by other businesses performing similar activities (i.e., selling similar products or providing similar services). This can provide information on typical expenses, profit margins, pricing, and other relevant issues. Of course, to the extent a new venture is unique and provides something *truly* new, this information may not be readily available. But since nothing is totally new, data on companies that are somewhat similar can be helpful.

Finally, financial feasibility involves the overall financial potential of the opportunity the entrepreneurs plan to develop. If the potential markets are tiny, costs of getting started are high (e.g., expensive equipment is required), and growth in the industry or domain the new venture plans to enter is low, the ratio of effort and initial investment to future financial gains may be too low to continue. In short, if the upside potential is low, entrepreneurs—even if they find the opportunity highly attractive personally—should think again before continuing. Time and energy are limited, and if the years of effort spent on an opportunity will not even provide the entrepreneur with enough return to support themselves and their families the opportunity is probably not worth pursuing.

An overview of the major components of a useful feasibility analysis are shown in Figure 4.3. Please return to it often when considering the possibility of starting *any* new venture, because the questions it addresses are crucial ones for entrepreneurs.

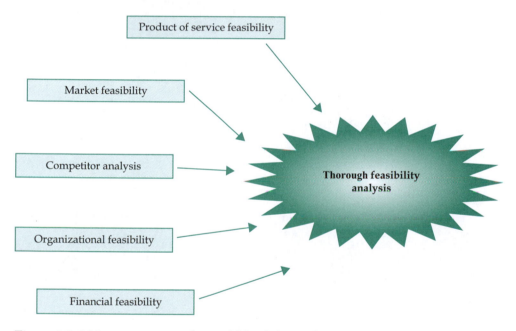

Figure 4.3 Major components of a careful feasibility analysis
A careful feasibility analysis involves gathering information on the issues shown here.

Is a feasibility analysis always necessary—or useful?

The information provided by a careful feasibility analysis is, without a doubt, very useful. It can help entrepreneurs decide whether to go ahead with developing an opportunity—which often requires a major investment of their time, money, and energy—or stop and think carefully about whether there is any chance of success. Basically, then, anyone thinking about starting a new business should gather such information. But this is one of those instances in which what entrepreneurs *should* do and what they *actually* do is often quite different. For instance, consider Ben Cohen and Jerry Greenfield, the founders of the well-known ice cream company, Ben and Jerry's Homemade Inc. Did they perform a detailed feasibility analysis? Not according to their descriptions of the early days of their company. What they did was use $8000 of their own money and $4000 they borrowed to open the first shop in Burlington, Vermont. They simply had the idea of providing a better product and more choices for customers, and reasoned that there would be a market for it (Figure 4.4). They were right—but more on the basis of their own intuition and experience than carefully gathered data.

Source: # Fotolia 16296396_M.

Figure 4.4 Do all entrepreneurs perform careful feasibility analyses?

For several reasons (e.g., they are individuals who want to get started *now*!), many entrepreneurs don't perform such analyses. Some succeed anyway (e.g., Ben & Jerry's Ice Cream), but by *not* performing a careful feasibility analysis they are reducing the likelihood that their new ventures will survive—and prosper.

So why do many entrepreneurs forge ahead without careful investigation of product, market, competitor, organizational and financial feasibility? Four major factors seem to play a role. First, many entrepreneurs have no formal training in entrepreneurship so they are not even familiar with the idea of a feasibility analysis. Second, they tend to be energetic "doers," impatient to get started (e.g., Pierro et al., 2012). Third, they simply *believe* that their ideas are great ones, and can't fail. And finally, they accept the widespread belief that there is a big advantage to being first to bring a new product or service to market (the first-mover advantage). Is this really true? The answer is complex. Sometimes, being first does offer advantages. It creates recognition among potential customers, and can set the standard for a new or developing industry or market. But it can also have important costs. Developing a new product or service is often expensive and given the pressure to be first, it might not be entirely ready when it is introduced. Similarly, many people don't rush to purchase or use new products or services—they adopt a "wait-and-see" attitude, and often delay until, as a result of competition, the costs goes down. As a result, companies that enter a market that is already developed or already growing rapidly may have a major advantage. Further, they may find it easier to obtain financing under favorable terms, since that market is known to exist. So, should entrepreneurs strive to be first? *Yes*, if they can enter with a fully developed product, and have performed a careful feasibility analysis. But *no*, if they can gain advantages such as a more fully developed product or service, more information on markets, and better terms of financing if they enter later. (Please see Chapter 11 for more information on the pros and cons of being first.)

Industry analysis: Why some industries are more favorable for new ventures than others

Suppose an entrepreneur has an idea for new product: a new kind of navigation system that provides real-time updates on traffic conditions in the area where the user is driving. This may be a very good idea, but there is a major problem: how can the entrepreneur persuade people to buy and use it? Many companies already provide similar information on GPS devices and through cell phones and other mobile devices. So how can the entrepreneur break into this market? Not very easily. In fact, in most industries or settings, new ventures are at a distinct disadvantage: major competitors exist and as noted earlier, will not readily surrender portions of their markets to newcomers. So another important factor entrepreneurs should consider is what is known as an "industry analysis"—careful examination of several important aspects of the industry they plan to enter. These features, and their relevance for entrepreneurs, are described below.

Industry structure: The costs of entry and the number and size of competitors

Industries differ greatly on a number of dimensions and together these constitute "industry structure." This structure, in turn, makes some industries more favorable than others for new ventures. Here are some of the key aspects of industry structure entrepreneurs should consider.

The costs of entry

First, some industries require more capital (financial resources) to gain entry than others. In a sense, the "entry fee" is higher. For instance, to enter the automobile industry, Tesla Motors, makers of high-quality electric cars (Figure 4.5), had to spend many millions of dollars. This was necessary because producing automobiles requires major facilities, and these costs were compounded by the costs of developing and producing the batteries all-electric cars require. Most new ventures—except, perhaps those that receive large amounts of support from investors (e.g., venture capitalists)—have limited financial resources, so the costs of entering an industry are a significant factor. Further, most new ventures do not generate high levels of cash flow from their operations, at least initially. So, they must rely on the resources they start with, and try to conserve these so that they don't run out of funds. Finally, when new ventures do obtain financial backing from investors, this is usually under relatively unfavorable terms. Why? Because investors realize that entrepreneurs know much more about their ideas and the company they are building than investors, so the investors require a "premium," to protect their interests in the face of this disadvantage.

The costs of marketing

Industries also vary in terms of the costs of marketing. While costs are low for some—for instance, companies that do much of their business on the internet—they are very high for others, who must promote their products through the media (television, print media) and in other ways. Brand recognition is an important aspect of marketing efforts, and establishing a well-known brand is often the key to success. This takes time, however, and involves relatively high marketing costs. Brand reputations are developed over time through repeated advertising efforts. As you might well expect, new ventures tend to be more successful in industries where the costs of marketing are relatively low.

Industry concentration

In some industries, a few large companies dominate—they account for most of the sales—and profits. The smaller the number of such companies, the greater the industry concentration. Trying to compete with large, dominant companies is very difficult for a new venture, which generally lacks the

Figure 4.5 An example of high cost of entry

Entering a mature industry such as the automobile industry requires very high entry costs. Tesla Motors was able to cover these costs, but few new ventures have the financial resources to do so. As a result, entrepreneurs should consider entry costs carefully before attempting to develop an opportunity.

resources to do this effectively. For instance, in many retail stores, shelf space is at a premium and most of it goes to large companies. For an entrepreneur to gain even a small amount of space, and therefore exposure to potential customers, in Wal-Mart, for example, is extremely difficult. Yes, giant retailers do take a chance on new products produced by small companies occasionally, but gaining their acceptance in this respect is difficult. Large retailers wonder whether the space given to new companies they are not familiar with will be wasted because, for instance, these new suppliers will not be able to keep up with demand if it is great.

Size of existing companies

Related to industry concentration, but somewhat distinct, is the size of the companies in an industry. By their very nature, new ventures are usually small, and as a result tend to do better in industries in which the average size of existing companies is also relatively small. One example is the biotech industry, in which many small firms compete to generate new products, for instance drugs. Many new firms enter this industry each year and some do indeed succeed; they develop a new drug and are able to either sell it or license it to a large drug company. In industries where most of the firms are relatively small, new ventures are at less of a disadvantage than in ones more most of the existing companies are large. This doesn't necessarily imply a high level of concentration by the way. For instance, many companies produce clothing yet none are dominant in a sense of having a large share of the total business. This is in contrast to, for instance, the automobile industry, where a relatively small number of companies account for most of the sales.

In sum, new companies have a much greater chance of attaining success in some industries than others, so this is an important factor entrepreneurs should consider before proceeding.

Industry life cycles: New ventures do better in young industries than mature ones

Industries, like people, have a life cycle. They emerge, grow, reach maturity and then, in some cases, decline or even disappear. This cycle is visible in many industries. For instance, consider the men's hat industry. It emerged many years ago (perhaps several centuries in the past), grew as a hat became a necessary accessory for men, but then declined and disappeared in the 1960s, perhaps because after President Kennedy did *not* wear a hat at his inauguration in 1961 wearing a hat was suddenly out of fashion (Figure 4.6).

The result for the companies that produced them, even the most successful ones, was disaster, and most simply disappeared. On the other hand, consider the industry that produces tablet computers. It emerged less than ten years ago, when Apple introduced the iPad, grew rapidly, and is now entering maturity as many other companies mount strong challenges to Apple's dominance. Will it decline? Perhaps, if some other product, even better, replaces tablets. This cycle is another important factor entrepreneurs should consider before proceeding because it has a powerful influence on both their ability to launch a new venture and new venture success.

Source: Fotolia # 46415189_M.

Figure 4.6 Industry life cycle—and one industry that met a sudden end

The men's hat industry was stable and mature for many years—until President Kennedy went to his inauguration without a hat. As a result, many men stopped wearing hats like the one shown here, and the hat industry quickly declined—and, except for baseball caps and similar products—disappeared.

As you can probably guess, new firms are more successful in industries that are young rather than ones that are fully mature. Why? Because they do better in markets that are growing rapidly than in ones that are growing slowly. This is due to the fact that only a small number of people adopt a new product or service as soon as it emerges. Most wait until it has been available for a while before purchasing it. This means that when an industry is new, growth tends to be relatively slow. Then, as the new product or service it offers gains acceptance, sales often rise rapidly. This opens opportunities for new ventures to enter, since the "pie"—sales—is increasing, and as one old saying puts it, "A rising tide floats all boats." In addition, when demand is rising rapidly, it may be difficult for existing companies to meet it fully; that too creates openings for new ventures. Finally, when an industry is relatively new, there may not yet be a dominant company or small number of dominant companies, and the market may be segmented. As noted earlier, that too can be a "plus" for new ventures.

When industries mature, however, the situation changes greatly. Strong, leading companies may emerge—ones with a large share of sales. Further, what is known as a "dominant design" often develops. Dominant designs are a kind of standard—one that all companies in that industry must adopt. For example, the internal combustion engine used in a very high proportion of automobiles is a dominant design. Yet, when this industry was young that was not the case. Engines based on steam and electric power were used and might well have become the dominant design. The internal combustion engine won this competition for several reasons—for instance, it was easier to refuel. The result was that as the industry grew, this engine became the dominant design and was—and still is—used in most cars. However, the situation is now changing, with electric engines leading the way. As noted earlier, one company—Tesla Motors—offers automobiles that are fully powered by batteries, but many other companies offer "hybrids," which have both an electric and internal combustion engine. And other kinds of engines also exist or are being developed—for instance, engines that burn natural gas. In short, a dominant design may not always be dominant; rather, it can be replaced by new technological developments.

The existence of a dominant design is important to entrepreneurship because new firms have a greater chance of success *before* a dominant design emerges—that is, when an industry is still young. Before a dominant design becomes entrenched, an entrepreneur can adopt whatever design she or he wants for the new venture's products or services so there is more room for something new and, perhaps, better. Once a dominant design exists, however, it is more difficult to be unique; all companies—young and old—feel strong pressure to adhere to this design. As a result, new ventures lose the important advantage of producing something *really* new. Further, existing large companies may be more efficient at making products that incorporate the dominant design. The key point? Entrepreneurs should think carefully before launching new ventures in a mature industry where a dominant design exists. Only in rare instances where the new venture's products or services are *noticeably* superior to the dominant design would they stand much of a chance of gaining success. However, this *can* happen. Dominant designs are sometimes less effective than other approaches to meeting various needs. For instance, back in the 1980s there was no dominant design for word processors or graphics programs. As a result, the market for these products was segmented, and many competing brands existed. For instance, I used a graphics program known as Harvard Graphics, and a word processor known as Word Star. This led to many problems: files in one program could not be easily used by files in another. When Microsoft introduced Word and PowerPoint, they were not necessarily better than what already existed, but once they gained a dominant position in the market almost everyone had to use them, and the competing companies disappeared—or were purchased by Microsoft. To this day, however, some people believe that the earlier products were better in various ways than the products that are now the dominant designs in their areas.

Why certain kinds of markets favor new ventures

How much do you need a new cell phone that is faster than the one you already have? Many people would say "Very much—I want the fastest one I can get." In contrast, how high is your need for a light bulb that lasts much longer than the ones in your home now? In this case, most people would say "Not very—this is no big deal." The term "customer demand" relates to these differences: the higher the expressed need of customers for a product or service, the higher the demand conditions. In these two examples, demand conditions are higher for the cell phone than the new kind of light bulb. Three aspects of demand conditions are important for entrepreneurs— factors they should carefully consider: market size, market growth, and market segmentation.

In general, new companies are more successful in large markets than small ones. For instance, returning to the biotech industry, new ventures do better if they concentrate on developing drugs that treat common diseases than if they focus on developing drugs that treat what are known as "orphan diseases"—ones that are relatively rare. This is because in developing new products, companies often have large costs. The bigger the market for their products, the greater the extent to which these costs can be amortized—that is, covered by relatively high sales. As a result, new ventures often have a greater likelihood of success when they focus on large rather than small markets.

In addition, and not surprisingly, new firms also perform better in markets that are growing rapidly than in ones that are growing slowly or even shrinking. This is true because in growing markets new companies don't have to lure customers away from established firms—they can concentrate on attracting new customers or ones that established firms are unable to serve (e.g., they live in such a small town that the volume of potential business is not large enough for, perhaps, a McDonald's restaurant).

Finally, markets differ greatly in terms of "segmentation." This refers to the degree to which customers want different features in the products or services they seek. In some industries, customers want very much the same thing—for instance, most people want the same features in home air conditioning: a system that is reliable and efficient. In other industries, however, segmentation is much greater. Clothing is a good example. Customers differ greatly in age, gender, and life style, and want very different products. Until very recently, people working in traditional offices needed suits and ties. Teenagers, in contrast, could dress any way they wished, and tended to prefer jeans and casual clothing (Figure 4.7). New ventures tend to do better in highly segmented industries because they can fill niche markets—relatively small, specialized ones—markets that larger companies view as not worth the bother. In addition, new—and small—companies are often able to respond to rapid shifts in customers' tastes and preferences. Recently, for instance, several new companies have responded to a new trend: men have suddenly begun buying colorful socks and ones with patterns. In the past, most men's socks were of a single color and had only muted patterns. But now, especially among younger customers, there is a demand for more varied styles, and new ventures have quickly moved to develop this opportunity. For instance, Happy Socks was launched a few years ago in Stockholm, Sweden, by Viktor Tell, who noticed that during the bleak Swedish winter, some of his male friends had put on colorful socks to lift their own moods. Mr. Tell founded his company to develop this opportunity, and it has attained rapid growth. The lesson for entrepreneurs is clear: if possible, seek opportunities that can be developed in highly segmented rather than unsegmented markets. It won't be necessary to try to take customers from other firms, and that can be a big advantage.

Source: Fotolia # 9709868_M.

Figure 4.7 Market segmentation: high is better than low for new ventures

Market segmentation refers to the extent to which customers want different features in products or services. The clothing industry, for example, is high in segmentation: men working in offices or several professions want formal clothing (suits, ties), while teenagers strongly prefer more casual apparel.

Other essential information: Being familiar with key government policies and regulations

When they start new businesses, entrepreneurs are, of course, focused on the businesses themselves. They want to accomplish basic tasks such as manufacturing the new products they plan to bring to market, building sales, managing current financial resources (plus obtaining additional ones if necessary), and hiring employees. As a result, many entrepreneurs don't devote much attention to government regulations and laws that might have a strong impact on their new ventures. Sadly, *that can be a serious omission*. Moving ahead to build a new company without considering these issues may, sooner than you might guess, result in major problems. If government regulations are not followed, and the appropriate agencies or departments charged with enforcing them learn of such violations, they may impose heavy fines and other penalties. Given that new ventures often have limited resources and cannot afford to have their operations delayed or even stopped, the consequences can indeed be serious. So many federal and state regulations exist that no entrepreneur could be familiar with, or understand all of them (at the federal level they are contained in a document more than 70 000 pages in length, and new regulations are currently being enacted at a furious pace). To do so— or at least, meet the most important standards and regulations—they must often obtain help from knowledgeable attorneys, accountants, and others. But even so, it is still crucial that entrepreneurs be familiar with some of the most important laws and regulations that can affect their businesses. To help you accomplish this task, laws and regulations with major implications for new ventures are summarized below. Please consider them carefully, because *ignorance of the law is no excuse*, and again, failure to follow these regulations can have serious negative consequences.

Regulations concerning employment practices: Preventing discrimination

Everyone in the United States (and many other countries) knows that discrimination on the basis of race, color, religion, national origin, sex, and pregnancy is illegal. This definitely applies to employees, so that new ventures must avoid violating this law (Title VII of the Civil Rights Act of 1964) in their hiring practices. If they don't, and persons who believe that they were *not* hired because of discrimination, can win penalties ranging from back wages through attorney fees, and all of these must be paid by the new venture. And this law applies to companies engaged in interstate commerce with 15 employees or more.

Another important law concerning employment is Title I of the Americans with Disabilities Act of 1990. This prohibits discrimination against persons with disabilities who, despite these limitations, can perform a particular job. Further, it requires companies to provide "reasonable accommodation" for such persons—conditions that allow them to do the necessary work despite their disabilities. For instance, reasonable accommodation for prospective employees in wheelchairs might include ramps to give them access to workplaces and, perhaps, lowering work surfaces so they can reach them (Figure 4.8). This law applies, again, to companies engaged in interstate commerce with 15 or more employees.

Source: Fotolia # 51512220_M.

Figure 4.8
Reasonable
accommodation: a
requirement of the
law

In the United States, the
Americans with Disabilities
Act makes discriminating
against persons with
disabilities who can
still perform a specific
job illegal. Moreover, it
requires that companies
provide "reasonable
accommodation" for
persons—conditions that
allow them to do their jobs
despite their disabilities.

Discrimination based on age is also prohibited and applies to employees over the age of 40. So, if an entrepreneur wants to hire only young, energetic people for her or his company and rejects older applicants on the basis of their age, the applicant can file a suit and win two to three years of back wages, or double this amount in certain circumstances. This law applies to companies with more than 20 employees (Figure 4.9).

Finally, consider the Equal Pay Act of 1964, which prohibits differences in pay on the basis of sex: equal pay for jobs that require equivalent skill, effort,

Source: Fotolia # 47079294_M.

Figure 4.9
Discrimination on
the basis of age is
illegal
In addition to sex, religion,
gender, and religious beliefs,
discrimination against older
persons is against the law.

and responsibility. This applies to companies with as few as two employees. And once again, penalties in situations where employees can prove the existence of such discrimination are considerable.

Many laws and regulations exist—ones requiring advance notice to employees that they may be fired or be part of a projected lay-off, regulations requiring that employers establish a drug-free workplace, that employees be given 12 weeks of leave for pregnancies (both women and men), without putting their jobs in jeopardy. We could continue because the list is indeed quite long, but the key point should be clear: entrepreneurs must be aware of—and obey—these laws and regulations because they apply to all companies once they reach a certain volume of business or number of employees.

Regulations concerning the health and safety of employees

In 1970, after a major accident in the coal mine that cost the lives of many miners, the federal government passed the Occupational Safety and Health Act (OSHA). This act requires that employers with as few as ten employees provide a safe and healthy work environment for their employees, and to keep records of injuries or illnesses that happen while employees are at work. These records must be retained for five years and must also be posted annually on a bulletin board for all employees to see. If employers violate these rules, they can receive large fines, and executives of the firms can be charged with crimes and sent to prison if convicted.

Fortunately, few new ventures experience serious problems in these areas—only a tiny fraction are ever cited by OSHA for violations. But still, as an entrepreneur, you should be aware of the fact that all businesses are subject to these requirements once they employ ten or more persons.

The Affordable Health Care for America Act: What it means for new ventures

In 2010, the US Congress passed famous—and controversial—legislation known as the Affordable Health Care for America Act. (Since it was sponsored by President Obama it is often known colloquially as "Obama Care.") The law was designed to provide basic health care coverage to millions of people who did not at the time have it. In fact, individuals—even those who are self-employed—are required to have health insurance or pay a fine. The law also has important implications for small businesses, and applies to companies with more than 50 employees. Clearly, many new ventures meet that criterion, so it is important for entrepreneurs to understand the basic provisions of this law, and the new requirements it establishes. The law itself is extremely complex (it fills more than 1700 pages of printed text), but the most important provisions for entrepreneurs to understand are these:

- **Employers must provide health care coverage for their employees**. If a company employs the equivalent of 50 employees or more it has the obligation to provide health care coverage for them. To help small businesses pay the costs involved tax credits up to 35 percent are offered. In other words, the government will share the costs of establishing health care programs with employers. (The implementation of this requirement was delayed, but not removed, in 2013.)

- **Small Business Health Options Program**. In the past, small businesses had higher costs for health insurance than large ones because of higher administrative costs (i.e., these costs are relatively fixed, so the larger the number of persons employed, the lower these costs per employee). To help reduce these costs, small businesses can join together to obtain lower rates from insurers.

- **Employee notification**. Employers also have the responsibility of informing their employees of health care options available through a newly created "Health Insurance Marketplace." In this marketplace, insurers compete to win contracts from companies, and offer several options with respect to the type of insurance available. Employers must make these options known to employees, and also notify them of the various plans offered by insurers. These rules apply to companies *with only one employee*.

- **Summary of benefits and coverage**. Employers must also provide employees with a standard form that explains their benefits and what their health care covers.

- **Ninety-day waiting period**. In the past, many companies required that individuals be employed by the company for relatively long periods of time before becoming eligible for health benefits. The new law limits such "waiting periods" to a maximum of 90 days.

- **Rewards for establishing workplace wellness programs**. Wellness programs offer employees rewards in terms of reduced insurance premiums if they meet specific requirements with respect to actions designed to improve their health—for instance, lose weight, stop smoking, reduce their cholesterol. Employers are rewarded for establishing such programs by reductions in the health care costs they must pay. (These reductions are covered by the government.)

These are only a few of the basic provisions of this new legislation; covering all of them would be impossible, and in fact, interpretation of the law is not yet clear. What *is* clear, however, is that (1) all businesses with more than 50 employees will have to provide health care plans for their employees, or face large fines, and (2) individuals who do not have health insurance through their jobs (e.g., they lose their jobs), *must* obtain basic coverage or also face fines. It is these requirements that make the law controversial. Some business owners, and many individuals, object very strongly to being told, essentially, that they have no choice: they must have health insurance. And many young people who have never experienced serious illness but are on limited budgets view the requirement that they obtain health care coverage as unfair. In fact, many prefer to pay the fines than obtain such insurance they believe they don't need. And the owners of small businesses—including many entrepreneurs—feel that their companies can't afford to pay for health insurance for employees, and that they should not be forced to do so. On the other hand, many individuals support the new law strongly, because they believe that health care is a *right* not a privilege—everyone should have access to it. Since the law applies only to full-time employees, many businesses are making many jobs part-time—less than 30 hours each week. The ultimate fate of the law is still in question because there is strong opposition to it, but as long as the law exists, entrepreneurs, like other employers, must comply with it—or risk the consequences.

We could go on to list other laws and regulations that can strongly affect entrepreneurs and their new ventures—for instance, laws and regulations concerning environmental hazards (pollution, toxic substances), and local laws concerning what kind of business can be operated where. The image of an entrepreneur starting a business in her or his basement or garage is a popular one, but whether it is possible today depends on the kind of business, and where it is located. Starting a company in a basement that actual *makes* physical objects (i.e., some kind of manufacturing) would probably not be permitted—in part because of the noise and other environmental hazards it would bring to a residential area.

By now, the main point of this discussion should be clear: starting a new ventures seems in some respects to be straightforward: have an idea, determine if it makes sense, and if it does, move ahead to develop it. But in fact, the "moving ahead" part is often complex; and one of the factors contributing to such complexity is a vast array of government regulations and laws. Since violating them can result in serious consequences, some basic knowledge of these regulations and laws should be included on any list of "must have" information for entrepreneurs. For an example of what can happen when entrepreneurs do *not* obey these laws and regulation, see "The Entrepreneurial Quest" case study below.

CASE STUDY

The Entrepreneurial Quest

How ignoring government regulations can kill even a good idea

About 15 years ago, a friend told me about a new company that was gathering financial resources so that it could start operations. The idea behind it impressed me as a very good one, because it addressed a major need—how to get rid of the huge number of used tires piling up in dumps all around the United States. These tires were an eyesore, and the technology used to eliminate them at that time was fairly primitive: either burn them—which produced dangerous air pollution—or tear them into little pieces for use in paving and construction, a process that used huge amounts of energy because the tires were so strong. The idea my friend described was based on something else entirely. A scientist who had recently immigrated to the United States from the former Soviet Union was a well-known expert in cryogenics—what happens to various materials at extremely low temperatures (e.g., –250° Fahrenheit). His idea was to freeze the tires, which then became brittle and easily pulverized. Valuable materials (e.g., nylon, rubber, steel) could then be recovered easily from the powder they produced. This idea impressed me as outstanding in several respects.

First, it would help eliminate a major environmental problem. Second, it would recover useful materials from what was now essentially waste. The icing on the cake was that many towns would pay a fee to get rid of the tires in their landfills. In short, the new company would not have to pay for its raw materials—it would actually be *paid* for receiving them!

The result was that I decided to invest in this new venture. Everything went well for a while, the Russian scientist provided the necessary expertise, and construction on the company's first building began. But then, suddenly, officials from the State Environmental Protection Agency came to visit . . . and closed the company down! All work stopped, and no more tires could be accepted. You are probably wondering what happened. The answer is simple: the founders (the scientist and two other persons who had previous experience as entrepreneurs) had failed to pay attention to government regulations. They did not know about various standards for sites that accepted used tires. On top of that, the founders had failed to find out about federal regulations concerning the use of the gases used in the freezing process.

And that, in short, was the end of the story. The company did survive, at least for a while, but it never managed to start operations, and investors (including me) lost their money.

This is a very sad story—especially for the investors—because in recent years, the basic idea of freezing tires and using the result to make useful products has been developed successfully by another company, Lehigh Technologies (Figure 4.10). As described on company's website: "Lehigh Technologies . . . turns end-of-life tire materials and other post-industrial rubber into micronized rubber powders (MRP) that are used in a wide range of . . . applications, including plastics, high performance tires, coatings & sealants and construction materials." Clearly, the founders of *this* company did not ignore government regulations and laws, and so have developed what was a good idea back in the mid-1990s into reality. And that, of course, is the essence of successful entrepreneurship!

CASE STUDY *(continued)*

Source: Photo from Baron, 2013, Figure 9.1, p. 172.

Figure 4.10 A good idea—that, *this* time is succeeding!

Fifteen years ago, a company was formed to recycle used tires, such as those shown above, by freezing and pulverizing them. However, the company failed because it ignored key environmental regulations. Recently, though, a company that follows all these regulations (Lehigh Technologies) is successfully exploiting this resource—and so helping to eliminate eyesores such as this one.

THE EFFECTIVE ENTREPRENEUR

Before proceeding to develop an opportunity, entrepreneurs should gather several kinds of important information. Together, this information can help inform the key decision about whether to move ahead—or seek another, better opportunity. To the extent that entrepreneurs gather the following kinds of information, their chances of success will be improved:

- Conduct as careful a feasibility analysis as time and resources permit. This can involve considerable effort, but the ultimate savings in terms of avoiding "dead ends" and opportunities that are unlikely to succeed can make this well worthwhile.

- Don't rush ahead with an opportunity that must be developed in an industry that is unfavorable to new ventures. That is, if the opportunity you have in mind would require entrance into a mature industry, one that requires high entry costs, and is dominated by a few large companies, pause and think again!

- Consider potential markets carefully too. If there is a well-established dominant design, if the market is unsegmented (most customers want the same thing), and industry is mature, this might not be

➡

← an environment in which to start a new venture.

- Find out about government regulations and major laws; if you violate them, the costs can be huge—and pleading ignorance is no help. If necessary, seek experts on these matters because again, although this can be costly it is still far less costly than learning, too late, that your new venture is in violation of important rules or restrictions.

SUMMARY OF KEY POINTS

1 Recognizing an opportunity is one thing; deciding whether it is worth pursuing is another. Before launching a new venture—or even thinking seriously about doing so—entrepreneurs should gather important kinds of information. A careful feasibility analysis, which considers product or service feasibility, market feasibility, competitors (current or potential), financial and organizational feasibility can help tremendously with this decision.

2 Some industries, and some markets, are more favorable to new ventures than others—that is, they offer greater likelihood of attaining success. Industries with many small competitors that are young rather than mature, in which a dominant design has not yet emerged, are growing rapidly, and in which customers want a wide variety of products or service, provide more fertile ground for the launch and growth of new ventures.

3 Government regulations and many laws are highly relevant to entrepreneurs and new ventures. These range from laws designed to prevent discrimination in hiring (i.e., discrimination based on race, religion, national origin, sex, age, or disabilities), to ones requiring that employers establish safe and healthy work environments for their employees. Failure to adhere to these laws can result in major fines and other penalties.

4 The Affordable Health Care for America Act (2010) requires all employers who have more than 50 employees to provide health care coverage for them. Employers must inform employees of these plans and various options, and allow them to enroll within 90 days of being employed. Entrepreneurs whose companies grow rapidly and reach the "magic number" of 50 full-time employees, must comply with these regulations or face stiff fines.

5 Overall, the moral for entrepreneurs is "Look before you leap" where pursuing an opportunity is concerned.

REFERENCES

Baron, R.A. (2013), *Enhancing Entrepreneurial Excellence: Tools for Making the Possible Real*, Cheltenham, UK and Northampton, MA, USA: Edward Elgar.

Mollick, E.R. (2013), "The dynamics of crowdfunding: Determinants of success and failure," *Journal of Business Venturing*, forthcoming.

Pierro, A., G. Pica, R. Mauro, A.W. Kruglanski and E.T. Higgins (2012), "How regulatory modes work together: Locomotion–assessment complementarity in work performance," *TPM— Testing, Psychometrics, Methodology in Applied Psychology*, **19**(4), 247–62.

5

Transforming ideas into reality: Careful planning . . . and improvising

 CHAPTER OUTLINE

- Business plans: Formal guides to creating value
  - Reasons for writing a formal business plan: Potential benefits—and potential costs
  - Business plans: Their key parts
  - Business plans: Is writing one related to new venture success?
- The importance of flexibility: Improvisation and bricolage
  - Improvisation: Its basic nature and relationship to firm performance
  - Bricolage: Making something from nothing?
- Effectuation: Using what you have to get where, perhaps, you want to go

If you don't know where you are going, you'll end up someplace else.
(Lawrence Peter "Yogi" Berra, American Major League Baseball player)

By failing to prepare, you are preparing to fail.
(Benjamin Franklin, 1706–90, one of the Founding Fathers of the United States)

[I]mprovising is wonderful. But . . . you cannot improvise unless you know exactly what you're doing.
(Christopher Walken, US actor)

As Yogi Berra (a baseball player and manager from 1945 to 1965) says so clearly: you can't get somewhere without knowing where you want to go, to which I would add—and without having a plan for getting there! This basic principle applies to many different activities and goals. For instance, in preparing dinner it's important to know what you want to cook and to have a plan for obtaining the ingredients and preparing them—in this case, a recipe. Similarly, when contemplating your retirement, it's crucial to have a specific goal (e.g., a specific amount of income), and to devise a plan for reaching it (e.g., save a given amount each year, etc.). In the field of entrepreneurship, careful planning is viewed as especially important. The "business plan"—a detailed, written plan explaining how entrepreneurs will actually convert their ideas into reality (a business that generates value)—is often viewed as perhaps the single most important activity entrepreneurs can perform before launching their companies. Entire courses are devoted to this topic and in many others, students must prepare business plans, in one form or another, as a key assignment. And certainly, to echo the words of Benjamin Franklin, if you don't plan you may well be headed for failure. For entrepreneurs, careful planning is often essential for obtaining the financial and human resources they need to actually launch a business and nurture its success. Just think about it for a moment: would anyone (e.g., venture capitalists) advance large sums of money to entrepreneurs who did not have specific plans for developing their ideas into actual businesses? And would anyone (especially individuals with high levels of talent, skill, or experience), come to work for a new venture that did not have clear and specific plans for attaining success? Probably not, because if they did, they might well be wrecking their own careers. In short, planning is essential and often *must* be part of the process of converting ideas into something new and useful.

On the other hand, it is clear that planning isn't all there is to entrepreneurship. A healthy degree of flexibility—a willingness to shift direction, change goals, and improvise—can also be important. For instance, consider a new venture that introduces products that are, when initially launched, superior to those offered by competitors. Will these other companies meekly accept this situation? Hardly! On the contrary, they will counter with various actions designed to combat this new threat to their own success, and entrepreneurs often can't predict the specific form these countermeasures will take, or the speed with which they will be introduced. For this reason, they must be ready to alter their own plans and strategies. Similarly, in many industries—especially high-tech ones—change occurs so quickly and unpredictably that detailed plans for running a new company may be outdated even before they are implemented; in such situations, clinging to old plans or strategies can prove deadly. For instance, consider what happened to Kodak, which once dominated the photography industry. In 1975, a Kodak engineer, Steve Sasson, invented the first digital camera. Yet, Kodak's management stuck to its existing plans—which were to produce cameras that used film, sell the film itself, and basically stick with "tried-and-true" technologies. In 1981, Sony introduced the first digital camera, and although Kodak conducted a large study of its potential—a study that clearly identified the appeal and potential of digital photography—Kodak concluded that it had at least ten years to move in this direction. The result? As digital camera sales grew, Kodak was left behind—and essentially rode its unwillingness to change and improvise to almost total ruin (Figure 5.1). Now however, even digital cameras are in decline as cell phones replace their basic function.

Source: Wikimedia: by unrestricted permission of the photographer.

Figure 5.1 What happens when even a large company fails to adapt to changing conditions

Kodak Inc. once dominated the photography industry. When it failed to adapt to the shift to digital cameras, however, it quickly lost market share and ultimately had to file for bankruptcy. It finally did shift to making digital cameras, but by then it was too late. (Recently, however, cell phones have begun to replace digital cameras.) *(Left-hand photo: a non-digital camera produced by Kodak; right-hand photo: a digital camera produced by Kodak).*

The same basic principle applies to entrepreneurship: although planning is indeed essential and often useful, there must also be room for "improvisation"—flexibility that allows for mid-course corrections and changes. Research findings indicate that many entrepreneurs engage in improvisation as standard practice, and that doing so can be very beneficial to their efforts to create successful new ventures (e.g., Hmieleski et al., 2013). As we noted in Chapter 3, not all opportunities exist "out there" in the external world; rather, entrepreneurs sometimes create them by their own actions. This idea is represented both in research on the importance of improvisation in entrepreneurship (e.g., Baker and Nelson, 2005; Hmieleski and Corbett, 2008) and in a unique approach to the issue of planning known as "effectuation" (e.g., Sarasvathy, 2001; Venkataraman et al., 2012). We'll cover both of these topics in later sections, but here, we should note that both suggest that detailed planning may not always be useful. Why? One reason is that entrepreneurs often operate in environments involving high degrees of "uncertainty"—environments in which the information necessary for careful planning does not exist and therefore cannot be obtained. As a result, they must essentially "make it up as they go along," and among the things they sometimes generate as they do so are new opportunities and new ways of developing them. Again, we'll return to these alternatives or modifications of careful planning in later sections.

Having made these basic points about planning and alternatives to it, we'll now proceed as follows. First, "business plans"—what they are, why they are important, and their role in entrepreneurship—will be described. This is a central activity for entrepreneurs, especially before they actually launch their new ventures, and as we'll see, it plays a key role in the process of obtaining essential resources (see Chapter 6). After that, we'll turn to improvisation, which involves the capacity to implement mid-course changes in strategy or actions in order respond effectively to rapidly changing conditions and new opportunities and to the related process of bricolage, which involves using available resources and recombining them in creative ways (e.g., Baker et al., 2003). Finally, we'll turn to effectuation and its implications for the traditional view—widely accepted—that entrepreneurship involves formulating specific plans and then implementing them. In contrast, effectuation proposes that entrepreneurs don't always need such plans; rather, they consider their available resources and then use these to create goals and opportunities. In other words, they don't respond to the world—they *change* it—a basic idea highlighted in Chapter 1.

Business plans: Formal guides to creating value

At most universities, high levels of enthusiasm—and excitement—surround yearly business plan competitions. Teams of students who have ideas for new products, services, markets, or means of production prepare formal business plans—documents describing how, in specific terms, they will convert these ideas into value-creating companies. The teams present these ideas to panels of judges (usually, highly experienced entrepreneurs and faculty members with entrepreneurial experience), who evaluate the plans and select the winners. Winning is more than simply an honor: most competitions provide substantial cash prizes—funds the winning teams can use to start or grow their new ventures (Figure 5.2). Further, winning teams can advance to national competitions in which they vie with teams from many universities for even larger prizes. Overall, these are very important events and are a central focus of entrepreneurship faculty and students alike. The reason for this is twofold: business plans are, of course, required for entry into these competitions. And winners not only receive prizes, they also often obtain offers of financial support from venture capitalists or even the judges themselves. (Many of the judges represent venture capital firms whose key activity is investing in new ventures.) These are strong reasons for prospective entrepreneurs to invest the effort required to prepare them; and make

Source: Courtesy of the Riata Center for Entrepreneurship, Oklahoma State University.

Figure 5.2 Business plan competitions: winning brings many benefits

The winners of business plan competitions not only receive cash prizes, they also gain access to investors who may provide financial resources for their new ventures.

no mistake—the effort involved is often substantial, involving long hours of work that many entrepreneurs—with their strong preference for "doing" rather than planning—find tedious. But winning business plan competitions and possibly obtaining financial support—although important—are not the only reasons for writing a business plan. We'll now describe some of the most important of these.

Reasons for writing a formal business plan: Potential benefits— and potential costs

As noted above, preparing a formal business plan involves a lot of hard work. In general, it requires many hours of careful thought, followed by the complex process of converting these ideas into a document that must follow a fairly specific format. While some people may enjoy such activities, many entrepreneurs do not. They want to move ahead to launch their business and make their ideas real. And many realize that once their new venture has been started it will rarely follow the steps and strategies outlined in the business plan. Further, they also realize that preparing such plans may not necessarily be closely related to their new venture's success, an idea supported by research findings as we'll soon describe.

With these obvious drawbacks to investing lots of time and effort in preparing a formal business plan, what is the "upside" of this activity? Should entrepreneurs expend the time, energy, and effort required to generate a first-rate business? In fact, there are two reasons that make this activity well worthwhile. First, excellent business plans do indeed often provide a foundation for acquiring valuable resources needed by a new venture: they help secure financial support from venture capitalists and others, and help attract excellent employees (see Chapter 6). In a sense, then, business plans are a "selling tool"—one that helps the entrepreneurs promote their ideas in ways that ultimately provide the resources needed to implement them.

Second, writing a first-rate business plan helps entrepreneurs refine their thinking about the opportunities they wish to pursue. Writing such a plan helps them understand the many complex issues and problems they will face. This, in turn, assists them in formulating clearer ideas about how they will meet these challenges and create a successful new company. And to echo the words of Benjamin Franklin once again, planning is usually crucial for success, and failing to plan leads instead to . . . failure! While that's not always true, in general it *is*, because while having clear goals is important, having a plan for attaining them is equally crucial. Writing an effective business plan requires an entrepreneur to formulate such plans, so the word "plan" is very appropriate: a comprehensive business plan describes the opportunity (e.g., what needs the new product or service will meet, what markets it will have), how the product or service will be produced or delivered, what skills and abilities the founding team brings to the new venture, how the new company will be structured, how the new venture will gain a competitive advantage, what critical risks it faces, what financial resources it needs, and so on. In addition, a well-prepared business plan contains a clear and well-developed "business model"—a model of how the new venture will actually operate, how it will compete, use its resources, develop relationships with other companies (e.g., suppliers), and interact with customers. We will return to business models in a later chapter, but here we should note that, in a sense, they explain how the company will create value and be profitable. In this discussion, however, we focus specifically on business plans.

Overall, the key point of this discussion of the benefits of writing a formal business plan is simply this—the effort invested in doing so provides entrepreneurs with enhanced understanding of what will actually be involved in converting their ideas into something tangible, and that is a major "plus." Being enthusiastic about the opportunities they have discovered or hope to create is not in itself enough and, in fact, can, if extreme, sometimes get in the way of attaining success. The careful thought required to prepare a detailed business plan may help to moderate these tendencies and so keep entrepreneurs on track. But entrepreneurs should also always keep in mind the fact that business plans are *not* set in stone—in fact, they are made to be changed, and any company that sticks too closely to its original business plan (or business model) as markets, technology, and other factors alter radically, can be headed for disaster.

Having summarized the benefits of writing a formal business plan, which are substantial, it's important to emphasize, again, that there is also a "downside" to this activity too. First, as noted above, it usually requires many hours of hard, focused work. As a result, entrepreneurs engaged in preparing a business plan have less time and energy available for other activities that may also be important to launching their new ventures—for instance, improving and developing their products, expanding their social networks (see Chapter 7), developing marketing plans, and so on. Second, and perhaps more important, the process of preparing a business plan may encourage the development of the kind of "mental ruts" described in Chapter 2: in essence, after spending many hours thinking about their ideas and resources required to develop them, entrepreneurs may become locked into thinking in certain ways. Thus, preparing an excellent, detailed business plan may tend to reduce entrepreneurs' capacity to think "outside the box"—in this case, a cognitive "box" created by their own repeated thoughts. These tendencies may be further strengthened by making many verbal presentations of their ideas not just in business plan competitions but also to venture capitalists and other potential investors. Research on cognitive processes indicates that frequent repetition of the information contained in these presentations can enhance one of the key cognitive errors described in Chapter 2—the confirmation bias, which involves a strong tendency to direct more attention to information that confirms our views than information inconsistent with them. That, in turn, can pose a serious threat to entrepreneurs' openness to important information.

Business plans—is longer (or at least more detailed) always better?

In recent years, there has been increasing recognition of the potential drawback described above, with the result that some entrepreneurs, at least, have adopted the strategy of preparing shorter, simpler plans. This raises an intriguing question: which of these approaches is better—long, formal plans, or shorter, less detailed ones? The answer, as you might well guess is "It depends." In some situations a detailed plan is necessary—for instance, when large amounts of funding are required to launch the new venture. Detailed plans are essential in such cases because in their absence investors may be very reluctant to provide the necessary funds. In other situations—for instance, when entrepreneurs will provide their own funding (an approach known as "bootstrapping"), as was the case for Ecovative, the company described in Chapter 3 that is offering a substitute for Styrofoam based on purely organic processes—a shorter and less detailed plan, or even no plan at all, may suffice. The guiding principle, then, is to *always* engage in careful preparation and planning, but to make flexibility part of the process, so that the plan is seen more as a reflection of the entrepreneurs' evolving thoughts and ideas—constantly adjusted in the face of new information—than as a rigid framework dictating how the new company will develop, operate, and create value (please see Chapter 11 for more information on these topics.)

Business plans: Their key parts

Assuming that entrepreneurs have decided that they do need a detailed business plan because they want to enter plan competitions and attract external funding, what information should be included? Business plans vary greatly in their specific contents and the way in which they are organized, but in general they generally contain information on the following issues:

- *What* is the basic idea for the new product or service? In other words, what is the opportunity being developed?

- *Why* is this new product useful or appealing and better than what currently exists?
- *Who* will want to buy or use it?
- *How* will the idea for the new product or service be transformed into reality—what is the plan for actually making the product (or providing the service), for marketing it, for dealing with existing and future competition?
- *What* is the business model—how will the new venture operate, compete effectively, use its key resources, interact with companies, and create value?
- *Who* are the entrepreneurs, and do they have the required knowledge, experience, and skills to develop this idea and to run a new company; what specific roles will they play?
- *How* will the new venture be structured, and how will it operate once it is launched?
- If the plan is designed to obtain financial resources, *how much* funding is needed, how will it be used, and how will both the entrepreneurs and other persons realize a return on their investment?

This is simply a list of some of the general issues that should be addressed. Usually, they are considered in much more detail in specific sections of the plan. These sections are shown in Table 5.1, where additional explanation concerning their content and structure is provided. While all parts of a formal business plan are important, perhaps the most crucial is the "Executive Summary"—a brief overview presented at the beginning. In fact, the Executive Summary is so important that it merits a closer look, and attention to *why* it is so crucial.

Have you ever heard the phrase "elevator pitch?" It refers to efforts to present—and promote—ideas to others in a very brief format; the name "elevator pitch" refers to the fact that the presentation should be one that can be made during an elevator ride—generally two minutes or less. (Of course, elevator rides in large office buildings can take a little longer than that, but the basic idea is clear: keep it short, simple, and to the point!) Similarly, in business plan competitions, entrepreneurs often have only a few minutes to present an overview of their companies (e.g., three to five minutes), and if they exceed that limit, a loud buzzer sounds and they must stop, even in mid-sentence! So in this context too, brevity is crucial.

In written business plans, the essence of an "elevator pitch" is contained in the Executive Summary. This part of the business plan—which should truly be brief (two to three pages at most)—provides an overview of what the new

Table 5.1 Basic sections of a business plan. Because the new ventures they describe are unique, business plans, too, are unique, but most contain the sections and information shown here

Section	Description
Executive Summary	*Brief* overview of the *idea* behind the opportunity—the idea for the new product or service? Why is it unique? Who will find it appealing etc.? No more than two to three pages
Background, purpose, and opportunity	A section describing the idea (the opportunity) and the current state of the new venture
Marketing	What is the potential market? How large? What is the existing competition and how will it be overcome, pricing, and related issues? (Sometimes this last topic appears in a separate section, and sometimes it is included in the marketing section)
Competition	If not included in the marketing section. Information on existing products and services, prices, market share, etc.
Development, production, and location	Where is the product or service right now in terms of development, how will it move toward actual production or delivery (service); where will the new venture be located and so on? Information on *operations*, too, can be included in this section (how the new business will operate, whether it will seek corporate partners, etc.)
Management (the entrepreneurs)	A section describing the human capital of the new venture's founding team—their experience, skills, and knowledge—and also what human resources they will need to acquire in the months head. Information on current ownership of the company, too, should be included
Financial section	Information on the company's current financial state, projections of future needs, revenues, and other financial measures. It should also include information on the amount of funding being sought, when this is relevant, and how these funds be will be used; cash flow and a break-even analysis
Risk factors	Various risks the new venture will face, and the steps the management team is taking to protect against them
Harvest or exit	Investors are interested in understanding precisely how they will gain if the company is successful, so information on this important issue (e.g., when and how the company might go public) can often be very useful
Scheduling and milestones	Information on when each phase of the new venture will be completed should be included, so that potential investors will know just when key tasks (e.g., start of production, time to first sales, projected break-even point) will be completed. This can be a separate section, or included in other sections, as appropriate
Appendices	Here is where detailed financial information, detailed resumés of the founding team should be presented, and detailed technical/scientific information can be included. These *should not* appear in the body of the business plan

venture is all about. In essence, it offers concise answers to several of the key questions listed earlier: what is the *idea* behind the opportunity—the idea for the new product or service? Why is it unique? Who will find it appealing (i.e., what is the potential market)? Why are the new venture's products or services superior to existing ones, and who is the competition? Can all this be accomplished in two to three pages? Absolutely. But doing so requires *very* careful writing. The effort invested in making this section not only crystal clear, but also interesting and persuasive, is well worthwhile: it represents the entrepreneurs' first and, often, *only* chance to generate interest among potential investors. If this section doesn't "grab" their interest they may stop reading right there, and won't even consider the rest of the business plan, no matter how excellent it is. Venture capitalists often receive hundreds or even thousands of business plans each year, so this is how they often proceed: they use the Executive Summary as an initial screening device, and only the few that seem especially interesting or potentially profitable, earn further examination. Truly, then, starting with a strong and persuasive Executive Summary is a crucial task.

After the Executive Summary major sections follow in an orderly arrangement. These can be organized in many different ways, but Table 5.1 offers one that is used in many traditional business plans and is quite logical. How long should a business plan be? In general, no more than 25–30 pages in the actual body of the plan (not counting appendices), and even shorter can often be better. An excellent business plan—one that is potentially prize-winning!— should present basic information succinctly, clearly, and persuasively, and these characteristics should be reflected in the verbal presentations made by entrepreneurs. This is a key reason why, in preparing for such presentations, the guiding principle should be *practice, practice, practice*, so that the presentation itself is clear, fluent, and fits within whatever time limits are imposed. I have attended business plan competitions where each team of entrepreneurs was given only two or three minutes to provide an overview of their ideas and business model. Some teams were ready and completed their presentations exactly on time, or with just one or two seconds to spare. Others, however, were stopped by the clock, and were unable to make key points. Needless to say, this did not impress the judges and none of them won a prize.

Business plans: Is writing one related to new venture success?

As noted above, preparing a detailed, formal a business plan offers important benefits: it opens the door to potential funding through plan competitions and is required by many venture capitalists before they will consider providing financial support. In addition, it helps entrepreneurs bring their own goals and business models into sharper focus. It's important to note though that these benefits, however, apply mainly to the very early phases of a new venture's existence, so another and very crucial question arises: "Does writing a detailed business plan also contribute to the new venture's actual success once it is launched?" In other words, does the effort invested in writing such plans pay off not just in the short term (e.g., prizes in business plan competitions), but in achieving the growth and success entrepreneurs seek? This issue has sparked a continuing debate in the field of entrepreneurship.

On one side are strong advocates of business plans, who contend that the benefits of completing this task far outweigh any potential costs. This view is currently in the majority. Virtually every program in entrepreneurship emphasizes the importance of developing excellent business plans and provides students with multiple opportunities in which to practice this activity. On the other side of this issue, however, are researchers and others who suggest that writing detailed business plans is only weakly related to a new venture's success. Why? For several reasons: new ventures often operate in environments of high uncertainty, which implies that accurate predictions are not possible despite efforts to make them; to contribute to success, the plans must be correctly implemented, which requires adequate resources, and the plans must be constantly updated—which means that the initial plan may have little bearing on the company's success. The arguments offered by both sides are persuasive, so this is clearly an instance in which the "evidence" portion of the title of this book is relevant. Basically, the only way to resolve this complex issue is through systematic research in which the long-term success of companies that started with a detailed, formal business plan are compared with ones that started without such a plan. Such research has actually been conducted, and, unfortunately, the results are as complex as this question itself. On one side are several studies indicating that preparing a formal business plan is only weakly related to firm performance (e.g., Lange et al., 2007). For example, in one study, Fernandez-Guerrero et al. (2012) found that the quality of business plans—their economic, financial, and organizational feasibility—was unrelated to the survival of new ventures three and six years after their founding. On the basis of these findings the authors concluded that unless entrepreneurs require a large amount of external funding they might be better off investing the time and effort required for preparing a detailed business plan in other activities such as basic (not detailed) financial planning, attracting customers, and planning actual operations of the company.

On the other side of the equation, however, is additional research indicating that formal business plans *are* related to new venture success (e.g., Burke et al., 2010). For example, Brinckmann et al. (2010) examined the results of 46 previous studies involving more than 11 000 companies started by entrepreneurs. Success was assessed by an array of standard measures—growth in sales, growth in earnings, profits, return on investment. The companies included in the review were divided into new start-ups or more established small businesses, and additional information on a key culture-related factor—the extent to which the culture in which they operated seeks to avoid uncertainty. Results indicated that companies that either had a written business plan or engaged in detailed processes of business planning were in fact more successful than ones that did not: they achieved higher rates of growth. However, these results were stronger for established firms than for new ventures just getting started. Further, the relationship between having a business plan and subsequent performance was weaker in cultures where uncertainty is looked upon as something to be avoided (e.g., France, Japan) than in cultures where uncertainty is viewed as more acceptable (e.g., the United States). One possible reason for this finding is that in cultures that seek to avoid uncertainty, entrepreneurs are reluctant to depart from the strategies described in their business plans, and so are less able to adapt effectively to rapidly changing conditions. In a sense, they feel "locked in" to the plans and this can reduce their willingness to improvise (see a later section), and hence, their overall success. In cultures that are more accepting of uncertainty in contrast, entrepreneurs may be more willing to depart from their original business plans, and so are better at responding to rapidly changing conditions. The result? Greater success.

One more issue is worth considering: even if there is a significant link between preparation of excellent business plans and subsequent firm performance, this might not, in itself, indicate that it is the business plans that contribute to such success. Rather, it might simply reflect the fact that entrepreneurs who are able prepare effective business plans are higher in skills or characteristics that contribute to business success than those who do not (e.g., see Chapter 8). Further, they may be higher in verbal and presentation skills, higher in social skills (useful in obtaining the help they need to prepare such plans). It might be these skills and characteristics, rather than the business plans themselves, that are responsible for their new venture's success. At present, conclusive knowledge on this possibility is not available, but it is one well worth considering.

So, what's the most reasonable conclusion? Should entrepreneurs devote long hours to preparing detailed business plans or simply not bother? As shown in Figure 5.3, there are "pluses" and "minuses" to both sides of this

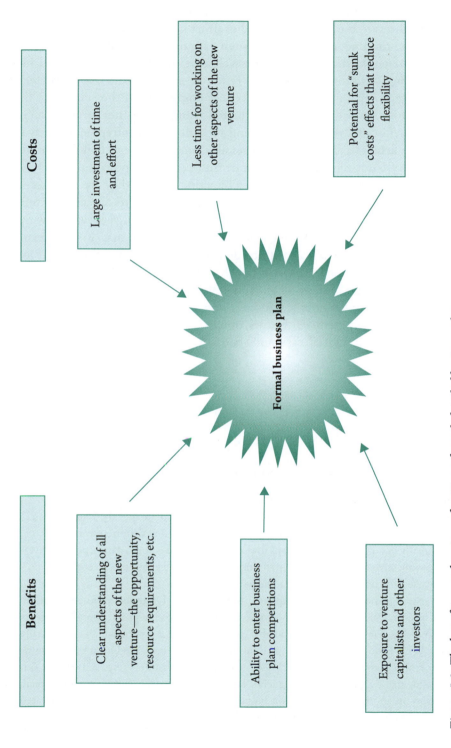

Costs

Large investment of time and effort

Less time for working on other aspects of the new venture

Potential for "sunk costs" effects that reduce flexibility

Formal business plan

Benefits

Clear understanding of all aspects of the new venture—the opportunity, resource requirements, etc.

Ability to enter business plan competitions

Exposure to venture capitalists and other investors

Figure 5.3 The benefits—and costs—of writing a formal, detailed business plan

As shown here, writing a formal business plan offers important benefits, but also has significant costs.

issue. The best answer, as suggested by available evidence therefore seems to be this: *yes*, they should invest this effort if they require large amounts of external funding to move ahead; such support is generally not available to entrepreneurs who do not have a well-developed and persuasive business plan. But if external funding is not required entrepreneurs may be better off spending their time on other tasks that contribute to the success of their companies. In addition, consider the following point: after investing a great deal of effort in the task of developing a business plan, entrepreneurs may feel very reluctant to depart from it. After all, doing so suggests that their original plans were not very good. The result: "sunk costs"—a powerful tendency to stick with past decisions or courses of action, even if they are not succeeding (see Chapter 2). And, the more time, effort, or resources invested in developing the business plan, the harder it may be change or withdraw from them. In other words, writing a detailed business plan may, to some extent, reduce entrepreneurs' capacity to demonstrate "improvisation"—the topic we turn to next, and a process that has been found to be strongly related to entrepreneurs' success (e.g., Hmieleski et al., 2013). (For an example of entrepreneurs who attained success outside the usual "prepare a business plan, present it potential investors, obtain financial support," please see "The Entrepreneurial Quest" case study below.)

CASE STUDY

The Entrepreneurial Quest

The wine cork: A success without external funding

Anyone who enjoys a glass of wine, even occasionally, has come face to face with the following problem: once a bottle of wine is uncorked it can deteriorate quickly. The problem is that air entering the bottle changes the wine (oxidizes it), so that within a day or two it declines greatly in quality. Many solutions to this problem exist—for instance, pouring the remaining wine into smaller bottles so there's no room for air to enter, special corks that supposedly seal the bottle. But none of them work very well.

A few years ago, however, one entrepreneur—Eric Corti—hit upon a different solution. Why not insert a small balloon into the bottle and inflate it to the point where it prevents air from entering (Figure 5.4). Corti was able to produce such a device, which he originally called the Wine Balloon, but later renamed the Air Cork. He presented it on the TV show *Shark Tank*, where the investors, impressed, made substantial offers (e.g., $200 000). But Corti, sensing that the product might generate large sales, declined to sell his equity. Instead, he appeared on another show—*Kitchen Inventors*—where again, the Air Cork generated lots of enthusiasm. As a result, he signed a licensing arrangement with a large distributor of

CASE STUDY *(continued)*

Source: Courtesy of Robert A. Baron.

Figure 5.4 The Air Cork—a product (and company) that did *not* rely on external funding

The Air Cork—a device designed to prevent opened bottles of wine from going bad—was presented on television (e.g., on *Shark Tank*) by its inventor, and received several offers of financial support. Ultimately, however, this entrepreneur decided to retain control of the company and *not* sell equity. Now, however, the Air Cork has been licensed to a large distributor that pays the company a fee for each one sold, and is generating substantial profits.

kitchen-related products—Lifetime Brands. This company has lots of "marketing clout" and may be able to generate a high volume of sales. It will pay Corti's company a royalty on each Air Cork sold, but he retains control of the company.

Does the product work? I have been using it for almost a year, and so far am convinced that it is in fact better than anything else I've tried. One drawback: the balloon has a relatively short life and must be replaced when it bursts. Aside from that, however, Mr. Corti appears to have developed a new product that meets a real need.

The moral of this story is straightforward: Mr. Corti did not receive offers of financial support or arrange a licensing deal on the basis of a high-quality business plan. Rather, he obtained these opportunities through his presentations on TV shows. In short, business plans are often helpful, but they are definitely *not* the only road to success.

The importance of flexibility: Improvisation and bricolage

Several times in this chapter we have noted that entrepreneurs often operate in environments characterized by rapid change and high degrees of uncertainty: not only are events and trends in these environments often unpredictable, also, the information needed to make such predictions is unavailable or may not even exist. Of course, entrepreneurs do not choose such environments by accident; as noted in Chapter 4, they enter them because such environments—and the industries in which they exist—tip the odds in their favor. That is, they are more favorable to new ventures than environments that are stable and low in uncertainty. Although such environments offer important advantages, they also place a premium on "flexibility." Entrepreneurs may start with a detailed business plan that provides a roadmap to reaching the goals they seek, but those working in high-uncertainty environments quickly discover that these plans and strategies must be adjusted or, sometimes, changed entirely. Basically, they have little choice: "adjust or fail" is the reality of life under such conditions. This suggests that entrepreneurs must be ready, willing, and able to "improvise"—to formulate new plans and strategies "on the fly" in response to unexpected events or trends (Baker et al., 2003; Hmieleski and Corbett, 2008). In this discussion we'll first consider the nature and advantages of improvisation, and then turn to a related but distinct kind of flexibility known as "bricolage" (Baker and Nelson, 2005). A basic distinction between these is that while improvisation involves being able to respond rapidly to changing conditions, bricolage involves "making do" with whatever resources are at hand and recombining them into something new and useful. As Baker and Nelson (2005) describe it, bricolage involves "creating something from nothing," which is, of course, a physical impossibility, but is, in another sense (primarily cognitive), something entrepreneurs often seem to do.

Improvisation: Its basic nature and relationship to firm performance

In the world of contemporary music—and perhaps, especially in jazz—improvisation is an important activity. It refers to instances in which musicians truly do what entrepreneurs frequently do—they "make it up as they go along." They do not simply play the notes written on sheet music, but instead whatever their musical skills and talents tell them to play. Improvisation is also an important aspect of entrepreneurship. When they start with a formal business plan, entrepreneurs have a detailed "roadmap" to follow, which they hope will lead to success. But even when they do not have such a plan, they generally have *some* idea of where they want to go (specific goals) and how to get there. Very soon, however, most find that they must depart from these initial plans. The world is too complex and too changeable to permit the luxury of moving through it according to a fixed plan (Mullins and Komisar, 2009). The result is that entrepreneurs often change their strategies, and even reverse decisions they have made in the past to respond to external changes and to take advantage of new opportunities that arise along the way. And, not surprisingly, the more flexible and open to change they are, the greater their success (Markides and Geroski, 2004).

More formally, improvisation is defined as deliberate, spontaneous (i.e., unplanned) actions to respond to a new problem, to handle situations to which no previously acquired rules or guidelines exist, or simply to try something new because it might work better than what was done in the past or is being done now. Although improvisation is described as unplanned, it is certainly not random. Rather, it is carried out to help entrepreneurs move toward key goals. As researchers studying this topic sometimes put it, improvisation does not occur in a cognitive vacuum—rather, underlying goals provide a general guide for its form and direction.

Again, it's important to emphasize that improvisation occurs in many different fields or areas of life aside from entrepreneurship. For instance, suppose you are on the road, driving to visit a friend. Suddenly, you encounter a slow-down in traffic, and looking ahead can see that a major accident is blocking your route and causing a major traffic jam. Do you just sit in your car and hope it won't be a long delay? Perhaps. But if instead you decide to leave your present route and try to find another one, you are engaging in improvisation. In a similar manner, entrepreneurs improvise when they encounter obstacles on the way toward their goals, whatever these may be. And being flexible— being able to improvise—can help them make progress, just as it helped you to reach your destination while driving.

This suggestion is strongly supported by research findings indicating that the capacity or, at least, willingness—to improvise—is important even in the first step of deciding to become an entrepreneur. Specifically, individuals who express a high level of willingness to improvise also report stronger intentions than persons lower in this tendency to become an entrepreneur (Hmieleski and Corbett, 2006). Willingness to improvise can be accurately measured by a brief questionnaire designed by Hmieleski and Corbett (ibid.; see also Figure 5.5). Sample items include: "I find new uses for existing methods or equipment," and "I deviate from plans in order to

SAMPLE QUESTIONNAIRE

1) I often invent things

2) I demonstrate a high level of creativity

3) I can figure out ways to move ahead with limited resources

4) I can readily figure out ways to recombine resources in productive ways

5) I can easily formulate new uses for existing products

6) I often think outside of the box

7) I am willing to take risks to produce new ideas

8) I identify many opportunities for new products or services

Figure 5.5 Measuring entrepreneurs' capacity to improvise

The items shown here are similar to those on a short questionnaire used to measure entrepreneurs' tendency to improvise. The higher their score, the more likely they are to improvise in situations calling for flexibility.

take advantage of opportunities in the moment." Individuals completing the scale indicate the extent to which these items are true about themselves, and research findings indicate that the higher the score of individuals completing this questionnaire, the higher they are in the intention to become an entrepreneur.

Improvisation and firm performance

The comments above suggest that the willingness and capacity to improvise are important "pluses" for entrepreneurs. In fact, however, it appears that often they have no choice: as noted above, it is either "improvise or "fail." Research evidence indicates that the capacity to improvise is significantly related to entrepreneurs' success (e.g., Hmieleski and Corbett, 2008). However, it also appears that this is *not* always the case. Rather, its benefits are *moderated* (i.e., influenced) by several other factors, so that improvisation is more of a "plus" under some conditions than others. Consider, for instance, a variable we will examine in Chapter 8: self-efficacy. This refers to individuals' beliefs that they can successfully accomplish whatever they set out to accomplish (e.g., Bandura, 1997). Entrepreneurs' self-efficacy has been found to be related to the success of their new ventures (De Noble et al., 1999), in part because entrepreneurs high in self-efficacy often show persistence: they don't give up when the going gets tough, because they believe that ultimately they will succeed (Baum and Locke, 2004).

This may be highly relevant to the benefits of improvisation because when they improvise, entrepreneurs are unlikely to "get it right" at first; they often need to adjust and re-adjust their new plans and strategies, and persevere in the face of initial setbacks. This suggests that improvisation may be more beneficial for entrepreneurs high in self-efficacy than low, and research findings (Hmieleski and Corbett, 2008) confirm this prediction. These researchers found that entrepreneurs' inclination to improvise (as measured by the scale mentioned above) was positively related to firm performance (sales growth) for entrepreneurs who were also high in self-efficacy, but was negatively related to firm performance for entrepreneurs who were low in self-efficacy. One possible explanation for these findings is that entrepreneurs who are low in self-efficacy lack the confidence to persevere in improvising until they find a combination of new plans, strategies, or resources that succeeds. Since they don't believe that ultimately they can succeed, their efforts at improvisation may be hampered by such doubts, and as result, their expectations come true: they *are* actually less effective than persons higher in self-efficacy. Whatever the precise reasons, it is clear that improvisation does not work equally well for all entrepreneurs; rather, it is more effective in boosting firm performance for some (e.g., those high in self-efficacy) than for others.

Additional evidence (Hmieleski et al., 2013), indicates that another important characteristic of entrepreneurs—their optimism (expectations of positive outcomes)—may also be relevant to the question of whether improvisation has beneficial effects on firm performance. Further, the kind of environments in which entrepreneurs operate—dynamic (changing rapidly) or stable, also plays a role. Hmieleski et al. (ibid.) obtained information on entrepreneurs' level of optimism and their tendency to improvise, as well as information on whether their new ventures were operating in dynamic or stable environments. Results indicated that all these factors played an important role in firm performance. In dynamic (i.e., rapidly changing) environments, entrepreneurs' tendency to engage in improvisation was positively related to the performance of their firms, but only for those who were *moderate* rather than very high in optimism. In stable environments, in contrast, entrepreneurs' tendency to improvise was not significantly associated with the performance of their firms, and that was true regardless of entrepreneurs' level of optimism. Together, these findings indicate that the tendency to improvise can indeed be beneficial, but only in dynamic (rapidly changing) environments and only when entrepreneurs are moderate in optimism—that is, when they have realistic expectations concerning possible outcomes.

Bricolage: Making something from nothing?

Years ago, I had the good fortune to live in France, in the city of Toulouse. I spoke some French, and worked hard to learn more, but soon after arriving I passed a store with a sign saying "Bricolage." When I looked it up in the dictionary, I found that it translated roughly as "do-it-yourself." In other words, it was a store that offered products people could use to make repairs or complete various projects at home, the equivalent of a Home Depot or Lowe's in the United States (Figure 5.6)

But what, you may be wondering, does this have to do with entrepreneurship? Actually, quite a bit. It is another way in which entrepreneurs can be flexible, and, in a sense, create "something"—something useful that generates value—from ingredients that, in and of themselves, are without much value. Specifically, the term "bricolage" (e.g., Baker and Nelson, 2005) when applied to entrepreneurship, involves three major components: (1) working with whatever resources are available, (2) recombining these resources into something new and useful, and (3) making do—doing what's possible, rather than seeking the ideal or some pre-existing goal (for instance, goals described in a formal business plan). Research on bricolage suggests, in a sense, that it is the ultimate expression of entrepreneurs' creativity. Perhaps a concrete example will make the nature of this process clear.

Tim Grayson was a farmer, and underneath his fields were many abandoned coal mines. This was a serious problem, because if a tractor broke through the roof of a tunnel the driver could be injured or even killed. He knew that there was methane gas in these tunnels, which was another problem, because it is both poisonous and explosive. But he wondered: given that this gas was present underneath his farm, could it be used in any way? To find out, he and a friend drilled a hole through the roof of one abandoned mine and attached a diesel generator they had converted to burn the methane that flowed through the hole. This methane gas could be used to generate electricity that Grayson then sold to a nearby utility. But he didn't stop there; his generator produced lots of heat, so he thought of building a greenhouse and using the heat to keep it warm. That worked very well, and Grayson grew good crops of tomatoes hydroponically—in water, using surplus electricity to heat the water too. Then he realized that he had lots of warm water filled with nutrients: couldn't he use that to raise fish? That was another good idea, and soon Grayson was raising—and selling—tilapia, a fish that is increasingly popular in the United States. Finally, even with all these uses, he still had surplus methane gas, so he sold that to a natural gas company.

Source: Wikimedia: with permission from the photographer, Enriquecornejo, for unrestricted use.

Figure 5.6 Bricolage—another way in which entrepreneurs demonstrate flexibility

Bricolage is the French word for "do-it-yourself." In the context of entrepreneurship it refers to making do with what you have, recombining resources into something new and useful, and working with whatever resources are currently available. (*Home Depot, Mexico City*)

It is hard to think of a more dramatic example of bricolage: Mr. Grayson had some unused resources at hand (under his farm), combined these into something new and useful, and making do with what he had, developed a thriving business (Figure 5.7). Research findings (Baker and Nelson, 2005) indicate that such bricolage is far from rare among entrepreneurs, and in fact, is often essential to their success.

Overall, then, it is clear that while planning is often helpful and in fact, in many instances essential (remember: business plans are the "entry card" to competitions and are required by venture capitalists), in many cases, improvisation and bricolage offer alternative routes to obtaining positive results.

Effectuation: Using what you have to get where, perhaps, you want to go

A basic principle of science is this: if we understand a phenomenon well enough to be able to predict it accurately, we can then often change it, at least to some degree. Traditional business plans take this principle of accurate prediction very seriously. They devote a great deal of attention to projections concerning many key issues: how quickly can a new product or service be developed, at what cost, who will want to purchase and use it, and how much value (financial or social) will it generate? Attempting to make such predictions seems very reasonable: after all, why proceed with development of an opportunity in the absence of any predictions concerning these and other issues? As a result, business plans often include sections that address these questions in detail—especially sections presenting financial projections of cash flow, profits, and "break-even" points—when, specifically, a new venture will begin to generate as much income as it spends.

But prediction is often a difficult task, especially in situations where knowledge is incomplete, a large number of variables are operating, and in fact, a complete list of all relevant factors isn't currently available. In other words, there are many situations that are so complex and in which uncertainty is so high, that accurate predictions are difficult if not impossible to make.

Entrepreneurship often unfolds in precisely such situations. Accurate predictions about central issues such as the cost of developing new products or services, the size of potential markets, or the reactions of competitors are almost impossible to make. Yet, they are included in business plans because potential investors generally—and reasonably—insist on their presence.

Source: Fotolia #_26078196_M.

Figure 5.7 Bricolage in action

A farmer, Tim Grayson, realized that he could use the methane gas in abandoned mining tunnels under his farm to generate electricity. He then used the heat produced in the process to warm a greenhouse for growing crops. Finally, he used the warm water to raise fish. This is a clear example of how entrepreneurs use bricolage to "create something from nothing."

This is the traditional approach, and the one reflected in most business plans. The guiding principle seems to be: predict whatever you can, and at least *try* to predict what perhaps you really can't! Is this the best approach? Recently a very different one has been suggested, an approach known as "effectuation" (e.g., Sarasvathy, 2001, 2008; Venkataraman et al., 2012). This approach starts with the idea that no matter what entrepreneurs say in their detailed business plans, they simply *cannot* make accurate predictions about many important issues. There are so many unknowns in the equation, and change happens so rapidly that accurate predictions are virtually impossible. Taking note of this fact, proponents of effectuation as an approach to entrepreneurship suggest that entrepreneurs should focus not on predicting the future but, rather, on *creating* it—on using the resources they have at their disposal to shape future outcomes. What are these resources? Basically, they include the characteristics, skills, and motivation of the entrepreneurs (or founding team), their knowledge and experience, their social networks—who they know, and of course, more tangible resources as well (e.g., financial resources, property, etc.). In contrast to standard "causal logic," in which entrepreneurs start by selecting specific goals (e.g., gaining a specified share of a market, obtaining a desired rate of growth) and attempt to identify means for reaching these goals, "effectual logic" (part of the effectuation perspective) suggests that entrepreneurs should consider their resources—the things they now have and can control—and on basis of these, formulate a set of imagined ends. In other words, effectuation proposes that entrepreneurs should ask themselves the following question: "Given what I have and can control right now, what can I hope to accomplish?"

Another way of putting these basic ideas is that since the future can be shaped by taking action, why bother trying to predict it? Instead, make it unfold in the ways *you* as an entrepreneur wish. This basic perspective suggests that in a sense, entrepreneurship is a "science of the artificial"—a field that explores not what exists but rather what is *possible*—what can be created through the actions of entrepreneurs. As Venkataraman et al. (2012, p. 24) put it: "A science of the artificial is interested in phenomena that can be designed . . . it is interested in a phenomenon's variables precisely to the extent we can intervene and change them. Design lies in the choice of the boundary values; control lies in the means to change them." In short, entrepreneurship is primarily concerned with creating or changing the future, not simply with predicting it.

The effectuation perspective also includes several other ideas; (1) entrepreneurs should focus on "affordable loss"—what they can afford to lose, given their resources, rather than on potential profits; (2) they should form partnerships with others in order to increase the scope of their resources—and therefore the range of outcomes they generate, and (3) they should view unexpected events as opportunities that open up additional possibilities for creative use of current resources—for creating or changing the future.

The ideas of effectuation (summarized in Figure 5.8) suggest a very different approach to the basic nature of entrepreneurship. Instead of choosing specific goals and then attempting to gather the resources needed to reach them—the traditional and widely accepted view—entrepreneurs can, instead, imagine

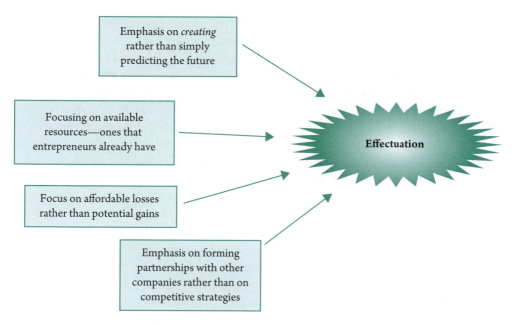

Figure 5.8 The basic nature of effectuation

Effectuation is an approach suggesting that entrepreneurs should not focus on attempting to predict the future but, rather, should seek to create it. This is the central idea of this perspective, but as shown above, it also involves several other components as well.

many different outcomes, based on their current resources, and then take action to make these outcomes actually happen. Again, the basic idea is that they don't try to predict the future, but attempt, instead, to create and control it—to make it unfold in various ways.

Do entrepreneurs actually operate in this manner—do they really use effectual rather than causal logic? This is still an open question, but some evidence suggests that sometimes, at least, this is how to proceed (e.g., Wiltbank et al., 2006). For instance, in one investigation (Dew et al., 2009), the researchers reasoned that as entrepreneurs become more experienced in starting new companies, they will gradually shift toward using effectuation as a basis for their decisions. In other words, they will focus more on "means-driven" (what they now have) rather than "goal-driven" actions, on affordable loss rather than potential gains, on forming partnerships, and on leveraging unexpected events rather than avoiding them through careful, detailed planning.

To investigate these predictions, Dew et al. (2009) asked two groups (highly experienced entrepreneurs who had founded on average 7.3 companies) and novice entrepreneurs (graduate students in business administration, most of whom had not yet started a new venture) to answer a series of questions about how they would develop an imaginary new product (a computer game focused on entrepreneurship). As they thought about each question, they described their thoughts out loud, and their comments were recorded and coded in terms of the extent to which they reflected either causal logic or effectual logic (for instance, the extent to which they reflected means-driven rather than goal-driven action, focus on affordable losses rather than gains, etc.). It was predicted that the experienced entrepreneurs would show greater reliance on effectual logic than the novice entrepreneurs, and this prediction was confirmed.

Although these findings seem persuasive, in fact there is a major problem: graduate students and highly experienced entrepreneurs may differ in many other ways aside from the amount of experience they have had in starting and running new companies. For instance, the experienced entrepreneurs are older, may have less education than the graduate students, and even, perhaps, had different diets during their childhood (Baron, 2009). Thus, comparing the two groups rests on somewhat shaky ground. On the other hand, additional studies do seem to support the idea that entrepreneurs often seek to create the future rather than merely predict it, so the central idea of effectuation is certainly both appealing and intriguing.

If entrepreneurship is indeed, to some extent, a field that deals with the possible, this suggests that detailed business plans, although very useful in several ways (e.g., in helping entrepreneurs clarify their own thinking about their ideas and the opportunities they want to develop), may be less useful in the actual process of entrepreneurship than has long been assumed. Writing such plans is certainly a key requirement to obtaining financial resources; after all, why would investors provide funds to entrepreneurs who don't have specific goals, but offer, instead, to create the opportunity they will develop along the way? But in other instances, where external funding is not essential, it may be better for entrepreneurs to focus not on predicting variables and outcomes that can't really be predicted, but instead on their own resources—and how these can be used to generate desirable outcomes. Only time and further research will resolve this issue, but it is certainly one worth considering, given the central role currently assigned to business plans, and to the detailed planning and predictions they involve.

THE EFFECTIVE ENTREPRENEUR

Planning is often essential for success in any field. In entrepreneurship, however, it may be especially important, because entrepreneurs are, by definition, breaking new ground and creating something that did not, in a sense, exist before. But how much planning is best? And what form should it take? Here are some guidelines that may help you become a more effective entrepreneur:

- If you want to obtain external funding, it's usually necessary to write a formal business plan. This takes lots of time and effort, but is required by most investors.
- You don't have to do it by yourself! Many universities have special centers that focus on helping students and faculty to develop new companies—and one of the services they provide is expert help in writing a business plan. So, *seek this help*—it can be invaluable.
- If you don't need or want external funding, a formal business plan may not be necessary, so resolve this issue first, before you invest lots of effort in preparing a plan.

- If you do write a business plan, remember that the "Executive Summary" is crucial. If this doesn't appeal to investors, they won't read any further, so make this part of the plan as clear, succinct, and persuasive as possible—even if that means many re-writes.
- Prepare a brief "elevator pitch" for your idea and company. Often (e.g., in business plan competitions) you will be given only a few minutes to explain what you plan to do, why, and what need(s) it will meet.
- Be prepared to improvise because even the best business plan doesn't provide a guaranteed formula for success. Rather, it must usually be altered—often significantly—after the company is launched and begins operation.
- Also be prepared to make do with what you have, and recombine existing resources into something new—that is, be flexible and follow the basic principles of bricolage whenever possible.
- Finally, remember that as an entrepreneur, you are not necessarily trying to predict the future—you may actually be *creating* it by your actions!

SUMMARY OF KEY POINTS

1 Careful planning is essential in many activities, and it plays a key role in entrepreneurship, where it is often expressed in formal business plans—detailed, written documents that explain how ideas generated by creativity will be converted into new products or services. Even the best business plan is "made to be changed," because once a company is launched, conditions change so rapidly that altering the initial plan is usually necessary.

2 Business plans generally address several key issues: what is the nature of the opportunity? What are the potential markets for new products or services? How will they actually be produced? Who are the entrepreneurs, and what skills, knowledge, and experience relevant to the new venture do

they possess? While all these topics are important, a crucial part of a good plan is the Executive Summary. Unless this is succinct, to the point, and persuasive, the rest of the plan may go unread.

3 Excellent business plans are required for entering business plan competitions and for attaining external funding. Writing them also offers other benefits, such as getting entrepreneurs to think carefully about how they will actually develop their ideas. Is writing a detailed business plan related to a new venture's success? Evidence is mixed, so it is important for entrepreneurs to decide whether they want to invest this effort on the basis of other factors (e.g., whether they require external funding).

4 Entrepreneurs must often engage in improvisation—formulating new strategies and actions as they move ahead. In addition, they can benefit from bricolage—a kind of "do-it-yourself" approach in which entrepreneurs recombine available resources in creative ways. These tactics are especially helpful in dynamic environments—ones that are changing rapidly.

5 In recent years, an alternative perspective on entrepreneurship known as effectuation has emerged. This view suggests that entrepreneurs should not focus on attempting to predict the future—a task that is often virtually impossible—but on shaping or controlling it. Some research findings indicate that entrepreneurs do in fact shift toward this approach as they gain experience in starting and running new ventures, but it is not yet clear to what extent this is true.

REFERENCES

Baker, T. and R.E. Nelson (2005), "Creating something from nothing: Resource construction through entrepreneurial bricolage," *Administrative Science Quarterly*, **50**(3), 329–66.

Baker, T., A. Miner and D. Eesley (2003), "Improvising firms: Bricolage, account giving, and improvisational competency in the founding process," *Research Policy*, **32**(2), 255–76.

Bandura, A. (1997), *Self-efficacy: The Exercise of Control*, New York: W.H. Freeman.

Baron, R.A. (2009), "Effectual versus predictive logics in entrepreneurial decision making: Differences between experts and novices: Does experience in starting new ventures change the way entrepreneurs think? Perhaps, but for now, 'caution' is essential," *Journal of Business Venturing*, **24**(4), 310–15.

Baum, J.R. and E.A. Locke (2004), "The relationship of entrepreneurial traits, skill, and motivation to subsequent venture growth," *Journal of Applied Psychology*, **83**(1), 587–98.

Brinckmann, J., D. Grichnik and D. Kapsa (2010), "Should entrepreneurs plan or just storm the castle? A meta-analysis on contextual factors impacting the business planning–performance relationship in small firms," *Journal of Business Venturing*, **25**(1), 24–40.

Burke, A., S. Fraser and F.J. Greene (2010), "The multiple effects of business planning on new venture performance," *Journal of Management Studies*, **47**(3), 391–410.

De Noble, A.F., D. Jung and S.B. Ehrlich (1999), "Entrepreneurial self-efficacy: The development of a measure and its relationship to entrepreneurial action," in P. Reynolds et al. (eds), *Frontiers of Entrepreneurship Research*, Babson Park, MA: Babson College.

Dew, N., S. Read, S.D. Sarasvathy and R. Wiltbank (2009), "Effectual versus predictive logics in entrepreneurial decision-making: Differences between experts and novices," *Journal of Business Venturing*, **24**(9), 287–309.

Fernandez-Guerrero, R., L. Revuelto-Toboada and V. Simon-Moya (2012), "The business plan as a project: An evaluation of its predictive capability for business success," *Service Industries Journal*, **32**(15), 2399–420.

Hmieleski, K.M. and A.C. Corbett (2006), "Proclivity for improvisation as a predictor of entrepreneurial intentions," *Journal of Small Business Management*, **44**(1), 45–63.

Hmieleski, K.M. and A.C. Corbett (2008), "The contrasting interaction effects of improvisational behavior with entrepreneurial self-efficacy on new venture performance and entrepreneur work satisfaction," *Journal of Business Venturing*, **23**(4), 482–96.

Hmieleski, K.M., A.C. Corbett and R.A. Baron (2013), "Entrepreneurs' improvisational behavior and firm performance: A study of dispositional and environmental moderators," *Strategic Entrepreneurship Journal*, **7**(2), 138–50.

Lange, J.K.E., A. Mollow, M. Pearlmutter, S. Singh and W.D. Bygrave (2007), "Pre-start-up formal business plans and post-start-up performance: A study of 116 new ventures," *Venture Capital*, **9**(4), 237–56.

Markides, C. and P.A. Geroski (2004), "Racing to be second," *Business Strategy Review*, **5**(4), 25–31.

Mullins, J. and R. Komisar (2009), *Getting to Plan B: Breaking Through to a Better Business Model*, Boston, MA: Harvard Business Press.

Sarasvathy, S.D. (2001), "Causation and effectuation: Toward a shift from economic inevitability to entrepreneurial contingency," *Academy of Management Review*, **26**(2), 243–63.

Sarasvathy, S.D. (2008), *Effectuation: Elements of Entrepreneurial Expertise*, Cheltenham, UK and Northampton, MA, USA: Edward Elgar, New Horizons in Entrepreneurship Series.

Venkataraman, S., S.D. Sarasvathy, N. Dew and W.R. Forster (2012), "Reflections on the 2010 AMR decade award: Whither the promise? Moving forward with entrepreneurship as a science of the artificial," *Academy of Management Review*, **37**(1), 21–33.

Wiltbank, R., N. Dew, S. Read and S.D. Sarasvathy (2006), "What to do next? The case for nonpredictive strategy," *Strategic Management Journal*, **27**(10), 981–98.

6

Assembling key resources I: Obtaining, managing, and using financial assets

 CHAPTER OUTLINE

- **Financial resources:** Where to find them—and how to obtain them
  - Types and sources of financial resources
  - Venture capitalists: How they make their decisions
- **Estimating financial needs:** How much will it cost to get started, and how will these funds be used?
  - Summarizing past performance: Balance sheets, income statements, and cash flow
  - Estimating start-up costs
  - Pro forma financial statements: Predicting the future
  - Break-even analysis: When will the company begin to earn profits?
- **Why obtaining financial resources is often difficult:** Overcoming investors' caution
  - Uncertainty problems: Which new ventures will succeed?
  - Information asymmetry: Entrepreneurs hold an important edge
  - How do investors protect themselves against these problems?

When I was young I thought that money was the most important thing in life; now that I am old I know that it is.
(Oscar Wilde, 1854–1900, Irish writer and poet)

You have to go broke three times to learn how to make a living.
(Casey Stengel, 1890–1975, Major League baseball player)

A good idea, evidence that it will work (from a feasibility analysis), and a plan for actually making it succeed, are all crucial ingredients in entrepreneurship. Without them, launching a new venture makes little sense. But important as these ingredients are, they are only the seed from which a successful new company *might* grow. To turn this potential into more than simply a dream, more is needed—crucial resources necessary for making this actually happen. In short, it's usually impossible to develop even a truly excellent opportunity without (1) financial resources, (2) human resources—a strong founding team, key employees and (3) well-developed social networks. Unless entrepreneurs can acquire these resources, the process may grind to a total halt. A key step—and one that must occur relatively early in the process—is that of obtaining (assembling) these resources (Figure 6.1)

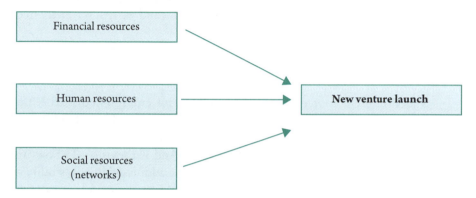

Figure 6.1 Essential resources required by new ventures

In order to develop the opportunities they have discovered or created new ventures must assemble the types of resources shown here.

In this chapter, we'll focus on the first—financial resources. These are certainly a key part of the new venture equation because although, as we noted previously, all entrepreneurs do *not* seek personal wealth, very little can happen, regardless of their motives, without sufficient finances. Oscar Wilde (one of the quotations above) almost certainly exaggerates this point (he was famous for exaggeration!), but it's clear that financial resources are often the basic engine that moves a new venture forward.

They are far from the entire story, however. Human resources—the skills, knowledge, experience, and effort—of the founding team and many others who soon join the new venture are also crucial. We'll examine these key resources in Chapter 7, but here we'll focus primarily on the financial resources new ventures need and must use effectively. Specifically, the chapter proceeds as follows.

First, we'll review various sources of financial support and how to obtain them. Then we'll turn to how to use them effectively, and how to keep track of them, in a systematic manner. As part of this discussion, we'll consider the question of how venture capitalists—a key source of financial resources for new ventures—decide which ventures to support. A substantial body of research has addressed this issue, and echoes themes developed in Chapters 1 and 2 to the effect that as human beings we don't always have clear and accurate understanding of *why* we make the decisions we do or act in specific ways. Venture capitalists are no exception to this rule (e.g., Dimov and Shepherd, 2005), so they are not always able to describe the criteria they use in choosing which new ventures to support. However, careful research has helped reveal the criteria they actually *do* use in making these decisions (e.g., Shepherd et al., 2003; Petty and Gruber, 2011), and we'll describe them here.

Financial resources: Where to find them—and how to obtain them

Many different sources of financial support for entrepreneurs exist. Before seeking such funding, however, entrepreneurs should first address two important initial questions: (1) do they really need it? Do they actually need financial resources from external sources? And if they do (2) how much, and in what form? These questions should be addressed in a feasibility analysis (see Chapter 4), but as the new venture develops and moves toward an actual launch, they become even more crucial. As you can readily guess, financial support, when it is obtained, is not free—at least not from many potential sources. As we'll describe below, when entrepreneurs accept external funding they must generally give up something in return—often, a large portion of the ownership (i.e., equity) of their companies. In addition, they may lose control over key decisions and even day-to-day operations. Since many individuals become entrepreneurs because they strongly value autonomy (e.g., Rindova et al., 2009), it's clear that the costs attached to external support can be substantial. How can entrepreneurs determine whether they need such funds, and if so, how much? A good way to begin is by estimating the costs involved in moving forward. In other words, what funds will be needed for further product development, initial marketing and promotion, rent, equipment, travel, supplies, postage—the list is almost endless and varies with the kind of company (and products or services) it seeks to provide. Forecasting such costs is a very, very tricky business and, in fact, is extremely difficult to do precisely. Unexpected costs almost always emerge, and unanticipated problems (requiring financial resources) seem to appear from nowhere. Given these uncertainties, a good rule of thumb is to estimate costs for a given period of time (e.g., the first year of operations) as carefully as possible—and then at least *triple* this figure. Entrepreneurs should then compare these figures with the financial resources available to them. If these resources are sufficient, seeking funding may not be necessary. If the estimated costs far exceed personal resources, external funding becomes a necessity rather than an option. Again, no precise or definitive answer to the question "Does a new venture need external funding?" exists, but carefully considering the costs involved in seeking and accepting such support is one every entrepreneur should perform at the start.

Now, however, assume that entrepreneurs have considered this question carefully and have reached the conclusion that substantial amounts of funding are required. Where and how do they obtain it? Those are the issues to which we turn next, and are often at the heart of the entrepreneurial process, especially in its initial phases. Again, these steps should be part of a thorough feasibility analysis, and if that activity has been completed in a careful manner, answers to these questions may already exist—or at least, be ones of which the entrepreneurs are aware.

Types and sources of financial resources

Two basic types of external funding for new ventures exist: equity financing and debt financing. Equity financing involves trading part of the equity of the new venture for financial resources—that is, transferring a portion of the ownership of the company to the investors who provide these funds. Debt financing, in contrast, involves a financial obligation to return the funds provided plus a scheduled amount of interest. Most entrepreneurs prefer equity financing for the following reasons. First, until they have generated positive cash flow (i.e., significant income) they may be viewed as "bad risks" by banks and other potential lenders. As a result, the terms of such loans are generally unfavorable (e.g., high interest rates). Second, debt financing at a fixed rate of interest encourages people to take risky actions because if the new venture fails, the entrepreneur can't lose any more than the funds he or she originally put into it; as a result, the downside loss is the same regardless of how much risk the entrepreneur takes. However, because the entrepreneur pays the same amount of interest on debt regardless of how well the new venture does, she or he keeps all of the returns from success. As a result, debt financing creates the incentive for taking risks.

These comments are true for what are known as non-recourse loans (or debt). Such loans are secured by tangible resources—for instance, buildings or equipment. However, the borrowers are not personally responsible for repayment. In recourse loans, in contrast, the borrowers are personally responsible for the debt, so if they don't repay the loan a lender has a legal right to their personal property. Needless to say, non-recourse loans are the ones entrepreneurs prefer, but lenders, in contrast, strongly prefer recourse loans, not only because they are more certain of repayment, but also because such loans remove the incentive on the part of borrowers (i.e., entrepreneurs) to take risky actions. Doing so might place all their personal assets in jeopardy!

Fortunately, entrepreneurs can draw on a wide variety of other sources aside from loans for the financial resources they need. Because these sources differ greatly in nature and offer mixed combinations of advantages and disadvantages, it is important to know what they are and when each type is most useful. Below, these different sources of capital (i.e., financial resources) are briefly described.

Personal savings and credit cards

The single most important source of capital for new ventures is the entrepreneur's own savings. Research findings indicate that approximately 70 percent of all entrepreneurs finance their new businesses with their own capital. These funds can come from personal savings, but in addition, many entrepreneurs "max" their credit cards, charging items until the limit for their accounts are reached.

Friends and family

Another major source of funding is friends and family members who are often willing to provide financial resources. The benefits of obtaining financial resources in this way are obvious: close friends and family members will often wait more patiently for a return on their investments than persons unfamiliar with the entrepreneur. Moreover, they are often willing to provide financial resources under terms much more favorable to the entrepreneur than other investors. For instance, they will accept smaller portions of equity in the company, or lower interest rates, if their help takes the form of loans. But the downside too is obvious: if things don't work out well and friends and family see little or no return on their investments, these relationships may be seriously disrupted, and entrepreneurs, in turn, may experience high levels of guilt over having disappointed the people who care about them most.

Recently, some entrepreneurs have obtained financing from their families in a new way: they ask their parents to provide them with their inheritance now rather than after their parents die. Although this may seem somewhat presumptuous, it is, as *The Wall Street Journal* recently reported, a procedure that has increased rapidly in recent years.

Business angels

Another important source of financial resources are business angels. These are private individuals, usually ones who are well-off financially, who invest in new ventures. The typical business angel is a former entrepreneur herself or himself, so they have an "insider's" view of the process. Their investments tend to be relatively small—typically $10 000 and $200 000, and such persons usually invest in new ventures located near their homes, since this gives them the opportunity to work closely with the entrepreneur, which is something they personally enjoy. Business angels typically require a lower return on their investments (e.g., less equity in the new venture) than venture capitalists, perhaps because they invest for many reasons aside from financial gain, and because they invest for themselves rather than on behalf of an organization.

Venture capitalist firms

Venture capitalist firms are companies that raise money, usually from large institutional investors such as university endowments and company pension plans, and then invest it in new ventures. The institutional investors or others who provide the money generally have little or no say in the venture capital firm's decisions or management. Individual venture capitalists associated with the venture capital fund make these decisions. Venture capital funds generally exist for a specified number of years and then liquidate. At this time, the venture capital firm returns the capital invested to the institutional investors plus a percentage of any profits from investing in the start-ups (usually 80 percent). The venture capital firm receives the remainder and also a management fee (typically 2 percent of the capital in the fund annually) for managing the investments.

In addition to providing money to new firms, venture capitalists provide many other forms of help to entrepreneurs, which, together, are known as non-financial value-added benefits. For instance, they provide legitimation— they add to the credibility and reputation of the new venture since an investment in it by a prestigious venture capital fund indicates it has undergone careful screening by highly selective experts. Other non-financial benefits include assistance with hiring excellent employees, introducing the founding team to potential customers, suppliers, and many others. In other words, venture capitalists help extend and strengthen entrepreneurs' own social networks. The venture capital firm may also help entrepreneurs develop effective strategies, and provide them with advice with respect to basic operations.

Although venture capitalists offer much to new companies, they require a lot in return. In general they expect a large share of the equity (i.e., ownership) of the venture. This amount varies with the perceived potential of the new venture: venture capitalists will accept a smaller share of a new venture they perceive as having very high potential. But since venture capitalists invest in only a small proportion of the new ventures they review—they are highly selective—they tend to view all the ones in which they do invest as relatively high in potential for success. Still, differences exist, and these are reflected in the proportion of equity the venture capital firm requires.

To protect their financial investments, venture capitalists also impose important restrictions on the actions of entrepreneurs. We'll review these in a later section, but here it's important to note that these protections are often built into the contracts they sign with entrepreneurs. For instance, venture capitalists often insist on forfeiture provisions—contractual terms that give them additional equity in the company if its performance falls below target goals. In essence, the entrepreneurs suffer penalties for not reaching their goals.

Given the demands that venture capitalists place on entrepreneurs and venture capitalists' focus on extremely high growth companies, there has been a recent trend for entrepreneurs to fund their own companies through bootstrapping and related procedures. Only those who require substantial funding seek to obtain it from venture capitalists because although the funds they provide can be substantial, the obligations they impose on the entrepreneurs can also be heavy.

Corporations

Many companies make investments in new ventures. By making these investments, they can obtain access to new products or technology owned by the new ventures. In return, the established companies provide important marketing and manufacturing support as well as improve the new venture's credibility. For instance, a new biotech company can gain considerable recognition and prestige if it receives financial support from a major drug company. Another advantage of corporate investors is that they generally offer better terms than venture capitalists and even business angels. However, entrepreneurs should proceed with care: large corporations provide favorable financial terms relative to other investors because they want to obtain access to the intellectual property and products developed by new companies. In a sense, they are giving with one hand (financial support) but taking with the other—and what they take may be the most valuable assets the new venture possesses. Moreover, their ultimate goal may be to purchase the new venture completely—thus putting it out of business as an independent company.

Banks

Commercial banks provide a variety of types of capital to new businesses. First, banks provide the companies with standard commercial loans. A commercial loan is a form of financing in which the borrower pays interest on the money borrowed. Second, banks often provide new companies with lines of credit—agreements to allow entrepreneurs draw up to a set amount of money at a particular interest rate, whenever they need it. Lines of credit are usually used to finance inventory or accounts receivable (bills the new venture must pay within a specific period of time). As noted earlier, bank loans are relatively rare for new businesses because they are viewed as bad risks, at least until positive cash flow provides the funds needed to pay interest on a loan.

Government programs

Federal and state governments offer a variety of programs to finance new businesses, and these are often very favorable to entrepreneurs. Perhaps the most important of these is the SBIR—the Small Business Innovation Research Program. Under this program new businesses can receive funds from government agencies to evaluate and then develop a technical idea. The program proceeds in three phases. Phase I is a six-month period used for a feasibility study. The new venture must demonstrate that the proposed innovation is feasible and has the potential to be commercialized. During this phase, new ventures can receive from $75 000 to $100 000. During Phase II, the business receiving government funds is required to develop and test prototypes of the innovation(s). Because this can involve considerable expense, the SBIR Program provides up to $750 000 during this phase, which can last as long as two years. Finally, Phase III involves moving the innovations to the marketplace. The SBIR Program does not provide funding during this phase; rather, the new venture must find funding or financing in the private sector. The SBIR Program has assisted literally thousands of small companies and is viewed by many as a highly successful government program—one that has truly helped entrepreneurs launch new ventures. Funds provided by the SBIR Program are grants—they do not have to repaid, even if the new venture fails, and do not require any interest. These are important advantages, and make this program highly attractive to entrepreneurs.

Another federal program is the 7(a) Loan Guarantee Program of the US Small Business Administration, which guarantees repayment to lenders of any capital that they provide to new businesses, up to a pre-set limit. The US SBA also provides the CAPLine Program, a system for guaranteeing loans to new and small businesses to finance inventory or accounts receivable. Lastly, Small Business Investment Companies (SBICs) are organizations that the US SBA licenses and to which it lends money.

Business plan competitions

Yet another source of start-up funds, plus the opportunity to obtain more substantial support are business plan competitions. As we noted in Chapter 5, these competitions offer cash prizes, and these can be substantial. In addition, they expose the entrepreneurs and their ideas to many potential investors, some of whom may be judges of the competitions. In short, this is a route to attaining financial resources well worth considering—although, as noted in Chapter 5, it does require preparation of an excellent, formal business plan.

Microfinance: Changing lives through very small loans

Individuals who live in poverty often have limited or no access to banking services. They can't apply for loans because they have no collateral and often don't even have any kind of account. Many live in undeveloped countries, but there are many persons in this category even in highly developed ones. In recent years, many organizations have been founded to change this situation. For instance, Accion USA provides microloans to entrepreneurs who can't get funding in other ways. The loans are small, $10 000 or less for brand new businesses, but can be as high as $50 000 for businesses that are already established and profitable. These are much smaller amounts than venture capital firms or even angel investors generally provide.

Perhaps the most unique organization providing small (very small!) loans to would be-entrepreneurs is Kiva. It makes loans as small as $500 to borrowers who want to start their own business using from individuals who want to help such persons escape from poverty through entrepreneurship, but that must repaid. There is no interest on the loans and in fact, almost 99 percent are repaid in full. Once lenders are repaid, they can use the funds to help other entrepreneurs, or withdraw them. Kiva has made loans to very large numbers of people; for instance, in one recent week, 33 465 loans were initiated, so it is making a difference in the lives of hundreds of thousands of people living in poverty. To date, Kiva has recruited almost 1 000 000 lenders worldwide, and has loaned over $467 000 000. In short, it is helping large numbers of persons move from merely surviving to a better life—and being able to realize their dreams.

Crowdfunding: A new approach to venture funding

Recently, and as we noted in Chapter 4, some new ventures have used crowdfunding to raise funds. This is obtained using the internet in several different ways. For instance, the entrepreneurs may seek small loans from large numbers of people. Alternatively, they may sell small amounts of equity to investors, again over the internet. It is not yet clear whether this is a useful route for entrepreneurs to follow because many legal issues have been raised about it, and new government regulations concerning its use may be enacted soon. For these reasons, it is probably best for entrepreneurs to approach it with caution, at least for now. An overview of the various sources of financial resources for new ventures is shown in Figure 6.2 (for an example of how one new venture proceeded to obtain the financing it needed, please see "The Entrepreneurial Quest" case study below).

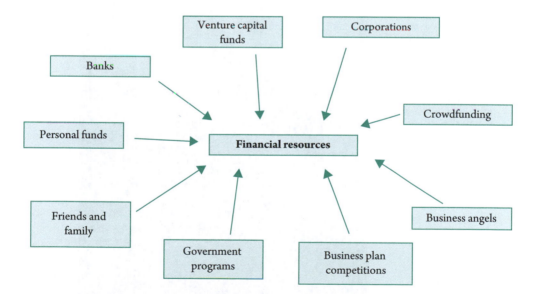

Figure 6.2 Potential sources of funding for new ventures

As shown here, many different sources can provide financial resources to new ventures.

CASE STUDY

The Entrepreneurial Quest

Clean NG: Helping make natural gas the fuel of the future

Have you ever driven behind a truck or bus that announces on the back "This vehicle burns clean natural gas" or something to that effect (Figure 6.3)? Perhaps you have, because in recent years there has been a major effort to develop ways in which all vehicles—trucks, buses, and even passenger cars—can burn natural gas instead of gasoline. The advantages of natural gas are many: for instance, it exists in abundance—in fact, there is actually an *oversupply* at present, and it produces far less pollution than gasoline. Yet, to date, it has not found use in commercial vehicles, such as trucks and buses. Why? One major reason for this situation is that existing storage tanks can hold only limited amounts of natural gas, thus restricting the range of operation for such vehicles—they run out of fuel too soon.

Source: Fotolia # 42601179_M.

Figure 6.3 Making natural gas an alternative to gasoline

One new venture, CleanNG, has designed a new storage tank for natural gas that increases the range for vehicles burning this fuel. This promises to greatly increase the use of natural gas for this purpose; a number of service stations are already equipped to provide this fuel because it has become popular for large trucks.

CASE STUDY *(continued)*

In 2010, however, a start-up company, CleanNG, began to tackle this problem head on. The result was a new kind of tank that could safely hold a much larger amount of natural gas under higher pressure than existing tanks. As a result, the driving range for vehicles using NG could be extended, thus making this fuel more practical than in the past. The new kind of tank weighs only 185 pounds, which makes it suitable for application in passenger vehicles. Interestingly, natural gas is already being used as a fuel in many countries around the world (e.g., Iran, Pakistan, Argentina)—ones that don't possess the large refineries that turn oil into gasoline. But in the USA only a tiny fraction of existing vehicles burn this fuel. As a result, CleanNG has a huge potential market to tap, and if further development results in a storage tank that meets current safety requirements, the company may be well on the way toward major success.

Why do we focus on this company here? Because it illustrates one important route to obtaining financial resources—and a chance at success. CleanNG won first place in a yearly business plan competition held at Oklahoma State University—thus earning a $25 000 cash prize. In addition, the publicity it received soon resulted in seed (i.e., initial) funding from a venture capital firm, with the promise of more to come as development of the company's products moved forward, and its customer list expanded. To speed this process along, Clean NG is also working on ways to convert vehicles that currently burn gasoline so that they can use natural gas instead—or perhaps both fuels.

In short, this company illustrates one key way in which a new venture can obtain the financial resources it needs: identify a promising opportunity, develop an excellent business plan describing how it will be developed, enter it in business plan competitions, and win, thus opening the door toward additional funding and opportunities limited only by the entrepreneurs' imagination!

Venture capitalists: How they make their decisions

Many entrepreneurs view venture capitalists (VCs) as the best or at least most important source of external funding for their new ventures. There are good reasons for this belief. Venture capitalists do indeed have the capacity to provide large amounts of capital, *if they wish*. The emphasis on the last three words is intentional though because, in fact, venture capitalists usually fund only a small proportion of the ventures that approach them seeking financial support. This varies greatly by region, state, and country, but in general, only 1 percent of proposals receive financial support. We have already considered another important reason for pursuing funding from venture capitalists: they also provide many other forms of non-financial support, from help with recruiting high-quality employees, through assistance with day to day operations.

Given these important benefits, it is not surprising that successful venture capital firms—ones with a strong track record of supporting new ventures that have achieved great success—are literally deluged with business plans from entrepreneurs. A key question then arises: how do they decide which ventures to support? This has been a topic of research in the field of entrepreneurship for many years (e.g., Fried and Hisrich, 1994; Shepherd and Zacharakis, 2005), and this work has yielded important insights into the criteria for such decisions and how they are actually made.

One way to answer this question, of course, is to simply ask VCs and other investors to describe the criteria they use in evaluating business plans and new ventures. As we noted in Chapter 2, however, people are *not* very good at recognizing or describing the factors that influence their decisions or at estimating the relative importance of each of these factors.

Is there any other way to answer this question—how to gain accurate insight into how VCs and other investors actually make their decisions? Two different methods have been used to address this question. One way of doing so is through the use of "policy capturing," an approach in which individuals are asked to make many decisions and then, *without* asking them to describe the factors that influenced these decisions, identify these factors—the ones that actually influence their judgments—through statistical analysis of the actual decisions. In other words, this method involves working backwards from venture capitalists' decisions to identify the factors that influenced these choices. In actual practice, the method works like this.

First, factors that are believed to play a role in the decisions being studied are identified. Next, these factors are built into various cases or examples in a systematic manner. These cases are then presented to the decision-makers (in this case venture capitalists) who rate the chance of success of each new venture described in the examples. Here's a concrete example. Suppose that one factor believed to affect VCs' decisions is "market familiarity"—the extent to which founding team members have experience in this market. The experience of the founding team would be described as high in some examples given to the VCs to evaluate but as low in others. A second factor might be the number of direct competitors for the new venture. The number of competitors would then be described as high in some cases given to the VCs but low in others. By combining several factors believed to affect VCs' decisions, many examples would be generated—examples in which the key factors are varied systematically (i.e., they are high in some but low in others).

Finally, by examining VCs' ratings of the companies in these examples, information about which factors are *actually* affecting their decisions can be obtained. For instance, if, across many different examples, VCs rate companies in which the founding teams have a lot of market experience more highly than companies in which the founding teams have very little market experience, that would suggest that this factor is indeed affecting the VCs' decisions. Moreover—and this is a key point—this would be the conclusion even if the VCs themselves are *not* aware that this factor influences their decisions—that is, even if, when asked, they do not name it as playing a key role.

Procedures like these have been used in many studies (e.g., Shepherd et al., 2003) and the findings of such research have identified several factors that actually *do* play a key role in VCs' decisions. These include familiarity with the market, leadership ability of the founding team, proprietary protection (the extent to which the product is protected by patents or other legal restrictions), the extent to which the process used to deliver the product or service is unique and difficult to imitate, "market growth" (percentage growth over last several years), the level of past start-up experience of the new venture team (how many other companies have they started in the past?), the number of competitors, and their relative strength.

One problem with such policy-capturing research is that it involves specially created (i.e., hypothetical) examples. Another is that it assumes that we already know what factors might be important. If we don't, other variables that could also play a role in venture capitalists' decisions can be overlooked. To avoid such problems, a different approach involving information on actual decisions by venture capitalists over an extended period of time has been used in recent research by Petty and Gruber (2011). This technique too provides information on the factors that actually influenced these decisions, rather than on the actors that venture capitalists *say* influenced their choices.

Combining the two lines of research described here—policy capturing (which uses hypothetical examples) and study of actual decisions by venture capitalists over an extended period of time—suggests that many factors play a role in their decisions (see Figure 6.4 for a summary). This conclusion, in turn, indicates that if they wish to maximize their chances of success in obtaining VC funding, entrepreneurs should focus on assuring that they—and their business plans—are high on these dimensions. Success, in short, goes primarily to those best prepared to meet the criteria venture capitalists actually use in their efforts to invest wisely—that is, only in new ventures that have the greatest likelihood of success.

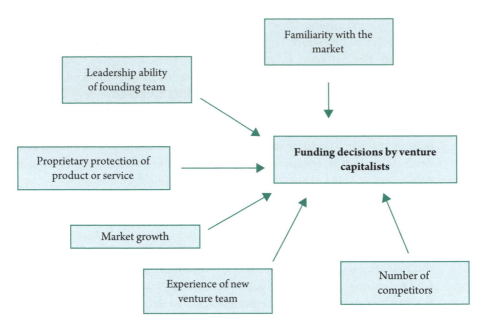

Figure 6.4 How do venture capitalists decide which ventures to fund?

Research using policy-capturing methods indicates that venture capitalists actually base their funding decisions on the factors shown here.

Estimating financial needs: How much will it cost to get started, and how will these funds be used?

Often, new ventures do not need large amount of capital to get started, but they do need some funds. A key question entrepreneurs face therefore is this: "How much money do I/we actually need?" Related questions are "What will it cost to obtain these funds?" (they are never free!), and "Once I/we have it, how will it be used?" As we noted in Chapter 4, part of the answer should be provided by a thorough feasibility analysis. However, once this preliminary process has been completed, it is usually necessary to consider the financial side of the new venture in more detail. Several tools can be used for accomplishing this task, and for providing the systematic financial information investors—who are usually very sophisticated about such matters—will want to see before providing funds. The most important of these tools are: (1) a careful record (or estimate) of start-up costs and how start-up funds will be used, (2) estimates of cash flow (for instance, estimates of the new ventures' income and expenditures), and (3) a break-even analysis—when the new venture can expect to reach the point where its income equals its expenses. Since, in many cases, the new venture does not yet exist—or at least, is not fully operational—there are often no data on previous results, so the financial information entrepreneurs develop must rely on estimates. This opens the possibility of painting a truly rosy picture of the new venture's future, but be warned: investors will recognize such "over-optimism," and insist on realistic projections. In contrast, if the new venture has existed for several years before seeking financial resources, it can provide basic historical data—financial records of how the company has actually performed in the past. Although in this chapter we will focus primarily on estimates or projections of future outcomes, we'll first briefly describe the nature of historical financial records, since a new venture will have to keep these after it has been launched and operating.

Summarizing past performance: Balance sheets, income statements, and cash flow

Historical financial records provide an overview of the new venture's past and current performance. There are three major types. "Balance sheets" provide a picture of the company's current assets and liabilities, and the owners' equity. Current assets include "fixed assets"—property, buildings, equipment, and furniture, plus assets that don't fit readily into these categories and are not tangible in the way buildings or equipment are (e.g., accumulated good will). "Current assets" include cash or other holdings that can readily be converted to cash if the need arises (e.g., marketable securities, inventories). "Liabilities" in contrast, include long-term liabilities, such as loans, mortgages on property the company is purchasing, and notes the company has signed promising to pay certain sums at certain times. Liabilities also include current liabilities—ones that are payable within a year, and the owner's equity—the equity owners invested in the company plus accumulated earnings (if there are any) that have been retained by the business. An example of a balance sheet is shown in Table 6.1.

A second key financial statement is the "income statement " (sometimes known as the profit and loss statement). This statement summarizes the results of a company's operations during a specific period of time. It includes income (revenues) and expenses during this period and indicates whether the company is taking in more money than it is spending—in which case it is making a profit—or spending more than it is receiving—in which case it is showing a loss. This statement typically includes "net sales" (sales minus returned goods and discounts the company has offered to customers, "cost of sales" (how much the company has spent to produce and deliver its products or services and so generate these sales), and "operating expenses"—which include administrative costs, marketing, and everything else not directly

Table 6.1 Example of a balance sheet. A balance sheet provides a summary of a company's assets and liabilities, plus owner's equity

	31 December 2005	31 December 2006	31 December 2008
Assets			
Current assets			
Cash and equivalents	100000	120000	130000
Accounts receivable less allowance for doubtful(s)	40000	50000	70000
Inventories	60000	90000	110000
Total current assets	200000	260000	310000
Property equipment plant			
Land	150000	200000	200000
Buildings equipment	200000	150000	150000
Total property equipment plant	350000	350000	350000
Less: accumulated depreciation	50000	40000	30000
Net property equipment plant	300000	310000	320000
Liabilities and shareholders equity			
Current liabilities			
Accounts payable	20000	25000	15000
Accrued expenses	5000	6000	7000
Total current liabilities	25000	31000	22000
Long-term liabilities			
Long-term debt	100000	75000	50000
Long-term liabilities	120000	110000	190000
Total liabilities	220000	185000	240000
Shareholders' equity			
Common stock (200000 shares)	20000	20000	20000
Retained earnings	10000	35000	40000
Total shareholders equity	30000	55000	60000
Total liabilities and shareholders' equity	250000	240000	300000

linked to producing and selling the company's products or services. An example of an income statement is provided in Table 6.2.

Finally, a third basic financial statement is a "statement of cash flow." This shows changes in the company's cash during a specific period of time. Thus,

Table 6.2 An example of an income statement. Income statements show the results of a company's operations during a specific period of time—an overview indicating whether it is making a profit or showing a loss

	31 December 2005	31 December 2006	31 December 2007
Net sales	550000	590000	650000
Cost of sales	300000	325000	350000
Gross profit	250000	265000	300000
Operating expenses			
Selling, general, and administrative expenses	110000	100000	90000
Depreciation	20000	18000	16000
Operating income	120000	147000	194000
Other income			
Interest income	2500	3000	3200
Interest expense	(8000)	(7000)	(6000)
Other income (expense) net	(3500)	(3000)	(2000)
Income before income taxes	129000	140000	189200
Income tax expense	35000	37000	45000
Net income	94000	103000	144200
Earnings per share	0.47	0.52	0.72

in a sense, it is like the statements provided by banks to their customers each month (or daily, if you bank online): deposits and debits (checks and withdrawals) are indicated, as well as changes in cash balance during the month. In the same way, statements of cash flow report "operating activities" for the company during a specific period of time—net income or loss, depreciation, other changes in current assets or liabilities, "investing activities"—any purchases or sales of fixed assets (equipment, real estate), and "financing activities"—cash raised during the period. by borrowing money, selling stock, and funds spend for paying dividends (rare in new ventures!).

Together, these three kinds of statements provide a very good picture of a company's financial health. Is it profitable? How do its assets compare to its liabilities—both current and future? And is the cash it holds increasing or decreasing? Please remember though that these forms can be generated *only* for companies that already exist and so have a record of past performance. They can't be generated for new ventures since, often, they haven't yet started operating.

Estimating start-up costs

As we noted in Chapter 4, estimating such costs is often difficult, but as the process moves forward toward an actual launch, entrepreneurs should try to make as careful and realistic a job as possible. Neither investors nor entrepreneurs like "big surprises" where these costs are concerned, so it is important to make the list of such costs as complete as possible. And remember: once this estimate has been made it is wise, as noted in Chapter 5, to double or even triple it because more costs are almost certain to emerge during the process. To be even in the "ballpark" such estimates should include the costs of necessary equipment, building an inventory of parts or whatever else is needed to provide the company's products, buying or renting space for the new venture, and almost anything else the new business will need during its first years of operation.

Once start-up costs have been estimated, the next step involves developing a plan for how these start-up funds will be used. Investors want to know that these funds will be put to good purpose—ones related to the launch of the new venture. So, for instance, investors may react negatively to large salaries or travel budgets for the founders, unless strong justification for such costs can be provided.

Pro forma financial statements: Predicting the future

The next step in the process is creation of the venture's *projected* financial statements. Such projections are reflected in "pro forma statements"—ones that project (usually for three years) the financial condition of the new venture based on information available at the time they are made. As we noted previously, if a company has existed for several years before it seeks financial assistance, it can provide historical data, summarized in balance sheets, income statements, and cash flow statements. If historical records don't exist, then future performance must be estimated—and again, as accurately (and reasonably!) as possible. Three basic forms are generally used for these purposes: pro forma balance sheets project financial structure of the business (its assets and liabilities), while pro forma income statements offer estimates of profit and loss for the new business. Pro forma cash flow statements predict the inflow and outflow of cash for the new venture.

Predicting the future is always difficult, and this is especially true for new ventures, which are, in a sense, exploring new business territory. But entrepreneurs can maximize the accuracy of such estimates in several ways. First, they should devote special attention to sales estimates, because sales play a key role in determining cash flow and income. In essence, sales are the foundation on which everything else rests. Second, the accuracy of future profits and losses depend heavily on accurate assessments of costs. And a major cost involves generating sales. These don't simply drop into the entrepreneur's lap; rather, effort and funds must usually be expended to obtain them. So, estimating these costs as carefully as possible is crucial.

Finally, entrepreneurs can base their projects of future cash flow and income on the results attained by companies operating in the same industry—that is, the results of competitors. Often these are available, especially if competitors have been in existence for several years and are public companies (i.e., ones whose stock is traded on stock exchanges). Of course, founders hope that the results for their new venture will exceed those of competitors, but, at least, information on the performance of these other companies can be helpful. The key principle for entrepreneurs, then, is simply this: do everything you can to make your pro forma statements—projections of the company's assets and liabilities, income, and cash flow—as accurate (and reasonable) as possible.

Break-even analysis: When will the company begin to earn profits?

Another important type of estimate entrepreneurs must make in order to obtain financial resources from investors is a break-even analysis. Basically, this involves calculating the volume of sales needed to cover all costs, so that the new venture no longer has to expend start-up funds to stay in business. This is a very important indicator of the potential of the new venture to actually develop into a profitable company, and as you can probably guess, the smaller the volume of sales needed to reach this point, and the more quickly it can be attained, the better. Calculating break-even point generally involves following these steps:

1. Determine the sales price of the company's products or services.
2. Specify the costs associated with the sale of each unit or service.
3. Subtract the cost per unit from the sales price to calculate the margin per item (how much more the company receives on each sale than it spends).
4. Estimate the business's fixed costs (e.g., for parts, rent, etc.).
5. Divide the fixed costs by the margin to calculate the break-even sales volume—the level of sales required to generate income equal to ongoing expenses.

As these steps suggest, the higher the proportion of costs that are fixed, the higher the break-even point—that is, the greater the volume of sales needed to attain break-even. For this reason, it's important for entrepreneurs to keep fixed costs as low as possible. So, elegant offices in high-priced locations, expensive company cars, and similar items are definitely a "no-no" for most new ventures (Figure 6.5).

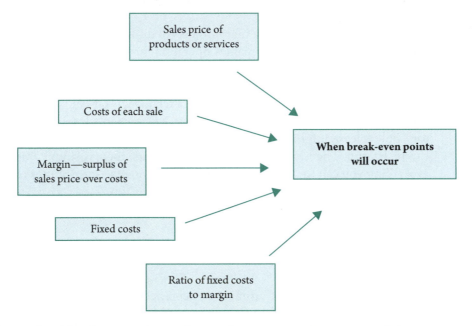

Figure 6.5 A break-even analysis indicates when a company's income equals its expenses

A break-even analysis provides information often crucial to potential investors. It indicates when, over time, a company's income will equal its expenses (costs). From that point on, the company will be profitable. The factors shown here play a key role in determining when this point will occur. The sooner break-even occurs, the better.

Why obtaining financial resources is often difficult: Overcoming investors' caution

Up to this point, the present discussion has focused on what might be termed "the mechanics" of obtaining and managing financial resources: where and how such assets can be obtained, how they will be used, and how to both summarize past financial performance and make projections of future performance. We have not, however, considered another important issue: is it easy or difficult for entrepreneurs to obtain financial resources? Not surprisingly, many entrepreneurs indicate that this was one of the hardest tasks they faced. Why? If they have identified an excellent opportunity, performed a careful feasibility analysis, and perhaps written a first-rate business plan, why is obtaining financial support so difficult? Is it simply that the competition is so fierce—hundreds of new ventures seeking support from a relatively small number of investors? While that is certainly part of the answer, much of the difficulty is built into the situation itself: entrepreneurs are asking investors to provide them with financing and since they believe in their ideas and their ability to turn them into profitable companies, they perceive these requests as reasonable ones. On the other hand, consider the situation from the perspective of an investor. They are probably not "in love" with the entrepreneurs' ideas, so they are not as certain that the new venture will succeed. In addition, they realize that the entrepreneurs have specific knowledge that they don't have, and this lack of information puts them at a disadvantage. In essence, these two kinds of problems that investors face—problems that make them reluctant to invest—are captured by the terms "uncertainty problems" and "information asymmetry problems."

Uncertainty problems: Which new ventures will succeed?

As was noted in Chapter 1, most new ventures fail—or at least disappear. This means that investors face a difficult task: somehow, they must choose the ones most likely to succeed. How can they accomplish this task? And how can they estimate the value of the opportunity the entrepreneur wants to develop? These are very difficult judgments and, in fact, investors may not even know what factors will determine the success of the new venture. Is it the basic idea behind the opportunity? The skills and knowledge of the entrepreneurs? The industry in which the new venture plans to operate? A financial or political climate favorable to the new venture? It is almost impossible for investors to know, so they are faced with a high degree of uncertainty; and as a result, investing funds under these conditions is a risky proposition.

As a result of these factors, investors must make their decisions largely on the basis of their own perceptions and experience. In this context, recall our discussion of how venture capitalists make such decisions: they may not even be aware of the factors that shape these decisions. And of course, entrepreneurs do everything they can to influence potential investors so that they will share the entrepreneurs' optimism and enthusiasm. To the extent they are successful in doing so, the investors may actually be making their decisions on the basis of factors they don't recognize—for instance, emotional reactions to the entrepreneurs and their presentations (e.g., Chen et al., 2009).

Information asymmetry: Entrepreneurs hold an important edge

When entrepreneurs request financial support from investors, they know all about their company. They were there from the very beginning, understand the idea and the opportunity it wishes to develop, know each other (members of the founding team) well, and in general, have much more information about their company than anyone else has or could possibly have. What is the implication of this for investors? Basically they are at a serious disadvantage. This disadvantage has several components.

First, entrepreneurs are reluctant to disclose all the information they have to investors; after all, if they release this information, the investors may decide to develop the opportunities themselves, or give it to someone else, and in a sense go around the entrepreneurs. Without the kind of protections discussed in Chapter 9, this is a real possibility. Moreover, investors have the capital necessary to exploit the opportunities—that's why entrepreneurs have approached them in the first place. So, entrepreneurs don't want to tell investors too much about their opportunities to avoid these risks. As a result, investors have to make decisions about financing ventures on the basis of incomplete information—less information than entrepreneurs have or could provide if they wanted to do so.

Second, the information advantage entrepreneurs have makes it possible for them to take advantage of investors. Entrepreneurs can use their superior information to obtain capital from investors and use it for their own benefit instead of the benefit of the company. For example, suppose an entrepreneur told an investor that he or she needed a car to get to clients' offices. The investor can't really know whether the entrepreneur needs the car for business or just wants something to drive on the weekends. Why? Because the entrepreneur supplies the information about the need for a car, and it might not be true.

Third, the investor's limited information about the entrepreneur and the opportunity creates the potential for a problem called "adverse selection." Adverse selection occurs when someone is unable to accurately judge which of two (or more) persons has a desired quality (one they are seeking). Because it's not possible to make these judgments perfectly, the person lacking in the desired quality has an incentive to misrepresent himself or herself and claim to have this quality. For example, some entrepreneurs have what it takes to build a successful new company and some don't. If investors can't tell one from the other, those without the ability to build successful companies will do everything they can to convince investors that they are highly competent, even if they are not. For instance, they will pretend to possess skills, information, or experience that they really don't possess. To protect themselves, investors have to charge a premium to insure against the losses that may occur if they decide to back the wrong people. Talented entrepreneurs with a very good opportunity don't want to pay this premium, so they withdraw from the financing market, leaving only the less competent entrepreneurs as candidates for funding—and this creates adverse selection. The bottom line is that investors have to choose among entrepreneurs very carefully; and after this choice, they must often implement techniques for ensuring that entrepreneurs do what they have promised to do, and work hard to make the new venture a success.

Why do we describe all these problems relating to uncertainty and information asymmetry in detail? Not to discourage entrepreneurs! Rather, they have been described to set the stage for explaining how investors and entrepreneurs cope with these problems. Now, therefore, we'll turn to these potential solutions.

How do investors protect themselves against these problems?

Given the difficulties described above (uncertainty problems and information asymmetry problems), you might wonder why investors ever provide financial resources to new ventures. Partly because many are highly sophisticated, and know various steps they can take to protect their interests. Among these, two are most important: contract provisions and staging of financing.

Contract provisions

To protect themselves against uncertainty and information asymmetry, investors often make a variety of provisions designed to guard their interests in contracts with entrepreneurs. First, they include restrictions on entrepreneurs' behavior. These are included as covenants (specific agreements) and often include restrictions that prevent an entrepreneur from purchasing or selling assets or issuing or buying back shares without investors' permission. They may also include mandatory "redemption rights," which require the entrepreneur to return the investors' funds any time they request them. Investors also employ convertible securities or other financial instruments that allow them to convert preferred stock, which gets preferential treatment in the event of a liquidation. Third, investors use "forfeiture" and "anti-dilution" provisions. These provisions require entrepreneurs to lose a portion of the ownership of their ventures if they fail to meet agreed-upon milestones. Fourth, investors give themselves control rights to the new ventures that they finance. "Control rights" are the rights to decide how to use a venture's assets. Investors typically take a disproportionate share of control rights—for instance, they own 30 percent of the shares of the company but take 51 percent of the seats on the board of directors (see Chapter 7). Finally, investors make it difficult for entrepreneurs to leave the company without investors' permission or to retain much owner-ship of the new venture if they do leave. Investors do this by requiring long periods during which time entrepreneurs cannot sell their portions of the company's equity.

Together, these tools minimize the likelihood that entrepreneurs will act against the interest of the investors, either by restricting the entrepreneur's behavior or reducing the incentive to act that way. They also make entrepre-neurs bear more of the uncertainty of the new venture, shielding investors against some degree of uncertainty. Of course, nothing can totally eliminate uncertainty or information asymmetry, but these steps can help investors to minimize both.

Staging of financing

Yet another technique often used by investors involves staging of financing. This means that investors provide financial support in stages, as the new venture meets various milestones—for instance, its first sale, break-even point, and so on. Providing financing in stages helps to minimize investors' risk because they can begin with a small amount of money and then see what happens to this initial investment. If they are not satisfied with initial results they can withdraw without providing further financial resources, and so minimize their losses; the most that they can lose is the small amount of the initial investment.

Staging of financing also helps to protect investors against efforts by entre-preneurs to use their information advantage to gain at the expense of the investor. By putting money into a new venture in stages, the investor has the opportunity to acquire information about how the venture is doing before making additional financial commitments. If the entrepreneur does anything that the investor doesn't like, such as using the money for private gain or the entrepreneur adopts a strategy investors consider too risky the investor can decide to withhold additional funds.

Finally, staging helps investors manage the uncertainty of investing in new ventures. In the very early stages of a new venture—soon after the discovery of the opportunity and before a product or service has been developed—new ventures are very difficult for investors to evaluate because so little information about them is available. Over time, however, as a new venture develops, information about the product, the entrepreneur's management style, the firm's strategy and so on become clearer, making it easier for investors to evaluate the venture. Because uncertainty is reduced as the venture develops, delaying most of the investment until after the venture has reached key milestones allows the investor to manage the uncertainty of investing in new ventures. The advantages of staging of financing for investors are summarized in Figure 6.6.

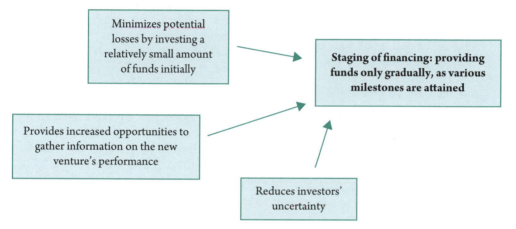

Figure 6.6 Staging of financing: one way investors protect their interests

By providing financial resources in stages—as various milestones are reached (e.g., first sale, break-even point)—investors protect their interests in the ways shown here.

In sum, although obtaining financial resources poses a major hurdle for entrepreneurs, there are ways of getting over—or around—this barrier. Moreover, these are designed to protect both the interests of entrepreneurs and investors. The result? Entrepreneurs provide the ideas, the energy, and the commitment, and investors provide the financial resources—the fuel—that propels the entire process, and sometimes (but not always), results in major success.

THE EFFECTIVE ENTREPRENEUR

Obtaining financial resources is a key task for entrepreneurs because although it's true that "money isn't everything," it *is* often important in starting a new venture. So, accomplishing this task effectively is a key step in the process. Here are some things you can do to be successful at acquiring these resources:

- First, if you don't need external funding, *don't* seek it! Many entrepreneurs are able to "get going" without outside financial support, and if you can do that, so much the better.
- If you *do* need external funds, remember that there are many potential sources; explore them *carefully* before you choose one. Yes, receiving funds from venture capital firms is prestigious, and many such firms will provide additional help other than money, but they will usually require a large share of your company, so you should consider this issue very carefully before proceeding on this path.
- Carefully explore various government programs designed to help entrepreneurs—especially the SBIR Program. If you can obtain a grant from the SBIR Program you do *not* have to pay it back, and the SBIR will not demand a share of your company.
- Remember that when estimating start-up costs, it is best to come up with a reasonable figure, and then to at least *triple*

it. That will probably be closer to the truth than your initial estimate.

- It is important to keep clear and accurate financial records. New companies, of course, have no historical data to report, but they do make projections of future sales, cash flow, and income, and it is important to base these on available evidence—and to be *realistic*. Investors are generally very sophisticated, and will view over-optimistic projections with considerable skepticism.
- An accurate break-even analysis is important too, both your own sake and for investors. No one is willing to wait forever for a return on their investment, so the sooner your company can reach break-even the better—and one secret to reaching this goal sooner rather than later is to hold costs to a *minimum*. Excessive costs are one of the most frequent causes of early "death" for new ventures.
- Obtaining financial support from external sources is definitely *not* a simple or easy task; investors are well aware of the disadvantages they face in this respect and will attempt to build "protections" into any offers they make. Be aware of these issues, and by all means, try to negotiate the very best arrangements you can. This is no time to be shy or reluctant to bargain hard because once a deal is made it is usually very hard to change it.

SUMMARY OF KEY POINTS

1 New ventures need financial resources to develop the opportunities they have discovered or created. There are many sources of such funds and each offers advantages and disadvantages.

2 Venture capitalists make their funding decisions on the basis of several

criteria (e.g., size of the market, experience of the entrepreneurs), and the ones they actually use have been clarified by policy capturing research.

3 A key step for new ventures is estimating start-up costs. If a new venture has existed for several years, its past performance is summarized by historical financial statements (balance sheets, income statements, cash flow statements). However, new ventures usually don't have such data, and so most estimate future performance in pro forma financial statements. An especially important type of projection is the break-even point—the point at which the new venture's income from sales equals its expenses.

4 Obtaining financial resources from investors is often difficult because investors recognize that they are exposed to uncertainty problems and also to information asymmetry. However, there are several steps they can take to reduce these problems.

 REFERENCES

Chen, X.-P., X. Yao and S. Kotha (2010), "Entrepreneurs' passion and preparedness in business plan presentations: A persuasion analysis of venture capitalists' funding decisions," *Academy of Management Journal*, **52**(1), 199–214.

Dimov, D. and D.A. Shepherd (2005), "Human capital theory and venture capital firms: Exploring 'home runs' and 'strike outs'," *Journal of Business Venturing*, **20**(1), 1–21.

Fried, V.H. and R.H. Hisrich (1994), "Toward a model of venture capital investment decision making," *Financial Management*, **23**(3), 28–37.

Petty, J.S. and M. Gruber (2011), "In pursuit of the real deal: A longitudinal study of VC decision making," *Journal of Business Venturing*, **26**(2), 172–88.

Rindova, V., D. Barry and D.J. Ketchen Jr. (2009), "Entrepreneuring as emancipation," *Academy of Management Review*, **34**(3), 477–91.

Shepherd, D.A. and A. Zacharakis (2005), "Venture capital," in M. Hitt and D. Ireland (eds), *The Encyclopedia of Entrepreneurship*, Malden, MA: Blackwell, pp. 245–6.

Shepherd, D.A., A.L. Zacharakis and R.A. Baron (2003), "Venture capitalists' decision processes: Evidence suggesting more experience may not always be better," *Journal of Business Venturing*, **18**(3), 381–401.

7

Assembling key resources II: Building a strong founding team, developing social networks, and obtaining expert advice

CHAPTER OUTLINE

- Building a strong founding team—and beyond: Developing the new venture's human capital
  - Resisting the lure of similarity—and why complementarity is often better
  - Cognitive heterogeneity: The benefits of different perspectives
  - Beyond the founding team: Attracting outstanding employees
- Developing high-quality social networks: Why who you know really *does* matter
  - Social networks: What they are and why they are crucial for entrepreneurs
  - Social capital: The benefits derived from social networks
  - How entrepreneurs build social networks—and acquire social capital
- Obtaining expert advice
  - Boards of advisers: Help from experts who *want* to help
  - Boards of directors: Help from experts with a legal role

The strength of the team is each individual member. The strength of each member is the team.
(Phil Jackson, former basketball coach, Chicago Bulls)

An expert is someone who knows some of the worst mistakes that can be made in his subject, and how to avoid them.
(Werner Karl Heisenberg, 1901–76, German physicist)

Although financial resources are certainly crucial, they are not the only kind new ventures need to get started—and move forward. These tasks also require an array of personal resources provided by the founding team: their knowledge, experience, skills, talents, and effort, to name just a few. Collectively these are known as "human capital" and are as essential as financial resources. (We say "founding team" by the way, because although many popular images of entrepreneurship focus on the efforts and talents of a single, "heroic" entrepreneur, most new ventures are actually launched by teams consisting of several persons.)

Human capital provided by the founding team is definitely a key ingredient, but it simply provides a beginning or foundation: after the new venture is launched, and especially if it grows rapidly, it faces the task of attracting high-quality employees who will add their own human capital to the new venture's resources. Finally, in order to grow and prosper, new ventures need one more key ingredient: information. Often, that is provided by other persons— individuals with whom the entrepreneurs have personal relationships. Thus, entrepreneurs also need strong "social networks"; in fact, the larger, and higher quality these networks are, the greater is the entrepreneurs' access to information useful for reaching key goals. In short, where new venture success is concerned, "who you know" is often just as important as "what you know." Once such information is attained, how can it interpreted and used effectively? Often, this involves obtaining advice and guidance from persons who are far more experienced in business and in entrepreneurship than the founding team. Fortunately, obtaining such help is not as difficult as it might seem because such persons often enjoy providing it, and are willing to serve on boards of advisors or even on more formal boards of directors. The help they provide can often be invaluable: research findings indicate that new ventures that secure such help are more likely to succeed than ones that do not (e.g., Reaume, 2003; Cohan, 2012).

The present chapter will focus on all these "people-centered" resources, describing their nature and how they can be obtained. Specifically, it proceeds as follows. First, the process of building a strong founding team will be examined. Get ready for some surprises in this regard, because existing evidence indicates that in many cases, novice entrepreneurs go about this task in precisely the *wrong* ways! Next, we'll turn to the nature of social networks and how these can be developed and used effectively. After that, attention will be focused on obtaining help and counsel from experienced individuals who are willing to offer their time and effort to help new ventures, often without any direct monetary compensation.

Building a strong founding team—and beyond: Developing the new venture's human capital

The new venture's founding team is, in a sense, the basic source of its talent, creativity, energy, motivation, knowledge, and skills. Clearly then, the bigger and deeper this pool of resources, the better. How important is the founding team? Many venture capitalists answer this question with comments like these: "I'd much rather have an *outstanding* founding team with a mediocre idea or opportunity, than a *mediocre* founding team with a top-notch idea or opportunity." And they continue by suggesting: "The outstanding team will make almost *anything* work, while the mediocre team will usually snatch defeat from the jaws of victory." But granted that the human capital brought to the process by the founding team is crucial, how can it maximized? How can entrepreneurs build a "dream team" capable of reaching the high levels of success they seek? Research on the role of founding teams in the development and growth of new ventures helps answer this question, and as we noted earlier, it also reveals that entrepreneurs often approach this task in precisely the wrong way. We'll now take a closer look at this question, considering both what many entrepreneurs actually do, and what, instead, they probably *should* do.

Resisting the lure of similarity—and why complementarity is often better

It is a fact of life that, in general, people tend to like and feel more comfortable with others who are similar to themselves (e.g., Baron and Branscombe, 2012). In other words, the old saying "Birds of a feather flock together" contains a large grain of truth. Further, such similarity can occur along a large number of dimensions—age, gender, ethnic background, attitudes, values, interests, field of training—and almost any others you can imagine. Not surprisingly then, all things being equal, most persons prefer to work with others who are similar to themselves in various respects. This is a very powerful tendency and is readily apparent in many areas of life. For instance, people tend to form friendships with, date, and even marry persons who are similar to themselves in various ways. Most individuals prefer to live in areas where their neighbors have similar backgrounds, levels of income, and other characteristics very much like their own; and their choice of social organizations, churches, and almost anything else you can think of, also demonstrates this same basic preferences for similarity. Does this powerful and general tendency have any bearing on entrepreneurship? In one very important way, it does. In fact, it often plays a key role in the formation of founding teams.

Think about it for a moment: how do founding teams emerge? How do several individuals come together to pursue an opportunity by launching and operating a new venture? Purely by chance? Because, for some reason, they have to? Such suggestions seem slightly absurd because people don't embark on such a serious journey by accident. In fact, the answer is straightforward and probably already obvious to you: a very high proportion of new venture teams—especially those formed at universities—consist of members who share a high degree of similarity (Figure 7.1). For instance, all may be of about the same age, gender, major, and even ethnic background. In our increasingly multi-cultural and multi-ethnic world, similarity with respect to these demographic variables is definitely declining, but it still exists. However, similarity in terms of training and interests cuts across these other differences and appears to still be dominant. As a result, most new venture teams are very homogeneous with respect to college major or training: three engineers come together to develop a high-tech product; several biologists join forces to develop a new drug; three or more persons who have been trained in finance unite to develop a new kind of investment tool. This pattern is certainly understandable: when founding team members are in the same basic field, communication between them is easier (they all speak the same language!), and they find working together relatively easy. The key question then, is not "*Why* are founding teams so homogeneous in certain respects?", but rather, "Does this high degree of similarity have beneficial effects?" In other words, does it contribute to the success of new ventures?

To answer this question, several studies have investigated the relationship between team members' similarity (both with respect to demographic factors such as age, ethnic background, gender, and so on) and similarity with respect to their basic fields of knowledge of training (e.g., Chowdhury, 2005; Kearney et al., 2009). The results are clear: similarity with respect to demographic variables has little or no bearing on new venture performance. In other words, the mere fact that team members are similar to one another in some respects is not related to the team's performance. And—perhaps more surprisingly—even similarity with respect to training or field of specialization is only weakly related to new venture performance. In fact, there is some evidence that the greater such similarity, the *worse* new ventures do. Given the powerful effects of similarity in other contexts, why doesn't it strongly enhance new venture performance? Part of the answer involves the fact that when all members of a founding team are highly similar, this means that they all tend to have the same knowledge and information, and also highly similar skills and talents. After all, they have gone through the same training. As a result, although they may find working together easy and relatively pleasant, they may be, collectively, lacking in some of the skills,

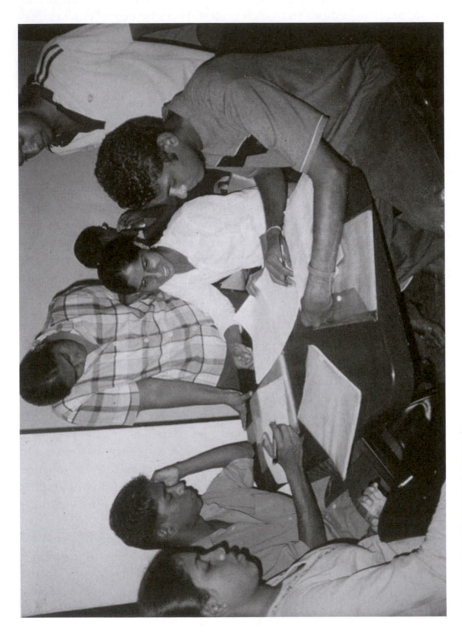

Figure 7.1 A high degree of similarity between founding team members: the most common pattern in new ventures

In many cases—perhaps the majority—founding team members are highly similar to one another in various ways.

knowledge, and experience necessary to launch and run a new venture. For instance, a group of engineers may be outstanding in terms of their capacity to plan and develop new products, but may have little or no idea about how to market them, or how to keep careful financial records. Similarly, a team of scientists may be experts in their field, but have little knowledge of the legal issues involved in founding and running a business. In sum, a high level of homogeneity among founding team members may mean that they do not have the broad array of knowledge and skills required to launch and operate a new venture.

This suggests that in building a founding team, entrepreneurs should indeed avoid the lure of similarity and be guided instead by the principle of "complementarity": they should seek partners whose knowledge, skills, and talents *complement* rather than overlap with their own. A "dream team" then might consist of a first-rate engineer, an expert in marketing, a member with knowledge of financial matters, and perhaps one with experience as a manager—someone who understands the day-to-day operations of a business (Figure 7.2). Unfortunately, this is rarely the case. Most founding teams consist of people

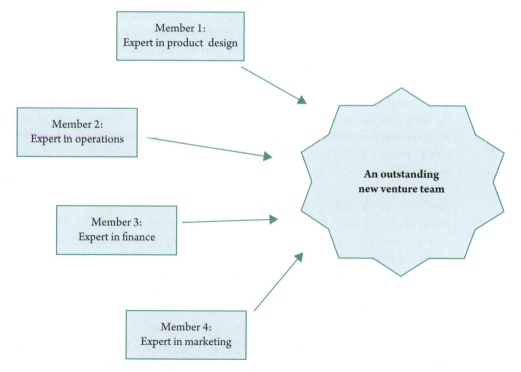

Figure 7.2 A "dream team" of founding entrepreneurs

Such a team would consist of members who have non-overlapping areas of knowledge, skills, experience, and talent.

who already know each other and have long-standing friendships—a totally reasonable preference. But as explained here, it may have high costs in terms of maximizing the human capital of the founding team and its overall versatility. This is one of those instances then in which what entrepreneurs actually do is distinctly different from what they *should* do.

Cognitive heterogeneity: The benefits of different perspectives

If similarity in training and background on the part of founding team members is either unrelated to or even negatively related to new venture performance, how should founding teams be created? As noted above, complementarity is one useful principle: teams should consist of members whose knowledge, skills, and talents do not totally overlap, but are, instead, complementary: what one has, the others lack, and vice versa. This is often far superior to forming a founding team on the basis of similarity, but recent research suggests still another approach that seem to be very beneficial—an approach involving what might be termed "cognitive heterogeneity." This research suggests that in creating a founding team—and increasing its overall strength—the extent to which members examine critical issues from a wide range of perspectives, consider different strategies, apply different decision criteria, formulate strategies by considering diverse approaches, and even hold contrasting views about what is important and should be carefully considered (Chowdhury, 2005)—is often very beneficial. These tendencies have been found to be positively related to many aspects of team performance—the quality and quantity of the team's work, its effectiveness at planning, its initiatives, and its overall performance. (Ratings of performance were made by the team members since external assessments of these variables is difficult to obtain, but of course, this introduces a degree of subjectivity into the measurement process.)

Similarly, other findings (Kearney et al., 2009) indicate that heterogeneity with respect to educational background (e.g., the extent to which founding teams consisted of persons from different fields appropriate to the new venture's industry) can also be very helpful. For instance, in the pharmaceutical industry, heterogeneity with respect to educational background might involve training in medicine, pharmacology, chemistry or biology; for new ventures in the telecommunication industry, heterogeneity might involve training in business administration, computer science, or engineering. Results revealed that diversity with respect to educational background—which would generate contrasting perspectives and hence cognitive heterogeneity—was positively related to various measures of team performance: efficiency, quality of innovations, productivity, and overall achievement.

In sum, it appears that founding teams whose members have complementary stores of knowledge, experience, information, and—most important—complementary perspectives—may be the strongest, and most likely to succeed. The general advice for entrepreneurs then is this: in building a founding team, it's important to resist the obvious appeal of a high degree of similarity, and to strive—whenever possible—for a team whose diversity with respect to perspectives and related cognitive processes—is high. Yes, this may result in team interactions that are somewhat less "comfortable" than is true when all members share many attributes and are very similar to one another, but this discomfort may be temporary, and well justified by superior outcomes. (For an example of a new venture that enhanced its success by strengthening its founding team through increased heterogeneity, please see "The Entrepreneurial Quest" case study below.)

CASE STUDY

The Entrepreneurial Quest

The Nobel Prize winner as entrepreneur—when even outstanding science is not enough for building a successful new venture

Careers take many different paths, and my own has certainly taken me to places and experiences I would never have predicted. One of the most enjoyable of these, however, occurred during a five-year period (2002–07) when I was privileged to team-teach a basic course on entrepreneurship with a Nobel Prize-winning physicist, Ivar Giaever. Ivar won the Nobel Prize for physics for his work on something I can only dimly understand: "experimental discoveries regarding tunneling phenomena in superconductors." But despite that, teaching with him was truly a pleasure, especially when he told the class: "Listen closely to what Prof. Baron says—it is very important." Ivar believed that entrepreneurship was the true wave of the future because it would help us to apply the findings of basic science to the task of improving human life.

In an effort to put these beliefs into practice, he and another physicist (Charles R. Keese) founded a company known as Applied BioPhysics. The company focused on developing devices to measure the electrical activity and movements of cells because research findings indicated that this information could be used to distinguish between normal cells and cancerous cells. The company received a grant from the SBIR, which provided sufficient start-up funds, so, working together, Giaever and Keese soon developed equipment (Figure 7.3) to detect the presence of cancer cells on the basis of cellular electrical activity, and tests indicated that it did so with greater accuracy than the techniques then being used (examining tissue under a microscope). As a result, the company appeared to be on the road to financial success, and—of course—to enhancing human welfare.

CASE STUDY *(continued)*

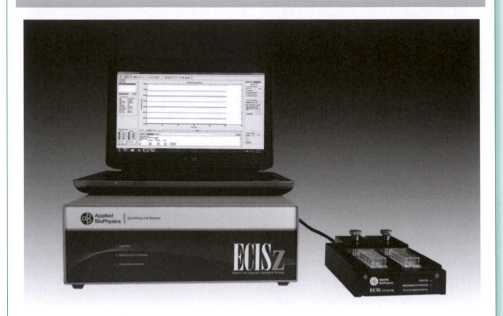

Source: Courtesy of Applied BioPhysics.

Figure 7.3 The importance of a strong and diverse founding team . . . even for Nobel Prize winners turned entrepreneurs

Ivar Giaever (a Nobel Prize winner) and his partner (Charles R. Keese) used their scientific knowledge to develop a device that measures the electrical activity and motion of cells—information useful in detecting cancers (photo). However, the company they founded did not begin to grow until they expanded the founding team to include a member with expertise in marketing.

Soon, however, serious problems emerged. Since the founding team (two scientists) had no previous business experience, they were unaware of the need to keep careful financial records and submit them to the appropriate state government. As a result, they soon received a notice from a state agency indicating that they were being fined $50 000 for "non-compliance " with certain regulations. To deal with this problem they hired an expert accountant who soon resolved the issue. Even more important, the equipment they produced was very expensive—more than $50 000 per unit. This greatly limited the market for it, since few potential customers (researchers working on cancer detection and treatment; hospitals) were willing to spend this much on a new kind of equipment that had no track record of success. Although the company—Applied BioPhysics— received lots of favorable coverage in the press, sales remained low, and the founders were at an impasse. What could they do to change this situation and make the company a success?

CASE STUDY (continued)

The answer was suggested by friends who *did* have business experience: "Recruit a marketing expert who can identify new markets and help convince potential customers to give your products a try," these persons advised. Giaever and Keese followed this advice and recruited a new partner who was an expert in marketing; soon, due to his efforts, sales increased greatly. The company then moved to new and larger quarters, increased the size of its staff, and ultimately became profitable.

The basic lesson in these events seems clear: all founding teams—including ones headed by a Nobel Prize-winning scientist—need a broad array of human resources to succeed, and the more diverse and complementary (i.e., non-overlapping) these resources are, the better.

Beyond the founding team: Attracting outstanding employees

Where human resources are concerned, the term "founding team" is highly appropriate: the founders are indeed the *foundation* of these resources. As just noted, the human and social capital they bring to the new venture play a crucial role in its success. But even if these basic resources are strong, once new ventures begin to grow, they soon need the talents, knowledge, and skills of additional individuals. In short, even modest growth quickly brings the founders face to face with an important question: how can they find, attract, and retain outstanding employees? Unfortunately, this is a complex and difficult task for all organizations, but is especially challenging for new ventures. As a relatively unknown company, a new venture may appear to be a high risk for the talented, skilled persons the entrepreneurs hope to attract. Funding from venture capitalists can help by boosting the venture's legitimacy, but even then, the task of finding and attracting excellent employees remains challenging. How do start-up companies overcome these difficulties? Partly through the use of their "social and business networks." We'll describe the nature of these networks and how they can be constructed in a later section, but for now we wish to note that entrepreneurs often utilize such networks to identify the highly talented and productive individuals they wish to hire. As we'll note below, this is an important reason why entrepreneurs should do their best to build strong networks.

Social networks, however, are often not enough in and of themselves: they may not be able to provide access to all the people a new venture seeks to attract and hire. Moreover, the tasks of finding and recruiting new employees—difficult and time-consuming as they are—are only part of the picture. Once such persons are hired, they must be retained and motivated to do their best work. This involves developing and providing appropriate employee benefits, establishing effective performance appraisal systems, setting up compensation plans that maximize employees' motivation and commitment, providing training when needed, and dealing with a wide array of interpersonal problems that always arise when individuals work together. We'll examine these processes in Chapter 10, but here it's important to note that they are very important for the growth and continued success of a new venture because no matter how talented, experienced, and knowledgeable the new venture team, it simply *cannot* do it all!

Unfortunately, entrepreneurs are generally much too busy running and building their companies to focus attention on these issues, crucial though they are, and, in fact, may not have the skills necessary to perform them effectively. (Remember: many founding teams consist of individuals with similar background and training; often, this does not include knowledge of human resource-related issues.) At some point then the wisest course for entrepreneurs may be to stop trying to do it themselves and decide to "outsource" these tasks—that is, hire someone else to perform them. A large number of companies exist that specialize in providing such services—hiring, attracting, training, motivating, and rewarding employees. Unfortunately, research findings indicate that entrepreneurs are often reluctant to take this action (e.g., Klaas et al., 2010). They feel that the new venture cannot afford the costs, and furthermore, because they view the new venture as "their baby," they are reluctant to delegate these tasks to others—especially people they don't know. Wise entrepreneurs will resist these tendencies because, as we noted in Chapter 4, there are many government regulations and laws relating to hiring employees, protecting their health and well-being, and many other issues. As a result, many persons who are experts in such requirements describe the situation as a "minefield"—one where it is very dangerous for those without sufficient knowledge to tread! The best advice for entrepreneurs then is simply this: seek advice and *don't* try to do it yourself. Delegating hiring and other processes to "outsiders" may seem hard, but the risks of proceeding without appropriate knowledge of such matters can be very high.

Developing high-quality social networks: Why who you know really *does* matter

At this point, let's return to the idea of building a "dream founding team"— one that possesses the human capital needed to maximize the new venture's chances of success. Human capital—the collective knowledge, experience, skills, motivation, and other resources of the founding team—is certainly important. But another strength too is necessary for success, and it reflects the new venture's need for high-quality information. No founding team—no matter how outstanding—can know everything. In fact, it needs information on everything, from where to locate the company's facilities and who are the best suppliers of needed parts or raw materials, through what new products competitors are currently developing, and even how to obtain a good accountant and a knowledgeable attorney. How can such information be obtained? As we noted earlier, through extensive, high-quality *social* networks (e.g., Aldrich, and Kim, 2007). What is the basic nature of these networks, and how can they be developed? These are the key questions we'll now consider.

Social networks: What they are and why they are crucial for entrepreneurs

What are social networks? Formally, they are defined as social structures composed of a set of members (which can be either individuals or organizations), and the ties between them—in essence, who knows whom, how well, and in what context. Social networks are important in many activities, from sports to science, but they are especially crucial for entrepreneurs. Because entrepreneurs are attempting to create something new, and are founding a business that didn't exist before, they have a great need for the benefits social networks provide. Among these, information is certainly central. As noted above, founding teams—even the best ones—can't possibly have all the information needed to successfully run every aspect of the new venture. For instance, perhaps the founding members are knowledgeable about the steps needed to develop and actually manufacture new products, but in contrast, may know little or nothing about accounting, or government rules concerning the safety or well-being of employees. An extensive social network can help provide such information.

To illustrate the value of social networks, here's an example of how they actually function, based on a popular television show, *Pawn Stars*. If you have ever seen this show, you know that it takes place in a Las Vegas pawn shop run by Rick Harrison and his family, The show centers around their negotiations with customers who bring an amazing array of items to the shop—everything from Super Bowl rings to centuries-old dueling pistols and articles of clothing owned by celebrities such as Elvis Presley. Often, Harrison or other members of his family know the value of the items, but in in many other instances, they do not. For example, they may be uncertain about the value of a rare book, a painting, or an old piece of jewelry. To find out, they call on people who are expert in such matters and who are part of their social network. These people come to the shop and both authenticate the item (determine if it is real) and also provide an estimate of its value. This gives Rick Harrison or other members of his family a basis for negotiations. For example, suppose that a customer brings a jade sculpture he or she wants to sell. The value depends greatly on its age, so it is essential for the pawn shop owners to get this information and an estimate of the item's value. Could they run their business successfully without this help? Probably not; they would have to avoid buying many items because they do not know their current value.

In precisely the same way, entrepreneurs often cannot run their businesses without information provided by other persons—ones in the entrepreneurs' social networks. Suppose, for example, that an entrepreneur needs someone who can provide help in gaining "shelf space" in a large retailer. Winning a place on this retailer's shelves virtually guarantees a high volume of sales, but the entrepreneur has no idea about how to proceed (Figure 7.4). To gain this information the entrepreneur might ask a number of persons in her or his network, and perhaps one of these individuals will either have the knowledge or at least be able to tell the entrepreneur who can provide such help. In this and many other instances, it is a broad and high-quality social network that saves the day.

Social capital: The benefits derived from social networks

It is clear that well-developed social networks can be very helpful to entrepreneurs in their efforts to launch and develop new ventures. A general term for the benefits they provide is "social capital." While human capital refers to the personal resources entrepreneurs bring to their new ventures, social capital refers to the wide array of benefits provided by social networks. Specific definitions of social capital vary, but most describe it as (1) the ability of individuals to obtain benefits from their social relationships with others, (2) these benefits themselves (Nahapiet and Ghoshal, 1998; Portes, 1998) or (3) the structure of individuals' social networks and their location in the larger social structure of the domain (e.g., industry) in which the entrepreneurs work (see, e.g., Aarstad et al., 2009).

Whatever its precise definition, social capital clearly derives from the social ties entrepreneurs have with others and the benefits they can obtain from these ties (Putnam, 1994). As you can probably guess, entrepreneurs with high levels of social capital (based on extensive and high-quality social networks) can more readily obtain information and advice they need, when they need it, than entrepreneurs lacking in social capital.

Source: Wikimedia: permission for unrestricted use granted by the photographer, lyzadanger.

Figure 7.4 Winning shelf space: crucial for many new ventures

How can a new venture manage to get shelf space for its products in large retailers? Help from the founding team's social networks can often assist with this difficult task.

In more general terms, social capital provides entrepreneurs with increased access to both "tangible" and "intangible" resources. Tangible resources include financial support and enhanced access to potentially valuable information. Intangible resources include support, advice, and encouragement from others, as well as increased cooperation and trust from them. While the benefits provided by these latter (intangible) resources are somewhat difficult to measure in economic terms, they are often highly valuable to the persons who obtain them. Overall, then, social capital is an important asset for entrepreneurs—one that provides major benefits.

The social ties on which social capital rests exist within social networks (Aldrich and Kim, 2007), and are often divided into two major types: (1) close or strong ties—for example, the strong, intimate bonds that exist between an entrepreneur and family members, very close friends, or other members of the founding team, and (2) loose or weak ties—social ties that are more diffuse, less intense, and often more short-lived than is true for close or strong ties. Generally, loose or weak ties develop between people who interact only in specific contexts (e.g., the entrepreneur and a supplier or an entrepreneur and an employee of a government agency from which the entrepreneur must obtain a specific kind of permit; e.g., Putnam, 1994; Adler and Kwon, 2002). The entrepreneur may see this person only once or twice a year, so any social ties between them are weak.

Close (strong) ties offer obvious advantages—for instance, they generate relationships based on mutual trust and can be a source of hard-to-obtain information. However, establishing and maintaining such strong ties can be effortful, and once developed, they are often difficult to maintain. Loose or weak ties too can supply information, but often it is not as important or hard to obtain as that supplied by close ties. On the other hand, establishing and maintaining loose ties often requires relatively little effort. Over time, loose (weak) ties sometimes develop into strong ones, in which case they would lead to relationships based on mutual trust.

Since social capital offers important benefits, and derives—to a large extent—from social networks, it is clear that one important ingredient in entrepreneurs' success is their capacity to build, and then reap benefits from, extensive, high-quality social networks. In fact, the social network perspective goes somewhat further, suggesting that an individual's position in a social network is by far the most important determinant of the information to which she or he has access. Persons with many weak ties have access to a broad range of information, while those with a few strong ties have access to a more restricted range of information—but it may be information that is closely held, hard to obtain, and is not readily available to others. Access to information often plays a key role in opportunity recognition. One view of this process is that it arises from "information asymmetries"—the possession, by some persons, of information that others do not have (e.g., Granovetter, 1973; Burt, 1992)—information that helps them identify or create opportunities. In this sense, therefore, the position an individual occupies in a social structure, and the kind of ties she or he has with others, strongly determine whether she or he will identify opportunities and so engage in entrepreneurial activity.

How entrepreneurs build social networks—and acquire social capital

Overall, it seems clear that social networks, and the information and other resources they provide, play a key role in entrepreneurship. Social network theory, however, does not directly address another important question in detail: how can individual entrepreneurs develop large social networks and hence a high level of social capital? Although social network theory does not focus on this issue, research findings on related topics offer two possible suggestions about how this process occurs.

First, as you may recall from the discussion in Chapter 6, venture capitalists often help entrepreneurs build and benefit from strong social networks. For instance, the best venture capital firms have huge social networks of their own, and so can put the entrepreneurs in touch with individuals or organizations who can help fill their needs, whatever these are. If, for instance, entrepreneurs need help with technical matters, the venture capitalists may know precisely the right sources of such help because they (the venture capitalists) often specialize in supporting only certain kinds of new ventures—ones in specific industries. Thus, the venture capitalists have ample opportunity to build social networks they can then put at the disposal of the entrepreneurs whose companies they choose to support. Further, venture capitalists often assist entrepreneurs—especially ones with little management experience— in running their new ventures. This can involve helping them hire excellent individuals who have the skills and knowledge the founding team lacks, and providing direct assistance and advice. In sum, although entrepreneurs can use many techniques to build their social networks—for instance, attending trade shows, conventions, and professional or business organizations—such efforts can be expanded and supplemented by venture capitalists (Figure 7.5).

Of course, only a small proportion of entrepreneurs obtain financial support from venture capitalist firms, because these companies only provide such

Figure 7.5 Entrepreneurs can build their social networks in many ways

Entrepreneurs can expand their social networks in many ways—for instance, by attending trade shows or conventions, as shown here. But introductions to key people by venture capitalists is often very helpful.

assistance to a small number of new ventures they have carefully chosen to receive such support. There is another important way in which entrepreneurs can build their social networks, however—one that emphasizes the personal skills or characteristics of the entrepreneurs themselves (e.g., Chi et al., 2013). This perspective focuses on what are known as "social" or "political" skills—skills that assist individuals in getting along well with others, and so in forming positive relationships with them (e.g., Ferris et al., 2007). The basic idea behind this approach is simple: people who possess certain skills (e.g., the ability to make a good first impression on others; to exert influence in subtle rather than overt ways) tend to be liked more than persons lacking in such skills, and as a result, find it relatively easy to establish relationships with others. Social and political skills, and their impact in a wide range of settings, including entrepreneurship, have been the subject of an extensive body of research, and we'll review its major findings in Chapter 8, where we consider the personal skills and characteristics that contribute to entrepreneurs' success. However, one recent study (Chi et al., 2013) is of special note because it has attempted to combine these two perspectives—social networks and social/political skills. This research obtained evidence indicating that in fact individuals high in such skills do indeed develop larger and better social networks than persons relatively low in these skills.

For now, however, the main point is this: in order to succeed in building their new ventures, entrepreneurs usually need a wide range of accurate information, and one of the most important sources of such input is other persons—people in the entrepreneurs' social networks. Developing such networks often involves considerable time and effort, but this is effort well spent, because once established, social networks and the benefits they confer, can make the difference between "a good try" and actually obtaining the success entrepreneurs seek.

Obtaining expert advice

Social networks can—and do—provide entrepreneurs with many kinds of valuable information. What they often don't provide, however, is continuous, detailed advice about how best to conduct the company's operations, key decisions, and overall strategy. Rather, social networks generally provide specific information on an "as needed" basis: in other words, entrepreneurs draw on this important resource when and how such help is needed. Is there any way to obtain information—and expert guidance—on a more regular basis? This can be invaluable to entrepreneurs, especially ones who are not experienced in running a business, which is, in fact, a large proportion of first-time entrepreneurs. Fortunately, there are several ways to obtain such help, and so supplement both the founding team's resources, and those provided by social networks. One is required by law when a new venture takes the legal form of a corporation (a board of directors) while the other is purely voluntary, but strongly recommended (a board of advisers).

Boards of advisers: Help from experts who *want* to help

Although many entrepreneurs start new ventures because they want autonomy—to be their own boss—those who are wise often seek the advice and guidance of individuals more expert than themselves in running a business, and especially a new venture. These individuals (often experienced entrepreneurs themselves) can provide such help by being asked to serve on a board of advisers, a group that meets regularly with the entrepreneurs, reviews the company's progress, and offers advice. These arrangements are often relatively informal: although specific meeting times and agendas are common, serving on such boards is completely voluntary, so advisers play a key role in determining what will be discussed, and when. Savvy entrepreneurs recognize the benefits of such boards: not only can they provide ongoing advice, they can also help entrepreneurs expand their social networks. In general, the individuals who are invited to serve on such boards (Figure 7.6) are carefully chosen by the entrepreneurs as those who offer skills and experi-

Source: # Fotolia 3344403_M.

Figure 7.6 Advice from the experts!

Entrepreneurs can often benefit from the advice and guidance of more experienced persons serving on boards of advisers or boards of directors for the new venture.

ence the founding team lacks. In most cases, board members serve without compensation—they help because they have been successful entrepreneurs themselves, and want to "give back" to their communities by helping others achieve the positive outcomes they have attained. In a sense, this is a classic "win–win" type of situation: entrepreneurs gain the help they need and want, while the board members gain satisfaction from helping entrepreneurs who are now making the same journey they made themselves in the past. Little wonder, then, that establishing boards of advisers is a step many entrepreneurs decide to take—and often, the earlier in the process, the better.

Boards of directors: Advice from experts with a legal role

While establishing boards of advisers for a new venture is purely voluntary, a board of directors is an entirely different matter. In many countries, laws require that any new company that begins life as a corporation appoints a board of directors—a group of individuals who are elected by the shareholders in the corporation and have the task of overseeing the management of the company (see Chapter 9 for a discussion of legal issues relating to new ventures). While the duties of such boards vary (e.g., they appoint officers of the corporation, declare dividends, provide financial oversight), their main contribution, from the point of entrepreneurs, is that of providing advice and guidance. Wise entrepreneurs choose members of their boards of directors very carefully, individuals who are knowledgeable and experienced in areas relevant to the new venture's operations. In other words, they are persons who have extensive experience in the industries in which the new venture operates, and moreover, have either held (or hold) important managerial positions in other companies, or have run their own new ventures. As a result, their advice and guidance can be invaluable to entrepreneurs.

But why, you may wonder, would experienced and perhaps famous individuals agree to serve on such boards for small, unknown companies? Clearly, for many reasons. For instance, since new ventures rarely have surplus cash, they may offer prospective board members shares in the company for their services. And then, as cash flow increases, they may also provide direct payment to these individuals. The amounts vary with the size and resources of the new venture, but can be substantial. The president of a university where I once worked served on the boards of several companies, and was reputed to receive large fees ($50 000–100 000) from each.

In contrast to boards of advisers, members of boards of directors have legal standing in the company. Their role and their powers are defined by the law. It is also important to note that if entrepreneurs receive financial support from venture capitalists, business angels, or others, these investors may require the right to appoint one or more board members. Given the problems of uncertainty and information asymmetry discussed in Chapter 6, the reason for doing so is clear: it provides investors with another useful means for protecting their investments.

The benefits to entrepreneurs, both in terms of advice they receive, and the legitimacy gained by having famous individuals on the board, more than offset the costs in terms of equity, direct payments to board members, and reduced control over their companies. So overall, having a strong board of directors is a big advantage for new ventures.

In sum, entrepreneurs, no matter how talented, dedicated, and committed usually cannot do it by themselves. Rather, they must seek help in many ways, and the better the assistance they secure, the higher the chances that their new ventures will survive and prosper.

THE EFFECTIVE ENTREPRENEUR

Financial resources are important, but they are not the only ingredient new ventures need to succeed. Human resources or capital—the skills, knowledge, experience, effort, and talent of the founding team members are also important. In addition, since obtaining information is crucial too, the social networks of founders—which are often a major source of such input—are also crucial. Here are some points to keep in mind to acquire and use these resources:

- Although it is tempting to build a founding team solely from friends or persons with similar backgrounds, training, and interests, this can be a serious mistake. If you do, the founding team may end up lacking skills and knowledge it needs to succeed. It is much better, therefore, to build a founding team that is diverse with respect to cognitive perspectives—a team that looks at problems and issues from different points of view, and has contrasting ideas about what is important and should be carefully considered.

- If a new venture grows and develops it will soon need additional employees, so attracting outstanding persons to fill these roles is also crucial.

- Information is often supplied by founders' social networks, so the broader and higher in quality these networks are, the better. Such networks can be built in many ways, such as attending trade shows, conventions, and other relevant meetings, and—importantly through assistance from venture capital firms or other investors.

- Additional help and guidance can be obtained from informal boards of advisers or, if the new venture is a corporation, from boards of directors, so recruiting highly experienced persons for these roles can be very beneficial.

SUMMARY OF KEY POINTS

1 Building a strong founding team is essential to the success of any new venture. Although most founding teams consist of persons who are similar to one another (e.g., they have similar background and training), this can be a serious error, because when team members are highly similar they share the same knowledge, skills, and knowledge. Thus, it is often better for there be some degree of heterogeneity, especially with respect to cognitive perspectives, among team members so that they bring non-redundant resources to the new venture.

2 Another key resource founding teams should have—or develop—is large and high-quality social networks. These provide important kinds of information and can be developed or enhanced in several ways—for instance, by attending relevant trade shows and conventions, and through help from venture capitalists or other investors. In addition, entrepreneurs who possess well-developed social skills are often more successful at building such networks than ones who are lacking in such skills.

3 Expert advice is often beneficial, and can be obtained from boards of advisers or boards of directors. The basic principle is this: the greater the human capital of a new venture, the greater its likelihood of success.

 REFERENCES

Aarstad, J., S.A. Haugland and A. Greve (2009), "Performance spillover effects in entrepreneurial networks: Assessing a dyadic theory of social capital," *Entrepreneurship Theory and Practice,* **34**(5), 1003–19.

Adler, P. and S. Kwon (2002), "Social capital: Prospects for a new concept," *Academy of Management Review,* **27**(1), 17–40.

Aldrich, H.E. and P.H. Kim (2007), "Small worlds, infinite possibilities? How social networks affect entrepreneurial formation and search," *Strategic Entrepreneurship Journal,* **1**(1–2), 1147–66.

Baron, R.A. and N. Branscombe (2012), *Social Psychology,* 13th edition, Upper Saddle River, NJ: Pearson Education.

Burt, R.S. (1992), *Structural Holes: The Social Structure of Competition,* Cambridge, MA: Harvard University Press.

Chi, L., R. Fang, M. Chen and R.A. Baron (2013), "Bringing social skills into social networks: Findings from a field study of entrepreneurs," under review at the *Journal of Management Studies.*

Chowdhury, S. (2005), "Demographic diversity for building an effective entrepreneurial team: Is it important?" *Journal of Business Venturing,* **20**(6), 727–46.

Cohan, P.S. (2012), "Is venture capital best for financing a start-up?" *Financial Executive,* September, 17.

Ferris, G.R., R.L. Treadway, P.L. Perrewé, D.C. Brouer, C. Douglas and S. Lux (2007), "Political skill in organizations," *Journal of Management,* **33**(3), 290–320.

Granovetter, M.S. (1973), "The strength of weak ties," *American Journal of Sociology,* **78**(6), 1360–80.

Kearney, E., I. Gebert and S.V. Voelpel (2009), "When and how diversity benefits teams: The importance of team members' need for cognition," *Academy of Management Journal*, **52**(3), 581–98.

Klaas, B.S., M. Klimchak, M. Semadini and J. Johnson (2010), "The adoption of human capital services by small and medium enterprises: A diffusion of innovation perspective," *Journal of Business Venturing*, **25**(4), 349–60.

Nahapiet, J. and S. Ghoshal (1998), "Social capital, intellectual capital, and the organizational advantage," *Academy of Management Review*, **23**(2), 242–66.

Portes, A. (1998), "Social capital: Its origins and applications in modern sociology," *Annual Review of Sociology*, **24**, 1–24.

Putnam, L.L. (1994), "Revitalizing small group communication: Lessons learned from a bona fide group perspective," *Communication Studies*, **45**(1), 97–102.

Reaume, A. (2003), "Is corporate venture capital a prescription for success in the pharmaceutical industry?" *Journal of Private Equity*, **6**(4), 77–89.

8

The central role of entrepreneurs: How their skills, motives, and characteristics shape new venture success

CHAPTER OUTLINE

- Essential skills entrepreneurs need—and should develop
  - Social skills: Acquiring social capital
  - Self-regulation: Choosing appropriate goals—and doing whatever it takes to reach them
- Are entrepreneurs really different? And if so, *why*?
  - Who becomes an entrepreneur—and who remains in this role: Why entrepreneurs may really be different
  - *How* entrepreneurs are different: Self-efficacy, risk, and personality
- Emotion and passion: The "feeling" side of entrepreneurship
  - The potential benefits—and costs—of being positive
  - Passion: The intense desire to be—and act—entrepreneurially

The world's greatest achievers have been those who have always stayed focused on their goals and have been consistent in their efforts.
(Dr. Roopleen, eye surgeon, author and motivational counselor)

Motivation is the fuel necessary to keep the human engine running.
(Zig Ziglar, 1926–2012, American author, salesman and motivational speaker)

Resilience is not a commodity you are born with, waiting silently on tap. It is self-manufactured painstakingly over time by working through your problems and never giving up, even in the face of . . . failure.
(Lorii Myers, Canadian entrepreneur and author)

Let's begin with a central question over which the field of entrepreneurs has long puzzled, and one we've mentioned before: why do most new ventures fail—or at least, quickly vanish, often without leaving a trace behind them? Many answers have been proposed, including all the ones below, which echo points made in previous chapters of this book:

- Failing to perform a careful feasibility analysis, so that, for instance, the entrepreneurs do not realize that there is actually no market for their new product service.
- Beginning with insufficient funds so that the new venture quickly runs out of money.
- The new products or services provided by the new venture offer no clear advantage over what currently exists so it has little or no competitive advantage.
- Expanding too quickly; growth is a wonderful thing, but not when it gets out of hand and can't be managed effectively.
- Entering an industry in which there are large established firms with huge resources and established customer bases.
- A lack of careful planning initially, followed by an inability to improvise and change.
- Very high overheads, which quickly exhaust the new venture's funds.

This is a far from exhaustive list, but it does draw attention to the fact that new ventures can get into serious trouble for many reasons. Although these factors are varied in scope, however, there is one underlying theme that pulls them together: they all involve *actions, judgments, miscalculations, or errors* by the founding entrepreneurs. Certainly, external circumstances beyond entrepreneurs' control can be, and often are, important. For instance, competitors may take unexpected actions, customer tastes and preferences can change suddenly, and technological advances sometimes leave the new venture behind. But in many cases, new ventures fail because the founders have not "done their homework," and haven't, in one sense, done what they need to do in order to attain success. In short, the fact that many new ventures fail can often be traced to actions—or inactions—on the part of their founders.

But what is the underlying cause of such errors, miscalculations, or misjudgments? Entrepreneurs are certainly *not* lacking in motivation, willingness to expend high levels of effort or enthusiasm concerning their ideas or vision, so why, despite these advantages, do the companies they start often fail? To reiterate: these sad endings to stories that start with high levels of hope and passion end in disappointment or failure because the entrepreneurs involved are lacking in essential skills or characteristics that, in the final analysis, are essential for attaining the success they seek. In a sense this is analogous to someone who sets out to perform a task but lacks the knowledge of how to accomplish it, the tools necessary for completing it successfully, or, perhaps, that confidence that she or he can reach this goal. Perhaps a concrete example will help clarify this suggestion; and, it's hard to imagine a better illustration of these points than the events that led to the development of the telephone—a device that truly changed the world.

Who invented the telephone? Almost everyone answers "Alexander Graham Bell," the famous entrepreneur who founded Bell Telephone and went on to become both famous and extremely wealthy. In fact, the story of Bell saying to his assistant, who was working in another room and couldn't hear him, "Watson, come here, I need you," but did hear Bell's request over the apparatus they were constructing, is famous. But was Bell really the inventor of the telephone? History indicates that in fact the credit should go to another person, Antonio Meucci. Meucci knew Bell, had worked with him, and had developed a functioning telephone several years *before* Bell filed his initial patent application. So why didn't Meucci receive credit for this invaluable invention? We'll never know for sure, but perhaps reasons that have little to with creativity or innovation, but rather, relate to how Meucci himself, played a role. He was an immigrant from Italy and did not speak English well. As a result, he was hampered in his efforts to convince investors to support his work. In addition, he was shy by nature, and reluctant to approach potential investors. On top of all this, he suffered from ill health, and lacked the vigor to actively develop and promote his invention. In contrast, Bell was a fluent and persuasive speaker, was well connected in the business world, and was known for his energy and vitality. The result? Bell triumphed because he possessed important skills and characteristics that Meucci lacked. For Meucci, the outcome was very sad: he died in poverty, not recognized until many years later for being first with this major invention (Figure 8.1).

In this chapter we will focus on the skills, motives, and characteristics that entrepreneurs need to succeed—to convert their ideas into real products or services. Again, it is fully recognized that factors relating to entrepreneurs are far from the entire story where success is concerned: external (i.e., environmental) variables and conditions are often crucial. For instance, no matter how skilled, motivated, and confident entrepreneurs are, they cannot succeed if they run out of resources or face obstacles and events that even the most careful planning could not predict. But it is assumed here that entrepreneurs *do* indeed play an important role in the process, and because they do, understanding how they differ and how these differences contribute to new ventures' success—or failure—can provide important insights into the entrepreneurial process.

Figure 8.1 Antonio Meucci: the real inventor of the telephone?

Existing evidence indicates that Antonio Meucci, *not* Alexander Graham Bell, was the inventor of the telephone. Why does Bell get credit for this invention? Perhaps because he was much more persuasive and vigorous than Meucci, whose inability to speak English made it difficult for him to convince investors to provide the financial resources he needed.

To provide you with a broad overview of the most important of these person-related factors, the present chapter proceeds as follows. First, it describes two key skills essential for attaining entrepreneurial success—social skills and self-regulation. Next, it turns to characteristics that, together, may make entrepreneurs different from persons in other careers, and may play a role in their success. As part of this discussion the question of *why* such differences might exist is also considered. Finally, the role of emotion and passion in the entrepreneurial process are examined.

Essential skills entrepreneurs need—and should develop

It has often been said (and it has been said before in this book!) that entrepreneurs create *something*—new products and services and the companies that provide them—out of *nothing*. In fact though, the "nothing" mentioned in this statement actually refers to important ingredients: entrepreneurs' creativity, talent, energy, knowledge, and skills. Of course, as we noted in earlier chapters (Chapter 6 and 7), they need many other resources to launch a successful new venture—for instance, financial resources and a strong founding team, but clearly, their own skills and characteristics are important too. We'll focus on several of these here, beginning with two that are especially important: social skills and self-regulation.

Social skills: Acquiring social capital

In Chapter 7, we noted that entrepreneurs often derive important benefits from their social networks. In fact, such benefits, stemming from entrepreneurs' relationships with others, are often a key ingredient in new venture success. This raises an important question, one we briefly mentioned in Chapter 7: how do entrepreneurs build their social networks? Part of the answer is that they receive help in doing so from investors who provide financial resources to their new ventures and also help them to make important "contacts"—people who can play an important role in their social networks. In addition, entrepreneurs often build their networks by attending trade shows, conventions, or other meetings in which they have an opportunity to meet—and form relationships—with other persons. But looking more closely at this question, how do entrepreneurs actually move from mere contact with others (e.g., a quick "Hello, my name is . . .") to forming relationships with them? A key answer provided by a large body of research is that they do so by using several "social skills" (also known as "social competencies"; Rubin et al., 2010)—skills that help them to get along with others effectively and form positive relationships with them. What is the nature of these skills and what role do they play in entrepreneurship? These are the issues we'll now consider.

The nature of social skills

As you certainly know from your own experience, some people are more popular and liked than others. Why? One important reason is that they are higher in terms of several social skills (e.g., Kotsou et al., 2011). These skills have been found to be an important "plus" in a wide range of settings—from politics and legal proceedings, to forming romantic relationships. In all these settings, they help the persons who have and utilize them to attain positive outcomes. The term "social skills" is the one we'll use in this discussion, but it's important that another one—political skills—is also commonly employed, and, with a few minor differences, refers to the same basic skills. The main difference is simply this: social skills is a general term referring to skills useful in a wide range of contexts; in contrast, "political skills" is focused primarily on work settings, and refers to skills useful in understanding others and in getting them to act in ways that enhance personal objectives (e.g., Ferris et al., 2007). Since the two terms refer to highly overlapping skills, we'll use the more general one—social skills—here. Below are brief descriptions of the most important of these skills:

- **Social astuteness (social perception)**. The capacity to perceive and understand others (their traits, feelings, intentions) accurately. Persons high on this dimension recognize the subtleties of interpersonal interactions, a skill that helps them develop effective, positive relationships with others.
- **Interpersonal influence**. The ability to change others' attitudes or behavior, through the use of a variety of techniques—for example, persuasion and other subtle techniques such as the foot-in-the-door tactic (starting with a small request and then escalating to a larger one).
- **Social adaptability**. The capacity to adapt to a wide range of social situations and to interact effectively with a wide range of persons.
- **Expressiveness**. The extent to which individuals can show their emotions openly, in a form others can readily perceive.
- **Impression management (including apparent sincerity)**. The capacity to make a good first impression on others through self-promotion (providing positive information about one's accomplishments or skills) or other-promotion, actions designed to induce positive feelings toward the person using them; these include various forms of ingratiation (e.g., flattery), and creating the appearance (if not the reality) of sincerity—presenting oneself as being honest and genuine.

Do social skills play an important role in entrepreneurship?

Are social skills important for entrepreneurs? Given their powerful impact in a wide range of contexts, it seems reasonable to suggest that they do. In a sense, they provide an extension of the benefits afforded by social capital. Social capital, once acquired, does indeed provide many benefits, including access to venture capitalists, potential customers, and potential employees. But once such access has been achieved—for instance, entrepreneurs gain access to potential investors or important customers—what happens next? Basically, the entrepreneurs must make the most of these opportunities so that the people involved are persuaded to provide what the entrepreneur wants: financial support, a large order, and in the case of potential employees, actually joining the new venture. In short, social capital does open doors, but once inside, outcomes depend strongly on the entrepreneurs' social skills—their effectiveness in interacting with, and forming relation-ships with others.

While social skills are important in many business contexts—for instance, it is often employees who are liked by their bosses who obtain the promotions—there are strong grounds for suggesting that such skills might be *especially* important for entrepreneurs. First, entrepreneurs meet and interact with a wide range of persons, many of whom are strangers not currently in their social networks. Social skills can be very beneficial to them establishing rela-tionships with these persons—making them part of their social networks.

Second, when presenting their "pitches" to venture capitalists, potential cus-tomers, and many other persons, entrepreneurs need excellent communica-tion skills and high levels of persuasiveness; these, in turn, often rest, to a large extent, on social and political skills. For instance, being persuasive often requires accurate understanding of the reactions of one's audience (i.e., a high level of social astuteness). Entrepreneurs also frequently face the task of gen-erating enthusiasm for their ideas, companies, or products in other persons; high levels of expressiveness may be helpful in this context. Finally, it is often essential for entrepreneurs to create good first impressions on others, since they and their companies are usually relatively unknown and have little or no existing reputation. Why, rationally, should potential customers take a chance on this unknown quantity? Perhaps because they form a favorable impression of the entrepreneurs, and are persuaded by them; and these out-comes are more likely to occur when entrepreneurs are high in social skills.

In sum, there are several reasons why high levels of social or political skills may be especially important for entrepreneurs. Is there any evidence that they actually are? The results of several studies offer support for this predic-tion (e.g., Baron and Markman, 2003). For instance, in one study (Baron and Tang, 2009), a measure of entrepreneurs' social skills was positively related to the performance of their companies. Moreover, others were better able to obtain valuable information and essential resources, than those lower in social skills. These resources, in turn, contributed to their success (Figure 8.2). The study was conducted with Chinese entrepreneurs working in many different businesses, so it also expanded the results of earlier studies, which were con-ducted in the United States in another and very different culture.

Perhaps the most intriguing evidence on the relationship between social skills and entrepreneurship has been provided recently by Obschonka et al. (2012). These researchers adopted a developmental perspective and sought to determine whether social skills early in life are related to becoming an

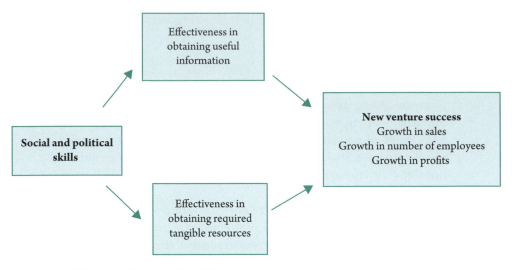

Source: Based on findings reported by Baron and Tang, 2009.

Figure 8.2 How entrepreneurs' social skills contribute to their success

Entrepreneurs who are high in social and political skills are more effective at obtaining useful information and essential resources than persons lower in such skills. These resources, in turn, contribute to the success of their new ventures.

entrepreneur and to success in this role. The researchers investigated this question in two different populations—one in the United Kingdom and one in Germany. The sample in the UK is especially impressive because it involved *every* child born in a particular week in 1970. The researchers obtained teacher ratings of the participants' social skills at age 5, 10, 16, and from self-reports of social skills at ages 30 and 34. Items used to measure social skills during childhood included these: "the child is highly popular with peers," "has many friends," is "very co-operative with peers," "does not tend to do things alone," and is an "extrovert." Ratings were made on 50-point scales, ranging from zero/not at all, to very high/all the time, depending on the item. When the individuals in the study were 34 years old, information on whether they were entrepreneurs or employed in another field was obtained; in addition, whether the participants continued in entrepreneurship for several years was also assessed, by determining whether they were entrepreneurs at age 30 and also at age 34. Success as an entrepreneur was measured by their income from entrepreneurial activities.

Results were clear: the higher the individuals were in social competence during childhood, the more likely they were to become entrepreneurs and to obtain success in this role (Figure 8.3). Similar findings were obtained with the sample from Germany too. The authors explain these relationships by noting that broad social skills in childhood may set the stage for effectively

Figure 8.3 Social skills in early life predict who will become an entrepreneur— and who will be successful in this role

Recent evidence indicates that the higher children's social skills, the more likely they are to become entrepreneurs as adults and to attain success in this respect. This suggests the importance of social skills in entrepreneurship.

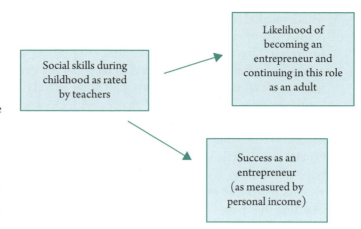

performing several tasks related to entrepreneurship in adulthood (e.g., leadership, engaging in business activities). Whatever the precise explanation, these results offer strong support for the role of social skills in both becoming an entrepreneur, and attaining success in this role.

Fortunately, social skills can be readily acquired or strengthened (e.g., Kotsou et al., 2011). Decades of research by psychologists indicate that with careful, guided practice, most persons can increase these skills (e.g., Kurtz and Mueser, 2008). One technique that is often helpful is making video recordings of individuals as they interact with others, and then having them view these recordings, while pointing out the shortcomings in their interaction style. Many people are surprised at their own actions, but can readily recognize the need for improvement in various ways. For instance, they may inadvertently be interrupting other persons, finishing their sentences for them, or may come across as "pushy" and overly ambitious—someone *not* to be trusted. After viewing the tapes they undergo training, guided by the psychologist, to improve these behaviors. In short, being better at understanding others, and interacting with them in effective ways can help entrepreneurs increase their own social capital.

Self-regulation: Choosing appropriate goals—and doing whatever it takes to reach them

Vince Lombardi, an American football coach many people consider to be the greatest coach of all time, once remarked: "The difference between a successful person and others is not a lack of strength, not a lack of knowledge, but rather a lack in will." The meaning of his words is clear: it isn't necessarily talent or knowledge that leads to success, but *willpower*—the capacity to do what's needed to attain it. Although success is defined differently in different fields (e.g., in art, it is being recognized as someone with unique talent; in surgery, it is having a very low percentage of patients who do not recover), for entrepreneurs it is usually defined in terms of the survival of their new ventures and its financial results (although as we noted in an earlier chapter, this is not the only kind of "success" many seek). Does willpower—the capacity to direct one's own behavior into the channels and actions that will bring success—really matter? In fact, evidence suggesting that these skills are truly crucial is overwhelming. Recognizing this fact, experts on self-regulation have noted that it is, perhaps, the single most important determinant of success in almost every human endeavor (Forgas et al., 2009). We'll now examine the basic nature of willpower—or, as it is usually described, "self-regulation"—and its important role in entrepreneurship.

Self-regulation: Its basic components

The term "self-regulation" refers to a collection of skills and capabilities individuals use to select key goals, monitor progress toward them, adjust their behavior (their thoughts, emotions, and actions) so as to enhance such progress. In a sense, such skills help individuals to "take their lives and fates actively into their own hands." What are these skills and capabilities? Research findings, reviewed in detail in later discussions, reveal that among the most important are these:

- **Self-control**. Performing actions that facilitate progress toward important goals (even if these actions are *not* enjoyable) while refraining from actions that *are* enjoyable but impede progress.
- **Focus and persistence**. Being able to maintain focus on key goals and work persistently (over time) to attain staying focused on key goals and working persistently toward them
- **Delay of gratification**. Being able wait for gratification (rewards) until the time at which they can be maximized (i.e., foregoing small rewards now to obtain larger ones later).
- **Accurate metacognition**. Being able to monitor and regulate our own cognitive processes and develop specific kinds of insight into our own capabilities, for instance, being able to recognize what we know and what we don't know.

Clearly, such skills are important for everyone, but there are several reasons why they may be especially valuable for entrepreneurs. First, in their efforts to create something new, entrepreneurs generally face situations in which there are few rules or guides to the best ways to proceed; they have no supervisors or teachers to show the way; rather, they must find it for themselves (although as noted in Chapter 7, they can be helped by other persons, such as boards of advisers). Second, because entrepreneurs fill many different roles, they must often perform tasks they have not performed before (e.g., planning sales campaigns, interviewing and hiring key employees). Thus, it is especially important that they have accurate metacognitive knowledge—for instance, to understand what they know and don't know, and to seek help when they lack the knowledge required for performing a specific task.

Finally, entrepreneurs, as a group, are very high in optimism and in positive affect (i.e., positive moods and emotions). These tendencies are often beneficial, but can also get out of control, so that entrepreneurs ignore negative information and are so eager to move forward that they skip over the careful thought and planning that are often necessary for success (Baron et al., 2012). In short, there are several reasons why well-developed, self-regulatory skills are especially important for entrepreneurs. Now, we'll review evidence suggesting that the aspects of self-regulation described above are in fact closely related to entrepreneurial success.

Self-control

Perhaps the component of self-regulation closest to the concept of willpower is self-control (e.g., Baumeister and Tierney, 2011). As noted above, this involves being able to perform tasks that we don't find interesting or enjoyable but are necessary for attaining key goals, while refraining from tasks we *do* enjoy, but which may interfere with attaining our goals. For instance, if an entrepreneur wants to run a successful business, she or he must keep orderly and accurate financial records—a task the entrepreneur may dislike—while refraining from spending too much time on activities she or he enjoys, such as working on the design of new products or meeting taking prospective customers to dinner.

Research on self-control indicates that people differ greatly in the capacity to exert self-control (Tangney et al., 2004), and that the ones who are high in this skill often attain better performance—and more success—than those lower in this skill (e.g., Baumeister and Alquist, 2009), in part because they are better able to exert the effort needed to attain true excellence, which often involves engaging in highly effortful deliberate practice that generates allows individuals to escape from being "average" and become instead exceptional at what they do (e.g., Duckworth et al., 2010). Another important finding with respect to self-control is that it appears to be a cognitive resource that is depleted by use; after individuals exert it in one situation or with respect to one activity (or temptation), their capacity to exert it again decreases. In short, well-developed skill in exercising self-control seems to be a necessary ingredient in attaining success (De Ridder et al., 2012), and it may be especially important for entrepreneurs who must often perform tasks they don't enjoy but help them reach important goals, and who have few, if any, external aids to doing what they should instead of what they enjoy (e.g., a teacher or supervisor who insists that they perform certain tasks and "keep their noses to the grindstone").

Is there any evidence that self-control actually enhances entrepreneurial success? Recent findings indicate that it does. For instance, in one study (Nambisan and Baron, 2013), self-control was found to be positively related to firm performance—the number of actual customers (and sales) for the products of high-tech companies. Overall, combining basic research on self-control with the recent findings of studies focused on entrepreneurs, it appears that self-control is indeed a valuable skill for entrepreneurs to develop.

Focus and persistence: Having clear goals—and working consistently to reach them

Another important self-regulatory skill involves two central components: (1) maintaining "consistent" interest in or focus on clearly defined long-term goals, and (2) demonstrating "persistence" in efforts to reach them (Duckworth et al., 2007). Together, these two components of self-regulation have been described by the term "grit," which was used in the title of a famous movie (*True Grit*). Although these two components are somewhat distinct, they have been combined in research (e.g., Duckworth and Quinn, 2009; Duckworth et al., 2010), so we treat them here as a single aspect of self-regulation. Existing evidence indicates that this combination of focus and persistence is strongly related to performance in many fields, and in fact is a key to attaining exceptional performance—performance far above the average (e.g., Duckworth et al., 2010; see also Figure 8.4).

Is this aspect of self-regulation relevant to entrepreneurship? One important reason why it is involves the fact that entrepreneurs rarely attain immediate success or rewards. On the contrary, these generally emerge only after months or even years of hard work. For this reason alone, being able to stay focused on and work persistently toward key goals are important skills for entrepreneurs.

Delaying gratification: Why waiting is often better

Many years ago (in the early 1960s), Walter Mischel (a young psychologist at that time), performed a series of famous experiments with three- and four-year-old

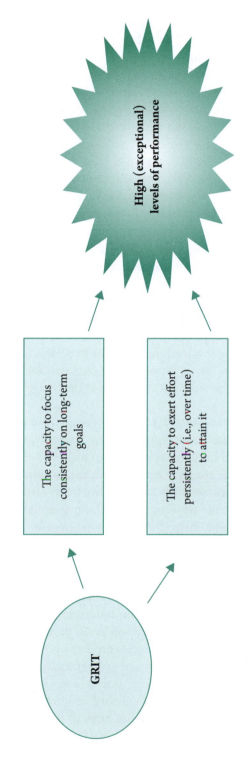

Figure 8.4 Self-regulatory skills and expertise

Recent evidence indicates that individuals who demonstrate exceptional performance in many different fields achieve their expertise through their ability to focus consistently on this goal and exert effort persistently to attain it (in current research, the combination of these components is often labeled "grit").

children. In these studies he placed a marshmallow in front of each child and told them, "You can have this one right now, but if you wait until I come back, you can have two. If you want me to come back right away, though, you can ring this bell." Then, he left the room and waited to see what the children would do. As you might guess, some of the children yielded to temptation and ate the marshmallow in front of them, while others were able to wait until he returned, and so received two. This simple experiment demonstrates clearly that people differ greatly in their capacity to "delay gratification"—to refrain from enjoying small rewards now in order to attain larger ones at a later time (Mischel, 1974, 1977, 2004, 2009). In a sense, the importance of this skill lies behind the advice often given by Dave Ramsey—a financial advisor who has a show on US radio. He often strongly criticizes people who live beyond (instead of beneath) their means, and fail to save for the future. In essence, what he rebukes them for is an inability to delay gratification—being unable to wait until the right time to begin enjoying various rewards, such as a fancy car or a larger house.

How important is skill in delaying gratification? Additional research by Mischel involved following the lives and careers of the children in his initial studies to see what happened to them. Results were dramatic: those who were good at delaying gratification age four experienced greater success in school, better careers, formed more stable personal relationships and were happier than those who were not successful in delaying gratification.

Further research provides insights into *how* people (not just young children) manage to demonstrate delay of gratification. Basically, they are good at regulating their own attention so that, for instance, they shift their thoughts away from the rewards available *now* to other topics. The four-year-olds who managed to wait for Professor Mischel's return, for instance, would cover their eyes, turn away from the tray containing the marshmallow, play with their hair—almost anything to help shift their own attention away from the treat in front of them. Research with adults indicates that similar but more sophisticated processes are at work. Adults, too, shift their attention to other topics and use their much more highly developed mental processes to accomplish this task. Similarly, if they can, adults attempting to delay gratification also remove themselves physically from temptations for immediate indulgence— for instance, if they are on a diet they will avoid passing their favorite restaurants or a bakery with delicious pastries on display. Similarly, entrepreneurs who want their new ventures to succeed may refrain from taking a large salary *now* in order to build the financial resources (e.g., working capital) of their companies. In fact, many entrepreneurs must resign themselves to living very frugally for months or even years, in the hope of much larger rewards in the future. As Mischel (2009) puts it, the basic trick to successfully exercising this self-regulation is "learning how to control your attention and thoughts" so that the lure of immediate rewards is reduced.

Metacognition: Understanding what you know . . . and don't

When someone on a diet is careful to avoid bringing high-calorie foods they love into their home, they are attempting to regulate their own cognition— to keep their thoughts away from these temptations. Similarly, when individuals want to avoid experiencing anger toward another person who has annoyed them, they may try not to think of this person or his or her actions. These incidents illustrate another important aspect of self-regulation known as "metacognition," which can be defined as thoughts, beliefs, and other cognitive processes used to assess and control our own cognitions—our own thinking. More generally, it refers to awareness of and efforts to regulate our own cognitive processes (Flavell, 1979).

Metacognition includes several different components (e.g., Haynie and Shepherd, 2009; Haynie et al., 2010) but here we'll focus on one that may be especially important for entrepreneurs: knowing what we know and do not know. This involves being aware of our own knowledge, how we can use it, and what tasks we are good—or poor—at performing. Recent evidence (e.g., Nambisan and Baron, 2013) indicates that this is a crucial skill for entrepreneurs. They found that a measure of this aspect of metacognition (Figure 8.5), was significantly related both to the performance of new

---

MEASURING METACOGNITION

1) I have *no difficulty* admitting that I do not know something, or do not know how to perform some task.

2) I am confident that I know what I need to know to run my business (practice, job) effectively.

3) I find it easy to ask for information, help, or advice from others.

4) I can usually tell if I have sufficient knowledge/skills to perform tasks I take on.

5) I am generally aware of what I know or don't know in any situation.

6) If I don't have enough knowledge or experience to tackle a task, I don't tackle it.

Figure 8.5 Metacognition: items used to measure it

Metacognition refers to our ability to understand and regulate our own cognitive processes. One important aspect of this process is recognizing what we know and don't know. The items shown here are similar to ones that have been used to measure this skill.

ventures and to entrepreneurs' subjective well-being—how happy they were with important aspects of their personal lives. These findings suggest that clear understanding of what we know and do not know is a key ingredient in developing entrepreneurial excellence. The same theme was proposed by McMullen and Shepherd (2006), who noted that an important task for entrepreneurs was determining which opportunities they might be able to develop successfully, and which they probably could not develop successfully. Making this judgment clearly involves being aware of our own knowledge and skills, so it refers to this aspect of entrepreneurship.

To summarize: a large body of research evidence indicates that self-regulation—skill in regulating and directing our own behavior—is important for success in many areas of life. It may be especially valuable for entrepreneurs who are attempting, to "blaze a new trail," and because they receive little or no direction or feedback from external sources. Thus, they must proceed on the basis of their own knowledge and judgment, and it is precisely under such conditions that self-regulation assumes truly major importance.

Are entrepreneurs really different? And if so, *why*?

I have often had this experience: I am a party or reception, and someone I'm talking to asks me: "What do you do?" When I say I am a professor, the next question is predictable: "What do you teach?" or occasionally, "What's your field?" When I say entrepreneurship, I can often see a new level of interest on the other person's face. Sometimes they then ask: "How did you get into that field?" My answer often involves the fact that I have been an entrepreneur myself and started a company based on my own research, which, in the past, focused on how the physical environment (temperature, air quality, lighting) influences human performance. At that point, they *really* get interested, and one reason why they do is that they assume that somehow I must be a unique or unusual individual because it is "well known" that entrepreneurs are a "breed apart"—very different from other people in several respects. Not only are some of them much richer (!), they are also especially creative, daring, and tenacious—they never give up. The source of these beliefs is clear: the entrepreneurs represented in the media do seem to be unusual people in various respects. From Henry Ford or Thomas Edison, through Richard Branson, Mary Kay Ash, Steve Jobs, and Elon Musk, they are far from ordinary. But what about less famous entrepreneurs? Are they, too, different from most other persons? And if so, why? Is it something in their genes—a view supported by some researchers (e.g., Shane et al., 2010)? Or are other processes at work? In fact, there are compelling reasons for suggesting that in some respects, entrepreneurs—as a group—may actually be somewhat different from others. We'll first examine the reasons why this may be so, and then turn to some of the differences that have been uncovered in careful research.

Who becomes an entrepreneur—and who remains in this role: Why entrepreneurs may really be different

Surprisingly, there is actually some evidence suggesting that the inclination to become an entrepreneur derives, at least in part, from genetic factors (e.g., Shane et al., 2010). But another possibility—perhaps one many people might find more acceptable—is that differences between entrepreneurs and other groups are largely the result of processes that lead to important differences between people who choose to work in different fields. For instance, consider dentistry: would everyone be attracted to this occupation? Probably not. And are dentists different in some respects from persons in other occupations? Probably so. Similarly, consider firefighters—are they different from, for instance, accountants? Almost certainly they are. And what about professional chefs, dancers, or musicians? Are they different from insurance agents or librarians? There is probably no need to continue with this list, because it seems clear that people in different occupational groups may well differ from each other. But why is this so? One compelling answer is provided by what is known as "attraction-selection-attrition theory" (e.g., Schneider, 1987; Schneider et al., 1995, 2013).

This perspective—the ASA model for short—is widely accepted in the fields of human resource management and industrial/organizational psychology. What it suggests, in essence, is that individuals are attracted to a particular career or choose to work for a particular organization because their personal characteristics, skills, or goals are closely aligned with the work or activities in that field or organization. (This is the "attraction" component of the ASA model.) However, among these persons, only some are selected to enter these careers. For instance, dental schools only admit individuals who have completed many courses in biology and express certain interests, while professional schools of dance or music only admit individuals who have demonstrated a high level of talent in these areas. (This is the "selection" component of ASA.) Finally, among these persons, only some find that they are actually suited for the field they have chosen, and only some are successful in their training programs or in the field once they enter it. As a result, some leave (either voluntarily or because they are invited to do so). (This is the "attrition" component of the ASA model.)

As a result of these processes—which operate in many different fields, especially those that are relatively selective—the individuals in a specific field, and especially ones that are highly selective, tend to be persons who were attracted to it in the first place, were successful in gaining entrance to it, and then chose, or were able, to remain in it.

Applying this model to entrepreneurs suggests that they may indeed be different from other persons, just as dentists, accountants, firefighters, and so on are different from each other. Entrepreneurs *are* different because (1) only some persons are attracted to becoming an entrepreneur, (2) only some actually become entrepreneurs (e.g., only some decide to actually attempt to convert their ideas and dreams to reality or launch new ventures), and (3) only some find that they are actually suited to this role, and so remain in it. For example, individuals attracted to the role of entrepreneur may be ones who strongly value "autonomy"—they want very much to be their own boss. Among these persons, however, only some are able to complete all the complex steps necessary to start a new company or act entrepreneurially, so only a portion of these potential entrepreneurs actually do so. Finally among this group, only some find that they actually function well as their own bosses—or start new ventures that survive. So, only they remain in this activity or role.

In short, the ASA process operates like a series of filters, with smaller and increasingly selected groups of persons passing through each stage—a process summarized by the phrase "Many are called but only few are chosen." Overall, this process of attraction-selection-attrition virtually ensures that people in different jobs, occupations, or roles differ in many ways.

So, returning to the questions we began with: are entrepreneurs actually different from other persons? And if so, why? The answer provided by decades of research on the ASA model (e.g., Schneider et al., 1995) is: (1) yes, they are different, and (2) they are different because of the same basic processes that almost guarantee that people in any given field are different, in various ways, from those in other fields. Entrepreneurs, like emergency room physicians, paleontologists, or government employees possess certain skills, characteristics, and interests—ones that suit them for their particular occupations or careers. An overview of the ASA model is presented in Figure 8.6, which illustrates why, according to the ASA model, entrepreneurs would indeed be expected to be "different" from other groups.

Now that this basic and crucial issue has been addressed, we'll turn to the question of *how* entrepreneurs are different—in what specific ways do they differ from persons in other fields? A growing body of evidence addresses this issue, and we'll review that evidence here.

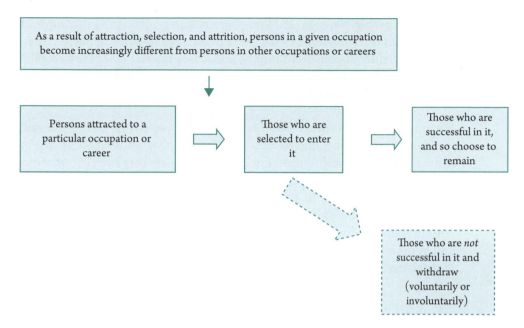

As a result of attraction, selection, and attrition, persons in a given occupation become increasingly different from persons in other occupations or careers

Persons attracted to a particular occupation or career

Those who are selected to enter it

Those who are successful in it, and so choose to remain

Those who are *not* successful in it and withdraw (voluntarily or involuntarily)

Figure 8.6 Are entrepreneurs different, and if so, why? ASA theory provides an explanation

Entrepreneurs, like persons in other occupational or professional groups are, as a group, highly selected. Only some are attracted to this role, only some of these persons actually become entrepreneurs, and only some find that they are suited to this role and remain in it.

How entrepreneurs are different: Self-efficacy, risk, and personality

At first glance, the question of whether entrepreneurs differ from others seems very straightforward. While many persons have ideas for something new and different, only a small percentage actually take steps to develop these ideas. This suggests that such persons are indeed a relatively select group, and almost certainly have skills and characteristics that differentiate them from others—the large majority who don't launch companies and develop opportunities. Interestingly, though, early studies designed to identify these differences yielded weak and inconsistent results. This led some researchers to conclude that, in fact, entrepreneurs do *not* differ from other persons, at least not in measurable ways. As explained earlier, ASA theory, on the other hand, suggests that such differences may well exist, and are the result of basic, well-understood processes (attraction, selection, attrition). So why didn't early studies obtain useful results? Because, they were seriously flawed in several respects. Rather than being designed to test predictions derived from existing theories or knowledge, they tended to be "fishing expeditions," which simply attempted to see if entrepreneurs differed from other persons in *any* observable ways. In addition, early research often used measures of various skills or characteristics that were neither reliable nor valid (i.e., these measures yielded inconsistent results, and it was unclear *what* they actually measured). Given such flaws, it is not at all surprising that these early studies yielded very little knowledge.

Fortunately, more recent research has avoided these errors, and as a result, we now have considerable evidence indicating that entrepreneurs are in some respects relatively unique. For instance, they are very high in optimism (Hmieleski and Baron, 2009), positive affect (i.e., positive emotions and feelings), and the tendency to search for opportunities (e.g., Tang et al., 2012). An overview of some of the most important of these differences between entrepreneurs and persons in other occupations or fields is provided below and in the section that follows, which is concerned with the role of emotion and passion in entrepreneurship.

Self-efficacy: Belief in our ability to "do it"

When individuals undertake virtually any task, they ask themselves: "Can I perform this successfully?" or, more generally "Can I accomplish what I set out to accomplish?" (Bandura, 1997, 2012). Such questions refer to what is known as "self-efficacy," individuals' beliefs concerning their ability to perform specific tasks and reach the goals they set for themselves. Not surprisingly, entrepreneurs are high on this dimension. That makes very good sense, because if they did not believe in their own capacity to achieve what they set out to accomplish, they might never begin! Many studies have confirmed this general suggestion (Zhao et al., 2005). So, overall, it seems clear that entrepreneurs are indeed higher in self-efficacy than persons in many other groups. More specifically, research findings indicate that there is a positive relationship between self-efficacy and the tendency to start new ventures (Markman et al., 2002; Zhao et al., 2005). In sum, entrepreneurs tend to be "can do!" individuals who believe in their own ability to reach important goals.

Risk: Are entrepreneurs really risk takers?

Entrepreneurs are often viewed as risk-takers—persons willing to pursue courses of action with a high probability of failure. Moreover, they often describe themselves in these terms—as individuals who don't mind taking chances when the rewards for doing so are potentially high. Are these views correct (e.g., Simon et al., 2000)? Overall, research results offer a somewhat mixed picture. Some studies indicate that entrepreneurs are high in their acceptance or tolerance of risk, while others find the opposite (Miner and

Raju, 2004; Stewart and Roth, 2007). What's responsible for these seemingly contradictory findings? One possibility is that entrepreneurs' willingness to take risks changes over the course of the entrepreneurial process. Initially, they almost *have to* accept high levels of risk; if they didn't the process would never begin. But later, after the new venture exists and must use its resources wisely, their willingness to knowingly take risks may decrease somewhat. After all, bills must be paid, employees must receive their salaries, and other obligations met. This doesn't imply that entrepreneurs become *low* in willingness to accept risk, but simply that this tendency may decrease over time. These suggestions are summarized in Figure 8.7.

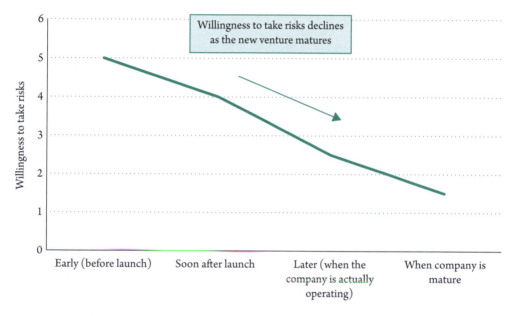

Figure 8.7 Are entrepreneurs really risk-takers?

Evidence on the question of whether entrepreneurs are high in their willingness to take risks is mixed, but perhaps one explanation is that this depends on when acceptance of risk is measured. Early in the process, entrepreneurs must be willing to accept risk or they would never get started. Later, however, they may be less willing to take risks since they must protect the resources of their companies.

So, are entrepreneurs really risk-takers? The answer depends on how and when we measure risk, and may vary greatly over the course of entrepreneurial activity.

Key aspects of personality: The "Big Five dimensions"

Two facts about people are clear: (1) they differ from each other in many ways, and (2) these differences are often consistent across time and situations. For instance, think of two people you have known: one is organized and orderly, and gets things done on time; the other lives in chaos, and never meets deadlines. These differences are readily visible and, moreover, they are apparent in many situations. The organized and orderly person shows these tendencies both at home and at work, and the same is true for the person who seems to thrive on disorder. Such consistencies in behavior or personal "style" are generally referred to by psychologists as "personality"—defined as consistent tendencies or dispositions in behavior (Larson and Buss, 2009). Personality plays an important role in many situations—especially ones that allow individuals to express their personal preferences or tendencies—what is known as "weak" situations. In contrast, it plays less of a role in situations where people are forced, by external factors, to behave in certain ways—what is known as "strong" situations. Here's an example: most people are polite and respectful when talking to their boss because they feel that this is required. In contrast, they may act in very different ways when talking to their friends.

Although individuals can differ in a very large number of ways, several decades of research indicate that there are, in fact, some basic dimensions that reflect these differences. These are known as "the Big Five" dimensions of personality (Barrick and Mount, 1991) and refer to very basic aspects of individual behavior—ones that are highly reliable, very stable over time, and can be readily observed and measured. The high ends of each of these dimensions are described below; the low ends are the opposite:

1. **Conscientiousness**. The tendency to be high in achievement and work motivation, organization and planning, self-control, responsibility (such persons tend to be orderly and organized in many different situations, and finish what they start—usually, on time!)
2. **Openness to experience**. The tendency to be high in curiosity, imagination, creativity, seeking out new ideas (persons high on this dimension are open to, and often seek, new experiences).
3. **Extraversion**. The tendency to be outgoing, warm, friendly, and energetic.
4. **Agreeableness**. The tendency to be trusting, cooperative, and altruistic in one's dealing with others (such persons start with the assumption that others are to be trusted, and only change this view if they receive evidence to the contrary).
5. **Emotional stability**. The tendency to be calm, stable, even-tempered, and, resilient after setbacks or when exposed to high levels of stress.

These dimensions have been shown to be related to a wide range of important outcomes, ranging from job performance (Barrick and Mount, 1991) to the size and quality of individuals' social networks. That they do indeed reflect very basic aspects of human behavior is indicated by the fact that when strangers meet for a few minutes and then rate each other on these dimensions, the ratings they provide correlate very highly with those given by individuals who know them very well—close relatives, spouses, co-workers, close friends. In short, where people stand on several of these dimensions is readily apparent even to casual observers, and in very brief face-to-face encounters.

Perhaps even more important, research findings indicate that several of these dimensions—conscientiousness, openness to experience, and emotional stability—are significantly linked to becoming an entrepreneur (Zhao and Siebert, 2006). Specifically, entrepreneurs are higher than other groups (e.g., managers) on all three of these dimensions. However, findings are mixed with respect to extraversion: although some results indicate that entrepreneurs are higher in extraversion than other persons (e.g., Zhao et al., 2010) some research results do not confirm this relationship.

Are these very basic dimensions of personality also related to entrepreneurs' success—for instance, the survival of their new ventures? Research evidence indicates that conscientiousness is positively related to firm survival. Surprisingly, however, there is very little evidence suggesting that openness to experience is related to entrepreneurs' success; in fact, some studies indicate that it is *negatively* related to their success. In addition, no significant links between the other three dimensions (agreeableness, extraversion, emotional stability) and entrepreneurs' success have been reported (Ciavarella et al., 2004).

Perhaps the most unexpected of these results is the possibility of a negative relationship between openness to experience and entrepreneurial success. One possibility is that persons high on this dimension have trouble staying focused; instead, they prefer change and something different—tendencies that may get in the way of maintaining the kind of consistent focus that is an important part of self-regulation. In other words, they are low in persistency, a key component of self-regulation (grit), as described above.

In sum, it appears that entrepreneurs do indeed differ from other persons with respect to certain aspects of personality, but not always in the ways we might expect.

Additional characteristics shown by entrepreneurs

Other evidence indicates that entrepreneurs are also higher than other persons in the need for "autonomy"—the desire to act independently, free from external constraint (Cromie, 2000; Rauch et al., 2005). In addition, they are higher in the "need for achievement"—the desire to excel in terms of meeting or surpassing standards of excellence (e.g., Stewart and Roth, 2007).

Still other differences between entrepreneurs and other groups relate to cognition (e.g., Mitchell et al., 2007). For example, entrepreneurs have been found to demonstrate weaker tendencies to engage in "counterfactual thinking" (imagining what might have been) than other persons (Baron, 2000). Apparently, their strong preference for focusing on the future reduces tendencies to look back and imagine different circumstances or outcomes from those that actually occurred. This is something that offers both advantages (e.g., it reduces the amount of time spent day dreaming about how things might have turned out differently—something almost everyone does occasionally), and disadvantages (e.g., it reduces efforts to learn from experience by imagining ways in which performance might have been improved; e.g., Roese and Olson, 1997).

In sum, it appears that entrepreneurs *are* different from persons in other groups or fields in several respects, and that some of these differences are related to their success. In the words of Niklas Zennström, founder of Skype: "If you want to be an entrepreneur, it's not a job, it's a lifestyle. It defines you." And clearly, some people, because of their personal characteristics, are more suited to such a lifestyle than others. (For a description of the unique characteristics of one famous entrepreneur, please see "The Entrepreneurial Quest" case study below.)

CASE STUDY

The Entrepreneurial Quest

Changing the world—but *not* by one idea at a time

Most entrepreneurs—even the ones that have been tremendously successful and acquired huge personal fortunes—have one or at most a few major ideas during their careers. It's possible to argue that Bill Gates, Michael Dell, and perhaps Mark Zuckerberg, built their fame, and wealth on the basis of one major idea. Elon Musk, however, is a clear exception to this general pattern.

Musk, who was born in South Africa but educated in the United States, has started several major companies—including ones that, at first glance, would seem to be extraordinarily risky. He began with Zip2 Corporation, a firm that provided content for new websites (it was 1992, and the web was just taking shape). He then moved on to found X.com,

CASE STUDY *(continued)*

which provided an online financial services company. After that it was PayPal, which in 2002 was sold to eBay for $1.5 billion; by then, Musk was a very, very rich person.

But he was far from done: his next project—SpaceX—was the first company to offer commercial space travel. This seemed somewhat far-fetched to some people, but the company has already received major contracts even from NASA. Then, using funds from these previous successes, Musk founded Tesla Motors, to produce fully electric cars. Although sales have been modest, the company's stock has zoomed and it is now worth many billions, and the company is currently set to introduce new models that may change this situation (Figure 8.8).

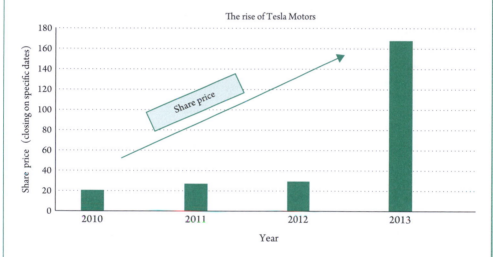

Figure 8.8 One of Elon Musk's many new ventures—and its road to success

As shown here, the price of shares in Tesla Motors, founded by Elon Musk, have risen since they were listed on a stock exchange, but recently have *zoomed* to amazing levels. Musk is truly a unique person who generates one creative idea after another—and many are successful.

So, what kind of person is Elon Musk, and which of his characteristics and skills have contributed to his success? The people who know him best (and those are relatively few), describe him as very outspoken, tremendously competitive (he doesn't want to lose—ever!), but incredibly dedicated to work, and capable of intense focus. He is also, perhaps surprisingly, a major hit at parties and other social gatherings. He is not humorous, but definitely has what is often called "presence"—people around him feel his intensity and recognize that this is a "different kind of person." He has been married and divorced twice and has five children (all boys), but visitors to his home—which he leases, rather than owns—notice that there is a lack of personal effects, such as photos and similar items.

CASE STUDY *(continued)*

Certainly, Musk is a complex person. But observing him from afar (humble professors are unlikely to enter his orbit!), it seems clear that he is extremely high in self-regulation—especially the capacity to focus intensely and exert effort persistently. He is also relatively good with people, despite a personal style that sometimes comes across as arrogant. He knows how to relax and enjoy himself, and that makes him good company in at least some settings. He is also supremely self-confident: the world may scoff at some of his ideas, but he "knows" that they will work—and the records show that they do. He is also a risk-taker—willing to invest a large portion of his personal fortune in starting his companies. And of course, his passion for inventing, starting, and developing new companies is obvious and it is also clear that he identifies himself—perhaps first and foremost—as an entrepreneur. Whatever his specific skills and characteristics, though, it is apparent that he is much more than someone who generates ideas: he also has the skill, energy, and judgment to turn them into reality—and that, of course, is the essence of entrepreneurship.

Emotion and passion: The "feeling" side of entrepreneurship

Can you imagine life without emotion—without joy, sorrow, or anger? Probably not because such an existence would be very strange, to say the least. The feeling (emotional) side of life is one of its most basic components. And, in fact, it is considered by many experts to be more fundamental than our rich and complex cognitive processes. Structures and systems within our brains that play a role in emotions are ones we share with many other species, while structures and systems that are more central to what are known as "higher mental processes" (reasoning, decision-making, planning, etc.) are ones that are either uniquely human or that we share only with a smaller number of species. What role do emotions and feelings (which are often termed "affect"—a more general term that includes moods as well as emotions) play in the entrepreneurial process? As we'll now see, a very important one.

Although research on this topic has investigated many issues, we'll focus here on two that are especially relevant to entrepreneurship: the potential benefits and costs of positive affect (positive moods and emotions), and the role of "passion," which has recently been defined as powerful identification with, and the intense desire to participate in entrepreneurial activities (e.g., Cardon et al., 2009; Murnieks et al., 2013).

The potential benefits—and costs—of being positive

Experiencing positive feelings or emotions is clearly preferable, in general, to experiencing negative ones. And a large body of evidence indicates that such reactions not only "feel" good, they are also related to many beneficial effects. The tendency to experience and express positive affect is related to outcomes such as (1) increased energy, (2) enhanced cognitive flexibility, (3) increased creativity, (4) greater confidence and self-efficacy, (5) use of efficient decision-making strategies, (6) increased use of effective techniques for solving problems, (7) improved ability to cope with stress and adversity (Weiss and Cropanzano, 1996; Ashby et al., 1999; Fredrickson, 2001; Lyubomirsky et al., 2005; Baron, 2008; Kaplan et al., 2009), and even (8) enhanced personal health. In addition, and more generally, high levels of positive affect have been found to be related to (1) improved performance on a wide range of cognitive and work-related tasks (Kaplan et al., 2009), (2) increased career success, and (3) the formation of more extensive and higher-quality personal relationships (i.e., networks; Lyubomirsky et al., 2005; Baas et al., 2008).

Given such effects, there appear to be strong grounds for concluding that positive affect either produces, or is associated with, a wide range of beneficial effects. The overall picture is not entirely rosy, however. Some research findings indicate that very high levels of positive affect increase susceptibility to cognitive errors (e.g., over-optimism) (Isen, 2000), and can interfere with performance on certain tasks, especially ones involving critical reasoning and logic (Melton, 1995; Bledow et al., 2011). In addition, high levels of positive affect have been found to reduce attention to negative information—especially information that contradicts currently held beliefs and attitudes (Forgas and George, 2001). Clearly, ignoring negative input can be a very dangerous tendency for entrepreneurs. Finally, high levels of positive affect—especially forms of positive affect that are high in both positive valence and activation (e.g., enthusiasm, excitement)—have been found to encourage "impulsiveness"—the tendency to act without adequate thought, abruptly, and with little or no regard for potential negative consequences (DeYoung, 2010). That too can be highly detrimental for entrepreneurs, whose new ventures generally have limited resources and cannot easily recover from the harmful effects of rash actions or hasty decisions by their founders (Khaire, 2010).

Overall then, the conclusion suggested by existing evidence is this: the relationship between positive affect and many important outcomes is curvilinear, not linear in nature. Up to a specific point, increases in positive affect are associated with beneficial outcomes, but beyond this level, they become "too much of a good thing," and can actually interfere with important aspects of cognition and behavior (Grant and Schwartz, 2011; see also Figure 8.9). In fact, recent findings (e.g., Baron et al., 2011) indicate that the level of positive affect expressed by entrepreneurs is related in precisely this curvilinear way to the performance of their new ventures. To a specific point, being "up" is a plus, but beyond some level it can interfere with firm performance, perhaps because entrepreneurs become overly optimistic, impulsive, and fail to consider negative information (which might interfere with their positive moods!) carefully.

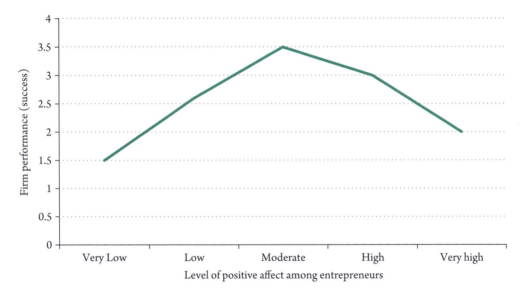

Source: Based on findings reported by Baron et al., 2011, 2012.

Figure 8.9 Is being enthusiastic and "up" always a plus? Perhaps not

Recent evidence indicates that the relationship between positive affect on the part of entrepreneurs and the performance of their companies is curvilinear in nature. Up to a point, higher levels of positive affect are associated with increased performance (success), but beyond that level they are negatively associated with performance.

These findings are important because, as a group, entrepreneurs tend to be very high in positive affect (higher, in fact, than any other tested group; Baron et al., 2012). While this is generally beneficial, it can, if too extreme, actually interfere with their performance, and with the success of their new ventures. In short, although positive affect is generally related to beneficial outcomes, there can be "too much of a good thing" with respect to such reactions, so that, ultimately, they generate effects that can interfere with the success of new ventures.

Passion: The intense desire to be—and act—entrepreneurially

In commenting on his own success, Albert Einstein once said: "I have no special talents. I am only passionately curious." History suggests that he was being too modest, but he was also insightful, because over the centuries, many thoughtful observers have suggested that a crucial component of success is "passion"— intense involvement in and love for whatever one does. This seems especially so in creative activities, whether building theories of the universe, generating art, literature, or—in the case of entrepreneurs—ideas for something new and better. Does passion actually play an important role in entrepreneurship? Many entrepreneurs refer to the importance of passion in their work, but until recently this remained a somewhat "fuzzy" concept because no clear definition of passion, and how it might influence entrepreneurship, existed.

This situation has been corrected recently by careful efforts to define passion clearly, and to understand its role in entrepreneurship (e.g., Cardon et al., 2009; Murnieks et al., 2013). These researchers define passion as a strong, positive inclination toward entrepreneurial activities, coupled with a powerful personal identification with these activities. In other words, entrepreneurs high in passion love what they do, and identify strongly with the role of being an entrepreneur.

Can such passion be measured? Cardon et al. (2013) have developed a brief questionnaire designed to assess entrepreneurial passion. Basically, it is designed to measure several aspects of passion: intense positive feelings about entrepreneurial activities (e.g., "I strongly enjoy trying to figure out how to make existing products better"), the extent to which being an entrepreneur is central to the individual's identity (e.g., "Owning my own company is very attractive to me") and identification with various roles that entrepreneurs play—inventor, founder, developer.

A key question, of course, is this: is entrepreneurial passion related to what entrepreneurs actually do and the success they achieve? Growing evidence suggests that the answer is "Yes." Passion, as measured by the scale mentioned above, is related both to entrepreneurial self-efficacy—the belief among entrepreneurs that they can accomplish tasks related to their entrepreneurial activities and to their behavior—what they actually do (e.g., the amount of their time they spend on running their new ventures versus other activities (Murnieks et al., 2013). At the present time, evidence concerning the question of whether passion is also related to entrepreneurial success is not available, but given the nature of passion it seems likely that this relationship too will be confirmed.

It's important to note though, that at least one recent study indicates that entrepreneurial passion may not necessarily enhance one important aspect of entrepreneurs' performance: their success in obtaining support (financial, human) for their ideas. Since entrepreneurial passion involves high levels of enthusiasm and enthusiasm often does "sell" it seems reasonable to expect that this would be the case. However, Chen et al. (2009) have reported that in making their "pitches" to venture capitalists and others, entrepreneurs' preparation may be more important than outward signs of their passion.

Does this mean that passion doesn't help with the task of obtaining financial resources? Perhaps, but it may also be that passion is more important in other ways. For instance, it may help entrepreneurs maintain their commitment even in the face of major setbacks (a topic we'll discuss in Chapter 12). Further, it is possible that this is yet one more instance of "too much of a good thing" where emotion is concerned. Up to a point, outward signs of passion may indeed help persuade venture capitalists and others to offer support for a new venture. However, beyond some point high levels of passion may be perceived as signs of insincerity or as overt efforts to sway an audience (e.g., by dazzling it with so much emotion that it becomes difficult to make rational decisions based on the facts—which is the key goal). Whatever the outcome of future research designed to investigate such possibilities, it seems clear that entrepreneurs' passion—their powerful commitment to their new ventures and roles they play in developing them—are an important way in which the "feeling side of life" influences the entrepreneurial process.

THE EFFECTIVE ENTREPRENEUR

There can be little doubt that entrepreneurs do indeed matter—they play a central role in the entire process. Clearly, then, their skills, characteristics, and emotions, are important. In this context, it's important to note that none of these are "set in stone"; they can all be changed—and improved. Here are some suggestions for using this information to become a more effective entrepreneur:

- Getting along with others is *very* important—perhaps crucial. Social networks are a major source of resources for entrepreneurs, and to build them, social skills are needed. These can be readily enhanced, but first you must have insight into where you stand in this respect. Friends can help, but if you are uncertain about these skills it might be worthwhile to consult a professional (e.g., a psychologist) for help.

It is one thing to desire success, but quite another to attain it. Doing so often requires a high level of self-regulation: self-control, being able to stay focused and show persistence, accurate self-knowledge (metacognition). These are *skills* and can be practiced and developed, so it is well worth the effort to work on doing so. ➡

- Entrepreneurs *are* indeed different from other persons—the attraction-selection-attrition process virtually assures that this is so. They tend to be highly optimistic, high in positive affect, and show various other characteristics. Again, these are not "set in stone" and can be altered, but it is important to understand where you fall on these various dimensions. Are you organized and orderly? An introvert or extravert? Gaining insight into these characteristics is important, and once you do, you should "play to your strengths"—seek situations in which you can use your personal strengths to good advantage. For instance, if you an extravert, you can arrange to interact with other persons frequently, and to address them as a speaker. If you are relatively introverted, you should avoid such situations as much as possible—or work on becoming extravert—it *can* be done.

- Another important characteristic of entrepreneurs is that they are high in positive affect—they tend to experience positive feelings and moods more often than other persons. This can be a strength in many situations, but can also lead to problems in some situations—for instance, by encouraging over-optimism, or a tendency to ignore negative information. So, while enthusiasm is often a "plus," entrepreneurs must learn to keep it in check in order to avoid the "downside" of being "up." Be sure that *you* don't fall into the trip of being too positive for the good of your new venture.

SUMMARY OF KEY POINTS

1 In order to successfully launch and run new ventures, entrepreneurs need many skills. Among the most important of these are social skills, which help them to develop strong social networks, and self-regulatory skills, which help them to stay focused on key goals, and do what's necessary to achieve them—and continue doing it over time.

2 Partly because of the operation of basic processes (i.e., attraction, selection, attrition), entrepreneurs *are* different in various respects from persons in other fields or groups. They are higher in self-efficacy, higher in their willingness to accept risk (at least early in the entrepreneurial process), and higher in certain aspects of personality—conscientiousness, openness to experience. They are also higher in optimism, and in the tendency to experience positive affect. This latter tendency is often associated with important benefits, but can actually have a detrimental impact at very high levels.

3 Entrepreneurs are also high in passion—a strong desire to engage in entrepreneurship and to fill several roles it involves (inventor, founder, developer).

REFERENCES

Ashby, F.G., A.M. Isen and A.U. Turken (1999), "A neuropsychological theory of positive affect and its influence on cognition," *Psychological Review*, **106**(3), 529–50.

Baas, M., C.K.W. De Dreu and B.A. Nijstad (2008), "A meta-analysis of 25 years of mood-creativity research: Hedonic tone, activation, or regulatory focus?" *Psychological Bulletin*, **134**(6), 779–806.

Bandura, A. (1997), *Self-efficacy: The Exercise of Control*, New York: W.H. Freeman.

Bandura, A. (2012), "On the functional properties of perceived self-efficacy revisited," *Journal of Management*, **38**(1), 9–44.

Baron, R.A. (2000), "Counterfactual thinking and venture formation: The potential effects of thinking about 'what might have been'," *Journal of Business Venturing*, **15**(1), 79–92.

Baron, R.A. (2008), "The role of affect in the entrepreneurial process," *Academy of Management Review*, **33**(2), 328–40.

Baron, R.A., and G.D. Markman (2003), "Beyond social capital: The role of entrepreneurs' social competence in their financial success," *Journal of Business Venturing*, **18**, 41–60.

Baron, R.A. and J. Tang (2009), "Entrepreneurs' social competence and new venture performance: Evidence on potential mediators and cross-industry generality," *Journal of Management*, **35**, 282–306.

Baron, R.A., K.M. Hmieleski and R.A. Henry (2012), "Entrepreneurs' dispositional positive affect: The potential benefits—and potential costs—of being 'up'," *Journal of Business Venturing*, **27**(3), 310–24.

Baron, R.A., J. Tang and K.M. Hmieleski (2011), "Entrepreneurs' dispositional positive affect and firm performance: When there can be 'too much of a good thing'," *Strategic Entrepreneurship Journal*, **5**, 101–19.

Barrick, M.R. and M.K. Mount (1991), "The Big Five personality dimensions and job performance: A meta-analysis," *Personnel Psychology*, **44**(1), 1–26.

Baumeister, R.F. and J.L. Alquist (2009), "Self-regulation as a limited resource: Strength model of control and depletion," in J.P. Forgas, R.F. Baumeister and D.M. Tice (eds), *Psychology of Self-regulation: Cognitive, Affective, and Motivational Processes*, New York: Taylor & Francis, pp. 1–35.

Baumeister, R. and J. Tierney (2011), *Willpower: Rediscovering the Greatest Human Strength*, New York: The Penguin Press.

Bledow, R., A. Schmitt, M. Frese and J. Kuhnel (2011), "The affective shift model of work engagement," *Journal of Applied Psychology*, **96**(6), 1256–7.

Cardon, M.S., D.A. Grégoire, C. Stevens and P. Patel (2013), "Measuring entrepreneurial passion: Conceptual foundations and scale validation," *Journal of Business Venturing*, **28**(3), 373–96.

Cardon, M.S., J. Vincent, J. Singh and M. Drnovsek (2009), "The nature and experience of entrepreneurial passion," *Academy of Management Review*, **34**(3), 511–32.

Chen, X.P., X. Yao and S. Kotha (2009), "Entrepreneur passion and preparedness in business plan presentations: A persuasion analysis of venture capitalists' funding decisions," *Academy of Management Journal*, **52**(1), 199–214.

Ciavarella, M.A., A.K. Bucholtz, C.M. Riordan, R.D. Gatewood and G.S. Stokes (2004), "The Big Five and venture success: Is there a linkage?," *Journal of Business Venturing*, **19**(4), 465–83.

Cromie, S. (2000), "Assessing entrepreneurial implications: Some approaches and empirical evidence," *European Journal of Work and Organizational Psychology*, **9**(1), 7–30.

De Ridder, D.T., G. Lansvelt-Mulders, C. Finkenauer, F.M. Stok and R.F. Baumeriter (2012), "Taking stock of self-control: A meta-analysis of how trait self-control relates to a wide range of behaviors," *Personality and Social Psychology Bulletin*, **16**, 76–99.

DeYoung, C.G. (2010), "Impulsivity as a personality trait," in K.D. Vohs and R.F. Baumeister (eds), *Handbook of Self-regulation: Research, Theory, and Applications*, New York: The Guilford Press, pp. 485–502.

Duckworth, A.L. and P.S. Quinn (2009), "Development and validation of the Short Grit Scale (Grit-S)," *Journal of Personality Assessment*, **91**(2), 166–74.

Duckworth, A.L., C. Peterson, M.D. Matthews and D.R. Kelly (2007), "Grit, perseverance and passion for long-term goals," *Journal of Personality and Social Psychology*, **92**(6), 1087–101.

Duckworth, A.L., T. Kirby, E. Tsukayama, H. Berstein and K. Ericsson (2010), "Deliberate practice spells success: Why grittier competitors triumph at the National Spelling Bee," *Social Psychological and Personality Science*, **2**(2), 174–81.

Ferris, G.R., D.C. Treadway, P.L. Perrewé, R.L. Brouer, C. Douglas and S. Lux (2007), "Political skill in organizations," *Journal of Management*, **33**(3), 290–320.

Flavell, J. (1979), "Metacognition and cognitive monitoring: A new area of cognitive-developmental inquiry," *American Psychologist*, **34**(10), 906–11.

Forgas, J.P. and J.M. George (2001), "Affective influences on judgments and behavior in organizations: An information processing perspective," *Organizational Behavior and Human Decision Processes*, **86**(1), 3–34.

Forgas, J.P., R.F. Baumeister and D.M. Tice (2009), *Psychology of Self-regulation*, New York: Psychology Press.

Fredrickson, B.L. (2001), "The role of positive emotions in positive psychology: The broaden-and-build theory of positive emotions," *American Psychologist*, **56**(3), 218–26.

Grant, A. and B. Schwartz (2011), "Too much of a good thing: The challenge and opportunity of the inverted U," *Perspectives on Psychological Science*, **6**(1), 61–76.

Haynie, J.M. and D.A. Shepherd (2009), "A measure of adaptive cognition for entrepreneurship research," *Entrepreneurship Theory and Practice*, **33**(3), 695–714.

Haynie, J.M., D. Shepherd, E. Mosakowski and P.C. Earley (2010), "A situated metacognitive model of the entrepreneurial mindset," *Journal of Business Venturing*, **25**(2), 217–29.

Hmieleski, K.M. and R.A. Baron (2009), "Entrepreneurs' optimism and new venture performance: A social cognitive perspective," *Academy of Management Journal*, **52**(3), 473–88.

Isen, A.M. (2000), "Positive affect and decision making," in M. Lewis and J.M. Haviland-Jones (eds), *Handbook of Emotions*, 2nd edition, New York: Guilford Press, pp. 417–35.

Kaplan, S., J.C. Bradley, J.N. Luchman and D. Haynes (2009), "On the role of positive and negative affectivity in job performance: A meta-analytic investigation," *Journal of Applied Psychology*, **94**(1), 162–76.

Khaire, M. (2010), "Young and no money? Never mind: The material impact of social resources on new venture growth," *Organization Science*, **21**, 168–85.

Kotsou, I., D. Nelis, J. Grégoire and M. Mikolajczak (2011), "Emotional plasticity: Conditions and effects of improving emotional competence in adulthood," *Journal of Applied Psychology*, **96**(4), 827–39.

Kurtz, M.M. and K.T. Mueser (2008), "A meta-analysis of controlled research on social skills training for schizophrenia," *Journal of Consulting and Clinical Psychology*, **76**(3), 291–304.

Larson, R. and D.H. Buss (2009), *Personality Psychology*, New York: McGraw Hill.

Lyubomirsky, S., L. King and E. Diener (2005), "Benefits of frequent positive affect," *Psychological Bulletin*, **131**(6), 803–55.

Markman, G.D., D.B. Balkin and R.A. Baron (2002), "Inventors and new venture formation: The effects of general self-efficacy and regretful thinking," *Entrepreneurship Theory & Practice*, **27**(2), 149–16.

McMullen, J.S. and D.A. Shepherd (2006), "Entrepreneurial action and the role of uncertainty in the theory of the entrepreneur," *Academy of Management Review*, **31**(1), 132–52.

Melton, R.J. (1995), "The role of positive affect in syllogism performance," *Personality and Social Psychology Bulletin*, **21**(8), 788–94.

Miner, J.V. and N.S. Raju (2004), "When science divests itself of its conservative stance: The case of risk propensity differences between entrepreneurs and managers," *Journal of Applied Psychology*, **89**, 3–13.

Mischel, W. (1974), "Processes in delay of gratification," in L. Berkowitz (ed.), *Advances in Experimental Social Psychology, Vol. 7*, New York: Academic Press, pp. 249–92.

Mischel, W. (1977), "The interaction of person and situation," in D. Magnusson and N.S. Endler (eds), *Personality at the Crossroads: Current Issues in Interactional Psychology*, Hillsdale, NJ: Lawrence Erlbaum, pp. 333–52.

Mischel, W. (2004), "Toward an integrative science of the person," *Annual Review of Psychology*, **55**, 1–22.

Mischel, W. (2009), "From personality and assessment (1968) to personality science, 2009," *Journal of Research in Personality* (Special Issue: Personality and assessment 40 years later), **43**, 282–90.

Mitchell, R.K., L.K. Busenitz, B. Bird, C.M. Gaglio, J.S. McMullen, E.A. Morse and J.B. Smith (2007), "The central question in entrepreneurial cognition research 2007," *Entrepreneurship Theory and Practice*, **31**(1), 1–28.

Murnieks, C.Y., E. Mosakowski and M.S. Cardon (2013), "Pathways of passion: Identity centrality, passion, and behavior among entrepreneurs," *Journal of Management*, in press.

Nambisan, S. and R.A. Baron (2013), "Entrepreneurship in innovation ecosystems: Entrepreneurs' self-regulatory processes and their implications for new venture success," *Entrepreneurship Theory and Practice*, **37**(5), 1071–97.

Obschonka, M., K. Duckworth, R.K. Silbereisen and I. Schoon (2012), "Social competencies in childhood and adolescence and entrepreneurship in young adulthood: A two-study analysis," *International Journal of Developmental Science*, **6**(3–4), 137–50.

Rauch, W., M. Frese and A. Utsch (2005), "Effects of human capital and long-term human resources development and utilization on employment growth of small-scale businesses: A causal analysis," *Entrepreneurship Theory and Practice*, **29**(6), 681–98.

Roese, N.J. and J.M. Olson (1997), "Counterfactual thinking: The intersection of affect and function," in M.P. Zanna (ed.), *Advances in Experimental Social Psychology, Vol. 29*, New York: Academic Press.

Rubin, K.M., W.M. Bukowski and B. Laursen (2010), *Handbook of Peer Interactions, Relationships, and Groups*, New York: Guilford Press.

Schneider, B. (1987), "The people make the place," *Personnel Psychology*, **40**(3), 437–53.

Schneider, B., M.G. Ehrhart and W.H. Macey (2013), "Organizational climate and culture," *Annual Review of Psychology*, **64**, 361–88.

Schneider, B., H.W. Goldstein and D.B. Smith (1995), "The ASA framework: An update," *Personnel Psychology*, **48**(4), 747–79.

Shane, S., N. Nicolaou, L. Cherkas and T. Spector (2010), "Genetics, the 'Big Five,' and the tendency to be self-employed," *Journal of Applied Psychology*, **95**(6), 1154–62.

Simon, M., S.M. Houghton and K. Aquino (2000), "Cognitive biases, risk perception, and venture formation: How individual decide to start companies," *Journal of Business Venturing*, **15**(2), 113–34.

Stewart, W.H. and P.L. Roth (2007), "A meta-analysis of achievement motivation differences between entrepreneurs and managers," *Journal of Small Business Management*, **45**(4), 401–21.

Tang, J., M. Kacmar and L. Busenitz (2012), "Alertness in the pursuit of new opportunities," *Journal of Business Venturing*, **27**(1), 77–94.

Tangney, J.P., R.F. Baumeister and A. Boone (2004), "High self-control predicts good adjustment, less pathology, better grades, and interpersonal success," *Journal of Personality*, **72**(2), 271–324.

Weiss, H.M. and R. Cropanzano (1996), "Affective events theory: A theoretical discussion of the structure, causes and consequences of affective experiences at work," in B.M. Staw (ed.), *Research in Organizational Behavior, Vol. 18*, Oxford: Elsevier, pp. 1–74.

Zhao, H. and S.E. Seibert (2006), "The Big Five personality dimensions and entrepreneurial status: A meta-analytical review," *Journal of Applied Psychology*, **91**(2), 259–71.

Zhao, H., S.E. Seibert and G.E. Hills (2005), "The mediating role of self-efficacy in the development of entrepreneurial intentions," *Journal of Applied Psychology*, **90**(6), 1265–72.

Zhao, H., S.E. Seibert and G.T. Lumpkin (2010), "The relationship of personality to entrepreneurial intentions and performance: A meta-analytic review," *Journal of Management*, **36**(2), 381–404.

Part III

Managing and building the new venture

Although most entrepreneurs do not found new companies because they want to become managers who spend much of their time overseeing their new ventures' daily operations, they usually find that they *must* fill this role. In order to manage their new ventures effectively, they need several kinds of knowledge: basic understanding of legal matters (e.g., non-compete agreements and intellectual property—patents, trademarks, and copyrights); basic knowledge of matters such as how to motivate employees so that they do their best work; how to exert influence over others; and how to make effective decisions. In addition, they must understand the processes of planning for, encouraging, and managing growth. This part of the book examines current knowledge concerning such issues.

9

Legal aspects of new ventures: Non-disclosure and non-compete agreements, intellectual property, and franchising

 CHAPTER OUTLINE

- **Can you legally start a new venture?** Not if you have signed agreements that limit your right to do so
  - Non-disclosure agreements: Protecting confidential information
  - Non-compete agreements or clauses: Preventing employees from becoming competitors
- **Legal protections for what you have created:** Copyrights, trademarks, and patents
  - Copyrights: Protection for the tangible expressions of ideas, but *not* the ideas themselves
  - Trademarks and service marks: Images symbolizing companies or products
  - Patents: The right to exclude others from developing or using ideas or inventions
  - When should entrepreneurs seek legal protection for ideas and inventions?
- **Other means of protecting the products of your creativity:** Trade secrets and complementary assets
  - Trade secrets: gaining protection by keeping information private
  - Control of complementary assets: Making it difficult for customers to benefit from potentially competing products
- **Franchising:** A new venture "in a box"?
  - Types of franchising
  - The benefits and costs of becoming a franchisee
  - Is franchising entrepreneurship? And is it for you?

The patent system added the fuel of interest to the fire of genius.
(Abraham Lincoln, 1809–65, 16th US President)

Great minds don't think alike. If they did, the Patent Office would only have
about fifty inventions.
(Scott Adams, creator of the *Dilbert* comic strip)

I hold three patents on my inventions, and two of them were very relevant to a company I started. The patents themselves are nice to look at—formal documents with blue ribbons attached (Figure 9.1). But, of course, much more important than the actual document are the rights the patents confer on me as the inventor. What are these rights, and once an inventor has a patent, do they always provide a strong guarantee that the products of her or his creativity will remain the inventor's property—that no one else can use them without the inventor's permission? And does a patent necessarily increase the value of the invention? These are complex issues, and the answers to them turn out to be equally complex. In this chapter, we'll examine various legal protections of what is known as "intellectual property"—a legal term referring to creations of the human mind. As we'll see, protections of intellectual property take several different forms, but all are designed to protect these outward expressions of human creativity by granting their inventors (i.e., creators) certain exclusive rights. For now, it's important to indicate that these creations include all of the following: inventions that perform some function, designs (e.g., the design of the classic Coca-Cola bottle), musical, literary, and artistic works, words and phrases (once they are expressed in some tangible form), new kinds of plants, and even symbols that represent a specific company. But before getting started, a concrete example of the complexities involved in protecting intellectual property may be helpful.

Have you ever heard of Joseph Swan? He was a British inventor and, in fact, history indicates that it was Swan, not Edison, who developed a usable light bulb—one that could function for hundreds of hours. Moreover, he did this several years before Edison came up with and patented (in the USA) what was essentially the same invention. Swan had filed for and received a British patent on his invention, and even described it in the magazine *Scientific American*, which was read (and still is) by very large numbers of persons. Edison knew about Swan's work, but proceeded to manufacture light bulbs anyway, and to build a system for delivering electricity to major cities. As a result, Swan sued Edison for infringing on his patent in the British courts—and won!—in the British courts Edison then had to make Swan a partner in his British electric company. But none of this stopped Edison from launching the General Electric Company in the United States, or from acquiring huge

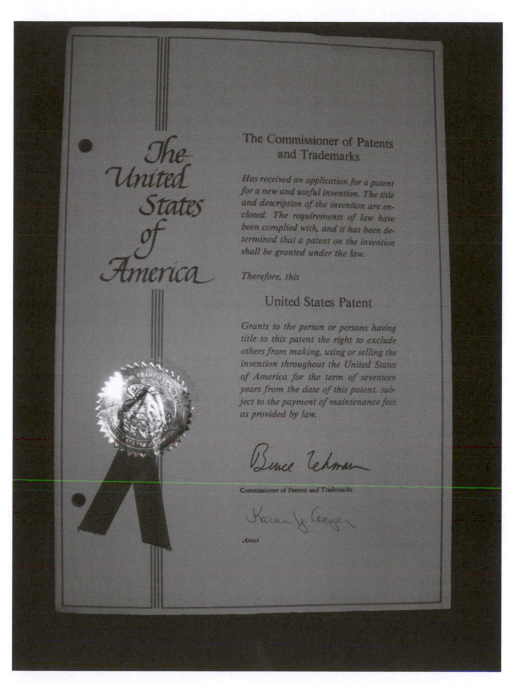

Source: Photo courtesy of Robert A. Baron.

Figure 9.1 The formal document granting a patent

This document is one of the author's patents. Obtaining this document requires a great deal of effort—and usually lots of money too!

wealth from exploitation of an invention that, in fact, may not have been his own.

This sad story had a happy ending, at least from Swan's point of view: the real inventor (Swan) was protected by a patent. But as we'll soon see, this is not always the case. For instance, if a very large company with ready access to skilled attorneys chooses to violate the patent of an individual inventor, the outcome may be something entirely different. In this chapter we'll examine several forms of protection—both legal and non-legal—of intellectual property. In addition, we'll examine the nature, the benefits, and costs of franchising—and address the question of whether it is a form of entrepreneurship. Franchising fits in the present discussion of legal matters related to entrepreneurship because it involves legal agreements between the franchisor (the company that grants the franchise), and the franchisee (the person who receives it)—agreements that may severely limit the franchisee's rights with respect to running her or his business. Before discussing these issues, however, we'll address an intriguing and even more basic issue: are individuals always free to start a new venture to develop their inventions or other products of their own creativity?

Can you legally start a new venture? Not if you have signed agreements that limit your right to do so

The question in the title above may seem puzzling: isn't it a basic right to be able to start a new company if you wish to do so? In general, the answer is "Yes," but there are two kinds of legal agreements hat may limit this right. One is known as "non-disclosure agreement," and although it is often an agreement between two companies it may also be an agreement between employees and their employer. The second type is known as a "non-compete agreement," and almost always involves an agreement between employees and their employer. Below, we describe both of these agreements and explain how they may restrict entrepreneurs' legal right to start a new venture.

Non-disclosure agreements: Protecting confidential information

Suppose you accept a job at a high-tech company. The company is working on several projects they hope will result in important—and potentially profitable—new products. As an employee, you work on one of these projects and gain information that the company would prefer to keep confidential—especially from competitors. After some period of time, however, you decide to leave and take another job. In your new position, your employer asks you to describe your former work, and in this way reveal some of the information your former employer wants to keep confidential. What should you do? Ethically, of course, you should keep the confidential information to yourself. But suppose the pressure to reveal it is high, and it is clear that if you reveal it, doing so will provide a big boost to your career. Aside from ethics, what you do depends, to some degree, on whether you signed a non-disclosure agreement with your former employer. If you did, you have agreed that you will keep this information secret, and if you violate that agreement you may be subject to legal action.

But what about a situation in which you want to start your own company, and this information might be useful—it will give you a jump on your competitors—including your former employer. A non-disclosure agreement may prevent you from doing this, because it may also bar you from using this information for your own benefit. In short, once you sign such an agreement, your right to start a new company that uses confidential information you obtained from an employer can be seriously restricted.

A related situation occurs when as an entrepreneur you want to tell investors or others about your ideas and new products. In such cases, it is wise for you to insist that they sign a non-disclosure agreement. If they don't, there is very little to stop them from using the information you provide for their own benefit—for instance, to use your idea to make products of their own. In short, non-disclosure agreements cut two ways: they can restrain a would-be entrepreneur from starting a new company, but can also protect the entrepreneur by preventing others from using confidential information she or he shares with them.

Non-compete agreements or clauses: Preventing employees from becoming competitors

Imagine again that you work for a company that is developing several new products. Then, at some point you decide to leave and start your own company. Can you do this? Yes, if you don't use any information you acquired at your former job, or if you start a business in an entirely different industry. But if you want to start a new venture in the same industry or type of business as your former employer, you may not be able to do so if you signed a non-compete agreement. Such agreements, which many companies insist that all employees sign, restrict you from starting a new business that will compete with your employer (Figure 9.2) or even from starting a business within a certain distance of the employer. Such agreements are binding and are often enforced. For example, in 2012, Acer Computers sued its former CEO, Gianfranco Lanci, who went to work at Lenovo, a key competitor, for

EMPLOYEE NON-COMPETE AGREEMENT

For good and valuable consideration the receipt of which is hereby acknowledged, _____ (Employee), the undersigned Employee hereby agrees not to directly or indirectly compete with the business of _____ (Company) and its successors and assigns during the period of employment and *for a period of* _____ years following termination of employment regardless of the cause or reason for termination.

Employee shall not own, manage, operate, consult or be employed in a business substantially similar to, or competitive with, the present business of Company or such other business activity in which Company may substantially engage during the term of employment.

Employee acknowledges that Company may, in reliance of this agreement, provide Employee access to trade secrets, customers and other confidential data and goodwill. *Employee agrees to retain said information as confidential and not to use said information on his or her own behalf or disclose same to any third party.*

This non-compete agreement shall extend for *a radius of* _____ *miles of* Company's present location and shall be in full force and effect for _____ years, commencing with the date of employment termination.

This agreement shall be binding upon and inure to the benefit of the parties, their successors, assigns, and personal representatives.

Signatures Of The Employee And Representative Of The Company Here:
Employee _____
Company Representative _____

Figure 9.2 An example of a non-compete agreement

Non-compete agreements, once signed by both the employer and employee, prevent the employee from starting a business that competes with that of their former employer after they leave employment. Such agreements can vary in the time they are in force, and the geographic area they cover. Basically, they restrict individual rights to start a new venture.

violating a non-compete agreement. If Lanci loses, he will be subject to size-able penalties, including cash fines.

In legal matters, it is a basic principle that *everything* can be negotiated, and this applies to non-compete agreements. The amount of time they are in effect can vary greatly (from a few months to several years), and the distance a new venture must be from the location of the employer can also be specified—for instance, a former employee can't go to work for a competitor or start a new company for three years, or can't go to work for a competitor or start a new business within 300 miles of the former employer. This is an important point, because potential entrepreneurs should bargain for the best terms they can attain.

In sum, although most entrepreneurs or potential entrepreneurs believe that it is their absolute right to start a new company whenever, wherever, and however they choose, their right to do so may be severely limited if they have signed a non-disclosure or non-compete agreement. So the main point is clear: think carefully before signing such agreements because they may come back to haunt you at a future time.

Legal protections for what you have created: Copyrights, trademarks, and patents

Inventors, authors, artists, musicians, and scientists want to protect their work, and understandably so. Generating their ideas and turning them into reality often takes a great deal of time and effort, so the persons who produce them feel that *they* and no others, should benefit from their work. But how can intellectual property—products of the human mind (or, as I prefer to say, products of human creativity) be protected? An important answer involves protections provided by the law. Legal systems differ from country to country, but most offer several kinds of protection for intellectual property. The most important forms of such protection are "copyrights," "trademarks," and—perhaps most important of all—"patents." We'll now review the basic nature of each of these forms of protection, and then turn to additional forms of protection that are not directly based on the legal system, but may still be highly effective.

Copyrights: Protection for the tangible expressions of ideas, but *not* the ideas themselves

When I was in college, I wrote a song, entitled "Ice Blue Eyes." I wasn't sure how to proceed, so I asked my uncle, who was in the music industry, what to do next. He suggested that I should copyright the song. Doing so, I soon learned, was simple and inexpensive—it merely involved sending a copy of the music and lyrics to the United States Copyright Office. A few weeks after I mailed these materials, I received formal notice indicating that my song was now protected by a copyright. The copyright meant that no one could use the song without my express permission.

Songs are only one of the things for which copyright protection can be obtained. Basically, such protection can be applied to anything that is: (1) original, non-functional (it doesn't *do* anything), and—most important—(2) is fixed in a *tangible* medium of expression. For my song, that simply meant writing it down on paper. Other items for which copyright can be obtained must also meet these two criteria. For instance, if someone writes a poem, a play, or a novel, they must put their words down on paper, or in some other tangible medium (perhaps a computer file), in order to obtain copyright protection. It must exist tangibly before it can receive a copyright. A wide range of items can receive this kind of legal protection: painting, photos, sculpture, computer software, rugs, and even wallpaper. To repeat, the key requirements are those shown above: the item must not do anything (the way an invention does), and it must be put into some tangible form. On the other hand, a copyright *cannot* be obtained for furniture because it is functional—it does something.

What rights do copyrights confer? Basically, they stop others from reproducing the work, distributing copies of it, performing it, or displaying it without the permission of the owner. If you've purchased a DVD of some movie or television show, you have probably seen a notice indicating that the material is copyrighted and so cannot be reproduced by anyone watching it. It's interesting to note that an "official" copyright from the US Copyright Office is not necessary: simply placing the symbol © or the word "Copyright," on the tangible expression of the work (which can be a song, book, painting, or even a term paper or PowerPoint presentation) can provide such protection. Copyrights are durable: the protection they offer lasts for the life of the author plus an additional 70 years, and for a work for hire (i.e., someone is hired to produce a book, a play, or piece of music), 95 years from the year of its first publication, and 120 years from the year of its creation. These features make copyright protection attractive, but again, it's important to remember that only the "tangible" expression of the ideas is protected—*not* the ideas themselves. For instance, although the words in a book are protected and others can't copy or reproduce them, the *ideas* expressed in the words are *not* protected. In other words, this book and others by the author are protected by copyright (Figure 9.3), but anyone can use the *ideas* expressed and even the way in which they are organized—as long as they don't copy

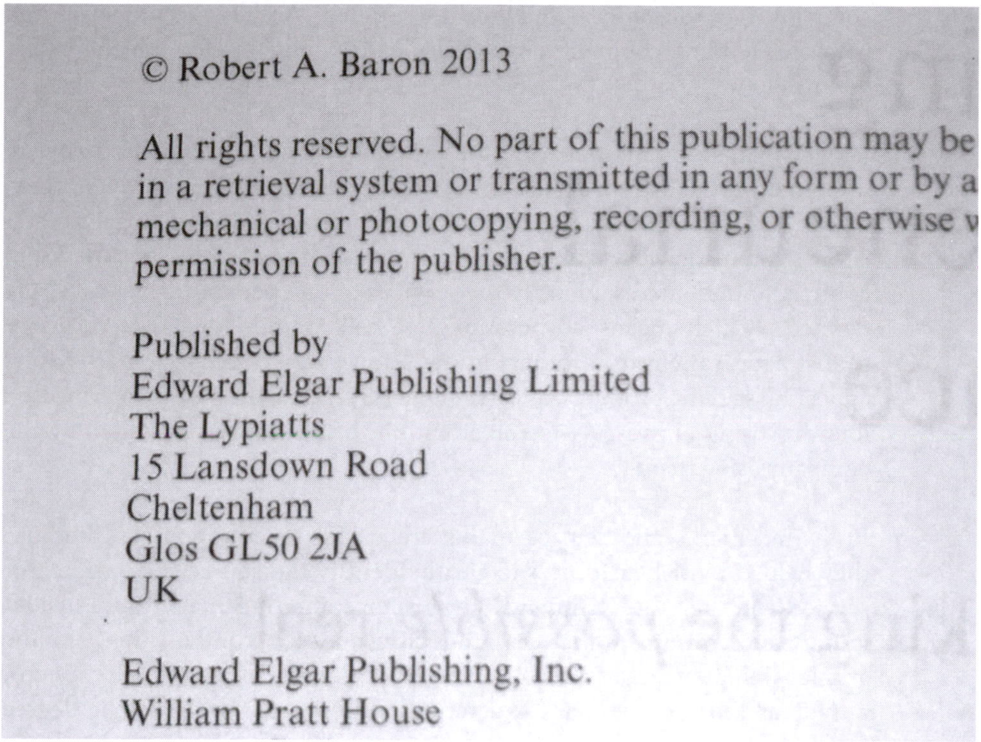

© Robert A. Baron 2013

All rights reserved. No part of this publication may be
in a retrieval system or transmitted in any form or by a
mechanical or photocopying, recording, or otherwise v
permission of the publisher.

Published by
Edward Elgar Publishing Limited
The Lypiatts
15 Lansdown Road
Cheltenham
Glos GL50 2JA
UK

Edward Elgar Publishing, Inc.
William Pratt House

Source: Courtesy of Robert A. Baron.

Figure 9.3 Example of a copyright page in a book

The copyright shown above is for one of the author's previous books. As you can see, the publisher has assigned copyright to the author.

the actual words. That has happened to me: other authors have adopted the same organization I used in some of my books, and they are within their legal rights when they do so. In short, copyright protection is easy to obtain, but—in certain respects—not very powerful.

Trademarks and service marks: Images symbolizing companies or products

Another and very different type of legal protection for intellectual property is a "trademark." This refers to a word, phrase, symbol, or design that identifies the products of one person (which, in legal terms, means an individual, partnership, corporation, or association) and distinguishes these products from those of other individuals (again, companies etc.). Trademarks can be placed on the actual products and identify them as coming from a particular company. For instance, McDonald's Golden Arches, Kentucky Fried Chicken's smiling colonel, or General Electric's blue circle with the letters GE inside.

Service marks do not appear on the products of a company, but rather are used in advertising. For instance, UPS places its service mark on its brown trucks, and Wal-Mart put its name and the phrase "Always Low Prices—Always" on its delivery trucks and signs outside its stores. Service marks, in contrast to trademarks, identify the services of one person (again, as legally defined—which means corporations as well as individuals)—and serve to distinguish them from others in the same industry. Service marks don't appear on specific products, as do trademarks; rather, they are primarily used for advertising purposes—to call attention to the services provided by the company using them.

Both trademarks and service marks are useful to entrepreneurs because they help potential customers to clearly identify the source of a product or service, and therefore its quality. For instance, the trademark "Intel Inside" indicates to consumers that the product in question contains the "genuine article"—chips manufactured by Intel Corporation. However, the value of a trademark or service mark is determined to a large extent by the degree to which it *uniquely* identifies products or services, and distinguishes them from those of other sources. The strongest trademarks are described as "arbitrary": they have nothing directly to do with the products or services offered. For instance, the trademark for Google is arbitrary: the word "Google" has nothing directly to do the services provided by this company. The symbol for Target Corporation is another; this target symbol is widely recognized, but is not directly related to the products and services provided by this chain of discount stores. The symbol for Apple Inc. is another—apples have nothing to do with computers, smart phones, or tablet computers.

Somewhat less strong are trademarks or service marks that are "suggestive" of the products or services they represent. For instance, Igloo Corporation makes a line of coolers, and the word "Igloo" is suggestive of cold. Even less useful are trademarks or service marks that are "descriptive" of the products or services they represent—for instance, General Motors and IBM, since both refer directly to the products the companies provide. Least useful of all are trademarks or service marks that are so well known that they have become "generic"—they are widely used to represent an entire class of products or services, and have virtually become a word in the vocabulary of most persons. A few examples include cellophane, xerox machine, thermos, zipper, kleenex, and escalator. All have lost their value as trademarks because they are now used generically—to refer not to specific products, but to all similar products (e.g., all copy machines are often described as "xerox machines" no matter who manufactured it (Figure 9.4)).

Trademarks and service marks can be obtained in two ways: by actually using the mark or by filing an application with the US Patent and Trademark Office. Actual use involves placing the appropriate symbol—®, TM, SM—on the trademark or service mark. The right to use a particular trademark—for example, the Coca-Cola name—belongs to the first party to register or use the trademark, unless there is a conflict over its use. If there is a conflict, the courts decide who has the rights to use the trademark. As with copyright, the costs of obtaining "official" trademark or service mark registration are modest, but it is required that they be put to actual use on products (trademarks) or advertisements (service marks) or the protection they provide will be lost.

Patents: The right to exclude others from developing or using ideas or inventions

Now we come to what is, perhaps, the most important legal form of protection for ideas or inventions: "patents." There is a great deal of confusion about what patents are and what they provide, so let's begin by making one point crystal clear. Patents grant the patent holder the right to *exclude* others from making, using, or selling an invention. They are granted by the government of a given country, and last for a particular period of time (in the United States, 20 years from the date on which a patent application is first filed). Recall that Thomas Jefferson was against the idea of patents—he felt that ideas could not be the exclusive property of the people who originated them. But in fact there is a strong rationale for the existence of patents: yes, the patent holder has an exclusive right to the invention and its use, but in return, she or he must provide *full disclosure* as to how the invention works. So, it is a kind of bargain: society grants the patent holder exclusive rights to the idea and inventions based on it, but only for a specific period of time, after which anyone can produce, sell, or use it. So, both parties gain: society gains valuable information and patent holders are given the exclusive opportunity to develop their inventions and ideas and profit from them.

Can all inventions be patented? Absolutely not. In the United States, and most other countries, three basic conditions must be met to obtain a patent: the invention must be "useful" (or least, potentially useful); it must be "new"—something that does not already exist; and it must be "non-obvious," meaning that it should not be an obvious extension of what already exists in

Figure 9.4 Trademarks that have become generic lose their value

When a trademark becomes generic—that is, it refers not to the products of one company but to an entire class of products, it loses its protective value. At present, most people refer to all copy machines as "xerox machines" so this trademark has become generic.

the eyes of anyone familiar with the field to which the inventions applies and existing products. If almost anyone working in a given field or industry could come up with the same idea because it is clearly suggested by existing products or services, then it cannot be patented.

A key term relating to these criteria is "prior art," which refers to all information that has been made available to the public in any form before a given date that might be relevant to a patent's claims of originality. If an invention has been described in prior art, a patent on that invention cannot be granted. So, for instance, if an invention has been described in the press, or at a convention, or discussed in a magazine article, it may not eligible for a patent. The reasoning is: why should society grant an exclusive right to someone for an idea or invention that is already known? Does this mean that an invention should be kept totally secret until it is patented? Yes and no. In the United States, the inventor has one year from the time information about an invention is made public to file for a patent. As long as the application is submitted during that period, the invention is still eligible for a patent.

This raises an important question: who determines whether an invention is or is not eligible for a patent? In other words, who decides whether an invention meets the criteria of being new, non-obvious, and useful? The answer is: the patent examiner—the person who evaluates a submitted patent application. Presumably, the patent examiner is someone with considerable knowledge in the field of the invention. For instance, if a patent application involves a new kind of air cleaner (as one of my own patents did), the patent examiner would, presumably, be someone with expertise concerning air cleaners, and existing "prior art" in that field. As a result, she or he can make an informed judgment about whether the invention is really new, useful, and non-obvious. Some very famous individuals have been patent examiners during their careers, for instance, Albert Einstein, and in general the people who hold this position are very careful and knowledgeable. But since the system involves "human judgment" there is lots of room for disagreement or even error. For example, consider the devices shown in Figure 9.5. Are they all useful? Truly new? Truly non-obvious? All actually received patents, but different people might well disagree about the extent to which they meet these basic criteria.

What kind of inventions can be patented? The list includes various kinds of machines, processes (i.e., start with a set of ingredients and through various actions, obtain various products), chemical formulas, software, drugs— virtually any new product. Among the things that can't be patented, however, are a business idea (e.g., the idea of selling fast food by means of a drive-through window).

Source: Patents that are in the public domain.

Figure 9.5 Patents that never resulted in actual products

Believe it or not, all of the devices shown here received patents but they were never developed and sold.

Snake-walking system

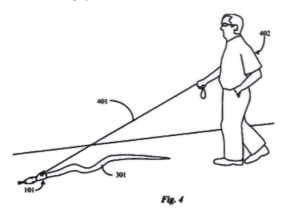

Fig. 4

Kiss shields

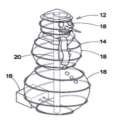

Instant snowman

Apparatus to give yourself a pat on the back

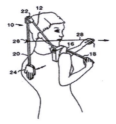

Patents on most inventions qualify for what are known as "utility patents"—patents for new processes, machines, devices, and so on—something in short that *does* something or at least, in which something (e.g., a process) happens. In addition, inventors can also obtain what are known as "design patents"—patents on original designs for manufactured products, for instance, the ornamental design or appearance of a functional item. The design of the classic Coca-Cola bottle is one item eligible for a design patent. While utility patents protect the way an invention works, design patents protect the way it *looks*; they are good for 14 years, rather than 20 years.

Another type of patent is "plant patents," which protect grafted or crossbred plants. For example, Tropicana recently sued Florida orange growers who used experimental varieties of oranges that Tropicana had developed for a particular brand of premium orange juice. Because Tropicana had patented these varieties, it argued that the orange growers should be barred from using these varieties without license from Tropicana. Finally, very recently, the courts have allowed inventors to patent "business methods," such as Amazon. com's "One Click" system, which permits repeat purchasers to make purchases without re-entering basic information about themselves.

The patent process

How are patents obtained? I have been through the process four times, and my overall comment is: *not* very easily. To obtain a patent, an inventor files an application with the US Patent and Trademark Office. The patent examiner assigned to the application then evaluates the invention in terms of the three basic criteria discussed earlier: newness, usefulness, and non-obviousness. The heart of a patent application is the "claims." These are legal statements about what was invented. Inventors and their patent attorneys write these claims very carefully and try to make them as broad as possible for the following reason: a patent precludes other people from duplicating or using *only* those things stated in the claims. For example, a claim in one of my own patents (Patent # 5,360,469) reads as follows: "We claim an apparatus for enhancing the environmental quality of work and living spaces consisting essentially of (1) a portable housing, (2) a high efficiency filter mounted in such housing, (3) a means of generating airflow through the filter, (4) a means for generating sound such that . . . the noise of the motor is eliminated by this sound." The patent examiner accepted these claims, and this gave us very strong protection, since *any* product that included these basic elements (e.g., a filter, a means of generating airflow, and a mechanism for generating sounds that "masked", i.e., reduced the noise of the motor), would violate this patent. If instead the claims had been more specific (e.g., they were restricted to only one kind of filter, one means of generating air flow, etc.), they would have been weaker. The strength of the claims in this product was one reason why my company was able to license this patent and the product it described to a large company who produced it and paid my company a royalty on each unit sold.

Unfortunately, patent is a long and often expensive process: it takes an average of two years to obtain a patent. Further, the costs are substantial: $10 000–$15 000 is not unusual, because patent attorneys are—to be frank—expensive! As a result, and because it takes on average two years for an accepted patent to issue (i.e., to be put in force), many inventors first file another kind of application, described below.

A provisional patent application

To help simplify the process and give inventors with limited resources a chance to protect their inventions, the Patent Act, which had been in effect for several decades, was modified in 1994, so as to allow what is known as a provisional patent application. The application for a provisional patent is a much simpler document, the costs are lower, and it does provide a record of the date on which the inventor had the idea. All that's required is a description of the invention (accompanying drawings are often useful). Detailed claims are not necessary. The provisional patent application is *not* examined to determine if the invention is patentable. However, the date of filing is on record, and that can be important in establishing that the inventor originated the idea, and when that occurred. That is very important because in the United States a patent can only be issued to the *first person to create an invention*. (In other countries, in contrast, the patent goes to the first person to file an application—even if someone else created the invention earlier.) The provisional patent application expires after one year, so the inventor must file a full patent application within that period. The fee for filing a provisional patent application is quite modest—about $130 recently. There are other ways of establishing the date on which the inventor created her or his invention; for example, public disclosure of the idea and invention in a newspaper or magazine. Once that is done, however, the inventor (in the USA) has only one year to file a patent application, after which she or he is no longer eligible for a patent on this invention. To summarize, the advantages offered by a provisional patent include: ease of preparation, lower cost, and—importantly— the right to include the phrase "patent pending" on actual products. This can discourage others from attempting to imitate it, because if a patent is received later, they may be legally obligated to pay damages to the original inventor.

Patents can be very valuable tools for entrepreneurs, but they do involve certain disadvantages. As noted earlier, they can be very expensive ($10 000–15 000 is an average) and defending a patent, once it is received, can involve truly huge costs. Patents also require fees at specific times to keep them active, and these, too, can be substantial. Further, although patents provide important protection for intellectual property, they are not 100 percent effective. Specifically, the fact that patents require full disclosure of the invention and how it works, can make it relatively easy for others to figure out a way to produce a very similar product that does not violate the existing patents; this is known as "inventing around a patent." In essence, inventing around a patent means coming up with a product that accomplishes the same things as the original invention but does not violate the claims in its patent. This is much easier in some industries and with certain kinds of products than for others. For instance, consider Apple's iPad. This was a breakthrough product when it was first introduced, and sales soon exceeded expectations. Needless to say, Apple obtained a number of patents to protect this invention and these prevented other companies from producing the same product. These patents, however, did not stop competitors from developing highly similar products. True, they differ from the iPad in various ways (e.g., they use different operating systems, offer different features), but still they provide serious competition for the iPad. The companies that produce these competing products used their own technical knowledge to "invent around" Apple's patents so that they could quickly offer similar products to consumers (Figure 9.6). In high-tech industries, where progress is often amazingly rapid, this is a common situation, and it is often possible for competing firms to invent around each other's patents.

It's important to note one more thing about patents. Patents are granted by national governments, so an inventor needs to obtain a patent in every country where she or he wants to protect an invention. In other words, there is no such thing as an international patent. This poses a major obstacle for entrepreneurs. Obtaining patents is expensive, and the need to patent in many countries means that these costs are multiplied. Second, failure to patent in a particular country means that it is legal for people in that country to imitate the invention. Since receiving a patent in the United States requires full disclosure about how the invention works, this means that if an inventor receives a US patent but does not seek patents in other countries, inventors and companies in those other countries know how the invention works but are not legally prevented from manufacturing it. Clearly, that's not a very favorable position for an inventor!

Source: Wikimedia: with permission from the photographer, Janto Dreijer, for unrestricted use.

Figure 9.6 Inventing around patents

Although Apple holds many patents on the iPad, it was possible for competing companies to invent around these patents and produce very similar devices of their own, such as the one shown here by Hewlett Packard.

Fortunately, a mechanism that simplifies obtaining patents in many different countries does exist. It is known as the Patent Cooperation Treaty (PCT) and allows inventors to submit a single application with the PCT Office. The application is then filed in a large number of countries, thus establishing a filing date in each of these countries. (Remember: in most countries the first person to file is the one who receives the patent—*not* the first person to come up with an idea for an invention.) The fees for this service can be very large and there is no guarantee that each country will grant a patent. But at least the overall process is somewhat simplified.

In summary, patents can, and often do, offer important legal protection for entrepreneurs: they effectively prevent others from copying or selling the entrepreneurs' invention. The strength of this protection depends heavily on the claims, however, and since patents require full disclosure of how an invention actually works, they also make it possible for potential competitors to invent around the patents. Whether seeking patent protection is or is not a useful strategy for entrepreneurs is therefore a complex issue, and entrepreneurs should *never* assume that paying the costs involved is a good use of their limited financial resources. We'll now examine this issue in more detail below.

When should entrepreneurs seek legal protection for ideas and inventions?

Take another glance at the inventions shown in Figure 9.5. Do you think they would have large markets if they were turned into actual products? Probably not. Yet, all they were granted patents. This calls attention to an important question that entrepreneurs should carefully consider before seeking a patent: "Does the invention have significant economic value?" In other words, is the potential economic value of the invention sufficient to offset the high costs of obtaining a patent? Only if it is should entrepreneurs invest the time, energy, and money required to obtain a patent.

Why, despite this fact, do so many individuals seek to obtain patents on inventions that in all probability will never lead to actual products, and even if they do, will not generate economic value (e.g., profits)? Perhaps because, consistent with and parallel to recent research on entrepreneurial "passion" (e.g., Cardon et al., 2009), they strongly identify themselves as inventors. They enjoy the role of coming up with something new, and don't really care if their ideas turn into anything real, or generate economic gains. Are such persons really entrepreneurs? They don't seem to meet the definition offered in Chapter 1, since they don't really care about converting their ideas into something real, useful, and better than what currently exists. They are certainly creative persons, but entrepreneurship requires more than formulating ideas—it also involves actively seeking to develop them. For this reason, pure "inventors" do not seem to qualify as being entrepreneurs. (For a description of what can sometimes happen to an entrepreneur even if she or has a patent on an invention, please see "The Entrepreneurial Quest" case study below.)

CASE STUDY

The Entrepreneurial Quest

Does a patent always protect an inventor's intellectual property? Often, but not always . . .

One night in 1953, Robert Kearns, a mechanical engineer, was struck in the left eye by a champagne cork. This accident left him blind in that eye, but years later it served as the foundation for a useful invention—the intermittent windshield wiper (Figure 9.7) As Kearns describes it, he was driving in a light rain, and found that the constant movement of the wiper blades interfered with his vision. This gave him the idea of intermittent windshield wipers—wipers that would operate only after an interval set by the driver. Kearns felt that this would imitate the human eye, which blinks every few seconds, rather than all the time.

In true entrepreneurial fashion, Kearns followed up on his idea and submitted patent applications for his invention. He received several patents and then demonstrated his invention to major automobile companies. His plan was to license his invention to them and receive a royalty on each one the companies installed in their cars. These giant auto-

Source: US Patent and Trademark Office; Patent # 3,351,836.

Figure 9.7 One patent that was ignored by large companies

Although the inventor of the intermittent windshield wiper (Robert Kearns) patented his product, large automobile companies ignored this fact and added it to their cars without obtaining his permission or paying him royalties. Kearns sued these giant companies and won—but only after many years of effort and expense. So, do patents provide total protection for inventions? Not always.

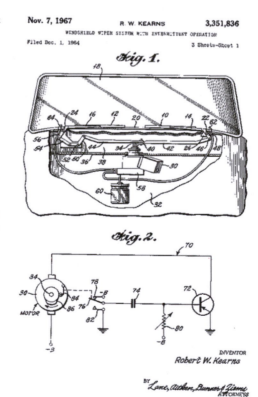

CASE STUDY *(continued)*

mobile companies declined to enter into agreements with him but—much to Kearns' surprise—began using his invention anyway. In 1978, Kearns filed a suit against Ford for patent infringement, and then in 1982 he filed a similar suit against Chrysler Corp. Beginning in 1990, he won these and other lawsuits, and ultimately received a total of more than $30 million from Ford, Chrysler, and other companies that were found by the courts to have violated his patents.

Sadly, though, these victories did not come quickly or easily. The large companies named in his suit had many attorneys on their payroll, and did everything they could to defend themselves against Kearns' legal actions. As a result, he had to spend a major portion of his time—and life—pursuing this battle, which he waged against large auto manufacturers outside the United States as well as within it. In addition, most of the damages he won went for legal fees, so when he died in February 2005, he did not leave behind a large personal estate. As Kearns puts it, however, winning cash awards was not his major goal. In his words: "the goal was not the magnitude of the money. What I saw (as) my role was to defend the patent system. If I don't go further, there really isn't a patent system."

It's hard to imagine a more dramatic illustration of the fact that patents do *not* provide total protection of intellectual property. If they are held by an individual with limited means, large companies that choose to violate them can do so for years, and reap huge profits in the process. Then, even if courts rule that they have acted illegally, the costs and fines imposed can still be far less than the profits they have generated by violating an existing patent. The overall lesson is clear: patents do provide important protection of intellectual property, but they are only as strong as their claims, and the will and means of the persons who hold them to protect their exclusive rights to their inventions.

Other means of protecting the products of your creativity: Trade secrets and complementary assets

Are copyrights, trademarks, and patents the only ways of protecting creations of the human mind—intellectual property? The answer may surprise you: definitely not. Although patent attorneys might answer differently, there are other effective ways of protecting inventions and other "products of the human mind" (or, as I prefer to say, "other products of human creativity and ingenuity"). These additional forms of protection are based primarily on business practices and strategies, and can be highly effective, although, of course, far from perfect. Two of the most important of these are "trade secrets" and what are known as "complementary assets."

Trade secrets: Gaining protection by keeping information private

Coca-Cola is, perhaps, the most famous soft drink in the world. As a result, there are many imitators of this product but, at least according to the Coca-Cola company, none of them equal the taste of "Coke" itself. Why? Because Coca-Cola keeps the formula for Coke secret. In fact, only a few top executives have access to it. Similarly, have you ever used WD-40, an all purpose lubricant that frees rusted parts, removes adhesives, cleans tools and parts? The formula for WD-40 is another trade secret, and has been kept locked in a bank vault since 1953, when it was first invented. So, once again, although there are many imitators, none completely match the properties of WD-40. Many other products are protected by trade secrets—the formula for Mrs. Fields' chocolate chip cookies, Kentucky Fried Chicken's "secret seasonings," and Krispy-Kreme Donuts, to name just a few (Figure 9.8).

Control of complementary assets: Making it difficult for customers to benefit from potentially competing products

At the turn of the twentieth century, it was not clear that gasoline-powered automobiles would become the "dominant design"—the approach adopted by all manufacturers. In fact, I played in an electric car when I was a boy, because it was parked in my Aunt's garage. When I asked what it was, she told me it was something used in the past but had turned out to be impractical. In later years, I came to understand that the problem was that these first electric cars could travel only 20 miles before they had to be re-charged. Moreover—and this is crucial—there were very few places to re-charge them. In contrast, automobiles using gasoline could travel long distances on a single tank of gas, and stations selling gasoline quickly mushroomed. In addition, drivers could take cans of gasoline with them, just in case they ran short of fuel while on the road. Together, this combination of factors doomed early electric cars such as the one shown in Figure 9.9, and they quickly disappeared from the roads.

This illustrates another way of protecting inventions: "complementary assets." These involve means that make it possible and convenient for customers to use a product. Gasoline-powered cars quickly developed such means—thousands of service stations selling this fuel. Electric cars did not, so customers quickly abandoned them for the more practical product. Interestingly, the same problem exists for the new generation of electric cars being developed and sold today (e.g., by Tesla Motors). At present, there are few places to re-charge such vehicles, although they

Source: Wikimedia: with permission for unrestricted use by the photographer, Zoha.Nve.

Figure 9.8 Trade secrets—another way of protecting inventions

Many products, such as that shown here, are protected not by patents, but by trade secrets—keeping information necessary to produce them confidential.

Source: Wikimedia: no known illustrator.

Figure 9.9 An early electric car

Electric cars were manufactured and sold by many companies in the early twentieth century. The one shown here was produced by the Baker Electric Company from 1912 to 1915. Electric vehicles lost out to gasoline-powered ones because they had very limited range (e.g., 20–30 miles), and there were very few places to re-charge them. In short, they lacked *complementary assets*. Gasoline-powered cars, in contrast, had these assets. Drivers could re-fuel them in many places and could also carry spare fuel with them on road trips.

are increasing, and some recent models can be fully re-charged in only 25 minutes. Also, the new electric cars can travel up to 300 miles on a single charge and receive high ratings from automobile experts. Still, until sufficient complementary assets exist—that is, until potential customers can re-charge their vehicles with ease and in many locations—they face major obstacles. In addition, these cars are very expensive—much more expensive than gasoline-powered vehicles, or hybrids that use both electric motors and gasoline-powered engines. Until the price drops to the point at which the benefits of using electricity as a fuel offset these costs, sales will probably remain modest. However, it is a mistake to underestimate the capabilities of companies like Tesla Motors and Elon Musk, its founder, so stay tuned for further developments: if the price of gasoline continues to rise, the price of all-electric vehicles decreases, and the number of places where they can be re-fueled increases, this situation may well change radically.

In sum, in some situations, other means of protecting inventions or other original works aside from those provided by the legal system (trademarks, copyrights, patents) can be very useful, and should be carefully considered by entrepreneurs.

Franchising: A new venture "in a box"?

In every corner of the USA—and increasingly around the world—many highways and commercial avenues are lined with businesses whose names almost everyone recognizes: McDonald's, H&R Block, Subway, Curves Fitness Centers, Domino's Pizza. Why are these businesses so common? Basically, because they have adopted a business model based on franchising. Franchising is a system in which legally independent business owners (franchisees) pay fees and royalties to a parent company (the franchisor) in return for the right to use its trademark, sell its products or services, and, in many cases, to use the business model and system it has developed. In other words, they pay to have a "business in a box," one they can open without having to go through all the steps in the entrepreneurial process. The franchisor often constructs the building in which the business is located, provides necessary equipment, supplies whatever raw materials or information is required, and often, extensive training to help the franchisees run their businesses effectively.

Franchising is tremendously popular: in the United States alone there are more than 3000 franchisors, which together operate more than 600 000 separate outlets (stores, restaurants, hotels, etc.). Further, the number is increasing rapidly: more than 300 new franchisors start each year, offering prospective franchisees everything from house-cleaning and pet care, through ready-to-eat meals and plumbing services—essentially anything you can imagine. In essence, franchising is a form of business organization in which a company that already has a product or service (the franchisor) licenses these products, services, trademarks, and methods of doing business to independent franchisees who actually operate the outlets for the company's products. We'll now take a closer look at the nature of franchising and both the benefits and costs it involves.

Types of franchising

One type of franchising "trade name franchising," involves giving franchisees the right to use or sell the franchisor's products and use its trade name (or trademark) in their business. In essence, the franchisee purchases the right to become identified with the franchisor's trade name. For instance, an automobile dealer becomes associated with the manufacturer of the automobiles it sells to customers—GM, Honda, Mercedes, Ford.

The second type of franchising, known as "business format franchising," involves providing the franchisee with a complete business system—a trademarked name, the products or services to be sold, the buildings in which the business will be operated, a marketing strategy, methods of actually operating the business, and assistance in actually running the business. This is the most rapidly growing type of franchising, and it is found in many different industries ranging from auto rentals to fast food. For their initial investments (which can be substantial—for example, an initial payment of $50 000 plus other costs that bring the total to over $800 000 for opening a new McDonald's). What do they receive for their investments? Important benefits; but they also experience major costs too.

The benefits and costs of becoming a franchisee

Although franchising is amazingly popular, it actually offers a mixed bag of benefits and costs for individuals who decide to pursue it. A summary of these pluses and minuses is provided below.

Becoming a franchisee: Its benefits

An underlying benefit to franchisees is that they benefit from the business model developed by the franchisor, who has, perhaps, already put this model into use hundreds or even thousands of time. Thus, franchisees can be quite certain that it works: if they follow the plan and operating procedures offered by the franchisors, the chances of success are very high. In addition, the franchisor offers specific benefits including: training and support for franchisees, standardized products and services, national advertising, buying power (the franchisors can buy in bulk and obtain lower prices), financial assistance such as helping franchisees form relationships with banks, and careful selection of locations for the business—ones where competitors are scarce or far away, and where customer traffic is high. The overall result is that if the franchisees follow these methods and work hard at implementing them, their likelihood of success is far greater than those of individuals who start businesses on their own (e.g., Bates, 1994).

Becoming a franchisee: Important costs

The benefits described are so appealing that many people decide to follow this route to owning their own business. However, life rarely offers easy decisions about important issues, so it's important for would-be franchisees to consider these important costs: franchise fees can be substantial, and then, once the business is operating, franchisees must pay royalties—a share of their profits—to the franchisor; the franchisor insists on standardization—franchisees can only sell products or provide services approved by the franchisor—and they definitely *can't* "do it their way"; market saturation may exist—successful franchisors may have so many outlets that they sometimes compete with each other; this is increasingly true because the best locations may already be taken. In sum, franchising, as a route to business ownership, offers a mixture of potential benefits and drawbacks.

Is franchising entrepreneurship? And is it for you?

The question shown in the heading above has sparked continuing debate: on one side are persons who believe that since franchising allows franchisees to open their own business it is at least entrepreneurial in nature; on the other, however, are persons who argue that since franchisees must follow the rules and business models of the franchisor, these businesses are not really independent in the way that businesses started in the traditional, individual way are independent. Further, as defined throughout this book, entrepreneurship involves coming up with an idea suggesting a business opportunity, and then taking actions to develop this opportunity. Franchisees, in contrast, use an idea and business model developed by the franchisor. In that sense, they are not entrepreneurs.

Yet, having said that, it's important to note that some franchisees are so successful that they open several outlets, and in a sense, operate a business of their own to oversee them. In this way, they attain at least some control over their own business practices. Further, many franchisees use the experience of operating a franchise to gain experience, and then move on to starting their own new ventures, which, if successful, may become franchisors themselves! In fact, this is how many large franchisors got started in the first place.

So, taking all these factors into account, is franchising for you? Or would you prefer to run your own business, make your own mistakes, and take the risks of learning as you go? Only each individual can answer this question, and to a large extent, it depends on the relative weights you place on (1) receiving expert help, becoming part of a going concern, and working with a tried and true business model, or (2) the personal freedom to run your business as you choose, and build it on your own. In short, the decision to become a franchisee is not purely an economic one, but rather one involving personal goals and preferences. Finally, it's also important to keep in the mind the fact that franchisees can, at least under certain circumstances (e.g., if they have been successful), surrender their franchise and start their own business. In short, it is *not* true that "once a franchisee always a franchisee." But if you decide to take the plunge and become a franchisee, it's important to consider these questions carefully. (1) What is the initial franchise fee? What other money will you be asked to provide (e.g., for construction costs, advertising, equipment)? What are the continuing royalty payments? Advertising fees? Other fees? (2) Is the franchisor growing rapidly? If not, stay away (Shane et al., 2010). What proportion of the outlets does the franchisor own? If this is high, it may be a sign that ultimately, the franchisor wants to own them all—and will rescind their franchise under conditions unfavorable to the franchisee—conditions that may have been specified in the original franchise agreement.

In sum, only move ahead if the answers to these and related questions are positive. The costs of becoming a franchisee—not just financial, but in terms of time and effort, too—are substantial. So the keyword for potential franchisees then, should be: caution!

THE EFFECTIVE ENTREPRENEUR

Ideas for new products or services originate in the minds of individuals who, if they actively pursue their development, become entrepreneurs. They would like to protect their ideas and inventions, so that *they*, not others, benefit from them. How can they accomplish this goal? And what factors should they consider? The points listed below may help you to resolve these important issues:

- Think carefully before signing non-disclosure or non-compete documents, and read them carefully, because they can greatly restrict your legal right to start a new venture.
- Protection for "products of the human mind" exists in several different forms and it's important to seek the one that is most appropriate for your ideas, inventions, and business.

➡

←

- One form of legal intellectual property protection is provided by copyright. A copyright protects the tangible expression of words, music, art, or of other creative products. But remember: they protect only the *tangible* expression of these items—*not* the ideas themselves, so it's important to write down, record, or otherwise give these creations tangible form.
- Another form of legal protection is provided by trademarks or service marks. These are symbols or images of a particular company that can be placed on products (trademarks) or displayed in advertisements, signs, and other forms (service marks). These symbols or images are protected in that no one else can legally use them. Such symbols or images are often important in establishing the identity of a company, so they are worth developing—and protecting.
- Patents are, in some ways, the most important form of legal protection of intellectual property. They grant inventors the exclusive right to their inventions for a specific period of time. But the inventors must disclose how their inventions work in their patent application. This means that at a later time (after the patent expires) anyone can produce, use, or sell the invention—or invent something similar that does not violate the existing patent. Patents are expensive to obtain, so think carefully about whether your invention has real potential to generate economic value. If it does not, it's probably not worth the time, effort, and expense involved in obtaining a patent.
- Provisional patent applications provide some protection for inventions, but expire after one year unless they are followed by a formal patent application. They do protect the date at which the invention originated, and that can be an important benefit.
- Other ways of protecting your invention involve trade secrets and complementary assets. If your invention involves some procedure, knowledge or "secret" formula not readily available to others you should work hard to keep it secret. Complementary assets are harder to obtain, and can usually only be obtained by large, successful companies, or entire industries that want to keep competitors from succeeding. So, it is unlikely that entrepreneurs can rely on complementary assets to protect their inventions. Franchising is a very popular way of attaining business ownership, but it offers a very mixed picture of benefits and costs. So, don't start down this road until you have considered these carefully—and especially have considered the strength and success of the franchisor.

SUMMARY OF KEY POINTS

1 Individuals considering the possibility of starting their own ventures assume that is their right to do so. However, if they have signed a noncompete agreement with their employer they may be barred from doing so—from starting a new company that will compete with the employer—for a specific period of time, or within a specific geographic area.

2 Sometimes, when seeking financial support from investors, entrepreneurs

must divulge information about their inventions. Before doing so, they should ask the persons who will receive such information for a non-disclosure agreement, which prevents them from sharing the information with a third party, and from using it themselves.

3 The law offers several means of protecting intellectual property—legally defined as products of the human mind. These include copyrights—which protect only if they are expressed in tangible expressions of human creativity, for example, written words, a musical score, and so on. They do *not* protect the ideas behind these expressions themselves.

4 Intellectual property can also be protected by trademarks or service marks—symbols or images representing a company and its products—for instance, the symbol shown on all Target stores, or the word "Tiffany" stamped on jewelry.

5 Perhaps the most important form of protection for intellectual property is patents, which grant the patent holder exclusive use of an invention for a specific period (e.g., 20 years). To obtain a patent, however, inventors must reveal the full nature of their invention so that after the patent expires, anyone can produce and sell it. Obtaining a patent is expensive, but entrepreneurs can begin with a provisional patent protection, which protects their inventions for one year.

6 Intellectual property can also be protected by trade secrets—keeping the ingredients or processes used in manufacturing a product confidential, or through control of complementary assets—means of delivering the product to consumers so that they can actually use it (e.g., places for all-electric cars to re-charge).

7 Franchising is a system in which legally independent business owners (franchisees) pay fees and royalties to a parent company (the franchisor) in return for the right to use its trademark, sell its products or services, and, in many cases, to use the business model and system it has developed. Although franchisees start businesses, it is unclear whether they are acting as entrepreneurs. There are both advantages and disadvantages in becoming a franchisee, so individuals should consider these carefully before adopting this role.

REFERENCES

Bates, T. (1994), "A comparison of franchise and independent small business survival rates", *Small Business Economics*, **7**, 1–12.

Cardon, M.S., J. Wincent, J. Singh and M. Drnovsek (2009), "The nature and experience of entrepreneurial passion," *Academy of Management Review*, **34**(3), 511–32.

Shane, S., V. Shankar and A. Aravindakshan (2010), "The effects of new franchisor partnering strategies on franchise system size," *Management Science*, **52**(5), 773–87.

10

Managing a new venture: What entrepreneurs should know to do it well

> *The best executive is the one who has sense enough to pick good people to do what he wants done, and the self-restraint to keep from meddling with them while they do it.*
> (Theodore Roosevelt, 1858–1919, 26th US President)

> *The key to successful leadership is influence, not authority.*
> (Kenneth H. Blanchard, motivational speaker)

Imagine that a survey was conducted with entrepreneurs who have recently launched a new venture, and it included the following questions: "Do you find the role of manager appealing—being someone who performs such tasks as motivating employees, assessing their performance, and—if necessary—firing them?" And "Do you want to be a leader—someone who either tells other people what to do, or inspires them to do it?" Almost certainly, a large proportion of the entrepreneurs would answer "No" to the first question—they do *not* want to be managers; and many (although in this case, perhaps, not so large a majority) would answer "No" to the second question too—although they may want to inspire others, many don't crave leadership in the way that politicians or generals do. As we noted in Chapter 8, entrepreneurs express passion for entrepreneurship and for being an entrepreneur, but in general, these powerful feelings involve their attraction to three major roles: "inventor," "founder," and "developer" (someone who helps "grow" a new venture). Neither the role of "manager" nor the role of "leader" are included on this list.

Yet, it is clear that although they may not specifically seek these roles, entrepreneurs must often fill them. Once a new venture has been launched, it must, like any other business, be managed effectively, and this involves everything from hiring and supervising employees, through keeping accurate financial records. Further, as founders of the new venture, entrepreneurs must, to some degree, serve as leaders; they must set the goals, coordinate efforts and activities to reach them, and exert influence, not simply over employees but on others too—customers, suppliers, and investors, to name just a few. So whether they like it or not, entrepreneurs are literally thrust into roles that were not, perhaps, ones they desired, or would have chosen.

These facts (and they are indeed facts of life for entrepreneurs) imply that running a new venture successfully requires entrepreneurs to do more than come up with ideas for something new and better, decide whether to pursue them, and if they do, acquire the resources necessary to develop them. In addition—and certainly after the new venture has been launched and is operating—they must both "manage" and "lead" it effectively.

In this chapter, we'll focus on the information and skills entrepreneurs need to meet these requirements—to be effective managers and leaders. Many different factors are involved, so it would be impossible to examine all of them here. Instead, we'll focus on three that are clearly among the most important: motivation, leading and influencing others, and decision-making Specifically, we'll proceed as follows. First, we'll examine motivation—its basic nature and how knowledge about it can be used by entrepreneurs to increase employees' efforts to do their best work. As part of this discussion, we'll also consider entrepreneurs' motives—why they chose this challenging role and activity and what they hope to gain from pursuing it. Next, we'll turn to leadership, again examining its basic nature, and then to the related question of how entrepreneurs can effectively exert influence over others. It makes sense to examine these topics together, since a key aspect of leadership is, in fact, influencing others—for instance, somehow getting them accept and work towards shared goals. Finally, we'll turn to decision-making—a key task entrepreneurs must perform, and one that ultimately can strongly influence the success or failure, of their new ventures.

Motivating employees—and understanding your own motives

One key task performed by managers—and by entrepreneurs—is motivating others. Most entrepreneurs are themselves incredibly high on this dimension: their motivation to make their new venture a success is often off the charts! But what, precisely, *is* motivation, and why is some basic knowledge of this concept useful to entrepreneurs?

The answer to the first question lies in the fact that people often engage in actions for which there appears to be no immediate or obvious cause. This is not necessarily true for entrepreneurs, because the reasons why they engage in this activity are often clear—although, as we'll soon see, these reasons may be more complex than is often assumed. In many other situations, however, the causes behind individuals' behavior are much harder to identify. For instance, Diana Nyad, 64 years old, has attempted to swim from Cuba to Florida four times. She failed on the first attempts, but continues to try. Why? What drives her to undertake such a dangerous task? There is no price for accomplishing it, yet she is willing to risk her life to reach this personal goal. Similarly, why do rock climbers attempt to scale sheer walls—ones from which a fall would result in serious injury or even death? And why do stamp collectors travel great distances, and great expense, to find a particular stamp that will let them complete a part of their collection (Figure 10.1).

In these instances, a basic question arises: *why*? Why do the people involved engage in activities that, to many others, seem puzzling? The answer offered by psychologists and others who investigate human behavior is that such actions stem from "motivation." Basically, this term refers to internal processes (cognitive, emotional, biological) that can't be directly observed, but that still exert powerful effects on what individuals think, plan, and do. Since these internal processes can't be directly seen, their presence must be *inferred* from overt actions. Rock climbers, for instance, may have a strong motive to attain high levels of stimulation. They enjoy the adrenalin "rush" that they get from their climbing and the danger it involves. Diana Nyad may be strongly motivated by the desire to do something no one else has done. Similarly, consider entrepreneurs, who often work 12 or 14 hours day, and only stop when

Source: Wikimedia: permission granted by the photographer, Stephen W. Wanju.

Figure 10.1 Motivation: its role in behavior

How can behavior such as travelling long distances at great expense to obtain a stamp for a collection be explained? Motivation, internal processes that energize, guide, and direct behavior provides an answer.

they absolutely must eat or sleep. These actions must stem from powerful motives that underlie them—but what are they? This is a complex question, and one we'll soon return to.

Whatever the origins of specific motives, once motivation is engaged, it has three crucial effects: (1) it provides the "energy" for overt actions, (2) it guides these actions, and (3) it causes them to persist until the motive is met or fulfilled. Consider again stamp collectors intent on finding the stamps they need to complete their collections. They actively seek the stamps they want, and often expend considerable energy—and money!—in doing so. These searches are directed: the collectors focus their efforts on places where the stamp is likely to be found—stamp shows, ads in magazines for stamp collectors. And their searches persist—they continue until the needed stamps are found.

The same basic principles apply to entrepreneurs. Their behavior too is energized, guided, and maintained by their motivation. But what goals do they seek to attain? Success? Fame? Wealth? Or, perhaps something else—independence or autonomy, to be their own "boss" and shape their own destinies? Whatever the entrepreneurs' basic motives (and several might be operating simultaneously), they lead them to exert energy and effort, to focus on actions that will help them reach these goals and to persist in these efforts for months, or even years. To recap briefly, motivation often plays a key role in human behavior and helps us understand—and explain—actions for which there are no obvious external causes.

Now that we have described the basic nature of motivation, we'll turn to two contrasting views about how it operates—views that suggest ways in which entrepreneurs can accomplish one of the key tasks involved in managing their new ventures: motivating employees to work—that is, to expend maximum effort to reach the new venture's goals.

The basic nature of human motivation

Assuming that motivation is indeed an important factor in all human behavior, a key question arises: what are its foundations? In other words, what factors lead individuals to have various motives? Decades of systematic research on this issue indicate, as you might guess, that motivation springs from several different sources. At the most basic level, biological factors play a role. For instance, hunger and thirst reflect basic bodily requirements, and everyone knows from personal experience that they can powerfully energize, direct, and maintain behavior. More important for our present discussion, however, are two other views of the foundations of motivation. Both relate not to biological factors, but to cognition—a topic we considered in detail in Chapter 2. Although these two aspects of motivation are distinct, each has important implications for ways in which entrepreneurs can increase their employees' motivation, and hence the success of their new ventures.

Expectancy theory: The "pull" of future events

In many instances, our current behavior is determined not by biological needs, but by our thoughts. Basically, our actions *now* are influenced by our thoughts about future events and outcomes. This basic reasoning underlies "expectancy theory," a highly influential view of human motivation.

According to this perspective, three factors play key roles in human motivation, and especially in motivation to work hard and expend effort on various tasks. The first is "expectancy," the belief that effort will result in improved performance. This is not always true; for instance, no matter how hard a young male athlete who is only 5'6" tall tries, it is unlikely that he will ever be able to become a professional basketball player. The second is "instrumentality," the belief that improved performance on key tasks will lead to desired rewards, whatever these happen to be. Again, this factor is not always present. In many organizations, the link between performance and raises or promotions is fuzzy at best. The third factor, "valence" refers to the value individuals place on these rewards. The theory further proposes that motivation is a multiplicative function of all three factors: expectancy × instrumentality × valence. The upshot is that people will work hardest and most persistently on various tasks when they believe that expending effort will improve performance, that enhanced performance will lead to desired outcomes, and that these outcomes themselves are ones they truly want.

The broad outlines of expectancy theory have been verified by a large body of research (e.g., Steers et al., 2004; Lambright, 2010), so it helps to explain why individuals—including entrepreneurs—sometimes invest countless hours of hard and often tedious work on specific tasks. Overall, expectancy theory suggests that they are willing to do so because they believe that these actions will help them to improve their performance, and that, in turn, will help them obtain the rewards or goals they desire. A key implication of this theory is that entrepreneurs, who often invest almost limitless time and energy in their new ventures, are doing so because they seek certain outcomes. We'll examine these outcomes, which are very varied in scope, in detail in a later section, but here I want to emphasize the "future-driven" approach of this perspective on human motivation.

Goal-setting: The pull of specific objectives

Another, and in some ways, related theory of motivation is known as "goal-setting theory." This theory, too, emphasizes cognitive factors but in this framework the focus is more directly on concrete goals (e.g., Locke and Latham, 2002). According to this perspective, individuals identify various goals (ones they choose themselves or ones assigned to them by, for instance, a supervisor, teacher, or entrepreneur). They then direct their effort and actions toward reaching these goals. A vast amount of research indicates that setting certain kinds of goals is, perhaps, the best single means for generating high levels of effort and persistence, and hence, for improving performance on a wide range of tasks. However, additional evidence indicates that goal-setting works best under certain conditions. It is most effective in boosting performance when the goals set are highly "specific"—people know just what they are trying to accomplish, the goals are "challenging"—meeting them requires considerable effort, but they are also perceived as "attainable"—people believe they can actually reach them. Finally, goal-setting is most successful when individuals receive feedback on their progress toward meeting the goals and when they are truly and deeply committed to reaching them. This last point is quite important; if goals are set by someone else and the people who are expected to meet these goals aren't committed to doing so, then goal-setting can be totally ineffective, and may even backfire, reducing rather than enhancing motivation. When the conditions described above are met though, goal-setting is a highly effective way of increasing motivation and performance (e.g., Locke and Latham, 2002). (An overview of both expectancy theory and goal-setting theory is provided in Figure 10.2.)

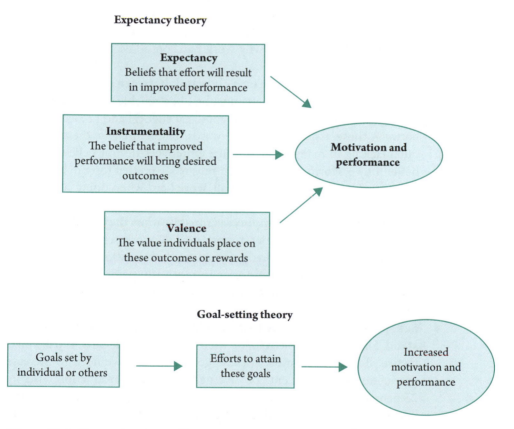

Figure 10.2 Two major views of human motivation: expectancy theory and goal-setting theory

Both of these theories emphasize the importance of cognitive factors—individuals' thoughts about future events or outcomes. Expectancy theory suggests that motivation (and performance) is a function of expectancy, instrumentality, and valence. Goal-setting theory, in contrast, focuses directly on goals and efforts to obtain them.

Putting these perspectives to use: Techniques for motivating employees

Now that we have described the basic nature of motivation and two important explanations for how it arises, we'll turn to the practical and important question of how entrepreneurs can use this knowledge to motivate their employees and others. Below is a summary of the practical implications of these views:

- **It is crucial to establish a clear link between effort and performance**. This means that it is important to make sure that employees have the resources (e.g., equipment), knowledge, and skills needed to perform key tasks. If any of these are lacking, they cannot achieve high levels of performance no matter how hard they work, and this can undermine their motivation. After all, why work hard on a task you can't possibly accomplish? Would you?
- **It is also crucial that there be a clear link between performance and rewards**. In other words, there must be (1) a reliable and valid means of assessing performance (is it poor, good, excellent?) and (2) a strong link between these assessments and rewards. Unfortunately, these links are often lacking in many organizations: employees do not believe that the better they perform, the larger their rewards. And that too can be fatal for motivation and effort. Why, after all, work hard when doing so won't be recognized or rewarded?
- **The rewards offered to employees must be ones they really want**. For instance, many people prefer a more flexible work schedule to a small raise; and others prefer more "personal days" or vacation to higher wages or even a promotion. A key factor in motivating employees then is to assure that the rewards offered for excellent performance match the ones they desire.
- **Set specific goals—ones that are clear and that employees understand**. Simply telling them to "do their best" or "work hard" is truly ineffective. Rather, goals more specific goals such as "We need to increase production by 10 percent" or "We need to reduce production costs by 25 percent" are much more effective. When such goals exist, individuals know what they are "shooting for" and can focus their effort and energies on obtaining them.
- **Never set goals that are unrealistically high**. For instance, telling employees who are already working hard that "We must double output this week," or "We have to reduce accidents to zero" are ineffective because individuals realize that they can't be reached—at least, not within the time frame suggested.

- **Provide feedback to employees on their work and performance**. In many organizations, feedback is provided only once a year, thus leaving employees largely in the dark about how well they are doing. Unless individuals are internally motivated (e.g., they want to do an excellent job even if the rewards for doing so are small), these conditions can undermine their motivation.

Entrepreneurs wishing to be effective managers in terms of motivating their employees should pay very careful attention to these points. If they don't, they may find themselves facing a workforce that does not share their own high level of motivation, and that performs well below expectations. Enhancing motivation, in short, is a key task for entrepreneurs, and one they should *never* overlook while trying to build their new ventures and attain success.

Entrepreneurial motivation: Why entrepreneurs make the journey

At first glance, the decision to become an entrepreneur and attempt to convert dreams into reality is somewhat puzzling. Many individuals who become entrepreneurs are employed by large organizations that provide them with a steady source of income, health insurance, and many other benefits. So, why do entrepreneurs decide to give up these conditions for what many realize are the uncertainties involved in starting their own business? In the past, it was widely assumed that they do so primarily because they are seeking financial rewards. But more recent research indicates that although this may be true for some entrepreneurs, it is far from the only motive behind their decision to "take the plunge." For example, some individuals become entrepreneurs out of necessity: they are downsized by their employers, or dismissed when companies they work for decide to move offshore. To make matters worse, they may be too young to retire. But on closer scrutiny it has become obvious that these are only two of the many motives that underlie the decision to become an entrepreneur.

In an influential paper, Rindova et al. (2009) suggest that many individuals choose to become entrepreneurs despite the risks involved, because they are seeking what these authors describe as "emancipation"—release from conditions that restrict their personal freedom or autonomy. In other words, they are seeking greater autonomy and independence—they want to take charge of their own lives and engage in the activities they choose, rather than remain in jobs they don't like, don't perceive to be meaningful, and in which their personal freedom is greatly restricted.

A more general way to express this view is to note that many entrepreneurs start new ventures because they are seeking "self-realization." They want to grow as individuals, motivate others, fulfill personal visions and dreams, gain independence, and do work they view as meaningful (e.g., Baron, 2010). Do these motives really underlie the decision to become an entrepreneur? Growing evidence indicates that they do. For example, a study conducted by Cassar (2007) examined data from a large national survey of entrepreneurs and prospective (nascent) entrepreneurs (the PSED). These data, which were collected from more than 64 000 people, included several motives that could, potentially, serve as a basis for entrepreneurship. Results were clear: the desire for independence was actually stronger than the desire for financial success among both prospective and actual entrepreneurs. Still another motive, the desire for recognition, which is closely related to motivation for achievement, was also fairly high in the ratings. A recent review of research designed to examine entrepreneurs' motivation (Franklin, 2013), indicated that this pattern has been observed in many separate studies involving thousands of entrepreneurs: overall, the entrepreneurs rated the desire for self-realization as higher than the desire for financial gains. Additional research indicates that such motives may have stronger effects on entrepreneurs' behavior than purely financial ones (e.g., Baron et al., 2013).

It's important to add that, in addition, some persons become entrepreneurs because they want to "do good"—to enhance human well-being, or at least, the well-being of people in their own communities, regions, or countries. Such persons are often described as being "social entrepreneurs," and although they realize that they must make a profit to stay in business and to continue their efforts to improve human welfare, they are *not* focused on this goal (Figure 10.3).

Before concluding this discussion, it's important to mention one additional point: individual motives, characteristics, and preferences are certainly important in the decision to become an entrepreneur, but they are definitely *not* the entire story. As we noted in Chapter 1, external (i.e., societal, social, economic) factors also often play a role. For instance, individuals are more likely to vigorously pursue entrepreneurial actions when (1) financial markets are favorable so that access to financial resources is readily available, (2) when government policies favor the founding and operation of new ventures (e.g., through favorable tax policies; Tung et al., 2007), and (3) when markets for specific new products or services are growing rapidly (Shane, 2008). These factors, too, are important because individuals do not choose to pursue their dreams through entrepreneurial activity in isolation

Source: Photo courtesy of Stovetec, Inc.

Figure 10.3 Social entrepreneurs: a focus on helping others, not financial gains

Contrary to the view that entrepreneurs primarily seek financial gains, many are more highly motivated by other goals—for instance, achieving autonomy or doing meaningful work. Social entrepreneurs, in fact, appear to be primarily motivated by the desire to help others. Shown here is a stove designed by social entrepreneurs that uses much less fuel, pollutes much less, and is much safer to use than the fuel-burning stoves that are currently used by more than 1.5 billion people every day to cook their food and stay warm.

from social and economic conditions in which they live. So, they too must be included in efforts to understand entrepreneurs' motivation.

Leading and exerting influence

As suggested in the introduction to this chapter, many entrepreneurs do not specifically seek the role of "leader." Rather, they want to gain autonomy and independence, and work on tasks they view as meaningful; they don't see themselves as heroic figures leading their followers to some kind of victory! Yet, whether they seek it or not, entrepreneurs *are* leaders. As founders of their new ventures they are in charge, and if the new venture grows, they must direct an increasing number of employees—setting goals for them, attempting to increase their motivation, and establishing an overall strategy for gaining competitive advantage (see Chapter 11). Often, they are the CEOs of their companies, which means, in a sense, that "the buck stops on their desks"—they have the ultimate responsibility for dealing with problems, for making key decisions, and in general *are* the leaders of their organizations.

Since they are often thrust into this role even if they do not actively seek it, it is important for entrepreneurs to perform it well—they must, as a vast literature on the nature of leadership suggests (e.g., Yukl, 2012), be effective in this role. One of the key tasks of leaders is that of exerting influence over others—not just their subordinates and followers, but others too. So in a sense, to be effective as a leader, entrepreneurs must also be effective at exerting influence—outside, as well as within the role of leader. In this discussion, therefore, we'll first focus on the nature of leadership and what makes some leaders more effective than others. Then we'll turn to the more general question of how entrepreneurs can be effective at exerting influence—for instance, somehow persuading potential customers to buy their products, investors to supply needed financial support, and potential employees to join the new venture.

Leadership effectiveness: Why some are more effective than others

There is, as described by experts on this topic, a kind of "romance" to leadership (Meindl et al., 1985). When we think of leadership, thoughts of famous leaders of the present and past and their great accomplishments come to mind: Alexander the Great, who conquered much of the known world, Queen Elizabeth I, who made England into a world power, and Bill Gates, who made personal computers a reality around the world by developing an operating system and programs that are relatively easy to use, or Steve Jobs, who changed the way many people live by introducing the iPad, the iPhone, and several other technological breakthroughs that have greatly changed everyday life for many millions of people.

Many of these leaders have been described as "charismatic" or "transformational"—persons who exert unusually powerful effects on their followers, and who truly *do* change their societies, their organizations, or even the entire world. But such individuals are rare, and in general, leaders are defined as the persons in a group or organization (including new ventures) who have the most influence—they set the goals, make decisions, and direct the group or organization in particular directions. In other words, as stated in one of the opening quotations at the start of this chapter, effective leaders depend more on influence than authority; they induce others to do what they want, not because they are the "boss" but because they *want* to follow the leaders' directives. According to this view, transformational leaders are simply ones who exert unusually high amounts of influence: they somehow persuade or convince others to do things they wouldn't otherwise do, and to follow the leader's guidance or directives with enthusiasm, whatever these may be. In addition, evidence indicates that charismatic leaders exert powerful effects by (1) expressing a clear vision of the future and how to get there, (2) generating emotional excitement in others, (3) gaining trust by demonstrating their own integrity, and (4) generating high levels of positive affect in followers (e.g., Conger and Kanungo, 1998; Waldman et al., 2001).

But putting aside the question of how charismatic leaders generate their powerful effects, another issue arises: why do specific persons become leaders? In other words, why do some people but not others assume this role? Over the years, contrasting views have been presented. One is that leaders possess specific skills or characteristics that qualify them for such positions, and that these skills or characteristics are much the same at all times and for all leaders; this view is known as the "great person" perspective. Although there is some support for the view that leaders do differ somewhat from other persons (e.g., Locke, 2011), it has become clear that, in fact, there is no short-list of "leadership traits"—characteristics that set leaders apart from others and help them rise to the positions they hold. Rather, modern views suggest that the following old Italian proverb is correct: "The right person comes at the right time." In other words, the characteristics, skills, and knowledge needed to become a leader vary greatly from one context to another. For instance, a military leader might need different skills and abilities than the CEO of a large corporation; similarly, in order to be a successful leader, the conductor of an orchestra might well need different skills and characteristics than an entrepreneur running a new venture. Regardless of who becomes a leader, however, it is clear that some are more effective than others, but why? It is to this important question we turn next.

Leadership effectiveness—and how entrepreneurs can attain it

What makes a leader effective—someone who helps the group or organization she or he leads to reach important goals? A large amount of research has been focused on this question, and results are complex. Moreover, as noted above, they suggest that a leader who is effective in one context might not be effective in another. Overall, however, research findings indicate that effective leaders are first and foremost flexible—they adjust their behavior or style to the conditions they face. For instance, they are "directive" (i.e., actively direct the actions of follower or subordinates) when this is necessary— during times of crises or high time pressure, and when subordinates need lots of direction because they are unsure what to do or how to proceed. Under other conditions (e.g., when the leaders don't have clear authority or when subordinates are already expert at their jobs) they adopt a "hands-off" approach, consulting with subordinates or followers rather than simply telling them what to do. (That point was noted in the first quotation at the start of this chapter.) Further, effective leaders make sure that subordinates perceive them as helping them attain both high performance and valued goals (Yukl, 2012). Finally, effective leaders also adapt their decision-making style to fit the situation: they don't seek or use feedback from subordinates when only *they* have the information necessary to make important decisions, rather, they simply make the decisions themselves. When they don't have such information, however, they invite input from subordinates—and listen to it!

These are only a few of the ingredients in effective leadership—there are many other components too. In essence, though, they suggest the following general guidelines for leaders wishing to enhance their own effectiveness:

- **Always keep your word—once you give it**. But don't give it until you are sure you can keep it. If you give it and then break it, subordinates' trust will be lost and may be very difficult to restore.
- **Always explain clearly to subordinates why they should do what you ask**. They will always ask themselves, "What's in it for me?" "Why should I work hard to reach the goals you have set?" Providing answers to these questions can greatly increase a leader's effectiveness.
- **Always be a true help to subordinates**. In other words, help them advance *their* interests, not just your own.

- **Do your best to remove obstacles from their path**. For instance, if they need equipment or other resources, supply it. If they don't have what they need to do the job, they can't—and won't.

These guidelines may sound like simple common sense, but amazingly, many leaders and many entrepreneurs don't follow them. The outcome is very predictable: poor results! Employees and other subordinates are not highly motivated, don't work diligently to attain key goals, and, on top of that, show little loyalty or commitment to the company. In contrast, if entrepreneurs follow these basic principles, they will be effective in the role of leader, and so contribute in important ways to the growth and success of their new ventures.

Exerting influence: Changing others' attitudes and behavior

Earlier, it was noted that leaders are often defined as the persons in a group or organization who exert the most influence, and charismatic or transformational leaders are ones who exert unusually powerful influence on others. However, we didn't fully define the term "influence." A general definition is that it involves efforts by one or more persons to change the behavior, attitudes, or feelings of one or more others (Cialdini, 2008). Such attempts are a part of daily life: advertisers try to convince consumers to buy or use certain products; politicians attempt to win voters' support, and charitable organizations attempt to win donations from as many people as possible. The task of exerting influence is one that entrepreneurs too often face. Within their own companies they want to influence current employees to work hard on their tasks and potential employees to join the new venture. Similarly, they sometimes attempt to influence their partners to accept their views concerning the firm's strategy, product development, marketing approaches, or many other issues. Entrepreneurs also often want to influence potential customers, suppliers, and investors so that they agree to buy their new venture's products or services, provide raw material or components at an attractive price or, in the case of investors, provide financial support. In fact, if entrepreneurs don't succeed in influencing these people, the new venture may quickly run out of resources and disappear.

There are many techniques for exerting influence—for somehow getting other persons to change their views or behavior. One of the most common is "rational persuasion," which is based on using logic and arguments to convince others that the views of the person doing the influencing are correct, or at least, the best available. This can sometimes be effective, but there is also considerable evidence that rational arguments often fail to change strongly held views; once people have formed their attitudes, they don't readily change them, even if there are rational grounds for doing so. Other techniques for exerting influence involve exchange: "You support me on this, and I will support you on that" (e.g., Yukl and Tracey, 1992). Perhaps the most extreme tactics involve pressuring others—making demands or even issuing threats. Although charismatic leaders may be able to use such techniques, most leaders cannot because these tactics often backfire, generating resistance rather than acceptance of the influencer's views.

Whatever form they take, efforts to exert influence often have the following goal: somehow, convincing other persons to say "Yes" to specific requests. This is known as gaining "compliance" (e.g., Baron and Branscombe, 2012) and many techniques are widely used to achieve it. Since knowledge of these can often be very useful to entrepreneurs, we'll examine several of them here.

Social networks and positive effects of social skills

One useful technique for gaining compliance from others—for getting them to say "Yes"—involves developing effective social networks; the persons in these networks will often agree to requests for help, information, and other resources. A high level of social skills often contributes to the development of such networks, because they generate high levels of liking for the person demonstrating them, and it has been found that the more people like an individual attempting to obtain their agreement to various requests, the greater the chances that they will in fact comply. This is another strong reason why entrepreneurs should develop social skills and use them to establish high-quality social networks.

Reciprocity: Repaying personal obligations

Another important technique for winning compliance from others is "reciprocity." This simply involves "calling in personal debts"—somehow reminding others of the benefits the requester has provided to them in the past. "I have helped you, so now it's your turn to help me" is the basic principle. Entrepreneurs can benefit from the use of this basic principle by providing help or assistance to anyone they hope to influence at a later time. For instance, they can offer prospective customers reduced prices, or accelerated delivery, and then later, perhaps, request help in return—for instance, a large order or increased shelf space.

Commitment/consistency

A third technique is quite different, and involves somehow gaining an initial commitment from the person or persons whose compliance to later requests is desired. Once people have made an initial commitment or decision they are often reluctant to change it, and so will be more likely to agree to later requests. This is a tactic often used by automobile salespersons. They negotiate a deal with a customer but then report that the Sales Manager won't approve it unless the customer agrees to pay more. The rational choice at that point is to walk away, but many people, having made the initial decision to purchase the car, are reluctant to do so, and agree to the higher price. As we'll note in a later section, making decisions is often difficult and effortful, so all else being equal, people tend to stick with them once they are made. Entrepreneurs can use this approach by offering very attractive arrangements to customers, suppliers, and others to obtain an initial order or terms, and then, once this initial commitment has been made, use it to attain compliance with later requests—for instance, new orders at a somewhat higher price.

Scarcity: Pressure to act before it's too late

Another technique for gaining compliance is one you are probably already very familiar with. It involves suggesting to the persons whose compliance is desired that if they don't act now, it may be too late—in other words, an opportunity that exists now will soon vanish. Department stores often use this tactic, suggesting that a sale will end at a specific time. This puts pressure on customers to buy now, which is, of course, what the stores desire. Entrepreneurs can use this technique by suggesting to potential employees that if they don't say "Yes" now, another person will get the job. They can use it in dealings with investors by indicating that if they delay, the entrepreneurs will turn to other investors who are "waiting in the wings." Overall, the principle is the same: suggest to others that they must act now or lose a desirable opportunity (Figure 10.4).

A large amount of evidence—much of it from research conducted by social psychologists—exists. This research indicates that such tactics really *work*: they are often highly effective in generating compliance with various requests. It's always important to remember, however, that attempts to exert influence work both ways: not only do we attempt to influence others; they often try to influence us. Entrepreneurs who want to be effective at exerting influence should always keep this thought in mind as they attempt to build their new ventures. (For an example of an entrepreneur who was a highly effective leader, and also unusually successful in influencing others, please see "The Entrepreneurial Quest" case study below.)

Figure 10.4 Scarcity—and approaching deadlines—an influence technique

As shown here, stores often claim that a current sale will last only until a particular time, thus putting pressure on customers to buy *now!* Entrepreneurs use similar techniques in their efforts to influence others—for instance, potential employees, customers, and investors.

CASE STUDY

The Entrepreneurial Quest

Creating the modern department store: Why the "customer *is* always right"

Nearly everyone shops at department stores sometime; the names of the stores vary from region to region and country to country, but in basic concept they are very much alike: all offer a wide range of products, from clothing to appliances, in one location. This is very convenient for customers, and from the stores' point of view, encourages them to spend all their money in one place! Perhaps surprisingly, department stores in their modern form did not exist until the early years of the twentieth century, when Harry Gordon Selfridge—an American entrepreneur—recognized an opportunity for creating them.

Selfridge was a colorful character, and something of a charismatic leader. He recognized that innovative marketing could bring large numbers of customers into his store (which opened in London in 1909), so after raising funds from investors—sophisticated individuals to whom Selfridge "sold" his creative ideas—he set about creating something truly new. Selfridge tried to make shopping fun, rather than a chore. He put merchandise on display so that customers could examine it at their leisure, used attractive displays both within the store and in its windows, and hired only attractive and socially skilled sales assistants. He also located various departments in carefully chosen positions—for instance, putting high-priced (and profit) perfumes near the entrance, so that customers would see them soon after entering the store (Figure 10.5).

Other innovative techniques involved establishing a roof-top café, from which customers had a panoramic view of London, and bringing celebrities to the store for special events. For instance, he invited Louis Blériot, the first pilot to fly across the English Channel, to visit the store, and even put his airplane on display.

The result was that Selfridge's soon became a major attraction, one native Londoners and visitors alike wanted to visit. But the success of Selfridge's wasn't due only to these innovative ideas: they also reflected his unusual effectiveness as a leader: he inspired employees with his vision of the future, and used a wide range of influence techniques to attract customers, win financial support, and basically, to obtain the results he sought. In short, Selfridge was a highly successful entrepreneur, and a major part of his success derived from his effectiveness both as a leader and as someone who could exert strong influence on others.

CASE STUDY *(continued)*

Source: Wikimedia: reprinted with permission of the photographer, Martin Addison; licensed for reuse under the Creative Commons Attribution-ShareAlike 2.0 license.

Figure 10.5 Inventing the modern department store

Harry Gordon Selfridge, an entrepreneur of the early twentieth century, came up with the idea of the modern department store. He tried to make shopping fun, and used techniques such as placing high-profit departments in locations where customers would be sure to see them. He succeeded in building a thriving business not only because of his creative ideas, but also because he was a highly effective leader, skilled in exerting influence on his employees—and customers. *(Selfridge's in London)*

Making effective decisions

Making decisions is often hard work, especially if the decisions are important, and each alternative offers a mixture of costs and benefits. Yet, this is an activity entrepreneurs must perform, often many times each day. Running a business involves countless decisions, everything from "How should available funds be spent (on product development, equipment, marketing)?" through "Which supplier should be chosen?" and "Which employee should be hired?" In fact, the necessity for making effective, accurate decisions is a constant, crucial activity for entrepreneurs. Are there guidelines that entrepreneurs can use to help with this task? Or are all decisions so unique that no helpful rules or procedures exist? While no definitive answer to these questions exists—decision-making is too complex to afford us that luxury—there are indeed some basic insights into the basic nature of decision-making, information on how to perform it effectively, and—just as important—insights into several dangerous pitfalls entrepreneurs should avoid as they develop their new ventures.

Basic strategies for making decisions

How do individuals go about making decisions? Part of the answer involves the question: "Are the decisions trivial, or important?" If a decision is fairly trivial, such as "Should I see one movie or another?" it is usually made quickly and without much thought or effort; after all, the consequences of the decision are minor. But as the importance of the decision increases, so too does our willingness to invest lots of cognitive effort in making it. This important dimension of "trivial to important" is not taken fully into account by one important model of decision-making—the "rational analytic model." Basically, this model (which derives primarily from economic theory as it existed in the past), assumes that decision-making is a rational process in which individuals engage in three distinct but related steps. First, they identify the decision that must be made—define the problem, their goals, and identify procedures for actually making the decision. Next, they actively generate alternatives, evaluate them, and make an initial choice. Third, they implement the decision—they put it into action, and then, finally, monitor the effectiveness of the decision and change it if results are negative. These basic steps are illustrated in Figure 10.6.

This model seems quite reasonable, but do individuals actually make decisions in this totally rational manner? Considering the limits of human cognition, and important role of emotions and feelings in our thinking, the answer seems to be: sometimes, but not always.

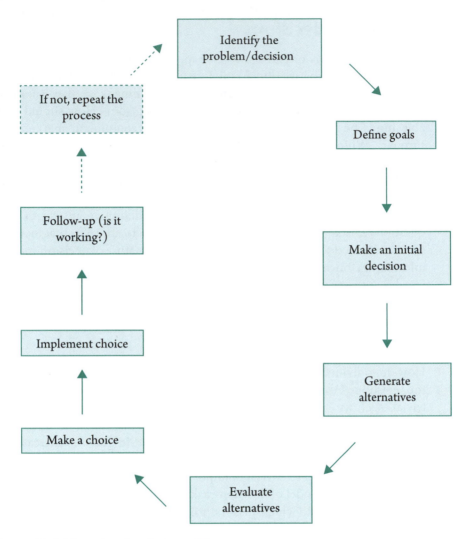

Figure 10.6 The rational analytic model

According to one influential model of decision-making, it proceeds in the orderly manner shown here. In fact though, actual decision-making often relies strongly on intuition, and is subject to important cognitive errors.

As noted above, when the decisions are trivial, people don't follow this careful, logical formula: the cognitive effort isn't justified. When decisions are of moderate to high importance—for instance, which of two similar jobs to accept—they may well follow the steps in this model. When the decision is crucial—perhaps life-changing (e.g., what career to follow; should I have children, and if so, how many; should I start a new venture?) most people seem to operate in a more intuitive manner. For instance, in deciding to make a life-time commitment to another person, few individuals proceed by means of the steps outlined in the rational analytic model above. They don't carefully weigh all the advantages or disadvantages of potential partners; rather, they tend to rely more on their feelings. Similarly, when considering whether to launch a new venture or not, it may be difficult for entrepreneurs to follow a purely analytic, rational process. Is the opportunity worth developing? Can I personally develop it? As we noted in previous chapters, emotions play a key role in our cognitive processes, and this is certainly true for decision-making. That's a crucial point, and one we'll return to several times in this discussion.

But what's the bottom line? In essence, the rational analytic model is sometimes used by individuals, but mainly for decisions that are of moderate to high importance. Truly crucial decisions, in contrast, tend to be made in a more intuitive, emotion-driven way. This certainly reflects our basic human nature, but as we'll now see, it also opens the door to many important sources of error and bias. Here, we'll focus on two of the most important.

Cognitive and emotional traps entrepreneurs should avoid

The French author Albert Camus once suggested that "our lives are the sum of all our decisions." If that's true, then it is crucial that we make these decisions effectively—that we choose the best options as often as possible. Unfortunately, our cognitive limitations (discussed in Chapter 2) add to the difficulty of this task. Since decision-making is basically a cognitive process, it too is subject to these limitations. In fact, it is subject to several kinds of error that, if ignored, can result in very poor decisions—and disaster for the entrepreneurs who make them. We'll now examine several of the most important.

Implicit favorites: The powerful—and lasting impact—of initial preferences

Decision-making, as noted earlier, is often hard work. When the decisions are important, and have potentially life-changing and long-lasting implications, people work hard to be as rational as they can. But how rational is that? When individuals face an important decision and try to consider all the obvious alternatives, they often discover that they have an initial preference. This is known as the "implicit favorite" (emphasis on *implicit*) because as noted in Chapter 1, people are often not fully aware of their motives or feelings, and may not even recognize that they are leaning in a particular direction. Yet, research on decision-making indicates that the impact of these initial preferences is very powerful; in fact, most people ultimately tend to go with their initial inclination or preference most of the time. Why? Because in the light of this initial preference they often tend to pay most attention to information that supports their implicit favorite. In a sense, their initial preference triggers the "confirmation bias"—the strong tendency to focus, primarily, on information that confirms our beliefs or views; and in decision-making situations one good way of doing this is to strengthen support for the initial favorite, while downplaying that for the other choices. Many studies provide evidence for this process so it is important for entrepreneurs to be on watch for it. If they are not, they choose the option they initially prefer, even if this is not really the best one.

Failing to recognize when it's time to get out: The dangers of escalating commitment

In our previous discussion of important cognitive errors (Chapter 2), we briefly described the powerful effect of "sunk costs"—the tendency to stick with bad decisions once they are made. Another term for this effect is "escalation of commitment," and, as it suggests, one reason people get trapped in bad decisions is that once these choices are made and they have invested time, energy, and effort in them, they soon reach the point where, cognitively, they feel that they have "too much invested to quit." In other words, they conclude that they can't reverse a previous decision, even if it is yielding negative results, because they are now too deeply committed to it to change. No one wants to admit that they were wrong, and this provides powerful pressure to continue, in the hope that, ultimately, the decisions turn out to be good ones.

This is a *major* danger for decision-makers, including entrepreneurs, and relates to one aspect of metacognition (our understanding of our own thinking): specifically, the ability to know when it is time to "get out"—to withdraw from a failing course of action or strategy. This is one major reason why so many new ventures fail; the entrepreneurs believe—often passionately—in their ideas, and in the business models they have formulated to develop them. As a result, they tend to be over-optimistic (another important key cognitive bias) and ignore or downplay evidence that things are not working out as they planned; rather, they continue to hope that the situation will soon improve.

Research findings indicate that knowing how much time and effort to spend on a chosen course of action before admitting that it was the wrong choice, is a major predictor of success in many situations (e.g., Jarvstad et al., 2012). For instance, assume an entrepreneur is developing a new product he or she plans to market, but despite the investment of high amounts of time, effort, and money, things are not going well—the product still does not work as expected. What should he or she do? Admit that they made an error, or continue? The temptation—a strong one—is to continue in the hope that success lies just around the corner. Quitting now, therefore, would be serious error, since it would waste all the resources already invested in the product. If the product never meets expectations, however, the result can be disastrous because, ultimately, so many resources are invested in a course of action that will never succeed, that the new venture lacks the resources to pursue other strategies.

Fortunately, we seem to be quite good at this task (Jarvstad et al., 2012) but only in relatively simple situations. In more complex ones, we are more susceptible to major errors (Kahneman, 2003). In view of such findings, it seems clear that effective decision-making involves not only choosing what seems to be the best available option, but also being able to recognize when this initial choice was not the optimal one, and having the courage—and flexibility—to admit this fact, and change course as quickly and effectively as possible.

What can be done to avoid getting trapped in sunk costs? One tactic is to decide, in advance, how much resources will be invested in implementing a decision; once this point is reached, the situation is assessed and if positive results have not been obtained, the decision is reversed. This is never easy to do, but setting a specific date or level of investment can help. Another is to separate the original decision from the decision to continue. For instance, if the decision was based on the strong support of one of the founders, this person will agree, in advance, that another member of the team will have the task of deciding at some point whether to continue. This can cause friction between the original decision-maker and the person who decides whether to continue, but it is better than pursuing a bad decision until it is too late to change.

Finally, the founding team can decide to let an outsider—for instance, an expert or an investor—play a key role. Since this person did not make the decision, she or he is not as cognitively committed to it, and can, perhaps, make the decision on more rational grounds. Whichever of these tactics entrepreneurs adopt, they can help protect the new venture from failure that could have been avoided. Given the fact that human cognition—although impressive—is far from perfect, entrepreneurs wishing to make effective decisions should do everything they can to avoid getting trapped in bad decisions.

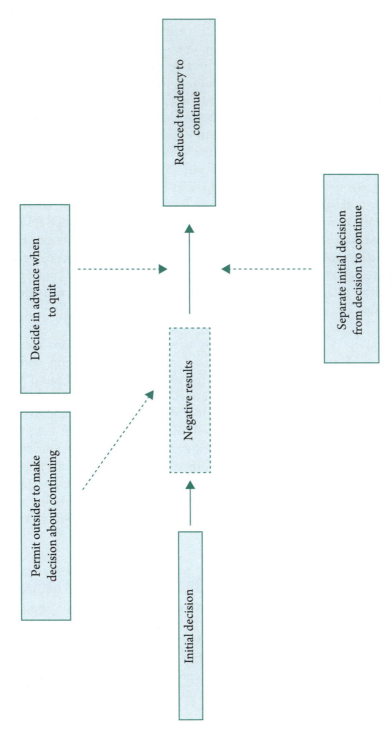

Figure 10.7 Techniques for overcoming the powerful tendency to stick with initial decisions

Many persons find it difficult to reverse past decisions. As a result, they become trapped in sunk costs (or escalation of commitment) in part because they feel they have too much invested to quit! Above are some techniques that can help to counter or at least reduce this tendency.

Decision-making strategies—and why some are better than others

Before concluding this discussion of decision-making, one other topic should be addressed: what basic strategy for making important decisions should be adopted? As described earlier, the rational analytic strategy, although useful, does not seem to work in many situations. Another possibility—the one many people seem to use in situations involving very important decisions, an approach based in intuition—may be subject to the serious errors noted above. What other approaches to decision-making exist? One involves the dimensions of maximizing and satisficing, and it offers important lessons for entrepreneurs.

Maximizing versus satisficing: Should entrepreneurs seek perfection, or "good enough"?

When you have to make an important decision, do you search carefully through all possible alternatives looking for the best one—the perfect choice? Or do you, instead, examine available choices until you find one that "works"—one that is acceptable, even though it is not ideal? Research evidence indicates that in making decisions individuals tend to adopt one or the other of these contrasting strategies. The first is known as "maximizing," since it is focused on finding the very best alternative. People who adopt this approach are described as being "maximizers." The second approach is known as "satisficing," because it involves searching for something that will work, even if it is not perfect or ideal (Schwartz et al., 2002; Schwartz, 2004). People who prefer this latter strategy are known as "satisficers."

Both approaches offer a mixture of costs and benefits. Maximizers engage in very careful and diligent comparison of all existing alternatives; this means that all else being equal, they tend to make good decisions—perhaps better ones than satisficers. But since maximizers seek perfection (or at least, the very best possible choice), they tend to take a long time to make decisions, and tend to be dissatisfied with their choices after they make them. Are they really perfect? That's a difficult question to answer, and leaves maximizers facing important doubts. Satisficers, in contrast, can generally make decisions relatively quickly and are usually pleased with the decisions since they do tend to work, even if they are only barely "good enough."

Overall, satisficers tend to be happier not only with their decisions, but with their lives overall. They tend to be higher in what psychologists term "subjective well-being" than maximizers (see Chapter 8). But what's the lesson for entrepreneurs? In general, they face situations that involve high levels of risk, and also high levels of uncertainty: all the information necessary for making a good decision is not available, and perhaps can't be obtained. Further, the opportunities they seek to develop may be available for only a limited amount of time, since someone may recognize and develop them at any time. These factors suggest that a satisficing strategy is often better for entrepreneurs. Of course, there is a downside to this approach: the decisions made may be far from ideal and require later adjustments. If satisficing is combined with the willingness to improvise described in Chapter 5, however, satisficing may offer the best combination of speed and effectiveness available. In sum, while the search for perfection is understandable and perhaps commendable in some situations, it may not be the best strategy for entrepreneurs in the chaotic, time-urgent situations they often face.

THE EFFECTIVE ENTREPRENEUR

Once a new venture is launched, entrepreneurs must take on many of the functions of traditional managers—that is, they must manage their new venture effectively. This requires a broad range of skills and knowledge; the most important of these are listed below, with suggestions for accomplishing them successfully:

- People—including employees—do their best work when they are highly motivated to perform it. Motivation can be increased in several ways: assuring that employees have the resources needed to do their jobs and that good performance is recognized and rewarded, with rewards employees really want; by setting specific goals that are both challenging and obtainable and providing accurate feedback about progress toward them. These points indicate that entrepreneurs should do everything they can to assure that such conditions exist in their new ventures. Doing so will enhance employees' motivation,

and therefore their willingness to work hard in order to attain the new venture's goals.

- Entrepreneurs are by definition if not personal desire, leaders as founders of their new ventures, and must provide direction and guidance to employees and others. Being an effective leader, therefore, is important to the new venture's success. Entrepreneurs can attain this goal by being flexible in their approach to guiding others, through leading by inspiration rather than decree or orders, and by following guidelines such as always keeping their word once it is given, making it clear that they have subordinates' interests at heart—not just those of the new venture—and by removing obstacles from employees' paths.

- Leadership involves exerting influence, and in fact, entrepreneurs must attempt to influence others in many different contexts—for example, they must try to influence potential customers to buy

➡

their new venture's products, to influence suppliers to provide basic resources at attractive prices. Many techniques exist for exerting influence, and especially for gaining compliance—getting others to say "Yes" to various requests. These techniques include: rational persuasion, which doesn't always work, and basing influence attempts on principles such as liking (people in our social networks are more likely to comply than those not in such networks), reciprocity (returning previous favors), and commitment (once people make a decision they tend to stick with it. Entrepreneurs should be familiar with these techniques and put them to use in their efforts to influence others.

- Another important task entrepreneurs face in managing their new ventures is that of making effective decisions. Although these are sometimes made through a totally rational approach, often decision-making is a more intuitive process.

- However they proceed, entrepreneurs must learn to avoid several cognitive traps that can lead to poor decisions. These include sticking with initial preferences and getting trapped in bad decisions, from which it is difficult to withdraw.

- In general, given the conditions under which they work, entrepreneurs should adopt a satisficing rather than a maximizing approach to decision-making—focusing on identifying an alternative that works, rather than searching for the ideal alternative.

SUMMARY OF KEY POINTS

1 Once a new venture is launched it must be managed like any other business. Thus, entrepreneurs must, whether they like it or not, perform many of the tasks carried out by traditional managers. They must seek to motivate employees, and can do so by assuring that certain conditions (e.g., close links between performance and rewards) exist, and by setting specific, attainable goals. Contrary to widespread beliefs, entrepreneurs do not enter this activity purely for financial motives; on the contrary, they often seek such goals at increased autonomy or independence. Whether they prefer this or not, entrepreneurs must often act as leaders and try to assure that they are effective in this role.

2 They must also attempt to exert influence on subordinates and many other persons (e.g., potential customers, suppliers, investors). They can reach this goal in many different ways aside from rational persuasion—employing the principles of reciprocity, liking, and commitment.

3 Entrepreneurs must often make decisions, so this is another task they should perform effectively. Although some decisions are made through a rational process, many others involve intuition and emotions.

4 However decisions are made, entrepreneurs must avoid important cognitive errors that can lead to poor decisions: sticking with initial (implicit) favorites, and getting trapped in sunk costs (escalation of commitment). They should also, in general, adopt a satisficing rather than a maximizing approach to decision-making.

REFERENCES

Baron, R.A. (2010), "Job design and entrepreneurship: Why closer connections = mutual gains," *Journal of Organizational Behavior*, **30**, 1–10.

Baron, R.A. and N. Branscombe (2012), *Social Psychology*, 13th edition, Boston, MA: Pearson/Allyn & Bacon.

Baron, R.A., H. Zhao and Q. Ming (2013), "Personal motives, moral disengagement, and unethical decisions by entrepreneurs: Cognitive mechanisms on the 'slippery slope,'" manuscript under review.

Cassar, G. (2007), "Money, money, money? A longitudinal investigation of entrepreneur career reasons, growth preferences, and achieved growth," *Entrepreneurship and Regional Development*, **19**(1), 89–107.

Cialdini, R.B. (2008), *Influence: Science and Practice*, Boston, MA: Allyn & Bacon.

Conger, J.A. and R.N. Kanungo (1998), *Charismatic Leadership in Organizations*, New York: Sage.

Franklin, R.J. (2013), "Motives, self-regulation, and entrepreneurial success," unpublished doctoral dissertation, Oklahoma State University.

Jarvstad, A., S.K. Rushton, P.A. Warren and U. Hahn (2012), "Knowing when to move on: Cognitive and perceptual decisions in time," *Psychological Science*, **23**(6), 589–97.

Kahneman, D. (2003), "Maps of bounded rationality: Psychology for behavioral economics," *The American Economic Review*, **93**(5), 1449–75.

Lambright, K.T. (2010), "An update of a classic: Applying expectancy theory to understand contracted provider motivation," *Administration and Society*, **42**(4), 375–403.

Locke, E.A. (2011), "Individualism, collectivism, leadership, and the greater good," in D. Forsyth and C. Hoyt (eds), *For the Greater Good of All*, New York: Palgrave Macmillan.

Locke, E.A. and G.P. Latham (2002), "Building a practically useful theory of goal-setting and task motivation. A 35 year odyssey," *American Psychologist*, **57**(9), 705–17.

Meindl, J.R., S.B. Ehrlich and J.M. Dukerich (1985), "The romance of leadership," *Administrative Science Quarterly*, **30**(1) 78–102.

Rindova, V., D. Barry and D.J. Ketchen Jr (2009), "Entrepreneuring as emancipation," *Academy of Management Review*, **34**(3), 477-91.

Schwartz, B. (2004), *The Paradox of Choice: Why More Is Less*, New York: HarperCollins.

Schwartz, B., A. Ward, J. Monterosso, S. Lyubomirsky, K. White and D.R. Lehman (2002), "Maximizing versus satisficing: Happiness is a matter of choice," *Journal of Personality and Social Psychology*, **83**(5), 1178–92.

Shane, S.A. (2008), *Technology Strategy for Managers and Entrepreneurs*, Englewood Cliffs, NJ: Prentice Hall.

Steers, R.M., R.T. Mowday and D.L. Shapiro (2004), "The future of work motivation theory," *Academy of Management Review*, **29**(3), 379–87.

Tung, R.L. and J. Walls (2007), "Cross-cultural entrepreneurship: The case of China," in J.R. Baum, M. Frese and R.A. Baron (eds), *The Psychology of Entrepreneurship*, Mahwah, NJ: Lawrence Erlbaum, pp. 265–86.

Waldman, D.A., G.C. Ramírez, R.J. House and P. Puranam (2001), "Does leadership matter? CEO leadership attributes and profitability under conditions of perceived environmental uncertainty," *Academy of Management Journal*, **44**(1), 379–97.

Yukl, G.A. (2012), *Leadership in Organizations*, Upper Saddle River, NJ: Prentice-Hall.

Yukl, G. and J.B. Tracey (1992), "Consequences of influence tactics used with subordinates, peers, and the boss," *Journal of Applied Psychology*, **77**(4), 525–35.

11

Building the new venture: Strategies for attaining growth

CHAPTER OUTLINE

- Why new ventures seek growth—and is it always the best route to success?
  - The allure of growth: Its potential benefits
  - The disadvantages of rapid growth
- Strategies for attaining growth
  - Internal strategies: Building the company from within
  - External strategies: Encouraging growth from the outside
- Entrepreneurial orientation (EO): A key strategy for new ventures
  - The nature of EO
  - Why new ventures adopt EO

The only way that we can live, is if we grow. The only way that we can grow is if we change. The only way that we can change is if we learn.
(C. JoyBell C., US author)

You will either step forward into growth or you will step back into safety.
(Abraham Maslow, *Motivation and Personality*, 1954)

The essence of strategy is choosing what not *to do.*
(Michael E. Porter, Harvard Professor, leading authority on company strategy)

In the business world, there is a widespread belief to the effect that unless a company grows, it will ultimately fail and vanish—or, perhaps turn into what is known as the "living dead"—companies that continue to operate but are totally stagnant have little chance of success. In short, growth is often viewed as an essential ingredient in business success. This is true to an even stronger degree with respect to new ventures. In fact, a few years ago, there was a widespread use of the term "gazelle" to describe certain new companies—a highly select few, in fact. A gazelle is kind of antelope able to run at 60 miles per hour, thus outdistancing many predators (Figure 11.1). As applied to new ventures, the image of a gazelle suggests that companies that grow very rapidly, and in that sense leave their competitors in the dust, are the models every new venture should try to emulate. Others, and especially the ones that plod along achieving modest growth, are boring, and, in fact, inconsequential; studying them is a waste of time.

This fascination with rapid growth continues to permeate thinking about entrepreneurship and although it is easy to understand its appeal, the overall picture may be more complex than it suggests. In this chapter, we'll focus on growth and on how new ventures can be developed into successful businesses by achieving rapid rises in sales, profits, number of employees, and many other respects. To consider the many complexities involved in rapid growth, we'll first consider why new ventures seek it—the benefits it offers. Then we'll examine its downside—its potential costs. After that, we'll describe specific strategies for achieving growth—ones focused on the new venture itself (internal strategies), and ones focused on factors and actions external to the new venture (external strategies). Finally, we'll focus on an especially important strategy through which new ventures can achieve growth—"entrepreneurial orientation."

Why new ventures seek growth—and is it always the best route to success?

When prospective entrepreneurs—individuals who have not yet started a new company but are thinking seriously about doing so—consider this possibility, what companies come to mind? Older traditional ones that have been around for decades (e.g., General Motors, Sears, General Foods)? Or do they instead focus on relatively new companies that have burst onto the scene recently and after doing so have gone on to grow at phenomenal rates? Clearly, the latter group is often the one that seizes their attention—companies such as Google, Home Depot, Amazon.com, and Wal-Mart, to name just a few. While these companies differ greatly in industry, products, and markets, they do share one key characteristic: rapid growth. In contrast, other companies that were once included in this select group, such as Microsoft, IBM, and JCPenney's, may now receive less attention because their rates of growth have slowed considerably—or even vanished. So, rapid growth after launch is a key goal for many entrepreneurs. Why? Intuitively, this seems reasonable. If they are seeking financial gains, then rapid growth offers the key to reaching such goals.

Source: Wikimedia: with permission of the photographer, Professor Berger, University of the Witwatersrand, Johannesburg South Africa.

Figure 11.1 New ventures that attain rapid growth are sometimes called "gazelles"

Gazelles are antelopes capable of amazing speed—up to 60 miles per hour when escaping from predators. New ventures that grow very quickly are sometimes described as gazelles because they leave their competitors in the dust!

But if, instead, they are seeking other goals—independence, meaningful work, or even helping others and their communities—then perhaps rapid growth is not for them. In the discussion that follows, therefore, we'll consider both the allure of growth—why entrepreneurs often seek it—and the potential costs it may involve.

The allure of growth: Its potential benefits

Given that rapid growth is a key goal for many entrepreneurs, a key question is: why is this the case? What is it about growth that makes it so attractive? Some of the key reasons are described below.

Advantages provided by rapid growth: Economies of scale, greater resources, and market leadership

One important reason new ventures seek growth is to obtain "economies of scale." This refers to the fact that as sales increase, the cost of manufacturing each item, or providing the company's service, decreases. For instance, consider a company started by an entrepreneur (or team of entrepreneurs) to produce a new kind of vehicle—one that combines a bicycle with an electric-powered vehicle. In fact, such a company exists, and produces the Elf (Figure 11.2). This vehicle is designed so that drivers pedal a bicycle when it is on a level surface; this charges the car's batteries. But then, when the driver encounters a hill, a 1 hp electric motor can be switched on to assist. The car can go about 20 miles per hour, and drivers not only get to their destinations, they also burn calories along the way—perhaps as many as 586 calories per hour. Right now, the Elf sells for $4995 and production is low—only 1500 have been manufactured—but if sales increase rapidly, costs will be reduced, and that will allow the price too to drop. In short, one important benefit of rapid growth is that it reduces the costs of production, and thus paves the way for lower prices—and even higher sales.

Finally, growth also contributes to the company's ability to develop new markets. As the new venture increases in size it has more funds to devote to marketing and sales, and as a result, recognition of its products among potential customers increases. It also provides the company with the ability to negotiate more favorable arrangements with suppliers. For instance, Wal-Mart can sell at low prices partly because it generates such a high level of sales that suppliers are willing to stock its shelves at low prices—which helps the company keep its own prices low.

Source: Courtesy of Organic Transit Inc.

Figure 11.2 The Elf: can it benefit from economies of scale?

The Elf is an ingenious vehicle, combining a bicycle with a small electric motor. At present it sells for $4995, which many buyers find quite high. However, if sales increase, economies of scale (lower cost per unit as volume increases) may reduce this price significantly.

The disadvantages of rapid growth

Given the advantages described above, it might seem at first that all entrepreneurs would seek it. In fact though, rapid growth has a significant downside too. First, consider the fact that many entrepreneurs do not start new companies to obtain financial rewards. Rather, they want independence, to be in charge, and to do work that they view as meaningful instead of the boring, and to them, pointless tasks they perform in their current jobs. Such entrepreneurs are often described as "life-style entrepreneurs"—they want the kind of life entrepreneurship can provide, but, as explained in Chapter 10, do not really want to become managers, as growth may require. For instance, I personally know one entrepreneur who sold her company for $300 000 000. When I asked what she would do with her newfound wealth, her answer was simple: "Sail my boat around the world, and see all the places I've always wanted to visit, but didn't have the time to see." Although her company had already experienced rapid growth she did not want to stay on board for even more.

Another reason why growth may not be for all entrepreneurs is that they know that they do not have the skills necessary to effectively manage a rapidly expanding company. As a company grows, the complexity of its operation also increases, and so too do the demands on the founder's time. They have to manage cash flow so that the company can pay its bills, and this is not always easy, since customers may demand that they be given 90 days to pay for products or services purchased, but the new venture may be required by its suppliers to pay *its* bills within 30 days. In addition, when growth is rapid, an increasing number of employees—including experts in various areas (marketing, production, product design, etc.)—must be hired, and many decisions must be delegated to these persons. Thus, inexorably, entrepreneurs lose some control over their companies—something many find hard to accept. Finally, rapid growth may make it more difficult to monitor quality of products or services, and this can boomerang, reducing the company's overall reputation.

So is rapid growth a goal entrepreneurs should always seek? In many cases, it *is* desirable, but in others it may run counter to the reasons why entrepreneurs have founded their companies in the first place; and it may also generate changes that, together, undermine entrepreneurs' enthusiasm and motivation—their passion. Each entrepreneur therefore should weigh these "pluses" and "minuses" carefully before adopting growth as their primary, overarching goal.

In short, growth does indeed generate a pie of growing size—more sales, revenues, and perhaps profits for a new venture. But, to continue the metaphor, the ingredients become more numerous and combining them successfully more complex. It is for these reasons that although growth is generally a good thing for a new venture, it comes at a significant cost—and entrepreneurs must be ready to meet the challenge of this cost if they wish to attain— and sustain—high levels of growth. When they are not, the results can be disastrous—as "The Entrepreneurial Quest" case study below indicates.

CASE STUDY

The Entrepreneurial Quest

When growth can be deadly

Merrill Lynch, AIG, Toyota, Starbucks, Dell, BP, Arthur Andersen, Lehman Brothers—all these companies were, and in some cases, still are, leaders in their industries. Yet several have disappeared, and others experienced some "rough spots" during which their profits declined precipitously. Despite the fact that they operated in diverse industries they all had something in common: all had become focused (perhaps "obsessed" is a better term) on attaining rapid growth, to the point that they lost sight of other important ingredients in success. One way to put this is to state that they failed to manage growth effectively. Rather, they sought it at any cost. The reasons for this emphasis on growth are obvious: stock markets reward increasing sales and profits handsomely. For instance, the stock of Tesla Motors, which makes all-electric vehicles, increased 19 percent in one day after the company reported profits of . . . 20 cents per share! This profit stemmed from increasing sales, and it is indeed a major reward for growth.

On the other hand, large companies can founder in the search for growth. Consider Borders Books. It ran a chain of bookstores throughout the USA and in many other countries too. The stores were attractive, the staff were helpful, and each had a café serving light snacks and beverages (Figure 11.3). I remember spending pleasant hours in a local Borders, which had well-stocked shelves and, seemingly, a wider variety of books, CDs, and other items than its key competitor Barnes and Noble. Yet, in 2011, Borders filed for bankruptcy and is now only a memory. Why? Many factors played role, including the chain's reluctance to enter the digital market. But rapid, uncontrolled growth also contributed to its downfall and disappearance. To grow, Borders opened many new stores—over 500 in the USA alone, plus 175 more that operated under the Waldenbooks trademark, and a growing number outside the USA. This proved to be too much for the company's management to handle, and as one bad decision followed another, profits declined; in fact the last time the company made a profit was 2006. Being focused on growth, Borders failed to move rapidly to make digital media a basic part of its business model, a failure that led to further declines as rivals developed this opportunity more quickly—and effectively. In short, Borders' focus on growth contributed heavily to its ultimate demise.

CASE STUDY *(continued)*

Source: With permission of the photographer, Serge Melki.

Figure 11.3 Did uncontrolled growth kill Borders Books?

Borders Books was a highly successful chain of bookstores, and it grew rapidly—perhaps too rapidly. As the number of stores and the complexity of running a large company increased, its top managers made important errors. It is possible that some of these stemmed from the fact that the company—and its executives—were not prepared for rapid growth and could not handle it effectively. Borders is now only a memory.

> **CASE STUDY** (continued)
>
> Entrepreneurs who launch new ventures also often focus on achieving rapid growth. This emphasis certainly makes sense, but only to a degree. If it leads them to overlook other important issues, the result may be major setbacks and unlike Toyota, Starbucks and BP, they lack the resources to recover.

So what does "smart" or effective growth involve? Basically, paying careful attention to these issues, even as the company seeks growth:

- **Managing cash flow**. Too much growth can add to expenses quickly, so that company soon runs out of operating capital. That can be deadly, since bills may then go unpaid and the company's credit may suffer.
- **Maintaining customer service**. Rapid growth may increase demand, but leave less time for servicing customers who, dissatisfied with their treatment, take their business elsewhere.
- **Developing human resources**. Intent on achieving growth, the company may have barely enough funds to meet monthly salaries, and no funds with which to reward excellent performance. As a result, the best people begin to look for another job.
- **Exceeding top management's limits**. Managers who could handle day-to-day operations when the company was relatively small, may find that they lack the skills to deal with the growing complexities generated by rapid growth.
- **Spending sprees**. As orders rise, management may be tempted to spend more, and use the cash generated to expand even more rapidly. The result? If there is even a temporary downturn in orders, the company finds itself with very high overhead—and few reserves to cover it.

These are only a few of the problems that can arise from rapid—and unmanaged—growth. Savvy entrepreneurs will assure that even as they attempt to grow their companies they will pay careful attention to these issues, so that growth does *not* become the rock on which their promising new company founders.

Strategies for attaining growth

As noted above, growth may not be for all entrepreneurs or all new ventures, but for those that choose growth as a primary goal other questions arise. How can it be attained? What steps and strategies are effective in generating rapid growth? Two major approaches to achieving this goal exist: "internal strategies"—ones focused on building the company from within, and "external strategies"—ones that focus, instead, on building the company by reaching outside it.

Internal strategies: Building the company from within

Internal strategies for achieving growth involve resources within the new venture—using what it has to fuel increases in sales and profits. Several of the most common—and successful—of these strategies are described below.

New product development

A basic strategy for attaining high growth is to introduce new products—ones not provided by competitors. In some industries this is truly a necessity; for instance, in high-tech environments, new products are introduced at a rapid pace, and any company that does not keep pace will soon be left behind. A new venture's ability to generate new products is based, in part, on its "dynamic capabilities"—its ability to change in response to rapidly shifting external conditions and environments (Eisenhardt and Martin, 2000). In general, the higher a company's dynamic capabilities, the greater its success in attaining growth, because it can rapidly shift gears to respond to threats from competitors and pursue new opportunities. Of course, large companies often have an advantage in this respect; they have research and development departments that conduct a continuous search for new products that the company can develop. To overcome this disadvantage, new ventures should (1) focus on markets they know rather than attempt to expand into ones they don't know; (2) develop new products or services that are related to ones they also provide; (3) be very careful about setting prices—too high, and customers may disappear, too low, and profits may be non-existent, and (4) make sure that quality remains high; reducing quality (and price) in pursuit of rapid growth can be truly dangerous, since it will quickly destroy the new venture's developing reputation.

Improving existing products or services

Recently, an ad for a luxury automobile stated: "The extremely new . . ." The implication is that previous models of this particular product were now obsolete, since the *new* version was infinitely better. Fortunately, most consumers recognize such claims for what they are: exaggeration. The word "new" is one of the most overused terms in advertising; a much more reasonable term—one that more accurately describes what has occurred—might be "improved." And in fact, improving existing products can be a highly effective way of attracting new customers and generating growth. Apple is a master at this game, introducing improved versions of its products very often. Many customers quickly trade in their older models for the new ones, which loudly proclaim their many new features. This has worked well in the past, but recently there have been growing signs that consumers don't think the "improvements" justify the cost of replacing the products they already have. Up to a point, however, improving a company's products in ways that consumers find attractive is a useful internal strategy for generating growth.

Expanding product lines

A related internal strategy involves expanding existing product lines. This can involve developing different models of the company's products, each designed to appeal to somewhat different customers. For instance, consider a company that manufactures tablet computers. The company can increase its product lines by developing models that vary in features, size, and price. The less expensive models might appeal to first-time buyers who want to use the computers mainly for entertainment, while more expensive (and fully equipped) models appeal to individuals who want to use them, at least in part, for their work. By expanding their product lines, new ventures can tap larger markets, and so attain growth. However, development costs can be very high, so the potential increase in sales and profits must be weighed very carefully against these costs.

Expanding market penetration and/or seeking new markets

Another way in which a new venture can attain growth using its own resources is through expanding the markets for its existing products. This can be obtained through better advertising and by identifying—and then focusing on—markets the company has not yet penetrated. The term "market penetration" refers to the extent to which the new venture generates sales in specific markets where it was previously not represented.

Entering international markets: Going global to achieve growth

When new ventures are launched, their founders tend to focus on markets they already know—often ones close to the company's home, or at least within their country. However, as they begin to grow, many recognize opportunities to generate sales in other locations—including international ones. One reason for this is clear: in recent years, the economies of many nations have become interlocked and interdependent, with the result that movement of goods and services between them has become much easier than in the past. For instance, in the European Union, a single currency and a relatively free flow of products and raw materials between the member states, now exists. These conditions can be enticing to entrepreneurs, who recognize that they can obtain growth by "geographic expansion," first to nearby regions, and then, perhaps internationally as well. This is a complex undertaking: different countries still have different laws, and cultures differ greatly, so that features attractive to consumers in one country may not necessarily be attractive to those in another. Further, advertising campaigns that are successful in one language may make little or no sense in another. For example, General Electric Corporation long had the following motto: "We bring good things to life," meaning we supply products that make life easier. When this is translated into Japanese, however, it reads: "We bring dead ancestors to life!" Another amusing example is provided by the Chevrolet Nova. When it was offered for sale in Latin American countries, the name Nova translated, roughly, as "doesn't go" (*no va*) (Figure 11.4). That certainly didn't help sales! While giant corporations can afford such errors, new ventures generally cannot, so the moral is: proceed into international markets carefully. In this regard, I have a relative who speaks several languages (German, French, Greek) as well as English. She has started a company that helps people recognize the subtle nuances between these languages, so that they won't make the kind of errors noted above. Often, these subtle differences in meaning are hard to discern—but ignoring them can lead to very embarrassing outcomes.

Innovative business practices

One more internal strategy new ventures can adopt involves "innovative business practices"—doing something competitors don't do that customers perceive as beneficial. For example, many consumers often have difficulty in assembling products they have purchased that come unassembled, in a box containing many parts. An innovative practice might involve providing a DVD that walks customers through this process one step at a time. Another would be setting up a website customers could visit to receive such information, and making it interactive—they could ask questions that would be answered immediately online by company representatives. If other companies don't provide these services, one that provides them might gain an important advantage in terms of sales.

An overview of the various internal strategies that new ventures can use to move toward rapid growth is provided by Figure 11.5. If used with appropriate care—and caution—all of them can contribute to reaching this key goal.

Figure 11.4 The Chevrolet Nova—and the complexities of "going global"

Entering international markets can be very enticing—modern economies are now closely interlocked so in some ways doing so is easier than in the past. But cultural differences—including language differences—can make this a complex task. The Chevrolet was a popular car in the USA, but failed to generate the expected sales in Latin America—partly because in Spanish *no va* means "doesn't go"—not something most people want in their cars!

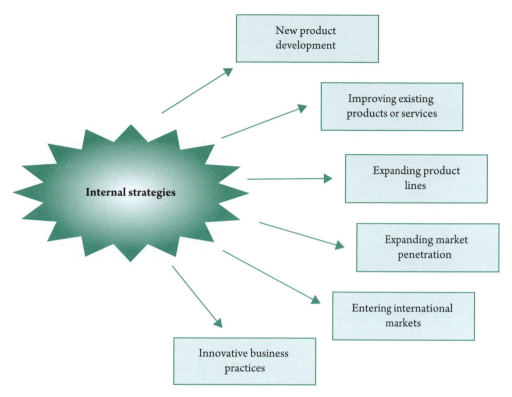

Figure 11.5 Internal strategies for attaining growth

The strategies shown here are ones based on resources within a new venture—using what it has to generate increased sales and profits.

External strategies: Encouraging growth from the outside

As we have just seen, new ventures can often attain high rates of growth through actions involving internal changes and effort—ones that take place primarily within the new venture (e.g., improving existing products and developing new ones; implementing innovative business practices). In today's rapidly changing business environment, however, another set of strategies is often virtually required. These involve efforts by the company to reach outside—to attain growth by use of resources outside the new ventures itself. Such tactics—generally described as "external strategies"—take many different forms, but in essence all involve leveraging the new venture's resources by entering into mutually beneficial arrangements with other organizations. Many such strategies exist, but here we'll focus on several that appear to be most effective: mergers and acquisitions, licensing of intellectual property, strategic alliances, joint ventures, and most recently, through joining innovative ecosystems—informal networks developed by a large company, in which smaller companies (often new ventures founded by entrepreneurs) work on further development of a basic innovation generated by the large hub company. Another external strategy—franchising—was discussed in Chapter 9.

Mergers and acquisitions

One external strategy for obtaining growth is, in some respects, the most extreme: it results either in the disappearance of the new venture, or its radical transformation. This strategy involves "mergers," in which two independent companies become one, often with a new name. For instance, Daimler-Benz, the German manufacturer of Mercedes Benz automobiles, merged with Chrysler Corporation in 1998 to form Daimler-Chrysler. Although, in fact, Daimler-Benz was larger, the two companies described their combining as a merger of equals. Although this was a merger of two giant companies, new ventures too sometimes merge. This is especially common in young industries where there are no dominant companies—for instance, biotechnology. In that industry, small companies often merge to combine their resources and knowledge so that both can grow.

A related strategy involves "acquisition," in which one company purchases another company outright. For instance, in recent years Google has purchased a number of companies including Android, Zagat, and Picasa. Similarly, Microsoft purchased Nokia in 2013 for more than $7 billion. Although many acquisitions do contribute to growth of the purchasing company, this is not always the case. For instance, when AOL purchased Time-Warner, hopes were high. Several years later, however, the combined company was losing huge amounts of money each year. The result: they separated, and after recovering its independence, Time-Warner went on to grow rapidly.

While mergers and acquisitions are designed to help both parties, they must be approached carefully. The advantages are clear: access to new markets may be developed, new products are added to the acquiring company's offerings, and important new knowledge may be gained by the company making the acquisition (after the acquisition, it generally owns all of the other company's patents and trademarks). However, sometimes there are "culture clashes" between the two sets of managers—especially top-level executives—and these can prove costly. For these reasons, entrepreneurs should approach mergers and acquisitions very carefully, because they are almost certain to involve a mixed pattern of benefits and costs.

Licensing: Granting access to intellectual property

A new venture's intellectual property—patents, trademarks, and copyrights—can be an important part of its value (see Chapter 9). One way of leveraging such property into higher rates of growth is through "licensing," an arrangement in which the party that owns the intellectual property grants use of it to another party under clearly stated conditions for specific periods of time. The author's company, Innovative Environmental Products, owned several patents, and it licensed this intellectual property to Holmes Products, Inc., a large manufacturer of small electric devices. Holmes then produced IEP's products and distributed them to large retail chains. They paid IEP a small royalty (2 percent) of the sales price of each unit sold. This was a fairly standard arrangement and it did help IEP to boost its sales in ways it would not have been able to do itself—for instance, by securing shelf space for these products in large retailers.

Several types of licensing exist, but two that are increasingly important are "technology licensing" and "merchandise and character licensing." Technology licensing involves granting the right to use knowledge contained in the licensing company's patents to another company—the licensee. In contrast, merchandise and character licensing involves licensing a recognized trademark or brand for use by another company. For instance, Starbucks has licensed its products for sale outside its stores in selected grocery chains. Starbucks has been very careful to limit such licensing because of the real risks involved in such arrangements. If a company licenses its trademarks or brand widely (i.e., to many different users), it faces a difficult problem: how can it assure that all these purchasers are meeting its quality standards? If they are not, the reputation for high-quality products built up by the licensing company over years, may be seriously damaged, with the result that sales decrease, rather than increase—which is the goal of licensing in the first place.

One of the most common forms of licensing involves professional sports teams that permit clothing manufacturers to use their insignia (their trademarks) on everything from t-shirts to ties or shoes (Figure 11.6); this is known as merchandise licensing. Another common form involves licensing of trademarks by franchisors to their franchise holders, thus permitting them to display trademarks that belong to the parent company, and that consumers recognize instantly.

Strategic alliances and joint ventures: Partnering for growth

Another external strategy for attaining growth derives from a basic principle of life: in many situations people can accomplish more by working together

Source: Wikimedia: with permission of the photographer for unrestricted use.

Figure 11.6 Merchandise licensing—a very common way of licensing trademarks

Sports teams often allow clothing manufacturers to display their symbol. This is an example of merchandise licensing.

than they can by working alone—in others words, by cooperating. Such alliances often occur between large, well-established companies; for instance, Chrysler and Fiat established a "strategic alliance" to manufacture small jeeps. Another is the strategic alliance between Disney and Hewlett Packard, an arrangement that benefited both companies. New ventures too sometimes participate in strategic alliances, and in many cases they can benefit greatly in terms of enhanced growth by forming cooperative relationships with other companies. Such arrangements can take several different forms. One that is becoming increasingly popular is a partnership between two or more companies that is formed to attain a specific goal or objective. In some industries, for example, high-tech fields, a majority of new ventures form such arrangements. The benefits of such arrangements can be substantial. Each party to the agreement shares risks and costs with the others, there may be significant economies of scale, each party can learn from the others, and the speed with which new products can be brought to market may be considerably increased. Of course, there is a potential downside too. Partners to a strategic alliance often share proprietary information with the other parties, they lose some degree of autonomy and independence, and of course, their own success or failure is now at least partly dependent on the performance of the partners. Overall though, strategic alliances appear not only to be beneficial for many new ventures, they may also be essential for them in many cases, especially if they want to attain high rates of growth.

Some strategic alliances involve cooperation in research and development—they are known as "technological alliances." This is very common in the biotech industry, where large pharmaceutical corporations provide funding to small start-up ventures in return for access to any new drugs they develop. Other strategic alliances focus more on sales, and often pair a company that has a well-developed distribution system with another that has a new product to sell but is lacking such a distribution system; both gain in such "marketing alliances" since the company with the distribution system now has additional products to sell and the costs of maintaining the system are relatively fixed regardless of the number of products. The company with the new products, in turn, gains access to customers without the costs of having to establish an entire distribution system. Once again, though, entrepreneurs must carefully weigh the potential benefits and costs of any potential strategic alliance and choose only the ones that offer the most favorable balance.

"Joint ventures," in contrast, are new business entities created by two or more companies that together create the new venture in which they both participate. The companies founding the joint venture remain independent, but they join forces to create this new business.

Innovation ecosystems

A relatively new external strategy for increasing growth has been developed in recent years. It is known as an "innovation ecosystem" and is a loosely interconnected network of companies that work together to develop the capabilities of a new innovation. Innovation ecosystems are generally established by a large hub (Moore, 1993; Iansiti and Levien, 2004; Nambisan and Baron, 2013), which defines and offers the basic innovation. The large firm wants to extend or strengthen this innovation, and network members work on these tasks. Often, the other companies in the innovation ecosystem are small—new ventures—and, as just noted, they work on tasks assigned by the central hub firm. The hub firm chooses the small companies that are invited to join, and establishes the rules and policies that will govern both value creation and value appropriation, and as noted above, sets the specific tasks on which member companies will work. The smaller companies in the network gain because the large hub firm promotes their products, thus increasing their sales. An important "downside" of such arrangements, though, is that the hub firm, by setting the tasks and goals, exercises considerable influence on the small companies (Iansiti and Levien, 2004; Nambisan and Sawhney, 2011). They are, essentially very junior partners in the ecosystem. Further, given the size disparities, the hub firm holds significant power over the small member companies and can "make or break" them through its decisions on membership, technology licenses, nature and extent of knowledge sharing, special alliances and collaborative initiatives, certification and promotion of partner's offerings, and so on. All of this introduces a level of tension into the relationship with the hub firm that poses several challenges for entrepreneurs who bring their new ventures into the ecosystem.

Does joining an innovative ecosystem actually help new ventures grow? A recent study by Baron and Nambisan (2013) indicates that it does. New ventures in such ecosystems showed higher sales than ones outside ecosystems. So, although there are significant costs to the new ventures in terms of reduced individual freedom, the benefits of being associated with a large and highly successful company (e.g., Apple, Microsoft, Boeing have all established such systems) can be more than offset by these disadvantages.

In sum, there are a number of strategies—both internal and external—new ventures can pursue if rapid growth is their key goal. It's important to remember, however, that not all entrepreneurs desire such growth. Some are more concerned with achieving other goals—such as simply being their own boss, or helping others. Assuming that growth is the "be-all, end-all" of all new ventures, therefore, can distort the actual picture, which is much more complex, just as human behavior and motivation are very complex.

Entrepreneurial orientation (EO): A key strategy for new ventures

New ventures are as varied and unique as the entrepreneurs who create them, so it is far from surprising that they can, and often do, pursue a wide range of strategies in their quest to gain competitive advantage—an edge over other firms. We have already examined several of these in the discussion of strategies for obtaining growth. Here, we'll focus on one overall strategy that captures the essence of how many new ventures seek to achieve rapid growth—and the success it often yields. This strategy is known as "entrepreneurial orientation" (EO for short), and in a sense, relates to the overall way in which new ventures operate—their approach to developing the opportunities they have chosen to develop. We'll now examine this overall strategy and explain why many new ventures choose to adopt it.

The nature of EO

This strategy, which has received a great deal of attention from entrepreneurship researchers (Covin and Lumpkin, 2011), has generally been viewed as involving three distinct but related features: "proactiveness," "innovativeness," and "risk-taking" (Miller, 1983, 2011). As a result of recent research, much is known about the nature of EO (Covin and Lumpkin, 2011), and its role in several important processes—for instance, organizational learning (Kreiser, 2011), the performance of family business (Dess et al., 2011), new business creation (Miller, 2011), and several aspects of firm performance (Rauch et al., 2009).

The term entrepreneurial orientation (EO) was first introduced as a construct by Miller (1983), and later refined, expanded, and clarified by Lumpkin and Dess (1996). According to these authors, EO involves the three distinct, but interrelated components noted above: proactiveness—a preference for highly competitive actions and for introducing new products or services ahead of competitors—in essence for being first; innovativeness—an emphasis on developing many new products, lines of products, or services (often through heavy investment in R&D activities); and risk-taking—a willingness—and perhaps an actual preference for high-risk projects, as well as willingness to take bold, aggressive actions, which include moving quickly to exploit newly emerged opportunities (Covin and Lumpkin, 2011; see also Figure 11.7). Although these components are distinct, they are correlated, so they are often combined into a single construct—a kind of overview of how many new ventures approach conducting their business (e.g., George and Marino, 2011).

Although the components of EO are correlated, it sometimes makes sense to consider them separately, because each may be more important in some situations than others. For instance, as one author puts it (Miller, 2011, p. 880), "Sometimes . . . the components of EO are more telling than the aggregative index." For example, risk-taking may be especially relevant to actually starting a business, because launching a new venture *is* risky, so a willingness to accept such risk is virtually necessary to get started. In contrast, innovativeness may be especially important to operating a start-up in a high-tech context, where changes occur rapidly, and a failure to keep up, and offer many new or improved products can prove fatal. Finally, proactiveness—attempting to be first—is important in industries or environments where change is rapid and being first can be valuable; it may be less crucial in industries or environments that are more stable and "being first" brings few, if any, advantages.

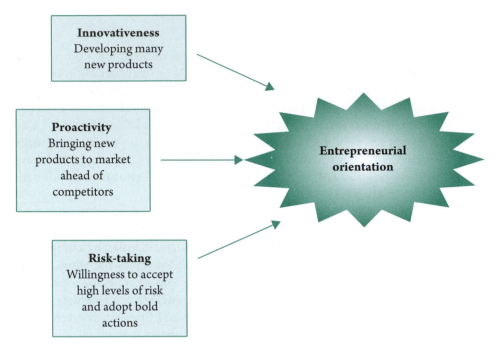

Figure 11.7 Basic components of entrepreneurial orientation

As shown here, entrepreneurial orientation—an overall strategy adopted by many new ventures—involves three major features.

Regardless of its specific components, a key question about EO is this: is it significantly related to firm-level performance, that is, to the success of new ventures? A large body evidence indicates that the answer is definitely "Yes." EO is indeed related to new venture success, although this relationship is somewhat stronger in very small (micro) organizations than larger ones, and in high-tech than low-tech firms (Rauch et al., 2009). On the basis of these and other findings, some authors (e.g., Simsek and Heavey, 2011) have suggested that adoption of EO is crucial for the new venture's ability to adapt to change and compete effectively. In short, EO appears to be one important strategy for new ventures. While nothing can guarantee success, adoption of the overall strategy does seem to be an important "plus."

Why new ventures adopt EO

Assuming that EO is indeed positively related to new ventures, it is not surprising that many entrepreneurs adopt it as a guiding. At first glance though, doing so is somewhat surprising. New ventures generally have limited resources, so how—when competing against much larger companies—can they hope to be proactive, that is, first to market? Similarly, how, with limited budgets for research and development, can they can hope to generate many innovative products and keep up, or even surpass, much larger companies with greater resources? And finally, given their limited resources, how can new ventures afford to take many risks? If such actions fail, the new ventures may find themselves . . . out of business! In contrast, large, well-established firms have sufficient resources to recover from even large losses. Given these points, why do many new ventures adopt EO as their basic approach to doing business?

At present, relatively little direct information on this important issue exists, but some findings point to intriguing answers. One informative study concerning adoption of EO was conducted by Simsek and Heavey (2011) who found that CEOs' core self-evaluations (a variable composed of self-esteem, locus of control, generalized self-efficacy, and emotional stability; Erez and Judge, 2001), was positively related to EO, at least in dynamic environments. These authors predicted that this would be the case because CEOs with high core self-evaluation would be more confident of their own abilities, and so more willing to take chances and adopt aggressive strategies such as attempting to develop and market highly innovative products. In addition, they would tend to emphasize the upside potential of entrepreneurial opportunities, and believe that they overcome major obstacles—thus being able to attain the ambitious goals identified by EO. Aside from this and a few other investigations (see e.g., Chiabaru, 2010), there is very little relevant evidence on *why* entrepreneurs choose to adopt EO.

Despite this fact, it is intriguing to mention several possibilities that may account for entrepreneurs' willingness to adopt EO in running their new ventures. For example, Baron et al. (2013) have proposed that entrepreneurs' self-regulation—their ability to monitor and direct their own behavior toward attaining important goals (see Chapter 8)—may play a key role in this process. Specifically, they predicted that the higher entrepreneurs' self-control, the less likely they would be to adopt all three components of EO—innovativeness, proactiveness, and risk-taking. This would be so because high self-control would keep them focused on reaching specific goals, and assist them to recognize that the goals of being highly innovative and first to market are probably beyond the new venture's reach; as a result, they would focus on other, more attainable goals.

On the other hand, certain aspects of metacognitive knowledge—entrepreneurs' understanding of their own cognition, and specifically, understanding of their own ability to recognize failing courses of action and withdraw from them—would be positively related to adoption of EO. In other words such self-knowledge would help entrepreneurs escape from the potential trap of sunk costs. Specifically, if it became apparent that the ambitious goals suggested by EO (e.g., being first to market) goals could not be obtained, the entrepreneurs would abandon these efforts and so minimize losses, rather than continuing with strategies that have little chance of success. In support of these suggestions, Baron et al. (2013) found that among a large group of entrepreneurs, metacognition was positively related to all three aspects of EO (innovativeness, proactiveness, and risk-taking), while self-control was negatively related to risk-taking. However, so far, these findings have only been obtained in one study so they should be viewed with caution.

Other possibilities that have not yet been examined relate to entrepreneurs' levels of optimism: those high in this characteristic might be more likely to adopt EO than those lower in optimism, who are, in a sense, more realistic! Similarly, entrepreneurs who focus primarily on obtaining gains (individuals high in what is termed "a promotion regulatory focus"; Higgins, 2000) would be more likely to adopt EO than those who focus primarily on avoiding losses (a prevention regulatory focus). These possibilities, although they have not yet been examined in actual research, seem reasonable in the light of existing evidence, and offer at least tentative insights into *why* some entrepreneurs adopt EO, and *who* would be most likely to do so (i.e., those high in promotion regulatory focus, and those high in metacognitive knowledge).

Regardless of the answers yielded by future research however, it is clear that EO is a strategy adopted by many entrepreneurs as a means of attaining the rapid growth that many (but again, not all) desire.

THE EFFECTIVE ENTREPRENEUR

Many entrepreneurs seek rapid growth and they employ a number of different strategies to attain this goal. However, all have a downside as well potential benefits, so an effective entrepreneur adopts them only after careful consideration of the balance between "pluses" and "minuses." Here are some guidelines to follow in choosing an effective strategy for obtaining growth:

- First, ask yourself if you *want* rapid growth. While this can increase sales and profits, it may require you to become a manager and oversee an organization growing in complexity. If this it not for you, then think again. If you decide that growth *is* what you seek, then choose the strategies for obtaining it carefully.

- Some strategies involve using existing resources of your own company to attain growth. These focus on improving existing products, developing new ones,

➡

expanding product lines, entering new markets, going "global," and developing innovative business practices—that other competitors don't or can't have. These internal strategies are ones your company can do by itself, so you may find them appealing and useful for this reason.

- Other strategies involve reaching out to other companies. Such external strategies include mergers, acquisitions, licensing of intellectual property (e.g., patents held by you company), forming strategic alliances with other companies, or entering into joint ventures with them. It can also involve joining an innovation ecosystem—a group of small companies who focus on developing improvements to the products of a larger company. Such ecosystems offer important benefits—the hub (i.e., founding) company can help new ventures boost sales, but it involves important costs too—a reduction in the new venture's freedom of action because it must work on tasks set by the hub company. Again, weigh the costs and benefits of each of these external strategies against your own goals before adopting them.

- Many new ventures adopt an overall strategy involving innovativeness (developing many new products) proactiveness (being first to develop and sell such products) and risk-taking (being willing to take risks and act aggressively to build sales and profits). Together, these are known as entrepreneurial orientation (EO) and describe the overall strategy used by many new ventures to seek growth. EO has been found to be positively related to such growth, but it too has a downside: developing many products and doing so ahead of much larger competitors may be difficult tasks for a new venture. So, it is useful for all entrepreneurs to consider the question of whether they can hope to accomplish the challenging tasks established by EO. If they can then by all means proceed. If they probably cannot, then this strategy should be approached with great caution.

SUMMARY OF KEY POINTS

1 New ventures often seek rapid growth and in many cases this is beneficial. However, growth has an important downside too. As a new venture grows, entrepreneurs must take on the functions normally performed by managers and some may find that this not to their liking. In addition, many entrepreneurs do not seek financial gain; rather, they want independence and an opportunity to perform work they find meaningful. Growth may be contrary to some of these motives.

2 If entrepreneurs do seek rapid growth, they can attain this goal through a wide range of strategies—both internal and external. Internal strategies employ the new venture's resources to attain growth (e.g., improving new products or developing new ones, moving into new markets). In contrast, external strategies involve resources outside the new venture

(e.g., licensing intellectual property, forming strategic alliances with other companies, joining innovation ecosystems).

3 Many new ventures adopt an overall strategy known as entrepreneurial orientation. This involves proactiveness—efforts to be first to develop and market new products—innovation—efforts to develop a steady stream of innovative products—and risk-taking, acceptance of high levels of risk. EO is related to new venture success, but given the limited resources possessed by new ventures, some of its major goals (e.g., being first to market with new products) may be very difficult to attain.

REFERENCES

Baron, R.A. and S. Nambisan (2013), "Entrepreneurs' self-regulation and firm performance: Cognitive processes inside the 'black box'," under review.

Baron, R.A., K.M. Hmieleski, C. Fox and C. Casper (2013), "Entrepreneurs' self-regulatory processes and the adoption of high-risk strategies: Effects of self-control and metacognitive knowledge," manuscript under review.

Chiabaru, D.S. (2010), "Chief executives' self-regulation and strategic orientation: A theoretical model," *European Management Journal*, **28**(6), 467–78.

Covin, J.G. and G.T. Lumpkin (2011), "Entrepreneurial orientation theory and research: Reflections on a needed construct," *Entrepreneurship Theory and Practice*, **35**(5), 855–74.

Covin, J.G. and D.L.P. Slevin (1989), "Strategic management of small firms in hostile and benign environment," *Strategic Management Journal*, **10**(1), 73–87.

Dess, G.D., B.C. Pinkham and H. Yang (2011), "Entrepreneurial orientation: Assessing the construct's validity and addressing some of its implications for research in the areas of family business and organizational learning," *Entrepreneurship Theory and Practice*, **35**(5), 1077–91.

Eisenhardt, K.M. and J.A. Martin (2000), "Dynamic capabilities: What are they?" *Entrepreneurship Theory and Practice*, **21**(10–11), 1105–21.

Erez, A. and T.A. Judge (2001), "Relationships of core self-evaluations to goal setting, motivation, and performance," *Journal of Applied Psychology*, **86**(6), 1270–79.

George, B.A. and L. Marino (2011), "The epistemology of entrepreneurial orientation: Conceptual formation, modeling, and operationalization," *Entrepreneurship Theory and Practice*, **35**(5), 989–1024.

Higgins, E.T. (2000), "Making a good decision: Value from fit," *American Psychologist*, **55**(11), 1217–30.

Iansiti, M. and R. Levien (2004), *The Keystone Advantage*, Boston, MA: HBS Press.

Kreiser, P.M. (2011), "Entrepreneurial orientation and organizational learning: The impact of network range and network closure," *Entrepreneurship Theory and Practice*, **35**(5), 1025–50.

Lumpkin, G.T. and G.G. Dess (1996), "Clarifying the entrepreneurial orientation construct and linking it to performance," *Academy of Management Journal*, **21**(1), 135–72.

Miller, D. (1983), "Two correlates of entrepreneurship in three types of firms," *Management Science*, **29**(7), 770–93.

Miller, D. (2011), "Miller (1981) revisited: A reflection on EO research and some suggestions for the future," *Entrepreneurship Theory and Practice*, **35**(10), 873–95.

Moore, J.F. (1993), "Predators and prey: The new ecology of competition," *Harvard Business Review*, **71**(3), 75–83.

Nambisan, S. and R.A. Baron (2013), "Entrepreneurship in innovation ecosystems: Entrepreneurs' self-regulatory processes and their implications for new venture success," *Entrepreneurship Theory and Practice*, **37**(5), 1071–97.

Nambisan, S. and M. Sawhney (2011), "Orchestration processes in network-centric innovation: From the field," *Academy of Management Perspectives*, **25**(3), 40–57.

Rauch, A., J. Wiklund, G.T. Lumpkin and M. Frese (2009), "Entrepreneurial orientation and business performance: An assessment of past research and suggestions for the future," *Entrepreneurship Theory and Practice*, **33**(3), 761–87.

Simsek, Z. and C. Heavey (2011), "The mediating role of knowledge-based capital for corporate entrepreneurship effects on performance: A study of small-to-medium-sized firms," *Strategic Entrepreneurship Journal*, **5**(1) 81–100.

PART IV

Dealing with adversity and leaving the new venture

Setbacks, disappointments, and shattered dreams are, unfortunately, an integral part of entrepreneurship; only rarely does this complex process go entirely smoothly. How can entrepreneurs bounce back from such experiences and learn from their mistakes so that they can do better the next time? All good things come to an end, and at some point entrepreneurs may conclude that it is time to leave their new ventures. This can happen voluntarily—the entrepreneurs choose to depart for any one of several different reasons—they want to reap the rewards of their hard work, start another company, or pass it on to others—family members or long-time employees. Entrepreneurs' departure from their companies may also be involuntary—they must close the company because it has failed. How can they recover from these experiences so that they can continue with their lives and, perhaps, try again? These issues are the focus of this, the concluding part of the book.

12

Endings . . . and beginnings: How—and when— entrepreneurs leave the companies they founded

 CHAPTER OUTLINE

- Different ways of saying "farewell"
  - Sale or transfer to persons inside the company: Shifting control to those who already know it well
  - Sale to people outside the company
  - Valuing a business: An essential ingredient in any sale
- Is taking their company public always the "golden ring" for entrepreneurs?
  - Going public: Potential benefits, potential costs
  - Going public: How the process unfolds
  - Going public: Other issues to consider
- Exit by necessity rather than choice: The effects of business failure
  - Why new ventures fail: Some all too common—but avoidable—reasons
  - Bankruptcy: The saddest ending to a company's life
  - Dealing with business failure: Surviving the end of a dream

There is no real ending. It's just the place where you stop the story.
(Frank Herbert, 1920–86, US science fiction author)

When one door closes, another opens.
(Arab proverb)

Never confuse a single defeat with a final defeat.
(F. Scott Fitzgerald, *Tender is the Night*, 1934)

As the title of this chapter and the quotations above suggest, in a sense endings are sometimes, beginnings. The end of one chapter of life is a prelude to what follows. For entrepreneurs this is often the case. In fact, many entrepreneurs (known as serial or, as I prefer, repeat entrepreneurs) open another company soon after one closes. In fact, I once knew an entrepreneur who sold his company for $700 000 000. When I asked him what he would do next he answered: "I'm already doing it—I started a new company even before the sale was completed." But not all stories concerning the ending of new ventures are quite so happy. Some close because, to put it simply, they have failed—they have run out of cash or even worse, are deeply in debt and can't continue.

In this chapter, we'll examine the full range of possibilities where entrepreneurs' departure from the companies they started is concerned. First, we'll examine sale of the company to others—either persons inside the company or outside it. Such sales raise a complex problem: what is the company worth? As we'll see, the question sounds simple, but answering it is often very complex. Then, we'll examine taking a company public—offering its shares to the general public by listing it on a stock exchange. Many people believe that this is truly the "golden ring" for entrepreneurs—the best possible outcome. But, in fact, this may not always be true for reasons we'll soon describe. Finally, we'll turn to the sad topic of business failure—when entrepreneurs do not close their companies voluntarily, but rather because the companies (and by extension, the entrepreneurs) have failed. Here, we'll examine some of the reasons why these unhappy events occur; bankruptcy, which is a consequence of business failure; and finally, the impact of such failures on entrepreneurs—which often includes financial, social, and psychological costs.

Different ways of saying "farewell"

We have already noted in previous chapters that many entrepreneurs have a strong and deep commitment to their companies. This is far from surprising; they think about them almost all the time and spend more time working in them than doing anything else; indeed, one complaint frequently heard from entrepreneurs' families is that they rarely get to see, let alone spend time with their spouses or, in the case of children, their father or mother. So why, given this deep commitment do entrepreneurs ever decide that they should exit? The reasons are as varied as human life. In some cases, the entrepreneurs simply want to reap the rewards they have earned and move on to other activities—such as starting another venture. In other instances the company is surviving but "limping along," with little prospect of future growth. A third reason is that they simply receive too good an offer to refuse. The main point is that there are many good and legitimate reasons, both economic and personal, why entrepreneurs may decide to cut the ties that bind them to their new ventures. What are the specific strategies or options open to founding entrepreneurs who decide to do so? Many exist, but most are variations on three major themes: (1) sell or transfer ownership of the company to insiders—people already in the company, (2) sell or transfer ownership to outsiders, or (3) take the company public through an IPO (initial public offering). We'll now take a closer look at each of these possibilities.

Sale or transfer to persons inside the company: Shifting control to those who already know it well

One obvious way for an entrepreneur to exit from the company they founded is through a sale to people already in the company but who aren't part of the founding team. Why would such people want to buy the company? Not, of course, if it is in deep financial trouble and sales are declining, but if the company is doing at least moderately well they may feel that they can do a better job of running it and see this as an opportunity to increase their own wealth—as well as to be in charge rather than a subordinate who follows "orders from the top." So, in fact, there are several reasons why insiders may want to become the top management team. There are several ways in which such a purchase can proceed, and they are described briefly below.

Transfers of ownership to successors and leveraged buy-outs

One very common way for entrepreneurs to exit from the companies they have founded is to turn over the reins to a group of insiders that they have very close relationships with, for instance, senior employees or members of their own family. This makes very good sense for several reasons. First, these persons (experienced employees, spouses, children, brothers and sisters, parents, etc.) have often helped to build the company either through financial support or by providing social support and encouragement to the entrepreneurs. Second, they often own large blocks of shares and know the company—and its business model—very well. They are also individuals the entrepreneurs most trust and have confidence in. For example, Henry Ford groomed his son Edsel to take over when he finally retired. Only Edsel's untimely death at the relatively young age of 50 prevented this from occurring. Years later, the Ford company produced a car named in his honor—the Edsel (Figure 12.1). Unfortunately, it was a dismal failure rather than providing a lasting tribute to Ford's son.

Finally, it's important to note that many entrepreneurs strongly wish to leave something of value to their children, grandchildren, and other members of

Figure 12.1 The transfer—and tribute—that failed

Henry Ford planned to transfer his ownership of the Ford Motor Co. to his son Edsel. However, Edsel died before he could take over from his father. Years later, the company produced a line of cars designed to honor Edsel's memory. However, the Edsel was a miserable failure and so did not provide the desired tribute to its namesake.

their families. So, turning the company over to these people, either by sale or in other ways, is a very reasonable way of reaching this goal. (Although, as noted below, there are other ways of attaining this goal.)

Succession: Gradual transfer to the next generation

Sale is not the only way in which entrepreneurs can provide a legacy for their children and others. Frequently, they accomplish this goal in a gradual manner; they begin to share power with their chosen successor, and to transfer blocks of shares to this person or persons. Gradually then, these individuals become the people making the important decisions, and, in fact, may own a large proportion of the company. Alternatively, and especially if they do not believe that their children or other family members are ready to take full control, entrepreneurs can form a "limited partnership" in which they transfer a majority of the shares to the family members but continue in a key role by acting as the general partner—the person who makes decisions and runs the continuing operations of the company.

A third way of transferring ownership of the company to family members or others is through a "trust." This involves a legal document that specifies that the company (or other property) will be transferred to the beneficiary of the trust when this person or persons reach some specific age or meet some other criteria described in the trust. A trustee (e.g., a bank) holds the assets in question until the person the trust was established for attains the criteria included in the trust. Why don't the donors just give these assets to the beneficiary immediately? For several reasons: they don't believe they are ready to handle them, they want to maintain control for some period of time, or, sometimes to reduce taxes. I personally set up a trust for my daughter's college costs when she was only nine years old, and directed that it pay her one fourth of the amount each year; that turned out to sufficient to see her through to graduation. Recently, I have done the same for my grandchildren.

Whatever mechanism for transferring ownership of the company the entrepreneur chooses, it is important that these plans be made, and that these plans are fully understood by all the persons involved. If they are not, disagreements—sometimes very serious ones—can arise between family members and others who believe that they have been short-changed in some way, and the greater the value of company, the angrier and therefore more difficult to resolve such disputes can be, sometimes resulting in costly legal battles.

Sale to people outside the company

While many businesses founded by entrepreneurs are sold or transferred to insiders, many others are sold to outsiders—people not currently in the company who want to acquire it. Several groups of potential buyers exist for any profitable business: "direct competitors" who want to expand their market share and eliminate one of their rivals, "non-direct competitors" (companies that do not compete directly with the entrepreneurs' company, but wish to enter to the markets it currently serves), and "non-competitors" (buyers who simply see the company as a good opportunity—a good place to invest their surplus cash and their management skills). From the point of view of the new venture, a sale to outsiders is often a very good strategy. For example, if a new venture becomes part of a larger company it is no longer necessary for it to maintain its own marketing.

If a business is profitable, there may be many potential buyers for it. Identifying these individuals, however, may be difficult. If the business is small, outside help—someone who specializes in matching buyers and sellers—may be required. If it is large, however, a sale may involve an investment banker—someone who can arrange for the large amount of financing needed for such a sale. If it is in financial trouble, finding a buyer may be extremely difficult. For example, in 2013, BlackBerry—once highly successful—announced that it was up for sale. The company, which did not keep up with its competition, was losing large amounts of money, and concluded that a sale was the best option. Here's what the company itself said (quoted from *The Wall Street Journal*, 2013): "the company previously known as Research in Motion (RIM) announced it had decided to 'explore strategic alternatives.' Buyers are being sought, though the company could also go private or be broken up. Few analysts expect a turnaround."

When a business is large (e.g., BlackBerry) selling it may require the services of an investment banker who can arrange the large amount of financing needed for such a sale. Whichever route is taken, sale of an existing business often involves preparation of a "selling memorandum," a document designed to attract interest in the business. Although it is designed to emphasize the company's strengths, it should be accurate because if it is not, buyers will often recognize this, and the trust necessary for reaching an agreement may be dissipated.

People selling their house are often advised by a realtor to make repairs, paint, or complete other improvements so that the house will be attractive to potential buyers. The same principle applies to sale of a company—the current owners should take certain steps to enhance its appeal to potential purchasers. Here are some steps entrepreneurs can take to make their company accomplish this goal:

- Sell when the company is on the way up and is growing rapidly, not when it has already reached its peak.
- Sell when the business cycle (i.e., the general economy) is strong.
- If the founding team of entrepreneurs intends to leave after the sale, some provision for transfer to a new group of managers should be made—for instance, the entrepreneurs agree to remain in the company for a definite period of time to smooth the transition.
- All intellectual property (patents, trademarks, etc.) should be fully protected—which often involves paying fees to keep them active.
- Appropriate accounting policies should be in place—ones viewed as appropriate in the company's industry.
- Resolve any disputes—legal or otherwise—that might put the financial future of the company in doubt.

Once potential buyers appear, a key factor that may determine whether an agreement can be reached is the "valuation of the company. What is it actually worth? This is such a complex and important issue that we'll now examine it carefully. As will soon be apparent, valuation is also complex, so there are no simple answers.

Valuing a business: An essential ingredient in any sale

How much is a business worth? This is a question that must be resolved prior to a sale to outsiders. As you can probably guess, entrepreneurs and potential buyers may differ greatly on this issue. Entrepreneurs have a great deal of energy, effort, and time invested in the business, so, like people selling their houses who add "sweat equity" into the equation, they tend to over-value their property (just as home owners often do when they put their houses up for sale). Entrepreneurs also understand "intangibles"—assets that the company has but that are difficult, if not impossible, to list on the balance sheet: goodwill the company has acquired with customers and suppliers, its reputation in the industry, its success in attracting and motivating first-rate employees. The result is that entrepreneurs often have difficulty viewing the business in purely economic terms, and when they think about a selling price, tend to set it very high—higher than the actual financial data would suggest. Buyers, however, take a much more rational approach to valuing the company, so the ultimate result may be that no sale occurs.

How can this important obstacle be overcome? In part by careful valuation of the company. Unfortunately, this is not a simple or straightforward calculation. In fact, even experts in valuing companies often disagree considerably. To cope with such problems, buyers and sellers often use several different methods to value the company, and then negotiate the actual price on the basis of all this information. Below are brief descriptions of some of the major methods used for this purpose.

Balance sheet methods

One basis for valuing a company is in terms of its balance sheet. In the simplest approach, net worth is calculated according to this simple formula: Net Worth = Assets – Liabilities. This sounds straightforward—a company is worth whatever would remain after all of its bills, debts, and so on, are paid. The problem with this approach is that it fails to take account of the fact that the true market value of some assets may not be reflected in the balance sheet. For instance, many companies carry land and buildings on their books at prices considerably lower than their actual value. Similarly, equipment and fixtures may be carried at higher or lower figures than their actual value—what it would cost to replace them. For this reason, valuation is usually computed by the "adjusted balance sheet technique"—in which the actual market value of assets is taken into account. This method yields a more realistic valuation than a simple balance sheet approach.

Earnings methods

Another approach is to value the company on the basis of its projected future earnings. A company generating a high level of profits is, of course, worth more than one that is generating lower profits, or even losses. When purchasers buy a business, they are, in a sense, purchasing not only current assets and liabilities, they are also buying future earnings. Thus, another way of valuing a business is in terms of its future earnings. Three different methods of calculating the value of a business in terms of its future earnings are widely used. Related to this is a comparison of the company's earnings with those of other companies in the same industry. If the company for sale is generating higher profits than its competitors, it is worth more. If it is generating lower profits, it is worth less.

Market method

A third major way of estimating the value of a business involves comparing the price/earnings ratio of the business to that of other publicly traded companies in the same industry. This is known as the "market value" or "price/earnings" approach. Several companies comparable to the company now up for sale are identified, and price/earnings ratios for those publicly traded companies are obtained. Price/earnings is the ratio between the price of the company's stock and its earnings. For instance, if a company earns $1 per share and its stock price is $10, then it is selling for ten times its yearly earnings, and the price/earnings ratio is 10.

One problem with this approach is that it is difficult to use unless the company for sale is listed on a public stock exchange. If it is, several publicly traded companies that are similar to it can be used for purposes of comparison. But if it is still private—still owned by the entrepreneur—this can't be done. Instead, several publicly traded companies similar to the one for sale can be chosen, and then a price/earnings ratio for those companies is used as a guide for valuing the company for sale. Another problem is that entrepreneurs may argue that the price/earnings ratio of public companies is not applicable to their company. In fact, they may suggest a higher ratio than exists for public companies, since they tend to over-value their companies. The result may be deadlock, and the failure to reach agreement.

In sum, there are several useful methods for valuing a company, and all offer both advantages and disadvantages. This is why both the sellers and buyers of a business often calculate its worth in different ways then discuss the methods that will actually be used. Overall then, determining what a company is actually worth is often a complex task, far more complex than determining, for instance, what a house or car are worth. Why? Because there are existing markets for houses and cars, and therefore it is possible to compare one with another. For instance, if comparable houses in the same neighborhood have sold recently for $300 000 then this is a good starting point for negotiations—one that both buyers and sellers may accept—although, like entrepreneurs, sellers may tend to over-value their home because of their personal connections to it (Figure 12.2).

Is taking their company public always the "golden ring" for entrepreneurs?

There is an old saying on Wall Street that is worth considering. Basically, it says that people who report having purchased shares in Wal-Mart when it first went public in 1970 and have held it ever since, are either tremendously lucky or . . . *liars*! If they bought the shares in the first place, they were buying a brand new company about which they, and everyone else, had little information. And few people hold on to a stock for decades; they usually sell long before this point, when the stock is, for instance, three or four times what

Source: Wikimedia: Canadian Register of Historic Places, unrestricted permission for use granted.

Figure 12.2 Sellers of companies—like sellers of houses—often over-value their property

Even though valuing a house for sale is a relatively straightforward task, sellers often believe it is worth more than it actually is, and ask an unrealistic price. The same effects are sometimes observed among entrepreneurs, who tend to over-value their companies, largely because of all the time, effort, and devotion (!) they have invested in them.

they paid for it. But imagine that you were one of the lucky ones. In 1970, you bought 100 shares at the offering price, which was $16.50, making your total investment $1650. Today, after 11 splits, you would be holding more than 20 000 shares and the recent price (August 2013) was almost $77. So your original $16.50 investment would now be worth more than $1 500 000. Not bad! (See Figure 12.3.) If these are the gains for investors, imagine what they are for the entrepreneurs whose companies go public and then grow phenomenally, as Wal-Mart did. Founders often hold a large percentage of the shares, so it is easy to see why the Walton family is among the richest in the world.

Stories like this one suggest that when companies go public—they offer a portion of their equity to the general public—the entrepreneurs who founded them can become fabulously wealthy overnight. For instance, when Facebook went public in 2012, its founder, Mark Zuckerberg, was suddenly worth billions of dollars. (The price of the stock soon dropped by 50 percent, however.) It is easy to understand, therefore, why many entrepreneurs view "going public" as the golden ring—the prize for which they are working so hard. But it's important to note that while a few entrepreneurs reap mind-boggling rewards when their companies go public, most new ventures who go this route do *not* see their stock rise. In fact, most show little or no gains, and many actually generate losses for investors (Table 12.1). So although going public seems at first glance to be an outcome to be fervently desired, the picture is far more complex than that. To understand these complexities, we'll now take a closer look at both the benefits, and potential costs, of going public.

Going public: Potential benefits, potential costs

As noted above, many entrepreneurs hope to take their companies public because this will make them wealthy overnight. But there are other important reasons for following this route. First, it is a way to gain new equity capital—cash that the company can use to grow. In fact, this is why Sam Walton decided to take Wal-Mart public: the company needed $5 million to build a warehouse system, so Mr. Walton decided to offer a small part of the company to the public. The shares sold quickly and Wal-Mart was able to proceed with its plans—and, importantly, without going into debt.

Another important benefit is that the shares of the company can now be traded on a stock exchange. This provides an easy way for individuals or institutions (e.g., retirement funds) to buy and sell the shares. Third, the task of valuing the company is now relatively simple: share prices are available virtually all the time, so multiplying the number of shares by their price provides a clear way of determining what the company is worth.

Figure 12.3 Sometimes, taking a company public produces astounding results for persons who buy its shares

If you had bought 100 shares of 'Wal-Mart when it went public your $1650 investment would now be worth more than $1, 500, 000. This is what *can* happen—but rarely does—when a company goes public.

Table 12.1 As shown here, many companies that go public do *not* experience major increases in the price of their shares

The companies shown in this table all went public in the United Kingdom recently. Although other companies showed large increases in share value, the dismal results for these companies are representative of what happens to the price of most new ventures that go public. In fact, many disappear within a few years of their initial public offering.

Company	% Change in Stock Price During First Year
Mercom Oil Sands	−93.20
Rialto Energy	−90.13
Latin Resources	−76.59
RusPetro	−69.59
Global Market Group	−69.23

Yet another benefit is that companies that have gone public gain prestige and recognition; since only a tiny proportion of new ventures attain this outcome, investors view the company as a very good one. This, in turn, can help the share prices rise.

Given all these advantages, why don't all entrepreneurs want to take their companies public? Because, in fact, there are several major *disadvantages* to "going public," ones many people overlook. First, of course, once they sell a portion of their equity in their company, entrepreneurs lose some degree of control over it. There are now many other owners, and they have clearly defined rights with respect to at least some aspects of the company's management. For instance, anyone who owns 5 percent of the shares has the right to inspect all financial records. Second, when companies "go public" they must disclose a great deal of information to the public—information concerning the company's operations, management, financial results, and related matters. This, too, reduces entrepreneurs' control of the companies they founded.

In 2002, the US government adopted legislation known as the Sarbanes-Oxley Act, which made public companies even more subject to regulation enforcement by the Securities and Exchange Commission and public stock exchanges. The Act requires that accountants and attorneys working for public companies follow strict rules and guidelines, all designed to protect the investing public from scandals that erupt from time to time, even among very large companies. Recall Bernie Madoff, who is now in prison after a gigantic fraud in which he used new investors' money to pay handsome dividends to previous ones. This is known as a Ponzi scheme, and eventually, of course, it falls apart. Presumably, legislation such as the Sarbanes-Oxley Act can help prevent such events.

A third disadvantage of "going public" is simple: the process involves very large fees. The cost of employing lawyers and accountants to prepare the required documents can be very high. In addition, the founders of the company must spend a huge amount of time and energy in promoting the public offering, thus taking time away from managing the company. The company must also do everything possible to put itself in the most favorable light—it must be profitable or have excellent opportunities to reach this goal, any law suits against the company must be settled if at all possible, and in general, the top managers (which generally include the founders) must demonstrate their effectiveness and efficiency.

In short, "going public" is definitely a mixed blessing. It can, indeed, generate large gains for the entrepreneurs who founded it, provide large amounts of new capital that can fund expansion and growth, and it make it possible to buy and sell shares in the company on a stock exchange. But it's important to keep in mind the fact that there are important disadvantages to going public too. So, although "going public" is certainly an attractive goal for many entrepreneurs, it is one that must be approached with caution and care and actively pursued only at the right time and in the right ways. (Figure 12.4 summarizes the advantages and disadvantages of taking a company public.)

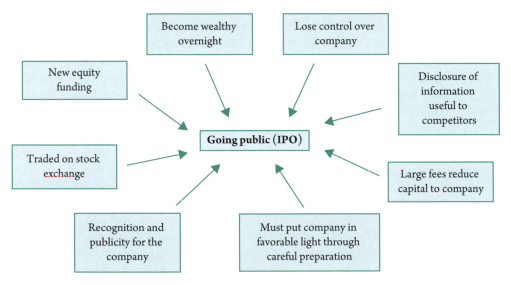

Figure 12.4 The advantages—and disadvantages—of going public

As shown here, going public has both advantages and disadvantages, and entrepreneurs should weigh these carefully before proceeding.

Going public: How the process unfolds

Initial public offering—the day on which companies go public—does not happen automatically or effortlessly. Far from it. In fact, there are four distinct stages in the process leading up to this important event, and each requires considerable effort and planning. During Phase 1, efforts are made to prepare the company for "L-Day" (listing day). This involves many steps designed to help the company to look its best so that its shares will sell very well on the day. Phase 2 involves working closely with experts who help make the stock offering possible (underwriters, investment bankers, attorneys). They prepare the required documentation (registration of the stock, prospectus, and so on). Phase 3 involves preparing the foundation for distribution of the company's shares. This usually involves visits by top management to many locations where they attempt to build enthusiasm among the brokers who will sell the shares to their clients. Phase 4, which can last for years, involves providing a constant flow of information to stock analysts and investors; this helps maintain public interest in the company and its shares to rise. Unfortunately, after the first three phases are completed, many companies find it extremely difficult to maintain these activities. Further, the top management team must return to the task of running the company—a true necessity given the time and effort they have spent during the process.

So, should entrepreneurs consider "going public" a viable exit strategy? Many experts agree that the answer can be "Yes" if the company truly needs large amounts of capital to grow and develop, *and* it is fortunate enough to possess an experienced management team that can handle the stress of the process and at the same time tell a great story to the public markets. Under these conditions, an IPO can provide entrepreneurs with the capital they need to fully realize their vision and, ultimately, with a very profitable exit route. On the other hand, many companies show excellent records of growth without an IPO (e.g., Cargill in the USA), so this is not a necessary ingredient in long-term success.

Going public: Other issues to consider

If at this point the process of going public seems complex, this is still only part of the total picture. In addition, several other important issues arise, and should be carefully considered.

Choosing an underwriter

When companies go public they frequently offer large numbers of shares to the public. How are these shares actually sold? Offered to the public? This task falls primarily to the "underwriter"—the company that actually offers the shares to the investing public. This role is crucial because many companies going public are relatively unknown to the general public. It is the underwriter's task to change this situation so that the potential investors learn about the company and choose to purchase its shares. Underwriters include banks, insurance companies, and brokerage (investment) companies. In the latter case, brokers have customers they have worked with and offer the shares to these individuals. If a company is viewed as one likely to be highly successful, there are often more potential buyers than needed to purchase all of its shares. Then brokers receive only a small number of the shares they requested, and divide these among their clients—with the best ones being given the opportunity to buy a larger number of shares. Underwriters don't provide these services for free, of course; fees are high, and these reduce the funds received by the company going public.

Despite the best efforts of the underwriters, not all public offerings are successful. The shares simply don't sell as well as had been hoped. In fact, if sales are truly dismal, the offering may be withdrawn. What determines whether the sale will be successful? One important factor is the timing of the offering.

Timing may not be everything, but it *is* important. Do you recall the financial crisis of 2008? During that period the stock market dropped precipitously and the shares of large banks virtually collapsed. For instance, Bank of America shares dropped from $52.00 per share to under $4.00! And many other companies in a wide range of industries experienced similar declines. The moral is simple: this was *not* a good time for a company to have an initial public offering. Buyers would be rare, and even those purchasing stocks would tend to stick with well-established companies that had a long-term track record. Clearly then, market conditions are an important factor entrepreneurs should consider before beginning the complex process required to go public. Choosing the right time—a period when stock markets are strong and prices are rising—is often the secret to success in this regard.

Registration of shares

If the discussion so far suggests that arranging for an initial public offering seems complex, it has still not considered one more major issue: registration of shares. In the United States and many other countries, companies must be registered with the appropriate government agency (the Securities and Exchange Commission in the USA). The SEC requires a full and fair disclosure of the company's financial status, presented in a document known as a "prospectus." This document is distributed to investors prior to the date of the initial public offering, and contains information on many issues, including: the nature of the company and its business, potential risks, how the money raised will be used, and roles and experience of the founding team members (the top management of the company).

In addition to the prospectus, other forms that provide financial disclosure are required. These, and the prospectus, are reviewed by the SEC, which may request additional information. And in any case, SEC approval is required before the prospectus can be distributed, and the shares offered for sale. Other legal requirements exist—for instance, in the USA each state has its own laws concerning public offerings.

Overall then, it is clear that although going public offers many opportunities to the companies involved, it also requires a great deal of preparation and hard work if it is to be successful. When it *is* successful, however, the entrepreneurs who have worked hard to build their company may become very, very wealthy overnight. But—and this is an important point—they are prevented by law from selling all their shares immediately and realizing their gains. Rather, they must retain them for a period of time; and in many cases, the founding entrepreneurs voluntarily keep their shares to reassure potential buyers that they are not going to "take the money and run." For instance, Mark Zuckerberg, founder of Facebook announced publicly that he would not sell any of his shares for at least a year; he did this partly in response to a significant drop in the price of shares below that in the initial public offering.

So, is "going public" the perfect ending to the entrepreneurial story? Although many people believe that going public should be a key goal for all entrepreneurs, it seems clear on careful examination that it is definitely not for all new ventures. Yes, there is a significant upside, but the steps required for an IPO are complex, effortful, and lengthy. And even if it succeeds, entrepreneurs may experience many disadvantages: loss of control over the company, the necessity of providing lots of information about their company (information that can be useful to competitors!) and the legal requirements of being a publicly traded company, to mention just a few. Together, these and other issues indicate that going public may not be the best route for all entrepreneurs to follow. Rather, it should be chosen only when the entrepreneurs considering this process find the ratio of benefits to potential costs to be high for them personally.

Exit by necessity rather than choice: The effects of business failure

Sale to insiders or outsiders; passing the company as a major asset to the next generation; arranging for an initial public offering—it would be very pleasant to be able to suggest that is how most entrepreneurs say "farewell" to the companies they have founded. In fact though, the situation is much less encouraging than this. As noted in Chapter 1, a large proportion of new ventures fail or, at least, disappear within a few short years. In short, many entrepreneurs exit from their new ventures not because they want to, but out of necessity: they have no choice. The company for which they had so much passion and happy dreams simply cannot survive. In this final section then, we'll examine the effects on entrepreneurs of such disappointing endings—but will retain an optimistic outlook by noting that failure is, indeed, often the prelude to later success—as noted in the title of this chapter, a beginning as well as an end. Specifically, we'll examine here related topics: (1) why new ventures fail, (2) bankruptcy—perhaps the most extreme type of involuntary exit, and (3) how entrepreneurs cope with failure and go on, perhaps, to try again.

Why new ventures fail: Some all too common—but avoidable—reasons

A question that continues to haunt the field of entrepreneurship is this: "Why do so many new ventures fail?" At first glance this is a very puzzling situation. Entrepreneurs work long and hard to develop their companies, are deeply committed to them, are passionate about their ideas, and are often highly talented in ways that should, presumably, pave the way to success. Yet, despite all these factors, most new ventures disappear within a few years of their launch. In one sense we have dealt with this question throughout the present book. For instance, we have noted the following points:

- Unless entrepreneurs identify and develop an excellent opportunity, the likelihood of success is low (Chapter 3).
- If they fail to conduct a careful feasibility analysis, they may invest their time and energy in efforts to develop products or services for which there are very limited markets (Chapter 4).
- If they start without enough financial resources, or a strong founding team, and fail to build excellent social networks, they will soon run into serious difficulties (Chapters 6 and 7).
- If they don't have the skills needed to stay focused on important goals

and defer rewards (Chapter 8), or if they lack essential management skills (Chapter 10), their new ventures may be doomed even before they start.

In short, the answer to the question above—"Why do so many new ventures fail?"—involves many factors. To bring these sharply into focus, here is a list of the key factors that, existing evidence (e.g., Baron, 2013) suggests, are strongly related to new venture failure:

- Starting the business primarily to "get rich quickly"—even if new ventures succeed, years of hard work are usually necessary before any significant financial rewards occur.
- Lack of a sizeable market for the new venture's product or services—no matter how good a product or service, if no one wants to buy it, developing it is largely a waste of time.
- Not enough start-up funds to survive high start-up costs, which can quickly result in disaster; unfortunately, many entrepreneurs greatly underestimate these costs, and that can be fatal mistake.
- No obvious competitive advantage over existing products or services—why, then, should anyone buy the new venture's products if they are not clearly superior to ones already available?
- Expanding too quickly—as noted in Chapter 11, growth is often a good outcome, but not always, and especially if careful plans for handling it effectively are lacking.
- Competing directly with established industry leaders—these companies often have vast resources, and can easily use them to block efforts by a new venture to build a large customer base.
- Lack of sufficient, high-quality planning—business plans are, in a sense, made to be changed, but still, they may provide good guidelines for the new ventures.
- An inability to improvise and use resources available—rapid changes require a degree of flexibility (see Chapter 5) and unless entrepreneurs can adapt to them quickly they may be left behind.
- Poor location—far from customers, suppliers, etc.
- Excessive optimism, enthusiasm (positive affect) coupled with unwillingness to reverse previous decisions and withdraw from failing courses of action or strategies before it is too late!

Together, these factors help explain why so many new ventures end up as memories or thoughts of "what might have been" rather than thriving businesses. Needless to add, many external factors not under entrepreneurs' control such as rapid technological advances, shifts in customer preferences, the actions of competitors, also play a role. But overall, a strong case can be made for the suggestion that many new ventures fail as a result of *faulty actions, judgments, miscalculations, or errors* by the founding entrepreneurs who lack the knowledge and skills necessary to succeed. To put it in different terms, many new ventures fail despite the fact that their founders are highly motivated, talented, and dedicated, because they *lack* certain tools essential for achieving success. Fortunately, all of these tools can be acquired by entrepreneurs, and perhaps, if they are, the rate of new venture failure can be reduced. But entrepreneurs won't attempt to acquire them unless they recognize their importance, and overcome their strong tendency to "do it now"—to get started at once, without carefully considering all the factors and potential pitfalls involved (e.g., Pierro et al., 2006). One overarching goal of this book is to help entrepreneurs recognize these factors, and strive to build them into their efforts to convert their dreams into reality. But what happens if they fail to do so? We'll now turn to the discouraging events that may follow.

Bankruptcy: The saddest ending to a company's life

Kodak, American Airlines, Polaroid, Hostess (manufacturer of "Twinkies"), GM—what do these companies have in common? All have filed for bankruptcy (Figure 12.5). As we'll soon see, this doesn't mean they will disappear entirely—many companies survive bankruptcy after reorganizing in various ways. But even in such cases, bankruptcy is a very serious matter—one indicating the company in question is in an extremely precarious situation. We'll now examine different kinds of bankruptcy, as well as strategies for turning around a failing business and making it, perhaps, profitable once again.

Bankruptcy: Its forms and consequences

The term "bankruptcy" is a legal term used to describe situations in which a company cannot pay its debts—it lacks the resources to meet its obligations. For most companies this is a dire situation from which the chances of recovery are slim. Indeed, about 70 percent of companies that enter bankruptcy must liquidate, distribute their assets to creditors; this is known as "Chapter 7 bankruptcy" and there is little or no chance of recovery from it. Companies that enter Chapter 7 bankruptcy cease to exist, taking entrepreneurs' dreams and hard work with them.

In contrast, another type, "Chapter 11 bankruptcy," offers much more hope. When companies enter Chapter 11 bankruptcy they engage in reorganization—efforts to save the company from liquidation. Chapter 11

Figure 12.5 Even very large companies sometimes go bankrupt

When they experience serious financial difficulties even giant companies can go bankrupt. For instance, TWA—a pioneer of commercial aviation—took this route to oblivion. However, if bankrupt companies can reorganize successfully, they may survive; this happened recently to American Airlines and Kodak. When new ventures go bankrupt, however, there is little chance that they will recover.

bankruptcy is only available to companies that have significant resources and some chance of recovery, so, in fact, only about 1 percent of companies entering bankruptcy are permitted to follow this route. It's important to note that it is not only small or relatively unknown companies that file for such bankruptcy; in recent years, major companies such as the ones listed above have found it necessary to enter this state. Some never recover, but others *do* emerge from Chapter 11 bankruptcy stronger and better able to compete. GM is an example: although it took assistance from the federal government to save the company, it did emerge from bankruptcy and has, to a degree, prospered since that time, repaying the funds it received from the government. Again, however, there is no guarantee that such positive results will occur, so the courts allow companies to enter Chapter 11 bankruptcy only when some reasonable chance of survival appears to exist. Otherwise, they must liquidate and use whatever resources they have to repay their creditors—the people or organizations they owe money to—in a legally prescribed order.

In short, the term "bankruptcy" is not a synonym for "total failure." This is often the result (in Chapter 7 bankruptcy), but in some cases at least, the courts and creditors give companies a chance to reorganize or pay their debts gradually, and as a result, they can—and often do—survive. Whether they will ever be profitable again, however, is always uncertain.

Is it possible to tell when a company is in danger of bankruptcy? Not perfectly, but there are several tell-tale signs that all investors—and other interested stakeholders—should notice. These include the sudden departure of top-level managers, who see the writing on the wall, large and increasing discounts to customers, demands from creditors that all payments be in cash, and growing complaints from customers about poor service and product quality. For instance, Sears Inc., a venerable firm that has been in business for more than 100 years, has recently closed many of its stores and shown sizeable losses. Moreover, the stores it still operates have a somewhat rundown atmosphere. Will it end in bankruptcy? Some observers believe that this is a likely outcome, but it is still too early to tell. In any case, when a company shows several of the signs listed above, it is probably *not* a place investors should put their money!

Dealing with business failure: Surviving the end of a dream

Winston Churchill, who in addition to being the leader who helped Britain survive its darkest hour, was also a keen observer of human nature, and he frequently commented on the nature of success and failure. Here is one of this observations: "Success," he once said, "is not final, failure is not fatal: it is the courage to continue that counts." In the light of growing evidence concerning the effects of failure on entrepreneurs, these words definitely ring true. Many successful entrepreneurs report that their first two or three attempts to launch new ventures failed—sometimes miserably. Yet, learning from their mistakes and finding the strength to continue, they ultimately *did* achieve success. In this chapter we'll examine the effects of business failure on entrepreneurs. In addition, we'll briefly consider some factors that, together, can help them bounce back from these sad and sometimes traumatic experiences, in order to try again.

Effects of failure: Financial, social, and psychological

Have you ever heard this saying: "What doesn't kill us, makes us stronger"? The basic message in these words is that if we survive adversity or hardship, we become stronger as a result of these experiences. We learn from our experiences, so that "next time" we can do better (e.g., Kray et al., 2006; Roese and Morrison, 2009). But what, specifically, are the effects of failure of their businesses on entrepreneurs? As noted by Ucbasaran et al. (2013), they fall into three different categories: financial, social, and psychological.

The "financial" costs of business failure are readily apparent: capital, time, and energy are all lost. If the entrepreneurs have used their own resources, the effects on their personal lives and finances may be ones they cannot readily recover from. The "social" costs of business failure are somewhat subtler but can involve a loss of reputation and, in extreme cases, may result in the entrepreneur being labeled as a "loser" to whom no one should listen or give support. The greater the extent to which entrepreneurs are blamed for business failures, the greater such social costs (e.g., Cardon et al., 2011). Overall, the loss of reputation associated with failures may make it more difficult for entrepreneurs to start again, even if they wish to do so. In addition it may weaken or reduce an entrepreneur's social network: no one wants to be associated with failures, so some persons in the network—especially those who have weak ties to the entrepreneur—may distance themselves from the person who has failed. Individuals the entrepreneur has strong ties with, in contrast, may offer support and encouragement.

The "psychological" costs of business failure can also be serious. They include strong negative emotions (guilt, anger, shame), reductions in motivation (e.g., feelings of "helplessness"), and high levels of stress. In addition, they may have adverse effects on the entrepreneurs' self-concept, reducing their self-confidence and self-efficacy—the belief that they can accomplish whatever they set out to accomplish. Such effects are weaker for entrepreneurs who have previously run successful businesses (Cope, 2011), and those who are especially high in confidence or self-efficacy (e.g., Hayward et al., 2010), as well as those who are very good at managing their own emotions—a form of self-regulation (e.g., Shepherd, 2009). But persons lower on these dimensions may experience very harmful effects.

Unfortunately, these financial, social, and psychological costs can combine so that, for example, financial losses intensify the emotional ones, and the psychological costs, in turn, may further discourage entrepreneurs from trying once again. Overall, business failure is a bitter experience for entrepreneurs, given their passion for and commitment to their new companies.

Countering the effects of failure: Effects of stress and how psychological capital may reduce them

The origins of business failure are complex and involve the influence of many factors. But one that may be especially important is the high levels of stress entrepreneurs often experience. Such stress derives from the environments in which they work—environments that are unpredictable and subject to rapid change, involve high levels of risk and uncertainty, and frequently subject entrepreneurs to major financial problems. Compounding these conditions is entrepreneurs' own tendency to work very long hours—sometimes to the point of total exhaustion.

Together, these conditions would be expected to generate high levels of stress. Stress, in turn, has been found to exert harmful effects on the performance of many tasks, cognitive processes (e.g., judgment, decision-making), and personal health. Thus, it seems reasonable to suggest that high levels of stress may contribute to business failure: entrepreneurs experiencing intense stress may be less effective in performing key tasks, making serious errors of judgment and faulty decisions. In addition, their personal health may crumble, making it impossible to fully meet their responsibilities.

Interestingly, recent research indicates that although entrepreneurs are exposed to conditions that would be expected to generate high levels of stress, they may also be highly resistant to such conditions (Baron et al., 2013). The reason for this is that, as described in Chapter 8, only

individuals who are tolerant of high levels of stress are attracted to entrepreneurship and remain in it. Those who are not tend to withdraw from
this process either voluntarily or involuntarily—when their companies
fail!

Although entrepreneurs may be relatively resistant to the harmful effects of
stress, the fact remains that they are exposed to high levels of this factor.
This raises an important question: how can they—and therefore their new
ventures—be protected against the negative effects of such conditions? One
answer involves what is known as "psychological capital." Psychological
capital is a variable based on four underlying factors: high levels of self-
efficacy, optimism, hope, and resilience (Luthans et al., 2005). Self-efficacy,
as noted before, involves the extent to which individuals believe that they
can reach important goals. Optimism involves the expectation that positive
results will be obtained in almost any situation. Hope refers to being able
to imagine multiple pathways through which challenges can be overcome,
thus reducing the likelihood that the persons involved will overwhelmed
by high levels of stress (Snyder et al., 1997). Finally, resilience results from
having successfully dealt with (or survived) previous setbacks or failures, and
involves the belief by such persons that they will be able to overcome new
obstacles both now and in the future (Tugade et al., 2004). Recent research
suggests that this combination of characteristics may provide an effective
shield against the harmful effects of stress (Figure 12.6). In addition, they
may help entrepreneurs to "bounce back" after failure—recover from these
traumatic events to the point where they are willing to try again. In fact, this
is precisely the route taken by many highly successful entrepreneurs: early
failure(s) followed by later, huge success. "The Entrepreneurial Quest" case
study below, describes how this process actually unfolded for several well-
known entrepreneurs.

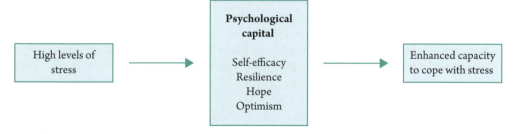

Source: Based on findings reported by Baron et al., 2013.

Figure 12.6 Psychological capital: a shield against the harmful effects of stress

Recent evidence indicates that psychological capital, consisting of high self-efficacy, resilience, hope, and optimism—
can protect entrepreneurs from the high levels of stress they often experience.

The Entrepreneurial Quest

Recovering from failure by learning from past mistakes

To quote Winston Churchill once again (he *was* a very keen observer of human behavior), consider this thought: "Success is stumbling from failure to failure with no loss of enthusiasm." In other words, the key to dealing with failure is . . . trying again without losing one's confidence that the final outcome will be positive. At the same time, however, it's clear that resilience and persistence alone are not enough: it's also essential to learn from past mistakes so that the next time things go better—perhaps much better. This basic process—failure, learning from this experience, and then trying again—has been part of the lives of many famous entrepreneurs. Here are a few examples:

Colonel Harland Sanders (founder of Kentucky Fried Chicken)
Colonel Sanders had a long, but not very rewarding career before coming up with the idea for KFC; in fact, he had been fired from more than a dozen jobs. At the age of 65 he hit upon the idea of making fried chicken his road to success. He developed a "secret" mix of spices and herbs, and then visited more than 1000 restaurants, trying to persuade the owners to give it a try. During this period he lived in his car and was essentially broke. Gradually though, he won some customers and the company was on its way. At the age of 75, he was able to sell it for $1.5 million, quite a lot for someone who began his career as an entrepreneur working out of his car.

Henry Ford
Ford—one of the most famous entrepreneurs of all time—was also not an immediate success. In fact, his first company—the Detroit Automobile Company—went bankrupt, largely as a result of trying to sell low-quality cars at high prices. He reorganized this company into the Henry Ford Company, but it too collapsed over a dispute with a partner. His third attempt was on the verge of failure when an angel investor swooped to the rescue with needed funds. Finally, after two disasters and a near disaster, Ford got it right and turned his efforts to producing high-quality cars that were low enough in price for millions of people to afford them. This car—the famous Model T—was an immediate success, and soon Ford was running a large and rapidly growing company.

Walt Disney
Today, Disney is a huge company, operating huge theme parks, producing films, and selling huge numbers of products, from toys to clothing. But its founder, Walt Disney, began with a series of defeats. Walt Disney always wanted to be a cartoonist for newspapers, but was told, repeatedly, that he had no good ideas worth pursuing. As a result of these rejections, he decided to found a company of his own to produce cartoons; unfortunately it entered into a

CASE STUDY *(continued)*

Source: Wikipedia: photographer unknown, unrestricted permission for use.

Figure 12.7 Many famous entrepreneurs experience failure before attaining success

Colonel Harland Sanders, the founder of Kentucky Fried Chicken, was not an immediate or early success. In fact, during one period he was so short of funds that he had to live out of his car! He founded Kentucky Fried Chicken during the 1930s (his first restaurant in Corbin, Kentucky is shown above), and the company went on to prosper greatly. Today, it has more than 18 000 outlets in 120 countries.

very bad business deal and went bankrupt. Disney then tried again, but during WWII he lost most of his employees to military service, and was on the verge of failure once again. At this point, however, he hit upon the idea of producing and distributing films in Europe, where costs were much lower than in the USA. This time he experienced modest success, and this, in turn, provided funds for expansion at home. Gradually, the characters Disney invented for his cartoons—Mickey Mouse, Donald Duck, Goofy and others—became cultural icons with vast popularity. The result was the founding an entertainment giant, which today has a presence all over the globe.

CASE STUDY *(continued)*

We could easily continue, because, in fact, most successful entrepreneurs have had very similar experiences: early setbacks and failures, a strong ability to bounce back after such defeats, followed, ultimately, by major success. The key question is this: what do these stories of defeat followed by victory tell us? Basically, they offer two important lessons: (1) resilience and faith in one's abilities are *key* ingredients in entrepreneurial success; but (2) these characteristics must be combined with a readiness to learn from past mistakes so that the will (and ability) to try again is coupled with the knowledge needed to do it "right"—or at least better—the next time.

One final point before concluding: the key components of psychological capital—self-efficacy, hope, and optimism and resilience—are all ones that can be strengthened; they are not "traits" that people either have or don't have; on the contrary, they can be enhanced and if they are, they can then provide entrepreneurs with increased capacity to cope with high levels of stress, and to reduce its adverse effects on their performance and cognitive processes. The overall result? One factor that often plays a major role in

THE EFFECTIVE ENTREPRENEUR

"All good things," one old saying goes, "must come to an end." That is certainly true for many entrepreneurs who, for various reasons, conclude that the time has come for them to exit from the companies they founded. This can be accomplished in many ways, and entrepreneurs should consider these carefully before proceeding, because they all offer a mixture of costs and benefits. Here are some points effective entrepreneurs should follow in this, the final phase of the entrepreneurial process:

- A sale to insiders can make sense, *if* they have the funds, experience, and knowledge to run the company successfully. If they don't, they will still run it—but run

it into the ground, which is something no entrepreneur wants. So, consider offers from insiders very carefully before proceeding.

- A sale to outsiders can be an excellent way to proceed, but in order to maximize the benefits of such a sale, entrepreneurs must time it carefully: ideally, a sale occurs when markets are high, the company is in excellent shape financially, and its customer base is secure. If these conditions don't exist, selling to outsiders can be major mistake.

- A key component of any sale to outsiders is an accurate valuation of the company; this is the basis for negotiations with the buyers so

←

it must be done carefully, and be anchored in reality; buyers won't pay for the entrepreneurs' deep commitment to the company or similar factors.

- Passing a company to successors—usually family members—can be a good way to proceed but *only* if a careful plan for such succession is prepared. If it is lacking, bitter disputes among the persons involved may erupt, even if they are closely related.
- Bankruptcy is a very sad ending for any company, in fact the best advice for

entrepreneurs is: don't let it happen! Either sell before it is imminent, or close the company and leave with your reputation intact.

- Business failure stems from many sources, but it is not necessarily the end of an entrepreneur's career. Many famous entrepreneurs experienced major failure before founding successful companies. So, effective entrepreneurs should remember that as long as they learn valuable lessons from these experiences, they are not necessarily fatal, and can lead to doing better—much better—the next time.

business failure—levels of stress that overwhelm entrepreneurs' capacity to cope—can be reduced.

SUMMARY OF KEY POINTS

1 When entrepreneurs decide to leave the companies they founded they can accomplish this in several different ways. They can sell or transfer the company to people inside it, sell to outsiders, or transfer it to members of their own family.

2 In any sale, a key issue is valuation—how much is the company worth? This is a complex task for privately held companies. Many entrepreneurs believe that taking their company public through an initial public offering (IPO), is a goal toward which they should actively strive. Although an IPO can, in fact, make entrepreneurs rich overnight, the process is long and difficult, and requires a great deal of preparation. In addition, timing is crucial; an IPO when markets are weak may fail to raise the capital it seeks, and may, if markets are very weak, fail entirely.

3 Sometimes entrepreneurs exit not by choice, but by necessity: their companies fail. This can occur for many reasons, but when it does the company may, depending on the size of the debts, be forced to enter bankruptcy. Several forms of bankruptcy exist, but all occur only when a company is in very serious trouble. Entrepreneurs whose companies fail must cope with this painful event.

4 A high level of psychological capital—a combination of self-efficacy, resilience, hope, and optimism—may help them to recover and, perhaps,

try again. This pattern—early failure followed by major success—is one experienced by many highly successful entrepreneurs, so failure, although painful, is not necessarily the end of entrepreneurs' dreams.

REFERENCES

Baron, R.A. (2013), *Enhancing Entrepreneurial Excellence: Tools for Making the Possible Real.* Cheltenham, UK and Northampton, USA: Edward Elgar.

Baron, R.A., R. Franklin and K.M. Hmieleski (2013), "Why entrepreneurs often experience *low*, not high, levels of stress: The joint effects of selection and psychological capital," *Journal of Management,* **20**(2), 1–27.

Cardon, M.S., C.E. Stevens and D.R. Potter (2011), "Misfortunes or mistakes? Cultural sensemaking of entrepreneurial failure," *Journal of Business Venturing,* **26**(1), 79–92.

Cope, J. (2011), "Entrepreneurial learning from failure: An interpretative phenomenological analysis," *Journal of Business Venturing,* **26**(6), 604-23.

Hayward, M.A.L., W.R. Forster, S.D. Sarasvathy and B.L. Fredrickson (2010), "Beyond hubris: How highly confident entrepreneurs rebound to venture again," *Journal of Business Venturing,* **25**(6), 569–78.

Kray, L.J., A.D. Galinsky and E. Wong (2006), "Thinking inside the box: The relational processing style elicited by counterfactual mind-sets," *Journal of Personality and Social Psychology,* **91**(1), 33–48.

Luthans, F., B.J. Avolio, F.O. Walumbwa and W. Li (2005), "The psychological capital of Chinese workers: Exploring the relationship with performance," *Management and Organization Review,* **1**(2), 249–71.

Pierro, A., A.W. Kruglanski and E.T. Higgins (2006), "Progress takes work: Effects of the locomotion dimension on job involvement, effort investment, and task performance in organizations," *Journal of Applied Social Psychology,* **36**(7), 1723–43.

Roese, N. and M. Morrison (2009), "The psychology of counterfactual thinking," *Historical Social Research,* **34**(2), 16–26.

Shepherd, D.A. (2009), "Grief recovery from the loss of a family business: A multi- and meso-level theory," *Journal of Business Venturing,* **24**(1), 81–97.

Snyder, C.R., J. Cheavens and S.C. Sympson (1997), "Hope: An individual motive for social commerce," *Group Dynamics: Theory, Research, and Practice,* **1**(2), 107–18.

Tugade, M.M., C.L. Fredrickson and L.F. Barrett (2004), "Psychological resilience and positive emotional granularity: Examining the benefits of positive emotions on coping and health," *Journal of Personality,* **72**(6), 1161–90.

Ucbasaran, D., D.A. Shepherd, A. Lockett and S.J. Lyon (2013), "Life after business failure: The process and consequences of business failure for entrepreneurs," *Journal of Management,* **39**(1), 163–202.

Author index

Subject index